MW01172583

CARTOON VOICES OF THE GOLDEN AGE, 1930-70

CARTOON VOICES OF THE GOLDEN AGE, 1930-70

The Pioneers of Animation Acting

By Keith Scott

BearManor Media

2022

CARTOON VOICES OF THE GOLDEN AGE, 1930-70
The Pioneers of Animation Acting

© 2022 Keith Scott

All rights reserved.

No portion of this publication may be reproduced, stored, and/or copied electronically (except for academic use as a source), nor transmitted in any form or by any means without the prior written permission of the publisher and/or author.

This is an independent work of historical research and commentary and is not sponsored, authorized or endorsed by any motion picture studio affiliated with the animated films discussed herein. Promotional and publicity photos reproduced herein are from the author's private collection, unless noted. Most of these images are from the original time-frame covered by this work and were released to casting agents and radio producers for publicity purposes between the years 1930 and 1970. The images are for editorial and educational purposes and pursuant to the Fair Use Doctrine.

Published in the United States of America by:

BearManor Media

4700 Millenia Blvd.
Suite 175 PMB 90497
Orlando, FL 32839

bearmanormedia.com

Printed in the United States.

Typesetting and layout by BearManor Media
Front cover image: Leading voices in forties Hollywood cartoons, clockwise from top right: Arthur Q. Bryan, Mel Blanc, Billy Bletcher, Bugs Hardaway, Frank Graham, Sara Berner, Wally Maher and Bill Thompson.

ISBN—979-8-88771-008-2

Contents

Acknowledgments

My primary research associate from 1994-2010 was Hames Ware (1943-2018). Hames was based in Little Rock, Arkansas. He spent fifty years researching the topic of voice artists and was himself a voice-over veteran. In the late sixties, soon after he began corresponding with British cartoon buff Graham Webb, he met his lifelong idols on a 1969 trip to Hollywood: legendary cartoon directors Bob Clampett and Frank Tashlin, and actor Billy Bletcher, the famous voice of Disney's Big Bad Wolf. Hames was also co-author, with Jerry Bails, of *The Who's Who of American Comic Books*, and in 2000 he narrated a documentary that won an Emmy Award. In that year Graham Webb published *The Encyclopedia of Animated Cartoons* for which Hames and I were research associates. Hames died in 2018. He was a diligent student of comic artists and voice actors, and his gentle and kindly presence is missed.

Our initial childhood interest in the admittedly arcane subject of voice actors got a kick-start in the mid-seventies with the growing availability of vintage radio shows on audiotape. As the old programs found a new generation of fans who began trading tapes, some of us began noticing how many familiar cartoon voices kept turning up. And so for this author what began as a hobby based around animation and radio gradually morphed into an obsession, until it became a serious research pursuit.

Scores of rare radio shows from the thirties and forties (*The Joe Penner Show, The Eddie Cantor Show, Calling All Cars, The Jack Benny Program, The Fred Allen Show, Al Pearce and His Gang, Komedie Kapers, The Mirth Parade, Warner Bros. Academy Theatre, The Grouch Club, Tommy Riggs and Betty Lou, Fibber McGee and Molly, Paducah Plantation, Jubilee, The Charlie McCarthy Show,*

Mickey Mouse Theatre of the Air and many more) were supplied by Ken Greenwald, Ron Wolf and Martin Halperin of the professional institution Pacific Pioneer Broadcasters; PPB's complete set of *Radio Life* magazine featured useful biographical pieces on obscure artists who voiced cartoons.

A select band of early radio show collectors were unfailingly helpful. They include Don Aston, the late Dave Siegel, Skip Craig, Joe Webb, Bob Burnham, Tom Brown (Radio Archives), Dick Judge, Ron Barnett, David Kiner, and John & Larry Gassman of *SPERD-VAC* (the Society for the Preservation and Encouragement of Radio Drama, Variety and Comedy). That fine organization had the presence of mind to record lengthy oral histories of many now deceased radio folk, several with cartoon connections. Also helpful was John Dunning's monumental radio encyclopedia *On the Air*.

Audio historians like Ted Hering (Spike Jones's archivist), Jordan R. Young, Jack Mirtle and Milt Larsen of S.P.V.A. (the Society for the Preservation of Variety Arts) supplied us with an array of vintage music, comedy and children's records, while in pre-digital days video collector and film buff Lee Boyett of Little Rock, a friend of Hames Ware, provided scores of hard-to-find cartoons on VHS tapes along with a fourth set of ears finely attuned to character actors' voice prints. In the early days of this project he was responsible for certain identifications of unknown cartoon voices that were later confirmed to be accurate.

Graham Webb's years of sharing information with Hames Ware finally resulted in a pioneering article "The Moving Drawing Speaks" for issue No. 18 of *Funnyworld* magazine in 1978. Their notes formed the basis of the feature article as written up by editor Michael Barrier. That article became the chief inspiration for this book. Our research continued for years after that seminal piece was published, and I happily joined forces with Webb and Ware in 1994.

Much of our research was in the pre-internet days when snail mail ruled. Letters were sent to cartoon pioneers. Graham Webb corresponded with Mel Blanc, Bob Clampett, Chuck Jones, Robert McKimson, Gladys Holland, Jerry Hausner, Sid Marcus and others. From Australia I contacted Chuck Jones, Lloyd Turner, Thurl Ravenscroft, Robert Bruce, Janet Waldo, Jameson Brewer, Leroy Hurte and Walker Edmiston, while Hames Ware received invaluable letters from Bob Clampett and Billy Bletcher.

Years before the advent of email, long distance phone interviews were conducted with early voice artists like singer Bill Days of the Sportsmen Quartet, the legendary June Foray who recalled details of forgotten actors on such cinematic obscurities as *Speaking of Animals*, Lucille Bliss, Dave Barry, Nancy Wible, Daws Butler, Betty Lou Gerson, Bill Scott and Paul Frees. All of these talents are deceased. As the years passed getting to vintage people "just in time" became a priority. I live in Sydney, so aside from my numerous research trips to the USA, this book was slowly assembled over a long time.

The endless listening and video watching continued. Analog tapes slowly gave way to CD burns, just as VHS tapes made way for DVDs which were upscaled to Blu-ray: shiny discs could now house comprehensive cartoon collections. After the screening marathons were exhausted, primary sources became the main target. Several archival institutions proved invaluable in my quest.

Ever willing to assist was Ned Comstock at USC's Cinema-Television Library, which houses the Jack Warner and MGM Music Department collections, both of which yielded information we assumed had been lost to the ravages of time; Ned also provided clipping files on voice artists including columnist Hal Humphrey's papers. Excellent too was The Margaret Herrick Library and its helpful staff at The Center for Motion Picture Studies in Beverly Hills, and Sony Pictures legal which housed Columbia's records, via archivist Nick Szech. Thanks also to Robert Tieman & the late David R. Smith at Walt Disney Archives, where Graham Webb and later yours truly conducted key voice-artist research. Thanks too to Brigitte Kueppers, the gatekeeper at UCLA's Arts-Special Collections containing the Walter Lantz-Universal holdings; and to the staff who run the excellent clipping service at the Billy Rose Theatre Collection, a division of the New York Public Library at Lincoln Centre, probably the most essential repository for show business research.

Lifelong animation scholars were unfailingly helpful, particularly the inestimable animator Mark Kausler who for many pre-DVD years graciously screened hundreds of rare cartoons from his remarkable film collection. Back in the mid-nineties *The Whole Toon Catalog* was helpful as a quick and efficient source for laserdiscs and rare cartoon tapes in the now paleolithic pre-YouTube era.

The eminent cartoon historian Jerry Beck was always there to assist. In 1999 he was associate producer on the rare Columbia cartoons TV package *Totally Tooned In*, which also helped to spur on this book. Jerry's "Garage Sale" DVDs of hundreds of hard to find cartoons were another pivotal research aide. Milton Gray assisted by supplying cartoons to study in the early days of home-burned DVDs. George Feltenstein, whose video compilations of cartoons and shorts made the research task so much easier in the laserdisc era, deserves special kudos, especially since he later did the same thing for DVD and Blu-ray at Warner Home Video.

I'm grateful for helpful items sent by musicologist-author Daniel Goldmark, whose painstaking digging into music cues for theatrical cartoons is of tremendous benefit to future students. Historians Tom Klein, J. B. Kaufman and Leonard Maltin were also helpful to this long distance author.

Of major importance was animation's premier scholar / historian Michael Barrier, whose pioneering interviews with over two hundred animation veterans culminated in his essential book *Hollywood Cartoons*, published in 1999 by Oxford. Thanks to his endless generosity we examined key interviews conducted by Mike and his research ally, animator Milton Gray. An interview may have had just one or two tangential references to voices or the topic of cartoon dialogue recording but each anecdote imparted a great sense of what the voice acting experience was like in the early days of sound cartoons (and revealed how so much remains the same ninety years later).

Above all others, the main source of inspiration was the late Bob Clampett (1913-84), the legendary Warner Bros. cartoon director whose memory was amazingly sharp on even highly obscure voice talents. In a remarkable ninety-minute phone call arranged by Milt Gray in February 1972, Clampett supplied my associate Hames Ware with a raft of names which were the building blocks for all our subsequent research. Without Clampett's help, it is likely we might still be unaware of the existence of key voice artists like Frank Graham, Dave Weber, Berniece Hansell, Kent Rogers, Elmore Vincent, Robert Bruce, Bernice Kamiat, Sara Berner and many other forgotten voices. Without realizing how helpful he was, Clampett was indeed responsible for our being able to give all these unnamed voice people long overdue credit via this book.

Specialized information on uncredited actors was found in library works. Film scholars applauded the publication of the *AFI Catalog of Motion Pictures* (1931-40 and 1941-50), which noted the unnamed actors in hundreds of movies from original Call Bureau cast sheets. Motion picture and radio casting guides were also helpful, including Margaret Herrick Library's set of *Academy Players Directory*. Rare volumes of *National Radio Artists Directory*, and its successor *The AFRA Guide*, dating from 1940-56 were consulted. Thanks to the late Ken Greenwald, Dan Haefele, the late Will Ryan, Randy Skretvedt, Jordan Young, Ron Wolf, Jerry Williams, Karl Schadow and Bobb Lynes for supplying various photocopies. *Variety Radio Annual* (1937-41) was another reliable resource.

Thanks a second time to Mark Kausler for copying a complete set of *The Exposure Sheet*, the Leon Schlesinger studio's 1939-40 newsletter. This set came courtesy of their original owner, the delightful and sadly departed Schlesinger ink & paint lady Martha

Sigall. Mark also supplied a set of *Exhibitor Reports* for the decade 1931-40; Ned Comstock graciously xeroxed many editions of *Warner Club News*, 1944-50. Mark Kausler, Jerry Beck and Leonard Maltin were kind enough to read the manuscript for anything from factual inconsistencies to plain old typos.

With the advent of the internet emerged a diligent researcher known by the blog de plume "Don M. Yowp" who became this millennium's newest research associate. Thanks to his tireless and productive trawling through movie trade journals and newspapers, we learned many answers to questions bugging us for years. Yowp remains noteworthy in this endeavour and I am grateful for his willingness to share many items, no matter how trivial seeming.

Thanks also to Michael Dobbs of *AniMato!* magazine, who provided a useful forum for some of the early "vintage voice" articles by Hames Ware and me; once published, we were amazed to discover we weren't the only people interested in the early voice mysteries. The late David Mruz's enjoyable fanzine *Mindrot* was another prized publication, happily amateurish yet one of the earliest sources for obsessive cartoon minutiae from fine researchers like Will Friedwald and Paul Etcheverry. Among the younger generation of diligent classic cartoon experts are David Gerstein, Thad Komorowski, Devon Baxter. Here in Australia I've been gifted with nice cartoon upgrades by Anthony Kotorac.

Grateful thanks go to publisher Ben Ohmart for taking on this project for BearManor Media Books. He has been most gracious and helpful. And I am particularly indebted to Sarah Joseph for the excellent layout and typesetting and her swift attention to the tiniest details in the fiddly work of putting a large project like this together.

This book, more than most, remains a work-in-progress: there are still voice artist mysteries unsolved, more vintage cartoons to rewatch, hundreds more radio shows to unearth. The jigsaw puzzle of unidentified voices is truly an open case of Sherlockian proportions. The game's afoot and the research continues!

INTRODUCTION

In the wide and seemingly bottomless world of film studies, many of the more obscure corners within the movie industry have eventually been chronicled. Topics range from the lives of B-Western stuntmen to the first Vitaphone shorts in the mid-twenties, to composers of film music, character actors, genre encyclopedias, 3-D and drive-in flicks, and even studies of two generations of movie buffs themselves. There is, however, one esoteric subject from the movies' Golden Age of 1930-60 that has been shrouded in near-mystery, with little surviving documentation: the scores of early uncredited cartoon voice actors. Even after thirty years of the internet, many eccentrically gifted people who provided character voices back in the thirties and forties, with the exception of Mel Blanc, remain largely unknown.

This book attempts to identify many of the forgotten but talented actors who provided anonymous and zanily comic voices in the so-called "classic" era of theatrical cartoons. It covers the development of the art, studio by studio. Ranging from the struggling days of new-fangled "talkies," when animation staff members supplied squeaks and falsetto grunts for the primitive on-screen characters, to the gradual emergence of sophisticated comedy dialogue which needed the skills of professional voices, it ends at the dawn of the sixties as the first generation of television cartoons was gaining a huge following.

In that thirty years of theatrical cartoons the brand new occupation of "voice specialist" was refined to levels of enormous versatility, comic skill and acting subtlety. This book is the history of an artform that was an offshoot of radio acting, crossed with the broad comedy of the vaudeville stage.

It's hard to imagine from today's vantage point, when cartoon voices and their innumerable actors are discussed, debated, deified and dissed to the point of tedium in online threads, but there was actually a thirty-year period when professional "voices" weren't listed in a cartoon's credits. The most famous and gifted artist of his field, the incomparable Mel Blanc, eventually received the rare accolade of opening screen credit ("Voice Characterizations by") in the classic Warner Bros. cartoons of the forties. But even he had notched up seven years of total anonymity, during which time he slowly perfected the voices of the studio's famous starring trium-virate - Porky Pig, Daffy Duck and Bugs Bunny - long before his name was finally emblazoned on huge Technicolor movie screens for theatregoers to discover.

Indeed, so much was totally different back in the day. The sheer novelty of seeing funny animal drawings brought to life and cavort-ing on screen - let alone appearing to talk - was overwhelming to early cinema patrons, who delighted in the synchronized music and silly gags. At the time, just the existence of moving cartoons with speech seemed a little miraculous. From the dawn of sound in 1928 it was standard industry policy that vocal contributors, mainly casual artists for hire, went unnamed. Along with the cartoons, hundreds of live action movies boasted voice work by uncredited narrators, dubbing singers and eccentric sound animal imitators. Virtually all of them toiled anonymously, and for decades many tal-ents received zero publicity, known only by studio casting person-nel and the directors who needed their skills.

One reason for this seeming secrecy was offered in early 1935, in a rare *Los Angeles Times* piece about offscreen voices. In noting the Disney cartoons, author Philip Scheuer reported,

"Keeping it Secret: The Walt Disney studio prefers anonym-ity for its vocal performers, in accordance with a policy of not showing favoritism to anybody. Around the plant they speak of the various characters–Mickey and Minnie Mouse, Pluto, Donald Duck and the rest–as living personages, and they don't see why the rest of the world shouldn't do the same.

"As a spokesman for the company summed it up, kids of 12 and 14 don't believe in Santa Claus but they don't want to see him without his beard.

"Besides, we don't have more than a few words in our 'Mickey Mouse' and 'Silly Symphonies.' Other than to intimate that those few are spoken by people 'around the lot,' he refused to commit himself further."

Roughly translated, "If we mention their names, it will spoil the fantasy of our cartoons." Of course, cynics might suggest they really meant, "If we mention their names, they might hit us up for more money!"

Several books on Golden Age cartoons finally gave belated recognition to a range of talented animators, inspirational design artists, story specialists and supervising directors like Tex Avery and Chuck Jones. But aside from a few standout "voices" like Mel Blanc (Bugs Bunny), Jack Mercer (Popeye) and Pinto Colvig (Goofy), most of the vintage vocal contributors remained unchronicled. Today it is widely acknowledged that those unique character voices are in fact a major reason why the old cartoons have endured. It is simply impossible to imagine any of the classic cartoon stars minus their distinctive speech patterns.

This book, based on a lifelong study of the first thirty years of sound animation, before TV cartoons took off in the late fifties, is a first attempt to redress the balance. Volume Two of this book contains detailed filmographies with voice credits for each studio, and affords overdue recognition to the names behind the variegated tones of Droopy, Elmer Fudd, Woody Woodpecker, Betty Boop, The Big Bad Wolf and a noisy raft of other beloved characters.

***

The advent of YouTube has seen a new and growing audience discover these vintage cartoon films and become fans, even serious students, of that long-ago era. There are dedicated "pages" for fans of Fleischer, UPA, MGM and Lantz cartoons. Much of the ancient stuff can seem alarmingly dated, some is embarrassingly racist. Some of the cartoons, now eighty years old, sit happily alongside brand new CGI animated shorts on video platforms like Dailymotion. Some classic stuff is being aired on niche channels like MeTV, in sparkling restored prints.

Meanwhile the 21st century has seen the field of voice acting morph into a huge and highly competitive profession, running a wide gamut from television cartoons to areas like Gaming, Audiobooks and indie animation. And there are still the traditional bread and butter opportunities: ADR dubbing, promo announcements and voice-over commercials.

In today's multi-channel universe, it can often seem as though everyone alive now wants to be a "Voice Actor." Many of these folk, exposed to daily cartoons since they were in the crib, came of age with a burning desire to do animation voices. Nowadays, the bottomless pit of the internet is awash with a million voice wannabe's appearing in video selfies featuring their imitations of a hundred famous animated characters, or a hundred movie star voices. Some of these non-pros are surprisingly accomplished, although just as many shouldn't be giving up their day jobs anytime soon.

Certainly, thanks to the explosion of technology which emerged in the late eighties and grew by leaps and bounds with each succeeding year, this Millennium is media savvy to the point where people can be instantly jaded after a few days. Online in the year 2022, one is overwhelmed by endless short attention span entertainment options. For this aging author, it's often hard to recall how it felt growing up with just three black and white TV channels on a rickety home set. Home video wasn't even invented! In my youth I had to settle for capturing audio from old cartoons on a reel-to-reel tape deck ("What's reel-to-reel?" I can hear a bunch of folks ask).

A vast number of theatrical cartoons from 1930-60, the period covered by this book, were seen over and over in that early television era. After a few years, once the new made-for-TV cartoons were flourishing, the old theatrical relics totally disappeared for several decades. But now, in the 21st century, those early cartoon films are being uploaded anew, available on YouTube at the click of a mouse, ready for young fans and animators to discover and study.

It's not only superstar cartoon heroes of yore like Popeye who are now instantly accessible. Many less-remembered names like Andy Panda, obscure series like Scrappy, Herman and Katnip, forgotten animal icons like the Fox and the Crow: all are being discovered afresh by people whose great grandparents were their original audience.

Today's technology allows these vintage videos to be re-run scene by scene, paused frame by frame, in fact analysed to the point of obsession. Small wonder new viewers are now asking endless questions like, "Gee, I wonder who animated that scene?" or "Wow... who painted that gorgeous background art?" and especially, "OMG, who's doing that WEIRD voice?" Inquiring minds want to know, as these ancient shorts enjoy this completely unexpected renaissance.

Regrettably, online information for the old cartoons is often inaccurate or inadequate. With much film history, the 21st century has seen questionable guesswork accepted as gospel on social media. In particular, when it comes to identifying uncredited voices from those first thirty years of sound films, the misinformation can be rife. IMDb and Wikipedia are endlessly Googled on this arcane topic, and the answers provided are often plain wrong.

The detailed filmographies which make up Volume Two of this book, are my attempt to accurately record the many voice actor discoveries known to date. Some unconfirmed information is qualified as "likely" and unknown voices are noted. Frustratingly, most of the New York studios are not able to be included due to a lack of documentation. It is my intention to continue researching East Coast cartoons from Famous Studios, Van Beuren and Terrytoons. If and when credible information emerges, additional voice filmographies will appear in a revised edition.

This book ergo doesn't claim to be the ultimate word on the topic of vintage voice artists. Despite years of archival research, identifying various actors remains an unfinished task encompassing a vast field that was chronically under-documented. Surviving information is frustratingly incomplete for each of the studios. I regard this book as comprehensive, yet a work-in-progress. Do feel free to contact me regarding any additional facts that come to light for a revised edition. Unlike many of this book's subjects, you will actually get credit!

The period covered encompasses a finite timeframe from 1930-72, the lifespan of the original theatrical cartoons. Happily by 1960, with the flood of new TV cartoons like *Huckleberry Hound* and *Rocky & His Friends*, the actors providing all the great character voices, starting with hall-of-famers Daws Butler and Don Messick, were finally afforded screen credit, thanks to SAG union mandates. Today, half a century later, there are innumerable references to animation actors via insanely detailed online fan sites like Voice Chasers and specific Facebook pages.

As noted, work on this project began eons ago when most vintage cartoons were virtually impossible to view. This century boasts a totally changed media landscape, and, to the author's happy surprise, the world wide web is now a convenient video companion to much of this book. As a Tex Avery character from the thirties would put it, "Well … imagine that!!"

NOTE: Readers will see occasional repetition of names and historic milestones in more than one chapter. This was inevitable due to the overlapping use of the same voice talents and animation people at different cartoon studios throughout the Golden Age. In order to link each chronology, I have hopefully kept such reiteration of background and events as brief as possible.

Photos herein are headshots of the venerated voices, some of them very rare names, taken back in the day. They were scanned from ancient casting books. They are proudly "Lo-Res" because in many cases that's all I could locate! At least the ancient visuals will match the book's vintage timeframe.

PREAMBLE

The common link in each of the following Studio chapters is the early thirties, when theatrical cartoons with sound were a brand new "thing" and everyone who worked in animation, no matter which area, was learning something technical or artistic each day.

As the cartoons became a popular and anticipated part of a full movie program, dialogue was almost an afterthought for a few years. No-one was even thinking along the lines of witty wordplay and satire. For at least five years staff members supplied the majority of squawks, yells and limited dialogue, the obvious example being the undisputed industry leader Walt Disney. As everyone knows by now, Walt did the voice of Mickey Mouse.

The first professional voices hired for cartoons were singers from vocal groups - trios, quartets, soloists - who doubled on character voices. Margie Hines was one famous example, a vocalist hired for her squeaky imitation of entertainer Helen Kane when the Fleischer studio was planning to bring a female nightclub singer to cartoon life. That singer eventually morphed into Betty Boop.

Some archetypes were established early, like the baby-voiced and relentlessly cute female heroines from Minnie Mouse to Buddy's girlfriend Cookie, along with the endless falsetto-voiced male heroes: Oswald Rabbit, Krazy Kat, Bosko, Bimbo and human stars Buddy and Scrappy. With the notable exception of urban-oriented New York characters like Popeye and Betty Boop it was decided that talking animals, rather than humans, seemed to work best as cartoon figures,. And so voices were eventually found for internationally renowned pigs, ducks, rabbits, cats and a very long list of dumb dogs.

By 1935 Disney was widely regarded as the industry guru and his lavish cartoons like *Who Killed Cock Robin?* began to feature sophisticated soundtracks with interesting voices. When he teamed up Mickey Mouse, Donald Duck and Goofy he had three of the most famous cartoon voices of all time. Leon Schlesinger responded with Porky Pig, a genuinely different voice. Other producers took a while longer, but by the end of the decade great cartoon voices had become far more wide ranging.

Engaging professional voice talents from radio was the next logical step as comedy and clever dialogue, even repartee, began to accompany the animated stories. Radio's bottomless pit of comic stooge voices were suddenly on call, with expert wise-guys, foils and master mimics of funny accents vying for cartoons. Most famously, Mel Blanc took over the Porky Pig role and in the same cartoon he voiced a brand-new character who would develop into Daffy Duck.

Only a handful of these pros had the gift of great animation acting; it required a broad approach, larger than life, loud and high octane, full of exaggerated double takes, yells, shrieks and caricature, yet remaining wholly believable. It sounded easy, but it was an art. Pinto Colvig's Goofy and Billy Bletcher's range of villains were part of that development.

Technological aids helped, too, especially pitch change. Even already cartoonish voices could sound chipmunk-like when sped for comic effect. Celebrity impressions were also big in thirties animation, and certain imitations were caricatured vocally as well as visually, unless the celebrity was already "over the top," such as Joe Penner in the thirties or Red Skelton in the forties. Both of those zany comedians already resembled human cartoon characters.

Having noted these developments, the following chapters offer an in-depth history of how the art of character voices developed at each of the major movie studios. Their cartoon departments produced what is now referred to as Classic Era animation. The voices from that golden age, from primitive to hilarious, were truly pioneers of what is today a vibrant industry populated with several generations of voice artistry. It is to those enthusiastic torch carriers, still inspired by the Golden Age voice people herein, that this book is dedicated.

Chapter 1

WARNER BROS. CARTOON VOICES, 1930-69

Of all the Golden Age animation factories, Warner Bros. is the most significant to an historical survey of cartoon voice artists. Not only was it home to the gifted Mel Blanc for most of his fabled cartoon career, but the films themselves, in the quarter century from 1937 to '62, were the most dialogue driven in the industry. This reflected not only Blanc's huge influence, but quicksilver "gag men" whose flair for clever verbal parody matched their ability at visual jokes. In turn, outstanding directors like Bob Clampett and Chuck Jones made astute use of these prized story men in a body of work arguably unmatched by any other classic era cartoon shop.

At their best, the Warner cartoons set a comic standard in which the new art of "voice acting" would often reach the performance level of live action comedies. It's altogether appropriate that Warner Bros. was the main studio responsible for the birth of the sound movie; its cartoons soon mirrored the house style - brash, wisecracking, blue-collar, breathlessly fast - established in the make-or-break Depression days of the early thirties.

***

Background: Animation with Sound

The first cartoon films accompanied by sound were part of an experimental series called "Koko Song Cartunes" which began in

1924 as silent novelties designed for audience sing-alongs. A dozen titles in the series were made with sound from 1924-26 when producer Max Fleischer collaborated with the pioneering audio engineer Dr. Lee De Forest of Phonofilm fame. Each entry consisted of a vocal group, billed as the "Ko-Ko Quartette," recorded on film singing lyrics which appeared via animation on screen. A bouncing ball kept in time with the words. These sound cartoons, released by Fleischer's distribution company Red Seal Pictures, ran for two years.

Like so much of show business however, the timing was inexplicably wrong. The Phonofilm song reels could only be shown in the thirty six Red Seal theatres that had been equipped for De Forest's system. The films saw only limited success, despite the series being acknowledged a technical breakthrough.

A year after De Forest's first sound shorts Western Electric demonstrated a competing system of sound-film technology using high quality disc recordings. Warner Bros. Pictures was impressed enough to acquire the company in April 1925. After more than thirty years of silent cinema the prospect of sound married to image was at last approaching reality.

By the mid-twenties sound technology was being acknowledged as inevitable to the future of movies. Fleischer's song cartoons aside, the film industry was undertaking various experiments combining sound with live action over the next couple of years. A notable milestone was the Warner Bros. silent feature *Don Juan* starring the acknowledged master thespian John Barrymore. The lavish film had a symphonic score and sound effects added via Warner's "Vitaphone" technology. That movie did excellent box office, earning almost $1.7 million in the year 1926.

It was during this experimental period that a large body of vaudeville performers and musicians appeared in short films with sound. Seen today they are a kind of "time machine" peep back to an age that seems distinctly alien, odd novelties - comedians, dancers, singing groups, small orchestras - valuable mainly for preserving the voices and acts of many now forgotten stage entertainers.

But far beyond these examples of blending sound with image, it was the overnight success of Warner Bros.' feature movie triumph *The Jazz Singer* in October 1927 that left the film industry reeling. Warners had a major hit on their hands and the technical marvel was now fully recognized. The public was entranced with this show and its magnetic star Al Jolson, and suddenly "the talkies" were here to stay.

Despite the previous four years of Dr. De Forest's excellent sound-on-film experiments it was the Warner-Vitaphone sound-on-disc method of *The Jazz Singer* to which movie audiences responded with such enthusiasm. The term "wired for sound" became the new industry catchcry between 1927 and 1930, as theatres across the world were slowly and expensively converted and equipped.

It was during this flurry of activity that the animated cartoon was about to be revolutionized. By 1928 Walt Disney was already a five year veteran with successful silent cartoons like the Alice Comedies and Oswald the Lucky Rabbit to his name. Disney, always looking ahead, quickly intuited that synchronized sound, done imaginatively, would be the undisputed future of the motion picture cartoon. After making two silent cartoons with his new character Mickey Mouse, he meticulously planned the third entry, *Steamboat Willie*, to feature a closely-synched blend of animated drawings matched to music and novel sound effects. He sensed this was a make or break project.

While Fleischer had seen only limited success in marrying sound to animation in 1924-26, * another veteran cartoon producer, Paul Terry, tried a sound cartoon with a second East Coast entry in mid-1928, *Dinner Time*. It would be quite a stretch to claim that this first sound Aesop's Fable short featured any actual cartoon "voice," because the film was mainly an exercise in sound effects. The audio seems distinctly primitive: its mix of music and a raft of sounds, including faint voices that were really extra effects (a distant man yelling "Hey!!" and "Giddyap!") was unappealing and strident. Disney saw this short while he was in New York to record his own first sound cartoon, and he told his business manager-brother Roy it was "just a lot of racket." As before, audience reaction to Terry's effort was distinctly disappointing.

> * A small cartoon dog spoke one sentence in a reworked 1926 Max Fleischer Song Cartune, *My Old Kentucky Home*, via a newly recorded and animated opening produced by Fleischer's ex-partner Alfred Weiss. As first noted by Fleischer biographer Ray Pointer [1], this new material was made by Biophone in early 1929, a few months after Disney's success with *Steamboat Willie*. Although primitive, it would seem to be one of the first examples of cartoon mouth-and-lip synch, as the hound appeared to speak seven words while looking straight to the audience ("Follow the ball and join in…everybody!"). The short speech, though surprisingly good, meant little when seen in late 1929. Disney's far more ambitious, witty and entertaining film was the one that had so delighted both moviegoers and the industry months before.

It took Disney's famous *Steamboat Willie*, with its ingenious synchronizing of jaunty music with imaginative comedy action, to really show the way ahead for cartoons.

Disney's milestone cartoon was successful beyond its clever technical achievement. His film had been ingeniously worked around a series of musical gags that were not only innovative, but animated well enough to allow for suspension of disbelief. It appeared to the theatre audience that the various animals on the riverboat really were making the zany music and sound effects themselves. Moreover Disney's stars, Mickey and Minnie, were winsome and amusing. Their likability made the audience want to see them again.

A notable triumph, *Steamboat Willie* was a huge technological leap forward for animation. Disney, an ambitious young independent with obvious talent, was still busily establishing himself and anxiously seeking a release deal. The success of the cartoon was a terrific boost to his confidence. He was now a credible name in the movie colony, and was noticed by the major studios. The Warner brothers - Harry, Albert and Jack - already feted as the leading success story of commercially viable sound movies realized they needed a cartoon series.

Warner Bros. Cartoons: The Harman-Ising Years, 1930-33

From 1930 to 1933 the pioneering animation partners Hugh Harman and Rudolf Ising made the first Warner Bros. cartoons. They were ambitious ex-Disney staffers who signed contracts with distributor Charles Mintz in February 1928 to produce Oswald the Rabbit cartoons at the Winkler Pictures studio in Hollywood. That enterprise soon soured and Universal, which owned the Oswald character, decided to start up its own cartoon shop in 1929, on the Universal Pictures lot. After one year the Winkler Pictures staffers were let go. (Veteran New York animator and born self-promoter Walter Lantz became the producer of Universal's Oswald series.)

Since their Kansas City beginnings with Disney in the early twenties, Harman and Ising had talked of going into business together. Being suddenly out of work in early 1929 galvanized them. They formed a production company, Harman-Ising Pictures, using their marvellously serendipitous surnames.* "Talkie" cartoons were obviously the future: they had seen Disney's *Steamboat Willie* open to wild acclaim just months before, and that first Mickey sound cartoon was already regarded as *The Jazz Singer* of animation. Harman and Ising were eager to match Disney's considerable success.

* Animator-historian Mark Kausler knew Harman and Ising for years. They told him that the name "Harman-Ising" was first jokingly noted by Walt Disney.

Hugh Harman had already created and copyrighted his own cartoon character in early 1928. For months he worked on a "pilot" script with sequential drawings to feature this character, which he named Bosko. As sound took off, Harman decided to add dialogue to his script, intending to make a "talking" cartoon with synchronized speech. The first thing that Harman and Ising needed was a short reel to demonstrate their ability to produce quality animation which stressed clever synchronized dialogue.

It was decided to make the demo as a combination film: Bosko, a cheerful pen and ink cartoon imp, would interact with his live action animator, just as the silent Koko the Clown had done with Max Fleischer. Carman "Max" Maxwell, a background artist and scene planner, had been with Harman and Ising since their Kansas City beginnings. He was elected to provide the voice for Bosko, while Ising would play the on-camera animator who argues with the cheeky little character.

Vitavox, a small Hollywood recording firm, magnanimously gave the cash-strapped Harman free access to its audio facility. It was part of the Tec Art studio on Melrose and Irving. Tec Art was the same facility where Disney held his early recording sessions, according to Marcellite Garner, an ink and paint girl who did the voice of Minnie Mouse. Maxwell and Ising went before sound cameras one evening in May 1929.

For the animators' "mouth and lip" reference Maxwell was filmed as he spoke Bosko's dialogue. Of that historic session Harman recalled, "We had [Maxwell] speak hundreds of words. Lines, lines, lines - humorous lines." The team's tiny budget precluded a boom microphone, so Ising's voice sounds roomy and distant next to the clearly recorded voice of Maxwell as Bosko. [2] Animator

Rollin "Ham" Hamilton's sister Irene provided the piano accompaniment.

The animation of Bosko commenced soon after the live action shoot. Harman and Ising were assisted by two more ex-Disney / ex-Winkler animators, Ham Hamilton and Friz Freleng. The small but determined crew worked long hours on the film, which they named *Bosko the Talkink Kid* (1929). They worked from a Vine Street office in Hollywood's Otto K. Oleson building, just south of the Brown Derby restaurant.

The inventive four-and-a-half-minute show reel was completed by the late summer of 1929. Ising explained, "It was really made to illustrate the technique [of synchronizing dialogue]…we were selling animated lip motion." [3] Harman and Ising specifically intended to make sound cartoons which would outdo the ones starring Disney's mouse, by specializing in synchronous dialogue rather than merely showcasing a cacophony of music and sound effects.

In fact, Disney was already approaching what Harman and Ising were attempting to perfect: cartoons like *Mickey's Choo Choo* (1929), released as the Bosko reel neared completion, featured a small sequence of sync dialogue including what is thought to be the first example of Disney speaking for Mickey. It didn't deter Harman and Ising, though, who were aiming for a more sophisticated, lifelike semblance of speech and dialogue.

Meanwhile, Warner Bros., despite being one of the Hollywood majors, still didn't have their own cartoon series. Indeed, Warners was lagging behind. In 1929 three other studios had sound cartoon deals firmed: Universal was making Oswald the Lucky Rabbit, Paramount distributed Max Fleischer's Screen Songs and Talkartoons, and Columbia not only had Mintz's sound Krazy Kat cartoons, but were about to distribute Disney's next series, the musical Silly Symphonies.

Warner Bros. needed a cartoon release to compete with the double threat of Disney's already popular mouse and his newly launched musical series. Shrewd showman Jack L. Warner, the head of West Coast production, decided to approach Leon Schlesinger. Schlesinger was a successful showbiz veteran. In 1925 he acquired Pacific Title and Art Studio, the major supplier of inter-title cards and artwork for silent films. With sound taking off, he was looking to diversify and expand.

Schlesinger was always assured of a hearing from Jack Warner. His brother Gus was an executive at Warner Bros. and the studio itself had long worked closely with Schlesinger's titling company. In fact Pacific Title even designed the famous Warner Bros. shield logo. [4]

According to WB archivist Leith Adams, the brothers Warner probably felt they owed Schlesinger. The success of *The Jazz Singer* had so definitively established "talkies" that Schlesinger's inter-title business, so plentiful in the silent era, would inevitably shrink to just opening-closing titles. [5] Several accounts note that Schlesinger was in the Warners' good books beyond his titling business: Steve Schneider wrote, "according to legend, Leon had helped finance the Warner's risky, first-ever talkie, *The Jazz Singer*." [6]

In any event, it was Schlesinger's professional reputation with Pacific Title and Art, located on Bronson Avenue close by the Warner studio lot, which stood him in good stead. In 1929 he was tapped by Warners to supply a series of musical shorts for inclusion in their new *Vitaphone Varieties* program for the upcoming 1930 movie season. Warner suggested Schlesinger try to include a cartoon series.

Warner had recently passed on one cartoon proposal: Pinto Colvig's *Blue Notes* (1928) starring "Bolivar, the Talking Ostrich." Colvig, an eccentrically talented jack-of-all-trades later famous as the voice of Disney's Goofy, was a seasoned musician, ex-circus clown and writer of cartoon title gags for silent comedies. He also had experience as a newspaper cartoonist. Colvig had been experimenting with animation for some time, believing that the coming of sound would see cartoons replace two-reel comedy shorts. In 1928, close on the heels of Disney's *Steamboat Willie*, he self-funded a cartoon pilot with a partner named Walter Lantz, whom he met at the Mack Sennett comedy factory. By early 1929 Colvig attempted to sell his picture to Warner Bros. Although the cartoon's animation was ready, its soundtrack wasn't. Undeterred, Colvig proceeded to screen the film.

According to Colvig's studio biography, "[Colvig] finally got Jack Warner and [Leon] Schlesinger to look at it in a projection room. Pinto [would] furnish the sound effects himself. He sat down near the screen with an amazing array of film tins under his feet, cow bells, squawkers, his beloved clarinet, a battered trombone, and sundry other noise makers. The picture came on the screen and Pinto started doing his stuff. He had to keep his eye fastened on the screen in order to furnish the proper sound at the proper time. His spirits rose as he heard Warner and Schlesinger roaring with laughter in the back of the projection room. Finally, the screening was finished. Warner slapped him on the back. 'Son, you are all right,' he laughed.

"It was several months later that Pinto found out that Warner was laughing so hard at Pinto furnishing the sound effects he hardly saw the picture. It was finally sold to a small independent [distributor] a year later for about the amount Pinto had invested in it." * [7]

* During this experimental period, Walter Lantz began working as an animator at Winkler Pictures until, as noted, he took over production of the Oswald cartoons for Universal in 1929. Colvig joined Lantz's Universal outfit, before relocating to Disney's studio in late 1930. Coincidentally, Colvig had an office for a time in the same building where Harman and Ising made their earliest Looney Tunes. Animation was already proving to be a "small world" industry where the same names kept bumping into each other.

But despite Jack Warner nixing Colvig's *Blue Notes*, by late 1929 his studio was busy developing its large program of short films, and sound cartoons would inevitably be a must-have part of the mix. Bosko, a cartoon "star in waiting," was about to get lucky.

Following six months of frustrating sales effort peddling their demo reel, Harman and Ising met their future middleman Leon Schlesinger through a producer named Roland Reed. They had recently assisted Reed and his partner by helping to time the music, and draw the layouts, for a non-theatrical 16-millimeter home movie *Ham Berger and his Horse Radish* as one of a Kodak puppet series called Daffyland. Schlesinger was supplying its titles. [8] Reed suggested the cartoon makers meet Schlesinger at their office. (Schlesinger recalled crossing paths with Rudy Ising one year previous. Ising had been working as a cameraman and he shot some title art for Schlesinger: "It was [for] a Universal title of an airplane flying around the world [like] the *Tailspin Tommy* things" [9]).

When the entrepreneurial Schlesinger was shown Harman & Ising's *Talkink Kid* demo reel, he was enthused enough about Bosko's potential to borrow the print and approach Jack Warner. Schlesinger was quickly rewarded with a deal to supply Warner Bros. with one Bosko cartoon per month. An agreement between Schlesinger and the production company, Harman-Ising Pictures, was signed in late January of 1930. Hugh Harman and Rudolf Ising, along with the Warner Bros. cartoons, were finally on their way.

The jaunty little Bosko would star in an all-talking and musical cartoon series named "Looney Tunes," a branding umbrella title coined by Schlesinger to compete with Disney's "Silly Symphonies." Schlesinger installed his brother-in-law Raymond Katz as business manager at the Harman-Ising studio, in a further example of Hollywood's rampant nepotism; Katz ran payroll, attended story meetings and oversaw the cartoon budgets.

In 1929 Harry Warner, anticipating the ongoing popularity of musical feature films, had bought three huge music publishing concerns - Remick, Harms, and Witmark - in two deals totalling ten million dollars. [10] The plugging of songs owned by Warners' three publishing acquisitions was the *raison d'être* for the cartoons being commissioned. Cross-marketing was already underway. Warners required each cartoon to feature song choruses from their musical features, thereby generating healthy sales of Warner-licensed sheet music in an era when the player-piano and ukulele were still mainstays of home entertainment.

Schlesinger also signed to supply a second series for the Vitaphone Varieties shorts program. These were *Spoony Melodies*, live action mini-musicals again highlighting Warner-owned songs. A pilot, *Cryin' for the Carolines*, was shot in 1930. An eventual series of four shorts, renamed *Song'natas*, featured "organ music and song with animation backgrounds" and were released in the 1931-32 season.

With the cartoon deal underway, the first official Looney Tune, *Sinkin' in the Bathtub*, was made at a small facility on Western Avenue, two blocks from Harman and Ising's former workplace, the Winkler Oswald Rabbit studio. Both Ising and Maxwell recalled, "We worked on that [first *Bosko* Looney Tune] day and night for a very long while." [11] The result was an excellent cartoon, filled with ingenious gags highlighting precisely synchronized music and speech. It proved a solid hit, and Warner Bros. quickly picked up their option to continue the series for a full season of twelve. Harman-Ising Pictures could now relocate to a bigger studio. By April they were housed at 5663 Hollywood Boulevard in the new Cecil B. DeMille Building near Van Ness Avenue. Their studio was above Silver's dress shop and the Peters' drugstore, where the small crew ate.

An early news item on the *Bosko* cartoons appeared in the *Los Angeles Times* in December 1930. Entertainment reporter John Scott explained various aspects of the cartoon making process, noting how musician Frank Marsales, "worked hand in hand with the men who work out the story, the 'gags' and the plot characters. These story conferences are a treat for the uninitiated. A plausible plot is concocted, then shorn of sense and reason and made into a sort of nightmare. Trees do spring dances, animals become human, fish are given intelligent expressions, and so on. The most difficult part of the whole business is to present a logical story in a ridiculous manner, at the same time making it entertaining." [12]

Of all the Hollywood-based animation companies, it was Harman-Ising Pictures which pioneered the most sophisticated use of cartoon voices.

Harman-Ising: Voices and soundtracks

From the start Harman and Ising enjoyed free access to the recording facilities and standby orchestra at Warner Bros. Sunset Boulevard lot. [13] Rival producers Disney and Lantz weren't so lucky, incurring their own sound recording costs. The Warner studio also housed the Warner-owned radio station (KFWB), then five years old. The character voices for the Warner cartoons released between 1931 and 1933 would soon be supplied by a small group of regulars heard on KFWB, with only an occasional assist from outside talent.

Most of the early voices, however, belonged to in-house personnel. This was standard procedure at every cartoon studio in this experimental, pre-actor union era. Max Maxwell, who spoke for Bosko in the sales film, returned to voice the first Looney Tune, *Sinkin' in the Bathtub* (1930). Maxwell's Bosko voice was a vaudeville African American dialect, lifting attitudes and popular catchphrases ("Well, here ah is," and "I'se regusted") from the wildly popular radio comedy *Amos & Andy*, which had soared to instant national success in 1928. [14]

As before, while he was recording the voice Maxwell's face was filmed as reference for the animators to approximate Bosko's lip-movements. On camera, he wore black-face makeup and read Bosko's dialogue with exaggerated mouth actions ("He-ll-o, Hon-ey"). This practice, however, was abandoned after the first two cartoons. Harman-Ising's team quickly mastered the art of "track reading": pre-determining on a bar chart the precise frames of film - which ran 24 frames per second - where each vowel and consonant would start and stop, and where each word on the sound track would be. A metronome marked the exact timing of the musical beats.

For *Sinkin' in the Bathtub* Maxwell was teamed with a young ingénue named Rochelle Hudson, the earliest voice of Bosko's girlfriend, Honey. The cartoon was successful enough for Ms Hudson's agent to use it as bargaining power in obtaining a Fox Pictures studio contract for his youthful starlet. Like Maxwell she adopted a Southern dialect for her character and, while recording, was filmed in black-face makeup for "mouth reference." [15] She impressed Leon Schlesinger enough that he was still crediting her in interviews years later.

As the series continued, Rudy Ising recalled, "Maxwell would be painting the wash on a background, and Hugh would say, 'Time to go over to the recording.' He'd have to lay that [artwork] down and go." [16] Incidentally, Maxwell's long-time nickname "Uncle Boscombe" was the source for Bosko's name. [17]

Sound editor Fred MacAlpin recalled, "At first, a lot of the voices were being done by Maxwell, and Rudy, and Hugh." [18] Ising spoke for the Looney Tunes' various gravel-voiced villains, starting with *Big Man from the North* (1930). Voice acting was a function he continued for much of his cartoon career. Ising admitted, "I did a lot of heavies, [but] I could never come in on a beat; I'm not that much of a musician."[19] He was also heard giving broad imitations of then-famous bandleaders Ted Lewis ("Are ya listenin', hmmm?") and Ben Bernie ("You are now in the hands of the dear old maestro"). Actual dialogue remained minimal in the first year's releases. Wordplay was a poor cousin to visual gags, as the comedy conventions of the silent cartoons lingered, and because the music was being heavily emphasized.

Bosko's accent was de-ethnicized to a neutral falsetto after *Sinkin' in the Bathtub.* "Max" Maxwell was soon replaced on the soundtracks by Bernard Brown, a veteran musician and the recording supervisor at Warner Bros. since the twenties, when he worked on the earliest Vitaphone sound shorts. Bernie Brown was one of the important names in the early history of the Warner cartoons.

A news item from early 1931 described Bernard Brown as "the official voice of the 'cast.' He gives Bosco [sic] his beautiful tenor and bestows upon the heavy his frightening bass. He contributes Honey's soprano and he whistles for everybody. He can also laugh like a hyena. In short, he is a fellow of many talents. Mr. Brown is a violinist by profession but gives all his time now to providing 'Looney Tunes' with voice and song." [20]

Within a short time, the cartoons featuring the eternally cheery Bosko were proving consistently popular. They managed to compete respectably with Disney's films, admittedly by appropriating various Oswald and Mickey gags in their first year. It was a given that the Disney studio's technical and artistic progress between 1931-33 set the industry standard. This ensured that Disney's cartoons starring the hugely popular Mickey would soon outstrip all competition, both aesthetically and at the box-office. Even so, the Looney Tunes with their close ties to musicals and their excellent synchronization, remained a hit with audiences. The crucial exhibitor reaction was encouraging.

The studio's second series, christened Merrie Melodies, commenced production in 1931. That spring, well-known Los Angeles radio personality Johnny Murray joined the Harman-Ising voice team. Bernie Brown was always busy in the Warner Bros. sound department, but as handy as he was at doing various falsetto voices, he lacked a certain acting ability and a new voice was being sought. The upcoming Merrie Melodies series would need a more versatile range.

Rudolf Ising was already a fan of Johnny Murray's radio work. He encouraged Harman to listen to Murray's fast-paced *Hi-Jinks* comedy show, sponsored by Franco Baking, which originated at Warner Bros. own radio station KFWB. [21]

A lyric tenor, Johnny Murray was an ex-band trumpeter and vocalist who had done a stint with Gus Arnheim's famous orchestra at the Cocoanut Grove nightclub in Hollywood's swank Ambassador Hotel. In 1929 Murray dubbed the singing voice of star actor Richard Barthelmess for the hit Warner Bros. prison feature *Weary River*. The versatile Murray had talents beyond music and was soon a popular radio comedian.

Ising recalled, "[For the Merrie Melodies] we used Johnny Murray as the voice of nearly all the lead characters." [22] These included Foxy and Goopy Gear, making Murray one of West Coast animation's first "voice artists." Murray was a man of great humor, popular with both the radio public and industry pros. For one scene in the first Merrie Melodie, *Lady, Play Your Mandolin!* (1931) Foxy breaks into an Al Jolson imitation provided by Murray. This was one of the earliest examples of celebrity caricature and a reflexive studio in-joke, hallmarks of countless Warner cartoons to come. (Future director Bob Clampett recalled his earliest Harman-Ising assignment being this cartoon: he did some animation for a background crowd "with streamers and so on." [23])

Johnny Murray soon became an integral part of the overall Harman-Ising "sound." He took over Bosko's voice as the dialogue increased. For the curious, he can be seen on-camera in the Warner Bros. musical *Twenty Million Sweethearts* (1934), playing himself, KFWB radio announcer Johnny Murray; the movie often screens on TCM.

The Merrie Melodies effectively replaced Schlesinger's short-lived *Song'natas* package. The cartoons featured non-recurring characters in musical settings, staging humorous song and dance routines. Two vocal choruses from a Warner-owned song were heard in each entry. It was decided to divide the production duties: Merrie Melodies were made in a unit headed by Ising, while Harman took sole charge of the Looney Tunes with Bosko. With the workload increased to twenty-six cartoons a year, head animator and future Warner cartoon director Friz Freleng took on supervision of the character layouts for both units. Harman said that Freleng effectively became a co-director. Freleng recalled differently, insisting his only full "directing" job at this stage was on one instalment, *Bosko in Dutch* (1933).

The Harman-Ising cartoons have been criticised for being plotless, but in this early period "story" was beside the point: music matched to image was the attraction and a six-minute cartoon could only really be a musical incident, bolstered by the gags generated at an evening think-tank session with the staff. Before recording, the tempo of each scene was determined by use of the ever present metronome, the device which afforded a rhythmic relationship between action and music: in these cartoons, not only characters but buildings, trees and other objects would sway to a tempo.

The recording sessions were supervised by Harman and Ising, sound specialist Bernard Brown and editor Fred MacAlpin and their musician Frank Marsales, who had previously arranged the music for Schlesinger's Spoony Melodies. A *Herald Tribune* piece noted that Marsales had "fourteen musicians in his permanent orchestra." [24]

William Hanna, the nineteen-year-old head of ink and paint, joined the staff in 1930 while they were still on Western Avenue. Hanna possessed an innate flair for music - as a child he'd studied piano and saxophone - and a budding gift for lyrics, story and timing: he contributed special lyrics for various cartoons, crediting Ising as his mentor for the rest of his life. Even in his early twenties, Hanna showed the aptitude which would see him head the giant Hanna-Barbera corporation decades later.

Assisting on story work were British-born gag man Bob Edmunds, whose work visa had actually expired, and Otto Englander who later left for the Ub Iwerks studio before landing at Disney. A major contributor to the Merrie Melodies was Jonathan "Moe" Caldwell, a dance instructor and expert in tap. He had an office next door to the Harman-Ising studio. Caldwell soon wore the title of "dance director." He was largely responsible for the path taken by the Merrie Melodies, particularly in pure vaudeville entries like *Goopy Geer* (1932) and *Bosko's Picture Show* (1933). For the animators, Caldwell imitated dance steps of various performers like then-famous eccentric dancer Will Mahoney, whose unique routines are recreated by Bosko for *Bosko in Person* (1933). [25]

Caldwell, an enthusiast of Black jazz and swing music, would later contribute many musical ideas to Harman-Ising's MGM cartoons. [26] The improved dance animation was intricate enough to warrant Maxwell shooting pencil tests; also tested were various animated cycles, including animator Bob McKimson's superb rain effect. [27]

According to Maxwell, musician Frank Marsales at first wanted "to synchronize every syllable of every piece of dialogue, so there wasn't any [visual] freedom at all in our stuff then." [28] Scott Bradley, who composed the scores for Harman and Ising's later MGM cartoons, dismissed Marsales somewhat curtly as "not much of a composer - his instrument was tuba." [29] Maybe so, but Marsales's résumé included playing that instrument with no less than John Philip Sousa and arranging for Paul Whiteman's band. Hardly small-time credits.

Sidebar: Recording the early cartoons

Technically the cartoons were one long learning curve between 1930-32. In the earliest years of talkies, Warner Bros. was committed to its patented Vitaphone system of sound-on-disc recording. But the rest of the industry, impressed by Fox Film's Movietone process, was adopting the superior, less trouble-prone and less cumbersome sound-on-film method. Warner Bros. eventually went with the flow: in 1930 the spoken dialogue in Looney Tunes was pre-recorded on blank variable-area film. Pre-recording of the voices speaking dialogue occurred after the storyboard was approved, but before animation commenced.

Weeks later when the cartoon was almost finished, any last minute vocal effects (like an extra yell for "Help!!") and all the singing parts were added in a "post-recording" session where the actors, singers and musicians could see the action on a screen. Ising clarified, "The dialogue and the songs were separate [recording sessions]. Nearly all the music, [including] the singing, was post-recorded at the same time we recorded the orchestra, after the animation [was completed]. We did it the same day. We'd usually record the orchestra first, and get them out of the way, then we'd record [any extra pick-up] dialogue." [30]

Once the post-sound session was completed, the cartoons were dubbed. This meant each separate track - music, dialogue and sound effects - was combined. At first the final mixes were transferred to 16-inch Vitaphone discs. Dubbing director and editor Fred MacAlpin, assigned to the cartoons, recalled, "They realized [early] that they couldn't make cartoon tracks satisfactorily on discs alone." [31]

Describing the difficulties inherent in the early disc recording method, MacAlpin said, "If Bosko was running, I'd have to cut in each footstep, which took quite a bit of time. [That's why recording on] film was an advantage: you could pull it, squeeze it, turn it upside down, slow it down, speed it up [via] a series of belts on the film machine." [32] Indeed, some 1930 Bosko cartoons feature a gaggle of animals who get angry and "speak" in a sped-up chipmunk-like tone.

MacAlpin recalled, "In 1930, Warners owned one film recorder and one reproducer," [33] so it was decided that the requisite sound effects would be recorded on film during the dubbing sessions which took place at First National studios in Burbank. The early cartoons featured sound effects supplied by musicians, mostly the pit drummer who used a wood block for footsteps. The inventive MacAlpin, who had a radio background, was soon creating various effects from scratch. Max Maxwell said, "[MacAlpin] had a good knowledge of music, and he [had] a pretty good mechanical mind, too." [34]

The *Herald Tribune* article described the early drummer's effects kit: "[The drummer] has a veritable menagerie of sound devices at his disposal - auto horns, all kinds of whistles, fire sirens, a scheme for producing an airplane whirr, mechanical imitations of falling rain, an elephant's sneeze or a horse's neigh." [35]

Certain sound effects in the earliest cartoons seem hollow and obvious today. The art of mixing was being perfected daily, and primitive devices like incidental characters talking "backwards" were part of an overall experimentation in the early days of transitioning to sound film. In a 1936 magazine piece Schlesinger recalled "having access to Warner Bros. record libraries...a John Barrymore dialog record, played in reverse [and sped], has served for the gibberish of animal characters." [36]

These noises were matched by now-dated gags, like the constant blowing of raspberries and expectorating of tobacco juice, reflecting the earthy, rural background of the cartoon staff. As Friz Freleng summed it up, "We were all flying blind." [37] An art-based industry was being developed daily by trial and error. A palpable sense of enthusiastic "work-shopping" is apparent in each new entry.

The first year of Merrie Melodies featured the same distinctive "stage sound" heard in Warner Bros. feature musicals like *42nd Street* (1933). At first the microphones had selective limitations which forbade the recording of dialogue and music together, due to differences in reverb. However, recording equipment and techniques improved by leaps and bounds in this bustling laboratory period, and certainly by 1931-32 the cartoons boast well-balanced dubbing. MacAlpin said, "We got more film dummies [duplicators] so that I could put the dialogue on one and the sound effects on another and have probably three or four different tracks." [38]

The direct-to-disc recording process was phased out from March 1930 at Warner Bros. when First National abandoned the four-year old Vitaphone disc system and committed fully to recording sound-on-film. However, even after the changeover, soundtrack discs were still issued for a few years to service the thousands of theatres which had invested in the costly disc playback process. And to ensure the highest audio quality, all music recording was still mastered on shellac glass-based discs, then transferred to film stock.

***

Ising's high-spirited Merrie Melodies were far more musically driven than the Looney Tunes and required specialty talents. The first four Melodies, following Schlesinger's suggestion, featured "guest" big bands to boost projected music sales: Abe Lyman's Californians were in three cartoons, and Gus Arnheim's Cocoanut Grove house orchestra played in another. Frank Marsales would rehearse with these bands at their theatres of engagement before recording them on the Warner stage. [39] Musically Marsales had more to work with in the Merrie Melodies: each entry featured an irresistible hot jazz break, as the on-screen action intensified.

Contributing vocally were The King's Men quartet, consisting of top tenor Bud Linn, second tenor Jon Dodson, baritone Rad Robinson, and arranger-bass singer Ken Darby. [40] The group, who would become nationally famous in the forties for their weekly comic-novelty numbers on radio's *Fibber McGee and Molly*, were young staff singers at KFWB (in fact the quartet was named for station manager Jerry King [41]). They had a regular spot on the Warner station's popular Sunday night radio offering, *Franco Hi-Jinks*, hosted by Johnny "Bosko" Murray. In a rare, surviving edition of the show Murray introduces the quartet who sing "I Love a Parade," sounding exactly as they did in the cartoon of that title.

The quartet sang most of the mandatory choruses in the Merrie Melodies ("Smile, Darn Ya, Smile," "You Don't Know What You're Doin'") and contributed various speaking lines. They warble gleefully in cartoons like *Three's a Crowd*. Ising recalled, "The King's Men did practically all our quartet work; [they] also used to do some individual voices; there was a little guy who was a [Scotsman] in the quartet who did voices." [42] Leader Ken Darby, first heard as a hobo pig in the early Bosko entry *Box Car Blues* (1930), provided most bass voices, like the Emperor in *One Step Ahead of My Shadow* (1933), and court jester Goopy Geer's singing voice for *The Queen Was in the Parlor* (1932). A decade later Darby was established as one of Hollywood's top vocal arrangers, making important choral contributions to *The Wizard of Oz* (1938) and various Disney cartoon features.

Also prominent in the Merrie Melodies was the fine girl's trio The Rhythmettes. The members were Mary Moder, Dorothy Compton and Amy Lou Barnes; two years later Moder and Compton provided the high-pitched voices for two of Disney's *Three Little Pigs*. Prolific background performers in musicals and at the Warner radio station, the Rhythmettes were heard to charming advantage in cartoons like their first, *Red-Headed Baby* (1931) or *It's Got Me Again* (1932).

Ising recalled, "The girl singers and Johnny Murray could read music. And the King's Men [could], too. These people, we didn't have to pre-record [for songs], because [musician Frank Marsales] could write it out for them, and they could do it right to a beat. They could give it inflection." [43] From the start the Merrie Melodies were lively and relentlessly cheerful cartoons, technically proficient for their time. Their debut coincided with a vast improvement in Harman's concomitant Looney Tunes, with entries like *Bosko Shipwrecked!* (1931) and *Bosko the Doughboy* (1931) employing cinematic staging which left the Bosko cartoons of just a year before looking archaic in comparison.

The squeaky voices of Honey ("Ain't he cute!") and other female leads in the Harman-Ising cartoons were supplied by one of the girls from the Rhythmettes trio. It was probably Mary Moder, who specialized in "child voices," but this remains unconfirmed as Ising could not remember which girl it was. [44] Also unknown is the identity of the mimic providing the fine Maurice Chevalier impression heard in several cartoons, including *A Great Big Bunch of You* (1932) and *Bosko in Person* (1933), proving a most frustrating thorn in your author's side.

Ising told Michael Barrier, "We always had to get permission to do the [celebrity] caricatures." [45] * The Chevalier voice turns up again, after Harman and Ising's departure, in the 1934 cartoon *Buddy's Showboat*. Schlesinger revealed that having entree to Warner Bros.' record library meant that real stars occasionally "spoke" from cartoon mouths: "[Comedian] Joe E. Brown's wide-mouthed yell has been heard in cartoons as the roar of a hippo." Indeed in *Lady, Play Your Mandolin!* (1931) a yelling hippo was designed to resemble Joe E. Brown. [46]

---

* Ising recalled that several Hollywood drag queens auditioned once the Merrie Melodies were under way. Performers like Jean Malin, from BBB's Cellar - a gay Hollywood

speakeasy specializing in female impersonation revue - were eager to audition when Harman-Ising began using vocal imitations. Ising recalled of that less inclusive era, "One guy sang 'Life is Just a Bowl of Cherries' just like Tallulah Bankhead or whoever...Frank Marsales could never stand it when these guys showed up and would have to leave the room." [47]

One early Merrie Melodie was given the title *Crosby, Columbo and Vallee* (1932). The soundtrack obviously needed imitations of then topical radio crooners like Bing Crosby and Rudy Vallee. A seventeen-year old student who sang at Long Beach Junior College was contacted by Warner Bros. to do the impressions. His name was Art Scott, and a few years later he began a long career in animation, from Mintz to Disney and all the way to Hanna-Barbera.

Another vocal specialist came from the male choral group The Rangers, who sang background for Warner Bros. feature musicals. Basso profundo Jesse Delos Jewkes, whose résumé called him "Hollywood's premier bass," plays the pig that scats to "Sweet Adeline" before belching up an ear of corn in the Russian-flavored *The Booze Hangs High* (1930). Jewkes also sings "In Days of Old When Knights Were Bold" for *Bosko's Knight-Mare* (1933). According to Ising, "He had one of the deepest bass voices I ever heard." [48]

When the King's Men quartet relocated to New York as part of bandleader Paul Whiteman's radio package, The Singing Guardsmen, another excellent freelance quartet, replaced them in the last two Harman-Ising entries. The Guardsmen continued to sing for the Leon Schlesinger produced cartoons that followed, and why not: they, like all the other "voices," were doing a daily quarter-hour show on the Warner-owned radio station.

Occasionally, freelance artists like singer-ventriloquist Shirley Reed, who plays the homely queen in *Young and Healthy* (1933), and bird-animal imitator Purves Pullen, in *I Wish I Had Wings* (1932), were hired. Several vocal effects were done in-house by Fred

MacAlpin who recalled, "I'd run out onto the stage and do a cock's crow or a crow's caw or something like that." [49] Even Max Maxwell was still contributing an odd voice in Harman-Ising's last year, such as the Yiddish-accented baby in 1933's *Shuffle Off to Buffalo*.

In early 1933 the always restless Hugh Harman, frustrated by budgets considerably lower than Disney's, decided to break ties with Schlesinger and seek a better release deal elsewhere. He felt that Schlesinger lacked ambition and was "shallow." [50] After the first two years, Harman was eager to make less formulaic, less restrictive cartoons on bigger budgets, allowing for color and more sophisticated content. Harman always had a compulsion to compete with his former boss Disney, a desire that became somewhat obsessive and, buttressed by the vagaries of circumstance, ultimately futile.

Harman decided to approach the Warner Bros. head office in New York. But he was ambushed by the canny Schlesinger who had been tipped off by story man Earl Duvall, himself lobbying for a directing post. [51] Schlesinger beat Harman to Manhattan by taking a plane. He surprised Harman and called his bluff, saying he would build his own staff of animators. Harman was read the riot act and learned just how angry Warner Bros. was at this turn of events, recalling "Schlesinger was furious." [52]

In any event, Schlesinger, always a little flamboyantly egotistical, was eager to head his own cartoon studio rather than being the middleman for an out-source firm like Harman-Ising Pictures. He may even have fancied himself being thought of as another Disney: Harman and Ising had seen the writing on the wall three years earlier when Schlesinger added a "producer" credit for himself in the opening titles of their very first cartoon. [53]

The upshot of these moves saw the departure of Harman, Ising and most of their animation staff in the spring of 1933. Several months later, they secured an MGM release and the resultant "Happy Harmonies" series. Harman, with Universal's takeover of Oswald the Rabbit still fresh in his mind, retained rights to his own copyrighted Bosko character. As a trade-off, Warner Bros. not only kept the two series names, Looney Tunes and Merrie Melodies, but also the end trademark "That's all, folks!" A version of that tagline had been heard as early as the *Talkink Kid* demo reel which ends with Bosko drawling, "So long, folks... see y'all later."

Johnny Murray and the same vocal groups pop up in some of Harman-Ising's early Metro cartoons, as well as two freelance Cubby Bear entries, *Cubby's World Flight* (1933) and *The Gay Gaucho* (1933). Harman and Ising subcontracted on those two cartoons in mid-1933 for the New York-based Van Beuren studio; a third Cubby cartoon made by them, *Mischievous Mice*, wasn't released. Harman and his business manager Gordon Wilson then spent several hard winter weeks negotiating in New York City, signing off on the MGM distribution contract in February 1934. [54]

MacAlpin recalled the break with Schlesinger coinciding with an industry-wide sound strike: "All the sound men walked out."[55] He managed to cut the audio for Harman-Ising's Cubby Bear cartoons at the Moviola Company during the strike. By early 1934 MacAlpin, too, had left Warner Bros. and was cutting sound for Harman-Ising starting with their earliest Metro cartoon; he remained with MGM until 1948. Meanwhile, Leon Schlesinger was now on his own.

1933-1944: Leon Schlesinger Productions

It was mid-1933, and Walt Disney had just set new standards in the short cartoon field with the release of his enormously popular Silly Symphony *Three Little Pigs*. Schlesinger now had a tough act to follow. A frantic coast-to-coast headhunt for animation talent ensued before Schlesinger could begin his own series of Looney Tunes and Merrie Melodies. They were produced at Warner's Sunset Boulevard studio,* between Fernwood and Van Ness Avenues, in what Bob Clampett called "the Jolson building" (Al Jolson's old dressing room was part of the structure, right next door to Bernard Brown's large music room). [56]

> * Although it housed the KFWB radio station and the cartoon studio for twenty-two years, much of Warner Bros.' Sunset Boulevard lot was effectively a rental facility after 1933. Warner feature film production had long since transferred to the large First National lot eight miles away in Burbank (First National Studios was acquired by the brothers Warner between 1928 and 1931).

Schlesinger's brother-in-law Raymond Katz continued as business manager, his original function at Harman-Ising Pictures. In this early period, Schlesinger and his associate, producer Sid Rogell, also made a series of low budget "Four Star Western" features showcasing the young John Wayne. One entry, *Haunted Gold* (1932), featured eerie animated opening titles.

Assisting Schlesinger from the start was the seasoned recording supervisor and musician Bernard Brown, who we already met with Harman-Ising. Apparently, Jack Warner assigned him to Schlesinger's new cartoon venture because of Brown's useful friendship with industry leader Disney. In turn, Bernie Brown recommended his long-time friend and tennis partner, the Disney animator Tom Palmer, for the role of Schlesinger's production manager.

Of immediate concern, Schlesinger needed a cartoon "star" for his Looney Tunes. Newly hired Jack King, another ex-Disney animator, helped Palmer work on the replacement character for Bosko, a colorless young boy named Buddy. Buddy was created by Earl Duvall, who had been a gagman for both Harman-Ising and Disney. Buddy was a human cartoon star who would compete with Columbia's two-year old Scrappy series, which also starred a feisty young boy character. Unfortunately, Buddy seemed more like a young man in some entries, his age apparently as nebulous as his personality.

The makeshift conglomeration that made up Schlesinger's new outfit struggled mightily at first, with artists from several far-flung studios, at varying levels of draftsmanship, hastily adjusting to a new house style. The first few months saw the cartoon direction duties split between a motley collection of talent.

Although a respected animator, Tom Palmer clearly lacked story ability. Bernard Brown described his pal as "a serious fellow, in a way, and not too funny." [57] Palmer simply didn't work out, supervising just two cartoons, *Buddy's Day Out* (1933), the first of the new Looney Tunes, and the more successful *I've Got to Sing a Torch Song* (1933), the first new Merrie Melody.

Early previews of Palmer's first "Buddy" cartoon proved disastrous, with Warner's front office complaining loudly about its poor quality. Bob Clampett recalled Buddy's girlfriend Cookie resembling a girl in Disney's early Silly Symphony *El Terrible Toreador* (1929). Warner Bros.' New York office rejected *Buddy's Day Out* threatening Schlesinger's heavy investment in his new setup. Palmer's clumsy cartoon required costly reworking by Earl Duvall.

Schlesinger was desperate. Via a series of phone calls made by Ray Katz, he virtually begged Friz Freleng to come back and offered him a directing position. Freleng recalled Schlesinger panicking he "could lose the $30,000" he had just put into the studio. [58] Freleng had just finished work on Harman-Ising's Cubby Bear cartoons and had never been fully convinced of Hugh Harman's managerial flair. With a growing family and an ailing brother to support, he elected to return to the devil he knew. At the end of September Freleng was back in the Warner Bros. fold. Palmer was let go by Schlesinger and relocated to the Van Beuren Studio in New York, where he worked on the color Rainbow Parade cartoons.

Meanwhile, veteran Disney animator Jack King was, in Bob Clampett's words, "the number one cartoonist at the studio" [59] and had been overseeing all the animation until Freleng was back. Eager to help Schlesinger, Bernard Brown also pitched in; he was one of those jacks of all trades, quick to master a range of skills. After Palmer left, Brown supervised a couple of cartoons in consultation with the layout artists and gag men, along with overseeing each cartoon's dialogue recording.

Upon his return, Freleng brought Ben Hardaway over from Disney as a story man. They had known each other since their Kansas City Film Ad beginnings in the early twenties. Hardaway, whose lifelong nickname was "Bugs," supervised a few cartoons with Brown: while Brown prepared the exposure sheets for the animators, Hardaway worked on story and gags. Freleng also brought in other Kansas City veterans, like cartoonist-gagman Mel "Tubby" Millar.

Schlesinger's other ex-Disney hire Earl Duvall proved a competent director, but after he made *Honeymoon Hotel* (1934), the studio's first color cartoon, he became too big for his boots and was let go. Freleng recalled Duvall getting drunk at breakfast one morning in the spring of 1934, insisting he was worth more money following the notable success of *Honeymoon Hotel* with exhibitors. Freleng was all praise for Duvall's cartoon, but warned him to sober up before mentioning money matters with Schlesinger. However, the impetuous Duvall tipsily traipsed into the boss's office, where he was immediately given his marching orders. [60]

Meanwhile, Freleng helped re-work and re-time some poorly conceived Buddys-in-progress, including Duvall's *Buddy's Beer Garden* (1933). He then directed *Buddy the Gob* (1934) before taking over full supervision of the Merrie Melodies. Here Freleng felt right at home: a lifelong vaudeville aficionado, he had some musical knowledge and a natural affinity for song and dance. He timed the action in his cartoons on musical bar sheets. Freleng would eventually become the top man at Schlesinger's outfit. Various people including his future layout artist Hawley Pratt and animator Arthur Davis considered Freleng the political "spark plug" behind the Warner cartoon studio for the next thirty years. [61]

With Freleng now working exclusively on Merrie Melodies, Jack King was, a little reluctantly, appointed head of the Looney Tunes. King directed the most Disney-esque of the early Schlesinger cartoons featuring cute characters like the two puppies, Ham and Ex. His tenure lasted through April 1936 when he returned to the Disney lot to direct the newly launched Donald Duck series.

***

Schlesinger: Voices and soundtracks

Music still took precedence over character voices in the early years, as the Merrie Melodies attempted - not too successfully - to compete with Disney's increasingly impressive Silly Symphonies. As historian Michael Barrier revealed, by this point the Silly Symphonies had three times the Warner budget. [62] Since 1932, veteran musician and sound supervisor Bernard Brown had been partnered with Schlesinger and musician-vocal arranger Norman Spencer in a recording venture called Pacific Sound Service. Brown supervised all the cartoon recordings and "read" the tracks to exposure sheets, while Spencer composed most of the scores and contracted the vocal talent.

The cartoons at first featured in-house voices like the genial Bernie Brown himself: as he had demonstrated on the earliest Looney Tunes in 1930, he possessed a flexible high range which was used for the first voice of new star character Buddy, as well as providing the various "That's all, folks!" spoken at the end of each cartoon. Brown recalled, "I did the voice for Buddy a long time…I did it all falsetto…Then I [also] did the whistling and anything musical. And the female voices. I did some of those, too. I had a very clear falsetto voice. Many times, I'd be back East, and [doubting friends said], 'That isn't you,' and I'd say, 'Yes it is. I'll do it for you.'" [63]

Brown was regarded as a most easy going character with a happy disposition. Bob Clampett described him as "Constantly cheery."[64] Animator Norm McCabe recalled him as always pleasant, smiling, and carrying his ever-present violin around. McCabe also recalled Norman Spencer, describing him as "always with the cigar, a real Tin Pan Alley type." [65]

Schlesinger's first Merrie Melodie, *I've Got to Sing a Torch Song* (1933), had a topical radio theme and featured some effective caricatures of movie and air talents. It employed a cast of KFWB performers as voices: actress Noreen Gamill imitated Greta Garbo, Zasu Pitts and Mae West, while The Rhythmettes trio did a Boswell Sisters take-off warbling the title song.

One early voice performer would become famous. A newspaper item from mid-1935 noted that child star Jane Withers, the tomboy rival to good girl Shirley Temple at Fox Film, had recently become a big movie name in the 1934 feature *Bright Eyes*. In reviewing her career, the article notes that Jane, a precociously accomplished child actress and mimic, arrived in Hollywood in 1932.

> "[Jane and her mother] pestered casting directors for eight months, but not a tumble did they get. But the radio was still left. Here Jane had better luck. She was selected from several hundred youngsters to exemplify the "Nuisance" on KFWB's weekly *Juvenile Revue*. This led to her being hired by the animated cartoon people to dub in the voices of the little drawn figures. She did six months of Looney Tunes, also Willie Whoppers [for MGM], sometimes imitating as many as four voices in a single reel." [66]

Forty years later Clampett and Brown vividly recalled seven-year-old Jane Withers, accompanied by her mother, coming in to Brownie's music room to audition. Clampett reminded Brown that Norman Spencer accompanied the tot on piano, and "she belted out a song." In one news item Schlesinger clarified, "Jane Withers came from radio to double vocally for a child character, before any studio gave her a chance on her own."[67]

Other Schlesinger staff voices on call included veteran New York animator Jack Carr who had owned up to "some speaking for Buddy" in later entries. In fact, Carr, who had performing talent, had been a voice for Columbia's star character Krazy Kat, and after that was animating at Universal for Walter Lantz where he became one of the many staff voices. Clampett recalled Carr "leaving his animation desk to go and record Buddy's lines" [68] and even playing other characters like "the Rube rooster that carries some flowers to his girl-hen" in *Let It Be Me* (1936). Clampett also recalled director Jack King providing an occasional voice, identifying the Jack Mercer-like "human monkey" Professor in Tex Avery's *Plane Dippy* (1935). [69]

Versatile gag writer Ted Pierce, who joined the studio in 1933, began providing his whiskey-voiced characters for the cartoons, starting with a growling coach in *Along Flirtation Walk* (1935). Pierce graduated to larger roles like Captain Andy from *Into Your Dance* (1935), a take-off on radio's popular *Maxwell House Show Boat* variety gala.

Even late in the decade, when radio actors were being regularly hired, the use of in-house vocal talent was still commonplace. Examples include story men like Cal Howard who voiced Gabby Goat in *Get Rich Quick Porky* (1937) and Ben Hardaway who was Dizzy Duck in *It's an Ill Wind* (1939). Even director Bob Clampett supplied odd vocal effects for the bizarre Three Stooges creature in his avant-garde *Porky in Wackyland* (1938). [70] Baby-voiced ink-&-paint girl Ruth Pierce made some minor voice contributions, according to her work colleague Martha Sigall. [71]

From 1934, however, the films began relying much more on "voices for hire." For a few years, much of this talent included Hollywood's flexible session singers, trained in operetta. Vocal groups like The Singing Guardsmen (tenor Henry Iblings, second tenor Earl Hunsaker, baritone William Brandt, and basso Dudley Kuzzell) sang in 1934 cartoons like *Goin' to Heaven on a Mule*, *Rhythm in the Bow* and *Beauty and the Beast*. Other vocal groups included The Varsity Three in *Honeymoon Hotel*, The Rhythmettes in *How Do I Know It's Sunday?* (1934) and another fine girl's trio, The Debutantes (Marjorie Briggs, Betty Noyes, Dorothy Compton) who sang in *Mr. and Mrs. Is the Name* (1935). All these groups were heard on the Warner radio station and contracted for Merrie Melodies. They performed in bouncy but essentially forgettable scores composed by Brown and his associate Norman Spencer. Spencer was a veteran song writer and chorus master. His incidental music behind action scenes was functional but unimaginative (that overused woodblock!), aside from occasionally inventive jazz sequences. The only memorable tunes in some Merrie Melodies were the songs from the Warner musical features.

It was also in this early period that specialty baby-voice actresses like Carol Tevis in *Little Dutch Plate* (1935) and Berneice Hansell in *I Wanna Play House* (1936) began being heard regularly. Another important cartoon actor was the excellent Billy Bletcher, best known as Disney's "Big Bad Wolf." He provided the distinctively deep-voiced villains in some of the Buddy cartoons, starting with *Buddy of the Apes* (1934).

An early entry, *Buddy's Beer Garden* (1933), featured an unnamed convict villain who was voiced by a Bletcher sound-alike (possibly character actor Ferdinand Munier). Girlfriend Cookie was at first played by Shirley Reed and then Dorothy Varden, a member of still another girl's trio. Cookie's final voice was, however, Berneice Hansell, whose first of many Schlesinger cartoons were the 1934 entries *Country Boy* and *Buddy the Dentist*. A gifted animal imitator and whistling expert named Purves Pullen also worked for the studio. He had notched up three years as a novelty with Ben Bernie's band and performed vocal effects for the Metro feature *Tarzan and*

His Mate, which got him noticed by cartoon makers at the Disney, Harman-Ising and Lantz studios. [72] Occasional voices, like the burly cop in *Buddy's Trolley Troubles* (1934) were provided by live-action Warner Bros. contract actors. Those voices remain frustratingly unidentified in this period.

Little by little the Warner Bros. cartoons improved. In the spring of 1935 *Film Daily* reported, "Leon Schlesinger, producer of Merrie Melodies and Looney Tunes, has signed a new 3-year contract for the release of his cartoon films through Warner Bros. Schlesinger has had exceptional success with these short features, their popularity and quality having steadily increased the past six years, during which time he has made those pictures." [73]

By the 1934-35 season, as Schlesinger's directors sought to improve the films in a mostly vain attempt to keep up with Disney's impressive advances in the art of animation, the gate opened to outside voice talent. Friz Freleng, in particular, longed to get away from the ubiquitous falsetto staff voices which had proliferated in Hollywood cartoons since "talkies" first talked, from Mickey Mouse via Oswald the Rabbit to Krazy Kat, Scrappy, Bosko, Foxy and Buddy.

The final voice of Buddy was the husky vocalising of a real child actor, Jackie Morrow. But it didn't help; by this stage, it was all too clear that the studio's "human" stars Buddy and Cookie were terminally lame characters, despite some inventive gags in a few entries. When Disney's menagerie expanded to include the sensationally popular Donald Duck in 1934, Schlesinger became increasingly anxious for new anthropomorphic characters with which to compete. Indeed, Freleng recalled that exhibitors had begun insisting on cartoons with animal stars "along the lines of Mickey, Pluto, and Goofy."[74] It followed that cartoon voices as humorously likable as those in Disney's shorts were inevitably being sought. Adding to this pressure, Schlesinger's East Coast competitor Max Fleischer now boasted two of animation's all-time distinct voices in Betty Boop and the wildly popular new sailor man, Popeye.

It was Schlesinger himself who had a sudden brain wave. At a fall 1934 staff meeting he suggested a cartoon equivalent of the popular Hal Roach *Our Gang* series as a convenient way to introduce a group of new characters. Freleng's unit was assigned to bring this idea to fruition.

The cartoon that resulted was released in March 1935. Featured in the line-up of schoolroom would-be-stars in Freleng's Merrie Melodie *I Haven't Got a Hat* were puppies Ham and Ex, little Kitty Kitten, Oliver Owl, Porky Pig and Beans the Cat. Because some fresh voices were needed, Freleng suggested a stuttering impediment like that of movie comic actor Roscoe Ates for the pig. Schlesinger knew just where to look and he told Freleng to call Warner's casting department. [75]

Real-life stammerer Joe Dougherty was a Warner Bros. contract dress extra and make-up assistant. He supplied the sympathetically awkward voice of Porky Pig; he also voiced a stuttering stage performer in that season's *Into Your Dance* who attempted to sing the title song. Clampett remembered being in Schlesinger's office on the day Dougherty showed up to audition. Director Tex Avery, who came aboard in 1935, recalled Dougherty as "an older guy, he was grey headed." [76] Freleng's idea of a comical speech defect may have been influenced by an earlier cartoon he'd worked on. In the 1933 release *Bosko the Speed King*, Rudolf Ising did a stuttering character voice for the race starter, while the early Columbia cartoon *The Minstrel Show* (1932) starring Krazy Kat, had first caricatured well-known movie stammer-comic Roscoe Ates.

In April 1935, *Los Angeles Times* entertainment reporter Philip Scheuer wrote a profile for his weekly "Town Called Hollywood" column. It described movie voice-dubbing talents in a rare early example of publicizing these normally anonymous artists. The article, "Business of 'Ghosting' [Voices] is Now Hollywood's Oddest", covered various cartoon studios including the Schlesinger plant: "Leon Schlesinger, who sponsors 'Looney Tunes' and 'Merrie Melodies' says most of his voice specialists were reared on farms. He employs twenty-five persons who can approximate the 'talking' and 'singing' of dogs, cats, mice, elephants, cows, snakes and the like. There is no age limit: Jackie Morrow, the 'Buddy' of 'Looney Tunes' is only nine years of age, while Dorothy Varden, who 'talks' Buddy's companion 'Cookie,' is in her early twenties. Young Morrow's chief worry is that his voice will change. Billy Bletcher, an expert at barking and growling, is 'Bozo' the dog; and only the other day they could not resist hiring a man because he gave an elegant imitation of a stuttering pig. Now they have to [draw] the pig." [77]

Aside from Dougherty's distinct stutter, an important mechanical aid was suggested: by slowing the speed of the optical film recorder, then playing back the recording at its normal setting, Porky Pig's voice was amusingly speeded-up. This pitch change would prove extremely useful for many animated voices over the coming years, imbuing them with a cartoony "not of the real world" quality, and interestingly it was a technique mainly exclusive to Warner cartoons, if we don't count Woody Woodpecker in the forties. *

* Sound editor Treg Brown explained that the speeding technique was controlled by a rheostat with locked settings.[78] Until the advent of audio tape in 1947 the lock-in process wasn't infallible. This may explain why Porky sounds slightly different in certain cartoons: indeed, in *Ali Baba Bound* (1940), he sounds listless and almost non-sped when singing "The Girlfriend of the Whirling Dervish."

Following the schoolroom cartoon, Beans the Cat began a brief starring career in *A Cartoonist's Nightmare* (1935), released after the final Buddy entry that year, *Buddy the Gee Man*. The embryonic Porky Pig was featured in some of the Beans cartoons but would soon become the studio's new star character when it became obvious that Beans, like Buddy before him, was completely lacking in screen charisma.

Meanwhile, the latest in-house voice talent was Schlesinger's newly hired director Fred "Tex" Avery, formerly with the Walter Lantz studio at Universal. Avery had been dismissed for trying to help animator Preston Blair get a raise, and likely for displaying a little too much naked ambition in the eyes of studio chief Henry Henigson. After passing on an earlier job offer from the Charles Mintz cartoon studio, Avery landed at Warner's Sunset Boulevard lot in the late spring of 1935 to start up a third unit: Schlesinger had announced he would be increasing his annual output from twenty-six cartoons to thirty-nine. Avery's six years with Lantz and Bill Nolan prepared him well for Schlesinger, who hired him on the strength of a storyboard which Avery prepared at home, assisted by his Lantz colleague, the creatively uninhibited gagman Cal Howard. [79] The story Avery pitched featured the Porky character as an adult in a western spoof. It was approved for Avery's first Schlesinger cartoon, *Gold Diggers of '49* (1935).

Avery was housed at first in a separate small wooden building on the Warner Bros. lot, some two hundred yards from the main cartoon wing. He recalled "it was old dressing rooms." [80] His team included the restlessly creative young animator Bob Clampett, who effectively became Avery's sounding board / assistant, and a couple of weeks later the animator Chuck Jones. Both Clampett and Jones had apparently indicated to Schlesinger their displeasure at the lack of challenge and stultifying blandness of the Buddy oeuvre. They were joined a couple of months later by some of Avery's animators from Universal, like the skilled Virgil Ross who became a Warner cartoons mainstay.

Possessed of a unique comic mind, Avery quickly exerted a strong and defining influence: as he saw it, going a "different way" to Disney, rather than attempting to copy him. It was Avery's approach that slowly transformed the Schlesinger cartoons into their famous satirical mindset. If animators were often described as "actors with pencils," Avery was more of a "comedian with pencil." A lover of the silent slapstick movies he had grown up avidly watching, Avery possessed the comic gift, the same gag mentality that comedy writers (when asked how they "think up" jokes) explain away as a cockeyed take on life. When preparing a story, he would often ask his gag men, "What would an audience *least* expect?" The satiric influence of Avery would utterly transform the Warner cartoons in speed and comic conceit, though both he and director Frank Tashlin always pointed to Disney's Silly Symphony *The Tortoise and the Hare* (1935) as the biggest influence on this stylistic shift.

In somewhat Hitchcockian fashion, Avery's voice would appear fleetingly in several of his own cartoons. He had already done many voices for Lantz, and is heard as early as 1936 in Warner cartoons like *Page Miss Glory* ("I want service!!!") and *The Blow Out*. With his comedic bent, Avery had a natural flair for cartoon acting. Other unit directors later took advantage of this: his infectious, distinctive belly-laugh is heard, for instance, as the referee in Dalton & Hardaway's *Count Me Out* (1938) and as the crafty villain in his own *The Sneezing Weasel* (1938). Chuck Jones employed his resonant voice, encased in a layer of "reverb" echo, as the mischievous spirit in *Ghost Wanted* (1940).

Avery also laid claim to being the first cartoon maker to employ an off-screen narrator to point up the gags, citing *The Village Smithy* (1936), which featured commentary by movie and radio actor Earle Hodgins. In fact, Avery had forgotten his earlier 1936 Looney Tune, *Porky the Rain Maker*. It too featured Hodgins doing his patented carnival barker voice, but the opening was narrated by gagman Ted Pierce, who was very likely animation's first "off-screen" voice. As Avery saw it, the cartoon commentator was "the only thing that Disney's ever stole from me. All his 'How-To' cartoons used the offstage narrator." [81] Jones recalled Avery seeing the 1937 Silly Symphony *Little Hiawatha*, narrated by top radio announcer Gayne Whitman, and excitedly telling one and all that "Disney stole my off-screen voice!!" [82]

Soon, new "casual" voices for hire began to be used. Among the freelance players hired in the years 1934-36 were specialty bird whistlers like Marion Darlington in *Pop Goes Your Heart* (1934); radio comedienne Elvia Allman in *Porky's Moving Day* and *The Cat Came Back* (both 1936); sound effects specialist Count Cutelli who provided realistic animal sounds like roosters and cats in Freleng's mid-thirties Merrie Melodies; some child actors including Tommy Bond in *I Love to Singa* (1936), and former "Buddy" voice Jackie Morrow in *Toytown Hall* (1936) and the final voice for "Beans". After 1936 came child actress and mimic Bernice Kamiat, later known as Cara Williams; she did a Mae West in 1938's *Porky's Five and Ten*; "spoonerizing" radio comic Joe Twerp in *Gold Rush Daze* (1939); celebrity mimics like Lind Hayes* in *The Coo Coo Nut Grove* (1936) and Cliff Nazarro, mainly a well-known "double-talk" act. Nazarro does an Eddie Cantor for *Toytown Hall* (1936); character actress Martha Wentworth, who specialized in mothers and battle-axes older than her own age, in cartoons like *Pigs is Pigs* (1937); dubbing singers like contralto Jeane Cowan who sang the Helen Morgan caricature in *The Coo Coo Nut Grove* (1936). There were others in the mid-thirties, several of whom remain unidentified at this writing, the most frustrating mystery being the hick corn-fed voice heard both as *The Country Mouse* (1935) and as Papa scarecrow in *I'd Love to Take Orders from You* (1936).

* He was later known as Peter Lind Hayes

Most prominent were Billy Bletcher (1894-1979) and Berniece Hansell (1897-1981) who became regular visitors to the Warner Bros. soundstage; they also did cartoons for Lantz. Bletcher worked for Columbia's Mintz studio and was a top Disney mainstay. He recalled Tex Avery being "a great booster for me. He'd say, 'What are you fooling around for? Get Bletcher.'" [83] With his powerful bass voice and great comic delivery, Bletcher was perfect for the many gruff-voiced villains in the musical cartoons, like the menacing vinegar bottle in *Little Dutch Plate* (1935).

Berniece Hansell continued to be used by all the directors, often in short-lived starring roles like Beans's girlfriend Kitty, or Pinkie, the obnoxious nephew of Porky Pig. Clampett, who used her as the devilish Pinkie in *Porky's Naughty Nephew* (1938), recalled, "What amused me was this great incongruity to Bernice Hansen [sic]: this middle-aged bleached blonde with that pure little child's voice." [84] She worked throughout the thirties, her final Warner cartoon being Avery's *Wacky Wildlife* (1940). Berneice Hansell remains the most frustratingly elusive of voice artists: despite diligent archival research, it seemed there was practically nothing about her career to be found anywhere. *

* Thanks to tireless online digging by cartoon buff-blogger Don M. Yowp we were finally able to learn a little about Ms Hansell: in spring 1936 a news item provided a hint about her, although she was still unnamed: *"On the Merrie Melodies vocal list is a woman who does no other film work than speaking for Kitty the Kitten. A young extra stutters convincingly as Porky the Pig."* Then in 1937 Schlesinger revealed, *"A middle-aged woman who works on the [Warner] lot as a dressmaker does Kitty's voice. It's her own natural voice but it sounds like that of a very small girl."* Finally, an early reference to our mystery woman surfaced from December 1934, naming her as *"Berneice 'Giggles' Hansell, a seamstress"* who had spoken for Disney's Mickey Mouse cartoons. [85] To add to all this mystery, this book's research associate, the late Hames Ware, found Hansell's name listed in a Los Angeles telephone book back in 1972, but when he called she had just changed her address that week. [86] Any relatives with information on her life are hereby requested to contact the author, so she can finally be "de-mystified" for a revised edition.

By mid-1936, the one new character who augured well for Schlesinger was Porky Pig. Joe Dougherty's authentic stutter, however, was proving troublesome: he would frequently use up expensive raw film stock during recordings in that pre-tape era. Freleng feared the wrath of Jack Warner every time Dougherty was engaged. He remembered Dougherty's first session in 1934 vividly, thirty five years later: "The stutter was uncontrollable. I could not control his voice. He had to recite 'The Midnight Ride of Paul Revere.' He would get up to record, and 'L-l-l-listen m-my children and you shall hear da...brrrr da...beeerrr...daaaaa.' Then we would say, 'Wait a minute. Cut!' And that would make *him* nervous. We just ran hundreds of feet of film before we really got the thing down." [87]

Listening to Avery's 1935 *Plane Dippy* confirms that Dougherty's stammer could at times be almost painfully hard to control. Clampett recalled Avery having to coach Dougherty to read his next Porky script, *The Blow Out*, with more "sympathy" than before. [88] From the first, Freleng knew they would need a replacement Porky voice down the line. More trouble loomed: Clampett recalled, "There was criticism from the PTA about the stuttering voice." [89] The Parent-Teacher Association lodged a complaint hinting that Porky's voice might prove offensive to children with genuine stuttering problems. Poor Joe Dougherty's days were numbered.*

*Even Porky's cheery new ending, appended to the cartoons from the fall of 1937, was beyond Dougherty's limited acting chops. A newspaper piece noted, "Millions of movie-goers who never heard of Count Cutelli were familiar with his ingratiating 'Th-that's all folks,' with which Porky ended each picture."[90] Italian-born sound mimic Count Gaetano Cutelli's reading was sped up in pitch and used later. Cutelli had apparently recorded this just prior to Mel Blanc's arrival. Schlesinger thought highly of this now obscure sound effects man and animal imitator, autographing a 1937 photo of himself which read, "To Count Cutelli. A great artist and a fine fellow." [91]

During this period the soundtracks for Warner cartoons got more interesting, especially those made by Avery. His charming 1936 Merrie Melodie *I Love to Singa* featured fine voice-work by Billy Bletcher and Martha Wentworth as the concerned Austrian-accented parents of a young owl who prefers swing music over classical. This was audio acting, rather than just strained or funny voices. It also featured amusing work by specialty artists like Berneice Hansell and another stammer comic, Lou Fulton. Fulton was half of the country and western comic team Oscar and Elmer, two more regulars on the Warner radio station working with Johnny "Bosko" Murray. He did a somewhat funnier version of a Joe Dougherty type who attempts to recite "Simple Simon" as a hapless talent contestant. This early Avery classic boasted a well-judged balance between the dialogue and music. Genuine wit, of the professional radio variety, was beginning to infect the Schlesinger cartoons.

It was a big change from some of the Looney Tunes released just six months earlier, which contained little dialogue, and virtually none that was witty. Cartoons like *The Phantom Ship* (1936) consisted almost entirely of the frightened mutts Ham and Ex yelling, "Uncle Beans! Uncle Beans!" One Merrie Melodie, *The Cat Came Back* (1936), the final entry in the 2-color process, boasted quite the sloppiest soundtrack in the studio's history, with a single character being voiced by two different actresses (in a careless, interchangeable way that seems to indicate Freleng's contempt for this cartoon's gag-bereft material). There are also two characters speaking lines which are both sped and at normal pitch, but with no reason for the change. The only saving grace is the pleasant rendition of the title song by vocal trio The Rhythmettes. By year's end the improvement in the Warner cartoon tracks was distinctly noticeable, and not before time: Disney's soundtracks had been rich with excellent comic voices, music and effects for at least a year, in such elaborate Silly Symphonies as *Who Killed Cock Robin?* (1935).

In 1935 some of Freleng's Merrie Melodies seemed stuck in a rut. There was scant creative progress from one entry to the next and they relied heavily on the old musical formula, with singers still being the most prominent voices. They were enjoyable but repetitive. *The Lady in Red* features a male quartet, a female trio, and tenor Ric Ricardi, who does a good Rudy Vallee send-up. The first Freleng Merrie Melodie to feature an actual story was *Let It Be Me* (1936), a morality tale featuring a Bing Crosby imitator, after which several of Freleng's cartoons began to evolve into mini-plays, rather than just being seven-minute musical vignettes.

The same Crosby imitator starred in another parody, *Bingo Crosbyana* (1936), which had the crooner as an insect who is betrayed by an unexpected streak of yellow. This gag resulted in a slap on the wrist for Schlesinger, described in the *Hollywood Reporter* on August 5, 1936: "A potential blow to cartoon producers who caricature stars is seen in the legal threat by Paramount and Bing Crosby Inc. against Warner Bros. over the latter company's cartoon entitled *Bingo Crosbyana*. Through the law firm of O'Melveny, Tuller & Myers, the Crosby corporation has deemed that Warner Bros. cease distribution and exhibition of the reel. The demand states that the Crosby voice is imitated, and the character of 'Bingo' is shown as a 'vainglorious coward.'" [92] Interestingly Crosby imitations continued to appear until the early fifties. While this early, husky Bing voice is unconfirmed, it might be a singer named Billy Paye who claimed to have done a Crosby for Warner cartoons.

In early 1937, Paul Harrison's syndicated entertainment column featured an interview with Schlesinger which touched on various aspects of his cartoons, including a rundown on some prominent voices: "A stuttering character actor does the Porky dialog for a recording; then the record is speeded up so that the voice is about an octave higher when it reaches the film. Before they attained acting prominence, Rochelle Hudson and Jane Withers worked for Schlesinger, dubbing in their voices for those of cartoon characters.

"Hollywood has scores of people capable of imitating voices, and the producer never has any trouble finding talents for impersonating, in sound, the Crosbys, Stepin Fetchits, Garbos and other celebrities whom he frequently satirizes in Merry [sic] Melodies.

"If you saw *Coo Coo Nut Grove* you'll recall that Katharine Hepburn was caricatured as a horse. Schlesinger has heard that she was delighted with the impudence and went to see the picture three times." [93]

In the watershed year of 1936, top gagman Ted Pierce came into his own as a Warner cartoon staff voice. Pierce was the first head of the Screen Cartoonists Guild. [94] Popular with all the directors, he was adept at mimicry and did funny imitations of various radio comedians of the day. These included Al Pearce's timid door-to-door salesman character "Elmer Blurt," used as the goofy lead in *Jungle Jitters* (1938), Bill Comstock's addled female cook "Tizzie Lish," heard as Medusa in *Porky's Hero Agency* (1937), and celebrities like bandleader Ben Bernie for *The Woods Are Full of Cuckoos* (1937) and screen comic W. C. Fields for *At Your Service Madame* (1936). [95] Ted Pierce was heard far more often than is generally realized in Schlesinger cartoons and he remained a solid, if unsung, voice-man through to the early fifties.

Meanwhile, at the end of 1936, a new vocal talent named Blanc would help transform the Warner Bros. cartoons for all time.

***

In the 1936-37 release season, young dialectician and comic-musician Mel Blanc was heard in the cartoons. He had begun in radio in the Pacific Northwest ten years before and been in vaudeville as an MC. When Blanc started working for Schlesinger's in late 1936 he was just one of a veritable stock company of trick-voice specialists - Billy Bletcher, Joe Twerp, Don Brodie, Berneice Hansell, Elvia Allman - working for all the Hollywood animation houses. But Mel Blanc was more than a journeyman actor with a repertoire of party trick voices. He was a seasoned orchestra leader and musician, his larynx was uncommonly strong, his comic sense unique and original, and his talents far ranging, aptly described by author Steve Schneider as "extravagant gifts." [96]

In other words, Blanc had "that something extra" to quote from the 1937 movie *A Star is Born*. Most importantly, as animation historian Michael Barrier observed, Mel Blanc's vocal caricatures soon inspired both story men and animators to match that extravagance. [97] Slowly but surely, Blanc effectively plussed up the comedy level of the cartoons.

In the mid-thirties Mel Blanc was a regular "stooge voice" on local Los Angeles radio comedies including Johnny "Bosko" Murray's newest show on the Warner Bros. station, *Johnny Murray Talks It Over*. Blanc was attempting to crack the more prestigious, and far more lucrative, coast-to-coast network sponsored shows. In fact, he had already begun appearing on comedian Joe Penner's new CBS comedy program. Blanc quickly deduced that cartoons, increasingly popular and ever more dialogue-driven, could augment his income as he dreamed of the radio big-time. There were, indeed, over one hundred Hollywood-produced cartoons in the year 1936 alone. He was encouraged to try out for cartoon work by his wife Estelle.*

* Footnote: One biographical source states that the young Mel Blanc was already on call as a fill-in violinist in the Warner Bros. orchestra, presumably between infrequent radio acting calls. [98]

Mel Blanc's older brother Henry, whose industry nickname was "Hank Blanc," was already a professional radio announcer who billed himself as "Henry Charles." In late 1936, while working at station KFWB, Henry Blanc put in a word for his comic sibling with Treg Brown, the recently appointed head of sound editing at Schlesinger's. Brown informed Friz Freleng who was still fretting about the need to replace Joe Dougherty. [99] In December twenty eight year-old Mel Blanc auditioned for Treg Brown, who became an instant kindred spirit to the young voice-actor: both men were seasoned novelty band musicians, the type of creatures who swap war stories about bad gigs and bond like mothers in childbirth.

In 1933 Treg Brown had transferred to Leon Schlesinger's studio from the Warner Bros. dubbing suite. After offering Ray Katz a gag idea, he began working in the story room under senior story man Ben Hardaway. Treg Brown transcribed the gag department's dialogue onto exposure sheets following each recording session. While non-relative Bernard Brown and Norman Spencer were handling the music and sound effects, Treg Brown's main role was cutting the approved takes of their dialogue recordings into final form.

Treg Brown inherited Bernard Brown's recording position when the latter left for a supervisory role at Universal Pictures in early 1936. For the next three decades Treg Brown supervised all the dialogue sessions and sound effects for all the Warner Bros. cartoons, working closely with the directors and musician Carl Stalling who arrived later that year. [100] Treg Brown's audio work was most inventive; Tex Avery, who always considered sound effects critically important to a cartoon's overall comedy, praised Brown for his proficiency in servicing four busy units. [101] Bob Clampett added, "Treg was always involved in the music and sound recordings. For his time 'Brownie' [Bernard Brown] did good things, but Treg was much more ingenious."[102] Brown's sound effects become more intricate from 1936: in cartoons like *I'm a Big Shot Now* the tracks are complex, with police fire, buzz bombers, and car chases expertly blended with suspenseful music. These cartoons, now in striking full 3-strip Technicolor, must have looked and sounded most impressive on the big screens of plush picture palaces in the thirties.

One of Brown's regular tasks involved recording the voice talent auditions to have on file. Bob Clampett recalled, "We used to listen to five, six a week at least."[103] Near the end of 1936 it was Mel Blanc's turn. With the hapless Joe Dougherty already on borrowed time, Brown recalled his first question to Blanc being, "'Can you stutter?' He said, 'S-s-sure I c-c-can.' I said, 'OK, Mr. Blanc, let's go back into the story room and get set up.'" [104]

Mel Blanc impressed Brown with his comical "news of the world" routine, This was a sure-fire comedy piece Blanc had on standby for occasions such as this. It consisted of crazy burlesque dialects and vocal sounds; for his audition, Blanc was assisted by Ted Pierce. Pierce played straight man to Blanc's nutty roles. Brown became so enthused he insisted Blanc repeat the performance for the unit directors who were called in from a Christmas staff party-in-progress. They moved to a big projection theatre. [105]

Brown vividly remembered Mel Blanc's audition years later: "He had us rolling. I called the story men in, and the directors. And that was [the start of Blanc's take-off in cartoons]. I called up the different radio stations; he was over at Lantz's and MGM. I should have signed on as his agent." [106]

During his audition Blanc recorded some minor trick vocal effects, mainly crazy "woo-woos" and comical hiccups. Brown added these to his effects library as numbered stock, and they can be heard as early as *Porky the Wrestler* (1937), which still featured Joe Dougherty speaking as Porky Pig.

Tex Avery was already well aware of Blanc, explaining, "We would often go over to KFWB [to watch radio talent] and we'd see this 'Noisemaker of the Air' character played by Mel. He'd blow a note on his cornet, then drop it on the floor and do some crazy voice describing what was in that day's news." [107] Friz Freleng recalled that Blanc had already done a couple of bits for Frank Tashlin's cartoons:

he's certainly playing Petunia Pig when she shrieks "Who's excited?" in *Porky's Romance* (1937), * while those distinctive hiccups are also evident in *Porky's Road Race* (1937). [108] He may even have been at Warners before that: it sounds like Mel Blanc as one of the singing soldiers in *Boom Boom* (1936), while a baseball catcher in *Boulevardier from The Bronx* (1936) yells in a sped voice suspiciously like Blanc's. Sadly, archival recording logs for thirties cartoons are today presumed lost.

> *The "Who's excited?" voice was a take-off of a contemporary radio character named Judge Hugo Straight, played by stooge-comic Tommy Mack.

Following his auspicious audition, Mel Blanc was quickly contracted by Tex Avery for his first official job in *Picador Porky* (1937), in which his hobo character drunkenly warbles "La Cucaracha." Bob Clampett recalled that Blanc's comic hiccups were especially impressive to the audience of cartoon makers: "That day Tex Avery and I were [gagging] a story called *Picador Porky* in which we have a couple of tramps who get into a bull suit. They reach out and get a bottle of hooch, they drink, and they start hiccupping. Mel did these voices that he had done up in Portland. They weren't anything [special] that you know now. They were good but nothing we saw any [immediate] use for. But the one thing that he did was these wonderful hiccups: really juicy, bouncy hiccups.

"After the [audition] meeting, we said to Mel two things: 'We got a thing with hiccups in it. Maybe you could do some hiccups for us.' And then Treg Brown and I and this other fellow [Henry Binder] also talked with him about the Porky voice. We ended up giving him a disc to take home and listen to. First, he was to try and match it, so you wouldn't notice a change. Of course, he did it much better." [109] At Schlesinger's insistence Mel Blanc took over the role of star property Porky Pig, beginning with Avery's milestone cartoon *Porky's Duck Hunt* (1937) for which he would bring a more controlled and humorous stutter to the character.

It was this cartoon, a comedy breakthrough in many ways, that kick-started Blanc's long Warner Bros. tenure which would eventually see him enacting nearly all the studios' lead characters. He started with Porky and added another Avery creation, Daffy Duck, who appeared as the pig's still-unnamed nemesis in that *Duck Hunt* picture. Clampett said, "From then [Mel] was on call. He'd be around [town] doing radio shows, but any time we needed him then he would meet us not over in Hollywood where the [Sunset Boulevard] studio was, but over the hill at the Warner Burbank Studio where we did our recording." [110]

Soon after the audition, Friz Freleng tested Blanc's ability at various voices in two 1937 cartoons: *The Fella with the Fiddle*, for which he also demonstrated his singing talent, and *She Was an Acrobat's Daughter*. Blanc quickly realized he had to be sharp if he was going to constantly impress this smart team of directors. For the *Acrobat's Daughter* cartoon Freleng asked him if he could mimic Lew Lehr, the German accented comedian from Fox Movietone News, famous for his catchphrase "Monkeys is de craziest people!!" Blanc had to quickly find a theatre playing a Lehr short and study the voice. [111]

It was soon apparent to all at the Schlesinger cartoon studio that Mel Blanc had something indefinably extra that hadn't been heard in animation. The innately caricatured timbre of Blanc's voice, his facility with funny adenoidal sounds and voices, and the furious energy level he achieved in performance, gave his characters a broadly comic quality that was perfect for animated cartoons.

Once Blanc landed the all-important Porky Pig role, he began doing regular voice-work for the new "junior" Warners cartoon division, the recently established Ray Katz Productions. This unit was responsible for the black & white Looney Tunes. Here Blanc quickly gained the advantage he would hold over all his cartoon actor contemporaries: he became the go-to talent for most of the funny "star" voices.

Leon Schlesinger, on the lookout for anything that could compete with Disney, knew he had a second potential star in the insane little black mallard, soon to be named Daffy. Blanc, guided by Avery and gagman Ben Hardaway, refined the voice for the duck's next appearance in *Daffy Duck and Egghead* (1938). It was decided that the duck's bill would result in a unique way of talking. Blanc was asked to adapt the juicy, zany delivery he had given the title character of Avery's 1937 cartoon *Egghead Rides Again* (1937), a voice based closely on spit-lisping vaudeville star comic Charlie Kemper. [112]

Within months of Blanc's joining the Schlesinger stock company, Clampett was using him in cartoons like *Porky's Badtime Story* (1937). For the first time, Blanc alone supplied all the voices for a cartoon, although that would become more common practice from the mid-forties. While he did the voices of both Porky and Gabby Goat, he was still sharing a few characters at this point. The perennially inventive gagman Cal Howard supplied Gabby's voice for the next in the series, *Get Rich Quick Porky*, released a few months later. [113] But from the summer of 1937 the Schlesinger boys knew that Mel Blanc was a keeper.

A year prior to Blanc's arrival, another prominent cartoon voice expert had begun making waves in Hollywood movie studios. This man was Dave Weber, who in late 1938 changed his professional name to Danny Webb when seeking a more substantial on-camera career; Weber was possibly deemed too Germanic a name in the turbulent world political climate of the late thirties.

Weber did radio comedy, was frequently hired as a dialect coach for feature films, and dubbed countless voices in Schlesinger, Lantz and Columbia cartoons. A talented dialectician and mimic, he specialized in impressions of movie stars and air celebrities like the Edward G. Robinson and Fred Allen voices in Avery's *Thugs with*

Dirty Mugs (1939). Earlier, Weber supplied political voices on *The March of Time*, the famous radio docudrama series which required lifelike impersonations. His was the most frequent voice of Avery's Egghead character, which he did in an uncannily accurate impression of radio comic Joe Penner, then a top children's favorite in his weekly Cocomalt-sponsored series. In *A-Lad-in Bagdad* (1938) Weber's imitation was completed with a well-animated send-up of Penner's unique dance movements, as Egghead sings the current hit "Bei Mir Bist Du Schoen," the theme song from Warner's 1938 drama *Love, Honor and Behave*.

One of Weber's best cartoon roles was in Clampett's *Porky in Egypt* (1938), a take-off on the 1935 Charles Boyer mental health drama *Private Worlds*. Weber played the camel Humpty Bumpty, who goes crazy from the desert heat, in manic fashion ("It's the Desert MADNESS!!!"). The camel's sound was essentially Weber's own straight voice. To get the hollow, ethereal sound of ghostly phantoms needed in this scene, Treg Brown had the actors and Clampett put their heads in a washtub, "then we put it through an echo chamber." [114]

Dave Weber and Mel Blanc were something of a team in their many Schlesinger, Lantz and Columbia cartoons from 1938-40. When Blanc signed an exclusive Warner Bros. contract in 1941, Dave Weber, according to Clampett, did a voice test for Walter Lantz's Woody Woodpecker. Woody was originated by Blanc under Ben Hardaway's voice direction; in so many ways animation was, and remains, a small industry, with paths being crossed on a weekly basis. [115]

***

At the time of Blanc's audition for Schlesinger, the Warner cartoons were also on their way to becoming more musically sophisticated. When Bernard Brown accepted a prestigious offer to re-equip and run Universal's sound department, his musical associate Norman Spencer resigned. Spencer's solo scores, except in a few creatively challenging cartoons like *I Love to Singa*, had become formulaic and lazily repetitive. He left the Schlesinger studio* making way for a much more accomplished and creative musician in Carl W. Stalling.

* Norm Spencer later turned up as host of *Can You Write a Song?*, yet another radio show originating from station KFWB.

Stalling, enthusiastically recommended to Schlesinger by gagman Ben Hardaway, arrived at the end of July 1936. Famous as the musician behind Disney's pioneering *Skeleton Dance* (1929) and the earliest Mickey shorts, Stalling had notched up years of experience as a popular theatrical accompanist for silent films in Kansas City, and was fresh from seven years of animation work at the Disney and Iwerks studios. [116] Stalling's assured, witty scores began with *Porky's Poultry Plant* (1936), coincidentally the first cartoon for talented director Frank Tashlin who was replacing the recently departed Jack King. Stalling immediately elevated Schlesinger's cartoons to a new level. As the instigator of the Silly Symphonies, Stalling was finally able to bring to the Warner cartoons a musical quality to match the Disney shorts.

Easing the way for Stalling was Leo F. Forbstein, like Ben Hardaway an old colleague from Kansas City. Forbstein, always on the good side of production chief Jack Warner, now headed the WB music department and had recently set up a permanent studio orchestra. As comedy became the Schlesinger cartoonists' watchword, the resourceful Carl Stalling met each new challenge with great facility. He matched the on-screen mayhem with droll cartoon music that remains admired decades later.

Vocal groups remained important throughout the thirties as Schlesinger increased the musical Merrie Melodies output. By 1935

Black harmony quartets in the Mills Brothers vein were in vogue. They accompanied themselves on a single guitar and would vocally imitate other musical instruments. Beyond their constant employment in the thriving Central Avenue jazz club scene they proved popular in Hollywood niteries during the rise of the swing music era, and the cartoon studios followed suit.

Leroy Hurte's group The Four Blackbirds (Hurte, Richard Davis, David Patillo and Geraldine Harris) was first heard in *Buddy in Africa* (1935). Steve Gibson's Basin Street Boys (Gibson, George Thompson, Sam Huterson, and Percy Anderson) and Ben Carter's Plantation Choir were featured in cartoons like *Uncle Tom's Bungalow* (1937), [117] They were three of the most versatile groups. Freleng, now working with Carl Stalling, became more adventurous with his soundtracks from 1936, and used comic Ben Carter's excellent Black chorus, featuring Carter and basso Roy Glenn, for *Sunday Go to Meetin' Time* (1936); he followed that with *Clean Pastures* (1937) which engaged several fine African-American performers previously heard in Hugh Harman's "jazz frog" cartoons for MGM.

Easing the way for these black groups in an era of industry segregation were Ray Heindorf and Georgie Stoll, both top ranking arranger-conductors in the music departments of Warner Bros. and MGM. Both men were inveterate jazz aficionados well known for giving employment opportunities in the film industry for many minority musicians.

Novelty groups like The Playboys in *The Mice Will Play* (1938) and western combos like Bob Nolan's Sons of the Pioneers in *A Feud There Was* (1938) got cartoon jobs. The Rhythmettes remained the top female animation trio. Frank Tashlin used the Three Dots of Rhythm heard in *Porky's Romance* (1937), because his wife, Dorothy Hill, whom he met on a vocal audition [118], was a member of that group, along with Dorothy McCarty and Dottie Messmer (hence the trio's name). Still another girls' trio was the Three Symphonettes who sang the title song in *You're an Education* (1938); they had already warbled that number in a live-action Warner Bros. short starring bandleader Freddie Rich.

Filling the hole created by the departed King's Men was a similarly accomplished novelty group called The Metropolitans, who changed their name to The Sportsmen Quartet. The original line-up was top tenor Bill Days, second tenor Maxwell Smith, baritone and arranger John Rarig, and bass singer Art McCulloch, who was replaced by Thurl Ravenscroft who joined the group in 1937. They were part of the Paul Taylor vocal chorus heard each week on Bing Crosby's high-rated *Kraft Music Hall*. The full Taylor chorale was heard in cartoons like Avery's *Cinderella Meets Fella* (1938). [119]

From 1937, Paul Taylor's "Sportsmen" became the most prolific group heard in Warner cartoons, their fine harmony work enhancing films like *Dog Daze* (1937), *Porky the Gob* (1938), *Fagin's Freshman* (1939) and *Snowman's Land* (1939). They were particularly flexible in comic numbers and could also do character voices. The vocal numbers were scheduled in the music scoring sessions: Thurl Ravenscroft recalled, "We were always separate from the dialogue people. We did all the Looney Tunes." [120] Stalling told Michael Barrier that most full chorus vocal arrangements were written by a choral director from Warner Bros.' music department, like Dudley Chambers. [121] However, the Sportsmen quartet's novelty songs were vocally arranged by group member John Rarig. Occasionally a cartoon set in an exotic locale received specialty music: Treg Brown recalled contracting an excellent Mexican group, The Guadalajara Trio, to sing "La Cucaracha" for Clampett's *The Timid Toreador* (1940). [122]

Wisecracking dialogue was now common in the Schlesinger cartoons, a reflection of radio's heavy influence on the studio. Freleng said, "Not only did we take many of our gags from radio, but in some respect our cartoons *were* just glorified radio." [123] The various cartoons about radio crooners soon gave way to parodies of actual shows: *The Woods Are Full of Cuckoos* was an animated version of

Gillette's Sunday *Community Sing* program on CBS, which featured comic MC Milton Berle and crooner Wendell Hall, both caricatured in the cartoon. As a result, broadcasting talent was increasingly on call and several narrators, voice mimics and comic stooges became animation semi-regulars. *

*Many cartoons from this period contain now-alien references to contemporary radio catch phrases. Random examples include *Cinderella Meets Fella* (1938) wherein our heroine exclaims, "No squat, no squint, no stoop!" This was an advertising logo for the Philco Corporation's floor model radios. In several cartoons a character whines, "Mmmmmmm, could be" in a distinctive Yiddish tone; this was an imitation of comedian Artie Auerbach's "Mr. Kitzel" character, heard on Jack Haley's and Al Pearce's shows. In *Page Miss Glory* (1936) the title character ends the cartoon by exhorting, "Play, Don!" This was Jack Benny's weekly instruction to his then-bandleader Don Bestor in his 1934-35 radio season. Of course, this essentially topical humor was never intended to be available on home video collections some eighty years later, long after such shows had faded from the airwaves and people's memories.

One radio-inspired voice that recurs in the Warner cartoons in 1937-38 is an imitation of strangle-voiced movie actor Andy Devine. He was then a weekly regular on Jack Benny's top-rated radio show in the recurring cowboy parody skits featuring "Buck Benny" which began in 1936, hence the expression "Hiya, Buck!!" in the cartoons. Tex Avery again provided a funny in-house voice as the whining, tone-deaf Devine character for the porcine hero of Freleng's western *My Little Buckaroo* (1938). Freleng recalled that Avery, certainly no musician, simply couldn't stay in time with the beat of the title song. [124] Adding further to the radio connection, the cartoon was essentially a send-up of the regional cop show *Calling All Cars* which ran in Los Angeles every week from 1933-39. Freleng even hired the original radio narrator, Frederick Lindsley, to satirize himself in this cartoon ("Calling all sheriffs!"). Tashlin had already used Lindsley's urgently melodramatic voice in his 1937 cartoon *Porky's Double Trouble*, a take-off on the recent John Ford crime comedy *The Whole Town's Talking*. Lindsley, a tenured speech professor at USC, appeared on-camera in the 1936 Warner Bros. Ku Klux Klan social drama *Black Legion* as a "March of Time" style newsreel narrator.

As noted, many radio voices were found right on the Warner lot at station KFWB ("Right next door to us," noted Bob Clampett). [125] Indeed, this practice continued as late as 1939, when Jack Benny sound-alike Jack Lescoulie, Jr., who hosted the hip comedy show *The Grouch Club* on the Warner owned station, was hired by Chuck Jones to play Casper Caveman in his cartoon *Daffy Duck and the Dinosaur*. Jones recalled, "Jack Lescoulie was a close friend of [animator] Phil Monroe. They played tennis together." [126]

Thanks to Avery, several more *Grouch Club* actors appeared in the Warner cartoons, the most noteworthy being Arthur Q. Bryan whose lisping, sappy creation "Waymond Wadcwiffe" was "twanspwanted" to animation, and after a year or so found a permanent home as Elmer Fudd's timorous hunter voice. Another *Grouch Club* regular was actor Robert Bruce, who became the most familiar of the off-screen narrators in Warner cartoons.

Robert Bruce was first used by Avery as the narrator of *Dangerous Dan McFoo* (1939), for which he also contributed bit voices like the fight referee. In fact it was this cartoon that also marked Arthur Q. Bryan's animation debut. Bruce was trained as an actor and received a degree in speech and theatre from the University of Minneapolis. He said, "I think the first [cartoon] calls I got were the result of working at KFWB. Strangely enough, with all the great talent that Mel Blanc was, he wasn't a good straight man, a good narrator. Whenever there was a narrator of any kind, they hired me; but I also would help with some crazy voices, when [Mel] got too many of them in a show, or just for variety." Bruce maintained, "The reason I narrated so many cartoons is that I wasn't a straight announcer, I was an actor. I dramatized the narration more than a straight announcer would do, or could do." [127]

Robert Bruce became a favorite of Avery and Clampett, his vibrant commentary enhancing cartoons like the Oscar nominated *Detouring America* (1939), *Wacky Wildlife* (1940), *Farm Frolics* (1941) and *A Gander at Mother Goose* (1940). Bruce also did a very distinctive "old man" voice, heard in Freleng's *The Hardship of Miles Standish* (1940) and as the title character of Clampett's *The Chewin' Bruin* (1940). [128] Bruce wasn't the only narrator, though: Avery's *Cross-Country Detours* (1940), for instance, used Lou Marcelle, soon to be Warner Bros.' long-time movie trailer announcer.

Adding further to the talent pool was the new prominence of West Coast radio. By 1936 the major networks began regular transcontinental broadcasts, and Hollywood soon became the epicentre of big-time commercial radio, displacing Chicago and New York, the former main hubs of the broadcast industry. This happened just as theatrical cartoons were showing an increased sophistication in music, animation and, particularly at Schlesinger's, self-reflexive humor. The directors Avery, Tashlin and Clampett, abetted by their gaggle of eccentric joke-smiths, were gaining a reputation for making the funniest cartoons in Hollywood.

The young Bob Clampett began directing in a fourth unit, officially named Ray Katz Productions. Earlier, the pioneering producer Ub Iwerks, at the end of his Comicolor contract with independent producer Pat Powers, directed two Porky Pig cartoons in his studio, assisted by Clampett and Chuck Jones, who oversaw the work for Schlesinger. According to Jones, Schlesinger had offered Iwerks a "financial bailout" but "in fact it was a takeover."[129] Iwerks left to direct Color Rhapsodies for the Screen Gems studio, while Clampett, under what he recalled as an earlier promise from Schlesinger, was appointed the director of the new unit. The cartoons they made were the black and white Porky Pigs. Three months later Clampett, his animators Jones and Bobe Cannon and some of the old Iwerks crew moved from Iwerks's Beverly Hills studio back to the Warner Bros. lot, where Katz Productions officially commenced operations in March 1937.

Tex Avery's unit was soon assigned full-time to the color Merrie Melodies. An avid listener to radio comedy [130], Avery drew voices from some of the big variety shows. He employed comic talents like Joe Twerp as the tongue-tied iceman in *I Only Have Eyes for You* (1937); veteran ink and paint colorist Martha Sigall recalled this being made under the more accurate working title *I Only Have Ice For You*. In the 1938-39, Avery hired more new voices: NBC staff artist Cliff Nazarro as the double-talking MC of *The Penguin Parade* (1938), Rolfe Sedan as the Germanic hog-director Hamburger with an advanced case of "rolling rrr's" in *Daffy Duck in Hollywood* (1938), and Phil Kramer as the nasal Brooklyn MC of *Hamateur Night* (1939).

Avery recalled, "Phil Kramer just came along with a voice, and it was funny. He was, at that time, getting some radio work, and that's how we found him."[131] Chuck Jones remembered that Avery, whenever possible, "insisted on using the original talent," and not an imitation. [132] The zany radio shows of comics like Al Pearce, Joe Penner, Burns and Allen and the like, populated with funny "second bananas," proved fertile ground for cartoon voice casting. Robert McKimson said, "[Radio] had an awful lot of real good [supporting stooge] comics at that time." [133] Clampett added that constantly listening to the radio and seeing movies for potential "voice ideas" was part of the enthusiastic research cartoon making entailed. [134]

Some voices even came from pre-existing soundtracks. In October 1937, when Freleng departed for a directing position at MGM's new cartoon plant, Schlesinger promoted animator Cal Dalton to head a unit with gagmen Cal Howard and Ben Hardaway. Dalton prepared the exposure sheets and timed the cartoons, while Hardaway handled story, assisted on gags by Cal Howard. Their first cartoon, which credited Howard and Dalton as supervisors, was the musical treat *Katnip Kollege* (1938), the soundtrack of which was most unusual. It consisted of "lifts" from two live-action Warner musicals featuring singing trumpeter-comic Johnny "Scat" Davis and comic actress Mabel Todd, who later married comedian Morey Amsterdam. The number "As Easy as Rollin' Off a Log" was originally to feature in the 1937 movie *Over the Goal*, but was cut. The centrepiece song, "Let That Be a Lesson to You," was from the 1937 musical *Varsity Show* featuring Fred Waring's glee club. At this writing it is not known whether the cartoon used out-takes or alternate takes, but both types of feature off-cuts were occasionally deployed for live-action novelty shorts.

A similar use of borrowed live-action track occurred in the 1939 release *Old Glory*, a cartoon specially commissioned by Harry Warner for inclusion in a patriotic-historical short film series. The cartoon even used the live series' narrator John Deering, who does the voice for a most realistically animated Uncle Sam, while the Patrick Henry character is "lifted" from the 1936 live-action short *Give Me Liberty*, in which he was portrayed by actor John Litel whose voice we hear, and whose image was rotoscoped for the cartoon. The Paul Revere character ("To arms!!") is also audio from an older short. Blanc, as Porky, and Paul Taylor's Sportsmen quartet supply the newly recorded voices in this unique, non-comic entry. [135]

As with all animation studios, Schlesinger's tracks were prone to the essentially haphazard piecemeal method of cartoon recording. Certain characters ended up with two voices when extra recording on cartoon dialogue was necessary, often after animation was completed and the originally used actor was unavailable for the post-synch re-record. Just as often a quirky use of voices was simply director's whim: Tex Avery's jolly laugh was used for the bulky mail boss in *Porky's Phoney Express* (1938) but the same character's speaking lines were read by actor Billy Bletcher. Similarly, Bletcher played the surly boss in *Porky's Tire Trouble* (1939) but Blanc is obviously reading one of his lines. The latter is an example of the frequent use of an actor to "tag on" a changed or new line of dialogue for a previously recorded track, often while at a recording session for another cartoon.

When Pinto "Goofy" Colvig left Disney's employ in the autumn of 1937 after a falling out with Walt and Roy, he freelanced on radio and for several cartoon studios like MGM and Charles Mintz. At Schlesinger's by 1938, he joined old friend Charlie Thorson, an ex-Disney character designer. Colvig's talent for gags, sound effects and music enlivened several of Schlesinger's soundtracks including *The Hobo Gadget Band* (1939) in which his great Goofy voice is heard, along with his musical virtuosity on clarinet. He also co-wrote the excellent featured song "Swing Time Down in Hobo Town" which he sang, backed by the Sportsmen quartet. Colvig was an example of a multi-skilled talent who could obtain work in various areas.

In a 1938 letter to an Oregon hometown friend Colvig described one of the voice sessions: "I am back [in Hollywood] to do some recording for some Warner Bros. short subjects ... I was recording a comedy song a few weeks ago on the 'big' sound stage at Warner Bros.-First National studios, with a 45-piece orchestra - and from up in the glass monitor-room, the head sound engineer yelled at me [through] the loudspeakers: 'Hey Pinto - that's lousy - you haven't improved since you were in the O.A.C. glee club 25 years ago!' - I wondered 'Who the hell??' - looked up and saw a large, bald-headed man - later he came down on the stage and introduced himself as Dolph Thomas - he was also with the [Oregon] glee club 25 years ago with me!" Thomas was a top sound man credited on many Warner feature films. [136]

Soon after the hobo cartoon, Colvig and Thorson left for the new Miami-based Max Fleischer studio. Colvig was originally hired as the new voice of Popeye's hulking nemesis Bluto. Colvig and Ted Pierce, who left for Miami earlier (in fact Pierce breached his Schlesinger contract), [137] spent a couple of busy years gagging and voicing Popeye and Gabby cartoons, as well as the two Fleischer animated features, before returning to the Coast. Colvig's abrupt departure from Warner Bros. cartoons necessitated Mel Blanc's imitating the Goofy voice for a hick ghost character in Clampett's 1939 Porky cartoon *Jeepers Creepers*. It was a good imitation but proved that Blanc was better at some voices than others, Pinto Colvig's sound being truly unique.

By early 1938, the talented impersonator and dialect actress Sara Berner, who received her break on Eddie Cantor's *Texaco Town* radio show the previous year, was working for all the cartoon companies. Berner's first Warner Bros. job was for Avery's *Daffy Duck in Hollywood* (1938). He took advantage of her funny mimicry of such stars as Katherine Hepburn. Avery recalled, "Sara Berner did a lot of voices for us, when we were all copying from the movies - Bette Davis, Hepburn - the whole list. Another girl was Elvia Allman, a very clever girl, very sharp and funny." [138]

All these talents fit nicely into the increasingly satirical tone of the Warner Bros. cartoons, which were rapidly finding their own comic voice. The trend was encouraged by Schlesinger. To combat Disney's move to features Schlesinger had, by decade's end, four busy animation units. In March 1938 young animator Chuck Jones, who had been working on Clampett's Looney Tunes and aiming for direction, was promoted to supervise the unit originally run by Frank Tashlin who was defecting to Disney. Jones began with a cartoon called *The Night Watchman* (1938) and then developed a cute mouse character named Sniffles.

Jones found a new voice artist in a nearby puppet studio, and youthful Margaret Hill began talking for Sniffles. Her son Rhys Talbot wondered if her classmates at the Pasadena Playhouse might have urged her to try for cartoon work. Blessed with a childlike "little" voice that was tonally close to Berniece Hansell's, she would do several cartoons for Schlesinger and Walter Lantz before retiring in 1941 to raise a family. The Sniffles cartoon that displays her range and acting ability best is *The Egg Collector* (1940). [139]

Leon Schlesinger's output had now increased to some forty releases per season, almost all of which were being highly rated by exhibitors across America. For the September 23, 1938 *Film Daily*, Schlesinger, obviously proud of his studio's quantum leap in just five years, wrote with enthusiasm: "With the heaviest program of any cartoon producer for the 1938-39 season, I'm looking forward to a grand year for cartoons. With clever stories, original gags, glorious color and fine music, the modern cartoon emerges a film of beauty and excellent entertainment for young and old. Satire, screwball comedy, caricatures, and travesties of popular classics seem to be the answer in our case. We strive, however, in treatment of story and in technique to be as surprisingly original as possible. Throughout we aim to amuse." (Of course, as Mark Kausler noted, animators reading this PR piece would have been a little chagrined: the only thing Schlesinger forgot to mention were the all-important funny drawings!)

Warner cartoon voices in the forties: Mel Blanc's rise

By 1940 the Warner Bros. cartoons had achieved a uniform consistency, much of which stemmed from their uniquely identifiable soundtracks. Those tracks benefited enormously from the dedicated talents of Schlesinger's three major sound-artists: Carl Stalling, the remarkably prolific composer, Treg Brown with his ever-inventive and witty effects cutting, and finally Mel Blanc, whose comic acting became increasingly polished. These three artists had notched up years of live musical backgrounds - each was a veteran instrumentalist - ensuring they had the "ear" for the disciplines and rhythms of cartoons so finely wedded to musical beats, not to mention the rhythm inherent in all good comedy.

During this decade the cutesy Berniece Hansell characters vanish very early; Chuck Jones's Sniffles cartoons from 1944-45 are more comedic than his Disney-esque ones from 1939-40. World War Two had a big effect, as theatrical cartoons quickly became brash, frantic and loud, matching the escapist tenor of the times. Vocal groups also diminish, although The Sportsmen remain in several cartoons through the war years, providing a fine college glee club ambience for Jones's then-bold experiment in pose-to-pose animation, *The Dover Boys* (1942). This cartoon, thanks to Jones's influential layout artists John McGrew and Gene Fleury, prefigured the UPA studio in its stylization of movement and backgrounds.

The forties was the decade when the Warner Cartoons crew added new leading characters. In 1940 Mel Blanc provided the voice for the still unnamed Bugs Bunny in Avery's *A Wild Hare*. The Schlesinger studio had made several cartoons in the previous two years featuring a screwball rabbit which had a mix of character traits from a disparate bunch of story men including Avery, Ben Hardaway and several other gagsters. By mid-1939 studio PR and trade items were already referring to the rabbit character as "Bugs Bunny," including a review of the Merrie Melody *Hare-Um Scare-Um* in the *Motion Picture Herald*. However in the cartoons the rabbit was still unnamed, the public still unaware of any "Bugs" moniker.

The embryonic rabbit voice was a speeded-up crazy, "pixilated" goofball, essentially the early Daffy Duck in a rabbit suit. After a couple more cartoons with a zany voiced hare, it was slowed down for a Chuck Jones stab at the character in *Elmer's Candid Camera* (1940), for which Blanc was directed to voice the early Bugs with a goofy "bucktoothed" tone to emphasize the rabbit's pronounced overbite. Blanc recalled worrying that using this voice impeded the clarity of his line readings. [140]

It wasn't until 1940 and Avery's *A Wild Hare*, today acknowl-edged as the first true incarnation of Bugs Bunny as we know him, that the rabbit's famous personality fell into place. When working on the final voice with Blanc, Avery directed as he always did: "I usually had someone in mind - a radio personality, or an actor or actress - to give the guy a clue as to what we were after, and then [he could] vary it from there." [141] For the rabbit, he suggested a New York wiseacre approach along the lines of Warner Bros. character man Frank McHugh. Avery said, "I would see a lot of movies, and I would remember voices." [142] During the refining, as Avery and gag man Rich Hogan fine-tuned the character, story man Mike Mal-tese suggested a Brooklyn accent. Essentially Avery was after a more "human" sound for the character, not a "trick" cartoon voice like a Popeye or a Donald Duck. It had to have something that would con-trast well with Bugs's amusingly casual attitude in the face of danger.

Avery: "[The rabbit voice] was pitched very similar to Frank McHugh's. * And it was almost a straight voice. I wanted to try that [approach]." Avery had first noticed that a straight human voice got a big reaction as comic contrast, citing the dog in *Cross Country Detours* (1940) who embraces all the California redwoods, glee-fully yelling, "Trees, trees, and they're all mine!!!" As Avery saw it, "I thought that a gimmick voice wouldn't work. I thought let's do it like Errol Flynn would do it - real straight. And [that dog] got a great laugh. Looking back at Bugs, his voice is not a gimmick voice like Donald Duck or Goofy; it's just a high-pitched straight voice, and I think that's what helped the character." [143]

* While Avery cited Frank McHugh, he did not mean an exact imitation: he was after the McHugh attitude, a genial and slightly sassy smart aleck. It is possible to detect a lit-tle Bugs in McHugh's delivery in a movie like *The Roaring Twenties* (1939). Sometimes, however, the early Bugs voice sounds more like the New York comic hoods played by char-

acter actor Edward Brophy than the milder McHugh tones offered.

Bob Clampett recalled one aspect of Bugs's vocal delivery being a whiny quality like that of distinctive comedy actor Phil Kramer, alongside whom Blanc had worked many times on the radio shows of Joe Penner and Al Pearce. Kramer was already noted for his work in cartoons like Avery's *Hamateur Night*. While Avery flat-out denied Kramer being an influence on the Bugs sound, Clampett insisted differently; he even recalled Phil Kramer's grousing about Blanc stealing his signature comic voice. [144] Kramer's nasal pitch and side of the mouth New Yorker character have some similarity, but his patented voice was more slowly paced and more of a nebbish. Still, from such surviving memories and perceptions is much of the minutiae of film history to be unravelled!

Overall though, it was Blanc's interpretation of the Tex Avery / Mike Maltese guideline suggestions which soon resulted in the classic vocal signature for Bugs. In re-viewing the seminal cartoon *A Wild Hare* today it's apparent the voice was still being worked out. In the first half Bugs sounds different: the tough stinker aspect is played in a low key, and some of Blanc's line readings spoken while chomping on a carrot tend to be muffled with the carrot affecting his diction. Story man Don Christensen noted, "I was there once when Mel was recording. The old gag about him spitting out the carrots all over the floor, that's true. They'd have to clean up carrots after Mel recorded Bugs Bunny." [145] Blanc eventually stopped speaking for Bugs with his mouth full, and from then on recorded all his dialogue lines before adding some chomping noises. The actual carrot was soon discarded and his own lip-tongue sounds sufficed as "pretend chomping" from that point on, most familiar when the later Bugs occasionally delivered his signature greeting as, "Meeeeaaahh - chomp, chomp, chomp - what's up, Doc?"

The rabbit's voice was subtly modified over the next couple of years, ending up more like the wise-guy fox in Avery's *Of Fox and Hounds*, released a few months after *A Wild Hare*. Mark Kausler notes that in the early forties when Blanc did Bugs Bunny guesting on radio shows like *The Abbott and Costello Program* it was still a little tougher and slower than the final voice. What is apparent is that from the start, Avery and the other directors and story men always ensured that Bugs, via Blanc, was given top-drawer dialogue.

By the late sixties as the first TV generation of animation buffs came of age, the directors began doing interviews about their time in the classic era. So did Mel Blanc, whose career anecdotes naturally touched on Bugs Bunny's origins. Avery, Clampett and others soon noted a litany of factual errors in Blanc's many talk show appearances, especially the howler about Mel talking them out of naming Bugs "Happy Rabbit," but they let it ride.

Clampett told author Walter Brasch, "Mel's a performer, it makes a good story to say, 'I went and listened to the pigs in the barnyard' [for Porky's grunts], but there's no mention of the guy [Joe Dougherty] that did the voice two years before...you're up against good fables as against how [things] really happened." [146]

Chuck Jones had a boiling point, though, telling Mike Barrier, "Mel didn't even invent the [Bugs] voice. His description of it is wrong, too. He says that Bugs is [a mean stinker] and he talks with a Brooklyn accent, which is a crock. Bugs talks with a Brooklyn rhythm - only occasionally did he use "dese" and "dose." Some [directors] at the beginning would use very definite 'dese' and 'dose' types of things, but I didn't like that myself. Contrary to what Mel says, he didn't originate voices. He came in when the dialogue was written and when the character was developed." [147] This sentiment was echoed in interviews with Maltese and Avery, even though they invariably had endless praise for Blanc's acting and interpretive skills.

Whatever Bugs's full origins, his impact was undeniable. The cheeky rabbit proved an instant favorite with audiences, quickly out-stripping Disney's characters in box office popularity. He remained a firm favourite each year, becoming indisputably the most popular theatrical cartoon character of all time. Beyond any other role in his stellar vocal career, Bugs Bunny was the one which guaranteed Mel Blanc's motion picture immortality.

In the spring of 1941 Blanc took the next step towards leader-ship of his turf: he signed an exclusive contract with Schlesinger Productions, precluding him from any other animation work. Until then he had been heard in many rival cartoons for Mintz-Colum-bia, Lantz, MGM, and Paramount's Madcap Models and Speaking of Animals shorts.

On April 25, 1941 *Daily Variety* reported, "Mel Blanc, the grav-el-voice of Bugs Bunny Merrie Melodies, has been signed to term contract" adding that it set "a precedent in the animated cartoon field." The agreement, which could "not conflict with Blanc's radio engagements" [148] would be renewed several times over the next twenty years; a clause in the second renewal allowed for Blanc to receive screen credit for "any cartoons featuring Bugs Bunny or Daffy Duck." Blanc's loud and highly energetic voices, along with Stalling's ever-livelier scores, became the dominant audio signature of the forties Warner cartoons, perfect for the up-tempo escapism so avidly sought by wartime moviegoers.

Through the forties Blanc was scheduled once a week for car-toons, on a day he was free from regular radio commitments. He was now Porky, Daffy and the popular new rabbit, and he had become indispensable. His dialogue sessions fell into a regular rou-tine. At the Warner Burbank recording stage he would first read all of one character's lines, with, according to Treg Brown, "four or five different takes of a line." [149] He would then go back and record all the second character's lines, and so forth. Head animators would later listen to the playback dailies, and the cartoon's director chose the "hero" takes. These lines were transferred by Brown from film to an acetate recording for the animators' timing reference.

Layout man Bob Givens recalled that Blanc would often first read straight from the large storyboards while perfecting his delivery. [150] Story man Don Christensen said some writers didn't take part in the dialogue recordings: "All we'd do was write the dialogue on the story sketches." [151] Animator-Director Norm McCabe explained that the voice people were shown the story on boards, and meanwhile "some of the gals at the studio would type up the lines in script form [for the dialogue session]." [152] Any subtle changes of inflection, needed for timing or visual gags, were discussed by Blanc and the director until the session was completed. McCabe recalled that coaching was minimal: "[The actors] were very good. I can't remember any trouble, especially with Mel."

Blanc truly came into his own during World War Two, with highly charged performances which saw him reach his pinnacle and remain there for at least the next decade. His work for Bob Clampett, who graduated to color cartoons in 1941 when he took over Avery's unit, was particularly brilliant. Clampett enabled Blanc to employ his powerful throat and innate musical and comic skills to splendid advantage in roles like the foaming-mad Adolf Hitler of *Russian Rhapsody* (1944), or Daffy Duck imitating Danny Kaye's Russian dialect and "git-gat-geetle" singing in *Book Revue* (1946). This was indeed the ART of animation voice acting.

Norm McCabe took over the remaining black and white Clampett cartoons, until his service period came up. He described the often-makeshift method of cartoon recording at Warner Bros., Burbank: "[Sometimes] they would pick a place where there was a little [live-action] set, and there'd be a couple of walls; you'd be in the corner of a room - you didn't have that vast feeling of a great big stage. There would be a guy with a boom mike, and a guy at the controls, and that was all." Although it was common to get everything in one session, McCabe clarified, "If something came up [after the session]

- if you had an added thought - one of the other directors would pick it up for you. Lots of times it would be just one or two lines, and they would be recording within one or two days. That happened quite often. 'Pickup lines,' they used to call them." [153]

It was McCabe's idea to get John McLeish for the voice of the dove in *The Ducktators* (1942), after hearing him do the voice of Pluto's conscience in Disney's *Lend a Paw* (1941). "That's one guy I remember asking them to try to get hold of, and they did. [Production manager] Johnny Burton was the guy we used to talk to about getting [outside] talent." [154] The overripe McLeish, a brilliant but troubled Canadian graphic artist who left Disney during the labor strike in the spring of 1941, later worked briefly as a gagman at Schlesinger's. His distinctive narrative tones also enhance Chuck Jones's *The Dover Boys* (1942), a cartoon for which McLeish also made important story and design contributions.

But beyond occasional talents like McLeish, the bulk of the forties voice work now fell to Mel Blanc. His undoubted talents aside, Blanc's vocal ascendancy was due in equal part to studio economics and the inevitable cutbacks incurred by wartime mobilization. Over three years Blanc had proven his worth to Schlesinger by playing "star" character voices like Porky, Daffy Duck and the increasingly popular Bugs, each of which was developed under the precise vocal tutelage of directors like Avery, Clampett and Freleng.

While Jack Warner, according to several accounts, was a fan of Schlesinger's cartoons, he was, first and foremost, a hard-nosed businessman.* Apparently, it was he who decreed that Blanc be signed up not only for his starring voices in cartoons which were routinely being singled out for high praise by exhibitors, but for his ability as a one-man stock company. This meant that the larger ensembles of voice performers were now, cost-wise, a thing of the past. Indeed, only an occasional one-off project like Clampett's ambitious *Coal Black and De Sebben Dwarfs* (1942) would employ a large range of extra voices from this point.

*A widely circulated anecdote describes a philistine-like Jack L. Warner being totally ignorant about cartoons: in the fifties he allegedly told Chuck Jones that he thought the Warner animation crew made Mickey Mouse. But the truth, as ever in film "history," is the polar opposite to one of Jones's oft-repeated tall tales. According to Clampett, Jack Warner, himself an inveterate hammy joke-teller, loved the WB cartoons, and took the directors to occasional lunches where he would critique the various cartoons then in release. [155] Freleng added that Warner and Norm Moray, the New York-based head of sales, kept an eagle eye on exhibitor reactions to all Warner Bros. releases, be they feature, short or cartoon. And Avery maintained that it was Jack Warner himself who insisted Schlesinger make more Bugs Bunny cartoons following the outstanding success of *A Wild Hare* in 1940. If the Mickey Mouse line was ever uttered, it was simply Warner - the lifelong frustrated comic - attempting a little jokey sarcasm. On another occasion Jones attributed it to Jack's older brother Harry; whatever...the brothers Warner may have been proudly bourgeois, but dummies they weren't.

Mel Blanc's contract renewal stipulating that he be given generic screen credit for "Voice Characterization" became a reality in early 1944, his name first appearing in the opening to *Little Red Riding Rabbit* (1943). While an undoubted boon for Blanc's radio career, many have argued it was unfair. With one exception, Stan Freberg's "Vocal" credit in 1957 for *Three Little Bops*, none of Warner Cartoon's other vocal artists were accorded the honor until 1962; certainly, in the case of regular Arthur Q. Bryan, the long-time voice of Elmer Fudd, it seems a pity. June Foray always felt that Blanc bore some of the blame in not pushing for Bryan, at least, to get screen credit, [156] while in Freberg's bombastic opinion, "Mel's [solo credit] was simply illegal." [157] In fact, it was perfectly legal, and Blanc's success was well earned. Besides which, it was long established industry practice for off-screen voices to be uncredited. Freelance day players were referred to by casting personnel as "casual hire," and Blanc was the only voice specialist under exclusive contract to a major film studio; the characters he was voicing–Bugs, Daffy, Porky–were by then the most popular in movies. Blanc had become a valued talent, and that was the real reason his management felt he deserved screen credit.

Noel Blanc told Leonard Maltin that his father and Arthur Bryan enjoyed a warm relationship, [158] one which extended to their radio work as well. In fact, Blanc was a regular cast member of Bryan's 1942 starring vehicle *Major Hoople,* and the well-known recording session outtake for *What's Opera, Doc?* from 1955 reveals a relaxed, convivial rapport between both artists.

***

With the outbreak of World War II, the versatile thirties voice-man Danny Webb was drafted and spent time in the European theatre a USO troupe attached to a Red Cross unit ("he was dubbed the Atomic Comic by General Eisenhower"). Following the conflict, he relocated to New York in 1944 and a career in radio and early TV.

But Danny Webb's place in animation history is assured, both for his dead-on Joe "Egghead" Penner imitation, as well as his final Hollywood cartoon assignment. Bob Clampett employed him to play the frog-voiced Wicked Queen in the previously noted cult-classic *Coal Black and De Sebben Dwarfs* (1942). [159] This was a hilarious performance, a tour de force swansong for a voice artist who, had the war not intervened, may well have ended up with some latter-day recognition like his colleague Mel Blanc.

Coal Black is such a special one-shot cartoon that it warrants extended discussion. Its vocal cast was most unusual for the period. When Clampett attended Duke Ellington's stage musical *Jump for*

Joy at LA's Mayan Theatre in mid-1941, he was imbued with the spirit and zest of the music and performers. He met with the cast, including stars Herb Jeffries and Dorothy Dandridge, enthusing them about his idea for a musical cartoon; he began auditioning several cast members and musicians, with the help of well-known African American pianist and vocal coach Eddie Beal, who became a lifelong friend. [160]

Clampett and his animators, Virgil Ross, Rod Scribner and Tom McKimson, also conducted research at Central Avenue's famous Club Alabam and other Black music venues in Los Angeles, soaking up the atmosphere and observing and sketching the musicians and the patrons' smooth, flowing dance movements. As his storyboard reached approval stage, Clampett began hiring the performers for his lead roles: Eddie Beal recommended Vivian Dandridge, from the Dandridge Sisters vocal trio, for the role of So White, while her mother Ruby auditioned for both the fireside "Mammy" storyteller and the Wicked Queen. She was, however, replaced by Lillian Randolph and Danny Webb in those roles. [161]

Clampett also planned to use the great Louis Armstrong for the role of Prince Chawmin' and discussed it with Satchmo backstage at the Orpheum Theatre. But when Armstrong was stuck with a touring commitment, Beal recommended extrovert drummer-vocalist Leo "Zoot" Watson, long-time member of the famed thirties trio The Spirits of Rhythm, for the Prince's voice. After the recordings were completed in early 1942, Clampett invited the performers to view the cartoon-in-progress, and to perform on 8-millimeter film as reference footage for his animators. [162]

Webb and Blanc, who voiced the dwarfs, were the only white voice artists heard in the cartoon. Today this film, so obviously a pet project of Clampett's, retains an incredible energy thanks to the combination of outstanding loose animation, frenetic pacing and clever rhyming dialogue. It also boasted a splendid boogie and blues music track. Clampett, Carl Stalling and his arranger Milt Franklyn collaborated with several Black musicians, led by Eddie Beal, on the score for *Coal Black*. As Mike Barrier noted, Warner Bros. had a studio orchestra under contract and so they allowed only one scene for which Clampett could use all-Black musicians: the famous end kiss, with Leo Watson on drums and another on jazz trumpet. It was matched by Rod Scribner's effectively loose-limbed animation of the desperate Prince. [163]

Clampett quickly followed up with another Black musical, *Tin Pan Alley Cats* (1943), again assisted by Eddie Beal who supplied the musicians, including a hot trumpeter for the film's surreal "out of this world" number. To save costs, this sequence re-used footage from Clampett's own *Porky in Wackyland* (1938) along with the hep "Nagasaki" number from Freleng's *September in the Rain* (1937). Clampett recalled that Beal also recommended the vocalists who sang both the smooth harmony opening song and doubled as the mission singers. [164] Returning was Leo Watson as a scat singing trumpeter, while Beal cast Harland C. Evans, who surely owned the most delightfully damaged voice-box in Hollywood, for the raucously gravel tones of the "Cats Waller" lead character ("Wha's de motter wit' him?"). Evans had notched up several cartoons imitating notable vocalists since the mid-thirties.

Sidebar: Race imagery in Golden Age cartoons

In the vastly changed world of the 21st century, vintage cartoons featuring Black caricatures are problematic. *Coal Black* in particular can seem contradictory in its place in animation history. On the positive side it is important to note that Bob Clampett gave valuable employment to terribly mistreated performers who keenly desired breaking the vile show business color bar, which lasted well beyond the fifties. The jazzy music and most of the voices are authentic and they deserved a vehicle to showcase their performing talents. The problem arises with the cartoon's lazy adoption of dehumanizing clichés, including minstrel-like "comic" attitudes already passé in 1942 (such as dice for teeth and stereotyped hidden razors carried as weapons), which sit uneasily with any actual comedy present. Most seriously, the stereotypes render parts of the film degrading and insulting, and from its release date *Coal Black* was the topic of correspondence between studio boss Harry Warner and the NAACP, which wanted the cartoon withdrawn from theatrical exhibition.

A major objection was the depiction of the Black dwarf soldiers; so soon after Black conscripts were being regarded as a positive step forward in the long move to equality, the cartoon appeared to denigrate them as minstrel-style buffoons who all speak in Mel Blanc's cringeworthy white version of a "comic negro" accent.

Several white voice artists who spoke this faux Black dialect unimaginatively based it on the stage take-off of Lincoln Perry's "Step'n Fetchit" screen character, invariably missing any of Perry's own subtle satiric intent. Blanc's version, heard to even worse effect in Lantz cartoons like the Li'l Eightball entries and *Scrub Me Mama with a Boogie Beat* (1941), is always hard to take, adding as it does even more of the shiftless and whining quality that was hurtful to many Black patrons. This and other racial cliches finally overwhelm and dominate the cartoon today, preventing it from being appreciated for its many entertaining aspects such as the loosely elastic animation drawings, the breathlessly rapid comic pacing and its witty musical segues.

On a positive note, both of these Clampett cartoons celebrate the sheer verve of Black "jump'n'jive" dance music with accurate reverence and satiric humor. That was always Clampett's desire. While many Black audiences were able to laugh at the film then and now, we can never truly know their full reaction to these complex historical issues.

Other groups were also racially mocked during this period: when *Coal Black* was released the World War had been a harsh American reality for a year, and the enemies were clearly defined. Various cartoons with often grotesque Japanese and German caricatures were loudly cheered at the time as morale-boosting comedy. Today however the films - like *Tokio Jokio* (1943) or *Herr Meets Hare* (1945) - only work in historic context when concise explanatory disclaimers precede them. For a detailed treatise on the issue of race in animation this author recommends the book *The Colored Cartoon: Black Representation in American Animated Short Films, 1907-54* by Christopher P. Lehman.

***

Meanwhile, another cartoon voice star of the early forties was young actor-mimic Kent Rogers. Like Danny Webb, he was inducted into the Army Air Corps in World War II. Sadly, Rogers, who was being groomed by Bob Clampett for starring roles like Beaky Buzzard in *Bugs Bunny Gets the Boid* (1942) and Horton the Elephant in *Horton Hatches the Egg* (1942) was killed in July 1944, while he was backing up a light airplane during a training exercise. He was only twenty-one. His best cartoon showcase was Avery's tinsel-town take off *Hollywood Steps Out* (1941) for which he performed twelve fine movie star imitations. Kent Rogers, just reaching his prime, was also heard to advantage in cartoons for Lantz (as Homer Pigeon), MGM, Columbia and two early entries for Paramount's *Speaking of Animals* novelty shorts.

In the forties the bellicose-toned Billy Bletcher was still being billed as "the little man with the big voice." While lacking Blanc's range of zany characters, he remained one of the great animation actors. It was unfortunate that his own personality quirks were his Achilles heel: there was a falling out with Clampett, whom Bletcher sarcastically referred to as "little Bobby." Clampett described Bletcher as "a little man with some of the attributes of the Big Bad Wolf which he portrayed [for Disney]," explaining, "[after] doing the Lone Stranger voice for me [1939's *The Lone Stranger and Porky*] in those Depression days, he expected me to see that he got continuing work at Warners for the sake of his little daughter, etc. Many times, I suggested using him for various roles [but] Leon or Ray said 'No, Mel can do that voice and save us the money.'" [165]

Although displaced to a large degree by Blanc, Bletcher continued working in forties cartoons for Warner Bros., as well as Disney, MGM, Columbia and George Pal's Puppetoons. Several of his Warner performances, including the unctuous Lawyer Goodwill in Tashlin's *The Case of the Stuttering Pig* (1937), a film and performance so gothically scary it resulted in parental complaints to Schlesinger, and the wolf in Freleng's *Little Red Riding Rabbit* (1943), are classics of the voice acting art. Billy Bletcher ended his Warner Bros. career with a role perfect for his talents: the dysfunctional father with the extremely short fuse in Chuck Jones's funny Three Bears cartoons; in a twist he replaced Mel Blanc who played Father Bear in the first of the series, *Bugs Bunny and the Three Bears* (1944).

Once Blanc was under contract he was often asked for a voice out of left field, such as his role in *A Tale of Two Kitties* (1942). Clampett recalled, "Some voices Mel didn't do...one of the things that made me think of [the Abbott & Costello parody] was when I went to a nightclub and I heard a guy [possibly Eddie Bartell] who looked just like Lou Costello...he did this perfect Costello. I tried to use him. I go back to Leon Schlesinger and tell him I need to hire this guy that does Costello in the nightclubs. Leon's thing was that he paid a weekly salary to Mel to do all he could, no matter what. He says, 'Let Mel do it.' I called Mel on the phone. He said he'd never done [Costello] before, he couldn't do it. So, Leon says, 'Oh, he can do it.' In this case I got the discs of Abbott & Costello, I worked with Mel, we went through it, listened to it, every little thing that Costello did, and Mel [finally] did a beautiful job. Just by a little working he got it! The Abbott voice was done by Ted Pierce, one of our gag men." [166]

Blanc was not, essentially, an impressionist, although he could do a few good imitations, like Eddie Anderson's Rochester character from *The Jack Benny Program*; he worked so often on that top rating show, becoming a virtual weekly regular from 1943, that he had ample opportunity to absorb Anderson's unique vocal delivery up close.

Sara Berner provided many female voices in the first half of the forties. Clampett noted, "She was an important voice artist at Warners." [167] Berner effectively replaced the tiny-voiced actresses like Berneice Hansell who had been so prevalent in the previous decade of "cuter" storybook cartoons. Berner became, in Clampett's words, "our female Mel Blanc." She played Beaky Buzzard's Greek-accented mother in *Bugs Bunny Gets the Boid* (1942). Clampett recalled, "I didn't write that as being a Greek voice. Sara did a voice [to match the rube farm-boy Beaky] and it just wasn't funny...I asked her what else she could do. She used the Greek voice that she did on the *Jimmy Durante Show* ["Ingrid Matzarata"] and everybody on the soundstage roared with laughter. On the second Beaky cartoon we changed it to Sara's Italian voice. In those days there was nothing where the public says, 'Don't use an ethnic thing.' That was just part of comedy [then]." [168]

Berner also performed a range of excellent celebrity imitations, from Bette Davis in *Hollywood Daffy* (1946) to Lauren Bacall in *Bacall to Arms* (1946). She was prolific at MGM and, like Billy Bletcher, did Paramount's Puppetoons and *Speaking of Animals* shorts during this era.

From late 1942, Sara Berner was joined by another fine radio actress named Bea Benaderet. Famously, these two voice artists played the nasal, gossiping telephone operators for many years on Jack Benny's *Lucky Strike Program*. Benaderet began doing many cartoon voices, such as the obnoxious Red Riding Hood in Freleng's *Little Red Riding Rabbit* (1943), effectively sending up the raucous radio comedienne Cass Daley. She was all the female voices in Jones's *The Weakly Reporter* (1944). She would eventually became the first voice of dotty old Granny in the Tweety and Sylvester films.

In the late forties and into the fifties, Benaderet was Warner's leading female voice, essaying many straight roles like a housewife for *Wild Wife* (1954), a pet owner for *Feed the Kitty* (1952) and a range of more eccentric character voices like the put-upon Mama Bear in Jones's Three Bears series. Her radio expertise shone through in McKimson's Foghorn Leghorn cartoons, especially *Lovelorn Leghorn* (1951) where she voiced every hen in the coop, each with a unique personality. This cartoon also introduced "Miss Prissy" the sad Widow Hen. Her eccentric voice was based on Martha of the husband-wife team "Sam & Martha Harrison," played by Pert Kelton on radio's *Milton Berle Show*. It was frankly funnier on radio, because her husband was, like Foghorn, a motor-mouth who would finally stop his endless gabbing to ask her a question, to which she would invariably respond with just a vacuous "Yeeeeees."

Throughout the forties, Berner and Benaderet appeared virtually every week with Blanc on radio shows like *Burns and Allen*, providing a continuity of thespian fraternalism for their many cartoon assignments. Another girl with a natural baby voice, Marjorie Tarlton, played Sniffles in Jones's revival of his overly cute mouse from 1943-46.

An occasional Warner cartoon newcomer often provided a single performance that has since become a latter-day favourite, like mimic Dick Nelson's funny imitation of Edward G. Robinson in Freleng's 1946 *Racketeer Rabbit* ("What a pal, what a pal"; "Rocky's gettin' mad now!"). According to the in-house *Warner Club News*, while Nelson ("another voice artist and one of our better imitators"

[169]) was driving to the sound stage for this recording session, he was involved in a serious car wreck from which he emerged shaken but happily unhurt.

Another distinctive performance was that of comic Sammy Wolf, who did the zany dog in Clampett's *Hare Ribbin'* (1944) as a vocal imitation of "The Mad Russian." This famous character was created and played by Bert Gordon, and was heard weekly on comedian Eddie Cantor's radio show. Wolf, a former stooge for vaudeville headliner Ted Healy, was a "second banana" in 1943. He was performing at Slapsie Maxie's, a Hollywood nightclub which was patronised one night by Clampett.

He recalled Wolf begging him to do a cartoon: "I saw him there. He appeared with [comedian] Ben Blue; he was kind of like one of the little *entr'actes* that Ben Blue had. Sammy Wolf and I became friends, and of course he was excited about doing voices on cartoons, and I didn't have much for him, but this one time he said, 'Can't you use me? I need some money, and gee, I'd just love to do a cartoon.' So, I made the thing with the Mad Russian [dog], and I think it was just for Sammy I did it."[170] Wolf also did some imitations for Tashlin's *The Swooner Crooner* (1944).

Dick Nelson and Sammy Wolf weren't the only mimics in Warner cartoons. Another good imitator, Paul Regan, did voices for cartoons like *Brother Brat* (1944) and *Hollywood Canine Canteen* (1946). One of the more gifted impressionists hired by Clampett was Dave Siegel, professionally known, latterly in Las Vegas, as Dave Barry. Barry provided the excellent Humphrey Bogart imitation for the effective take-off of the 1944 movie *To Have and Have Not* seen in Clampett's *Bacall to Arms* (1946), opposite Sara Berner doing the sultry Lauren Bacall soundalike.

Clampett remembered, "We had animated it to [the] original track of Bogart and Bacall, but Bogart's contract with Warners did not allow a secondary use like that. After we got it finished Warners came back and said, 'Oh my God, we can't use the Bogart and Bacall voices!' So, what I had to do was locate two outside voice people and work with them. We ran the picture, ran the original voice of Bogart and Bacall. They listened to it and did it right after it, and we got it." [171]

Dave Barry, then in uniform with Special Services, corresponded with Clampett, writing, "I'm glad the Bogey turned out all right. Frankly, I felt in the mood, like I myself could creep and crawl with Bacall!"[172] This cartoon was a pretty strange admixture: when Clampett left the studio in mid-1945, *Bacall to Arms* was reluctantly completed by animator Art Davis, who graduated to director status taking over Clampett's unit for the next three years.

Among Dave Barry's other cartoon roles, he also supplied the deep and distinctive "Gildersneeze" floorwalker voice, which was slightly slowed down on the track for extra vocal depth, in Chuck Jones's Bugs cartoon, *Hare Conditioned* (1945).

From 1943-45, Mel Blanc was also the voice of Private Snafu in a government commissioned series of morale building cartoons, made by Frank Capra's Signal Corps unit. Leon Schlesinger won the contract for these by outbidding Disney. They were light-hearted instructional films for men in uniform, made by the Warner cartoon directors and story men, at first under writer Ted "Dr. Seuss" Geisel's supervision, at the old Fox Studio on Sunset and Western. After storyboard approval, actual animation took place a few blocks west at Warner's cartoon studio. The Snafu shorts were presented to servicemen as part of the *Army-Navy Screen Magazine.*

The raunchy cartoons, running under four minutes apiece, also featured the voices of narrators Frank Graham and Bob Bruce, plus voice actors Sara Berner, Billy Bletcher, and a couple of one-off performers. Freleng's *Hot Spot* instalment used Hal Peary, radio's actual Great Gildersleeve, normally imitated by others in theatrical cartoons. Chuck Jones's *It's Murder She Says* featured a gin-soaked mosquito, "Anopheles Annie" played by veteran stage actress Marjorie Rambeau. [173] Half a century later, Robert Bruce vividly remembered the recording session: "She gave a great performance, sounding like a real blowsy old tart." [174]

In 1945 a second series commenced for the U.S. Navy featuring a timid seaman named Hook. Clampett said, "Arthur Lake did the lead voice for me." Lake was famous as the bumbling Dagwood Bumstead in Columbia's long-running *Blondie* films. [175] As with the Snafu cartoons, Lake was supported by Blanc, Berner and Frank Graham. Blanc did an enormous amount of work for the war effort, also voicing the slob-like character Trigger Joe for the First Motion Picture Unit's instructional cartoons; Rudy Ising directed the first one, *Position Firing*. Blanc also played the klutzy comic strip character Private Sad Sack, created by Sergeant George Baker, on many Armed Forces Radio shows using his stuttering Porky voice.

Meanwhile, in-house talent continued to prove invaluable in the theatrical cartoons. Gag man and genial ham Ted Pierce was now happily back at the Schlesinger shop in 1942 after three years in Florida at the Fleischer Studio. He was now a top story man, doubling as a voice in various roles including his fine Bud Abbott take-off - very close to Pierce's natural whiskey voice - for Clampett's "Babbit and Catstello" cartoon *A Tale of Two Kitties* (1942). He also did a villainous character in *Fox Pop* (1942) and was "Daddy," an imitation of radio actor Hanley Stafford, in *Quentin Quail* (1946). That cartoon was a parody of comedienne Fanny Brice's radio vehicle *The Baby Snooks Show* for which Sara Berner imitated the Snooks voice. Pierce also voiced the great dumb dog named Sylvester, tormented by Bugs Bunny in *Hare Force*.

Another gifted story man Michael Maltese, in real life a droll Italian, contributed the funny Benito Mussolini take-off in the wartime entry *The Ducktators* (1942), while he and Pierce teamed to play the famished castaways in *Wackiki Wabbit* (1943). Earlier they co-voiced *The Aristo-Cat* (1943), as Maltese explained: "Ted Pierce and I did Hubie and Bertie, the two mice. I played Hubie and Ted Pierce played Bert. We did a couple. We didn't get paid; it was fun, we were hammy." Later, Maltese added, "a kid in an Army uniform came in to audition - a tall, skinny redheaded kid - and we gave him the job of doing Hubie, and we gave the other one to Mel Blanc. This kid was Stan Freberg." [176]

The Screen Actors Guild waived any objections to non-members supplying cartoon voices in a scheme whereby Warner Bros. paid a flat day-rate payment to the union. The payment went to an actor down on his luck. Johnny Burton negotiated these terms with actor and SAG representative Murray Kinnell. For instance, Maltese used his "trick voice" for Jones's cartoon *A Feather in His Hare* (1948), playing a whiny Indian fall-guy, and a payment was sent to the Actors' Union. [177]

Gag man Lloyd Turner played the Red Skelton-like worm in *The Rattled Rooster* (1948); Turner admitted to having a flair for voices and did a couple of fill-in bits at Warners, thanks to his story-mentor Warren Foster writing in a part for him. [178] The animator Richard Bickenbach provided a creditable Bing Crosby imitation warbling "When My Dreamboat Comes Home" for Tashlin's *The Swooner Crooner* (1944). Lloyd Turner recalled this casting as sheer convenience: "Dick used to sing a lot at his local church." [179]

The wispy Sinatra voice heard in *The Swooner Crooner* and *Book Revue* (1946) was also the work of Dick Bickenbach. A later caricature cartoon, McKimson's *Hollywood Canine Canteen* (1946), employed the excellent band vocalist Robert Lyons for a Sinatra soundalike but re-used Bickenbach's Crosby track from the earlier cartoon. *Hollywood Canine Canteen* also featured impressionist Paul Regan doing imitations like Edward G. Robinson and Jimmy Durante.

The outstanding radio talent Frank Graham, although heard mostly in MGM and Columbia cartoons, narrated several Warner Bros. titles starting with Bob Clampett's *Horton Hatches the Egg* (1942). He was also used by Freleng for *Foney Fables* (1942) and by Jones for *Fresh Airedale* (1945). Graham ended his cartoon career with a malignantly sepulchral reading of Freleng's *Each Dawn I Crow* (1949), as the hapless bird's insistent conscience, in the style of radio's omniscient "The Whistler." Sadly Frank Graham, one of the great cartoon voices, took his own life over a soured love affair in September 1950.

These fine talents aside however, Mel Blanc's starring voices had become completely dominant during and just after the war when a raft of new star characters were developed. These included Sylvester the luckless cat, Pepe Le Pew the amorous skunk, Yosemite Sam * and Foghorn Leghorn, to each of whom Blanc gave beautifully crafted voices. Indeed, the only continuing non-Blanc star character of consequence remained Arthur Bryan's Elmer Fudd, and even he was basically a straight man to Blanc's zany leads.

* Sidebar: Genesis of a character voice, Yosemite Sam

Mike Maltese and Friz Freleng developed fireball Sam's voice, basing its unparalleled loudness on a character Tex Avery featured in 1939's *Dangerous Dan McFoo*. In that cartoon, Blanc played a Yukon stranger who yelled everything at ear-splitting volume ("Well, WHAT OF IT????"). It so amused Freleng he remembered it five years later, requesting Blanc adapt it with a more Western feel for a belligerent Sheriff. [180] Thus, Sam's vocal origins combined the bullhorn Avery character with the similar but not-quite-so-loud lawman in the Bugs Bunny *Stage Door Cartoon* (1944). The latter voice, in turn, was based largely on Red Skelton's popular "Sheriff Dead Eye" radio character ("Aw c'mon, horsie, won'tcha please whoa?") which was first borrowed for Clampett's Western parody *Buckaroo Bugs* (1944). Combine all this with vaudeville / radio comics Jack Kirkwood and Red Ingle, both of whom had a lot of Sam and Skelton's Sheriff in their bellicose deliveries. Freleng also referenced the blustery character actor Walter Connolly, busy in thirties films like *It Happened One Night,* as still another vocal influence. And to top all this, Chuck Jones weighed in insisting that Cottontail Smith in his cartoon *Super Rabbit* (1943) was the template. [181] All these elements, along with input during recording sessions from writers Mike Maltese and Ted Pierce (with Maltese half-jokingly adding that tiny Sam was visually modelled on hot-headed director Freleng!) resulted in the ferociously funny Yosemite Sam. Understandably, Mel Blanc came to dread Sam's throat-pounding recording sessions of the fifties.

***

In his book *Hollywood Cartoons,* Michael Barrier writes persuasively of a bleakness and street-smart tone to many Warner cartoons of the late forties, [182] cartoons written, indeed dominated in this period, by story men from struggling East Coast beginnings. Self-reliance and Depression-bred insecurity gave their comedy the jaundiced eye: Barrier cites Warren Foster as a case in point. Foster's dialogue for several Bob McKimson cartoons is cynically funny, providing a virtual gabfest for the dextrous vocal talents of Blanc.

In cartoons like *The Windblown Hare* (1949), *Rebel Rabbit* (1949) and *Daffy Duck Slept Here* (1948) the talk is non-stop, loud and distinctly world-weary. After a solid decade of contact with the Warner crew, recording several hundred of their cartoons, Blanc was the perfect conduit for this tough humor. It was in this period that Blanc came to mean more to the success of the Warner cartoons than just being their chief voice; his influence on the writers is now palpably obvious, and their need for him appears to have generated much respect: in a column in *Warner Club News,* Mike Maltese called Blanc "our voice sculptor." [183] As Freleng noted, "We knew what Mel could do, and we would write the dialogue with him in mind." [184]

Maltese recalled working with Blanc: "When you had a new character, you'd do the voice for Mel, and he'd do it better; but you had to give him an idea what the character was about. (When) we'd record with the voice talent, Mel knew right away what you wanted. We'd have suggestions. I'd say, 'Mel, can you put a little more question on the end of that?' Whatever director I was working with, I would always go to the recording sessions with them." [185]

Another garrulously talkative character perfect for Blanc's delivery was the loudmouth rooster Foghorn Leghorn. Director Robert McKimson recalled this character's vocal genesis thirty years later in 1971: "Warren Foster, my story man, had a rooster story - an idea for one - and all of a sudden I told him, 'I was listening to the radio the other night, and there was this 'Senator Claghorn' [played by Kenny Delmar on *The Fred Allen Show*], and I said, 'He took his delivery from the old sheriff in the old *Blue Monday Jamboree*.' This business of saying, 'I say there, son' was because the old sheriff was deaf, and he didn't think people would hear him. I told Warren about it, and he was nuts about the idea. We sort of merged the two ideas of the old sheriff and Senator Claghorn and put them onto Foghorn Leghorn." [186]

The problem with this anecdote is that McKimson mis-remembered the timeline. The original Sheriff voice was indeed heard throughout the thirties, on Warner Bros.' own station KFWB and in regional Pacific coast comedies like *The Gilmore Circus*. The hard-of-hearing old law man was created by character actor Jack Clifford.

In fact the early Foghorn was fully based on Clifford's Sheriff, not Kenny Delmar's Senator Claghorn. The first rooster cartoon was well into production months before the Claghorn character was even heard on Fred Allen's show. In fact for his first cartoon, *Walky Talky Hawky* (1946), the rooster's voice actually sounded more like Yosemite Sam.

Originally McKimson hired somebody before Mel Blanc to try the voice, "and it didn't work out too well. I didn't think that Mel could do it, but when we showed Mel what we wanted, he went ahead and did it, and did a real good job of it. But it wasn't copied [exactly from] Claghorn." [187] Even this quote has McKimson struggling to recall accurately.

It was when the second cartoon featuring the bombastic rooster was in production that Senator Claghorn became a national sensation on radio's famous *Fred Allen Show*. Actor Kenny Delmar employed some creative comic business for the windbag Claghorn that was similar to Jack Clifford's earlier West Coast sheriff.

Indeed, it was actually *Crowing Pains* (1947), the second Foghorn cartoon, that combined the two radio influences. The old Sheriff, for instance, originated the "repeating, I say REPEATING!!!" mannerism, but it was Claghorn who appended "that is" to the end of some sentences and also used the expression, "That's a joke, son!" The rooster was finally a blend, but Senator Claghorn's is the voice that is widely assumed to be Foghorn's entire template, while the original radio Sheriff has been totally forgotten.

Despite Mel Blanc's primacy as Warner's chief voice artist, other professional talents continued to be hired in one-off support, including strong radio actors like Jim Backus as the fuss-budget Genie in McKimson's *A-Lad in His Lamp* (1948). As McKimson proudly noted, "In fact it was the first time [Backus] had done any cartoon voice." [188] The Genie was the same voice as Backus's rich snob Hubert Updyke, an amusingly broad character he was then playing weekly on radio's *Alan Young Show*. Incidentally, when Backus recorded the Genie voice he was a weekly regular on *The Mel Blanc Show*, a 1946-47 CBS sitcom with Blanc playing a trouble-prone fix-it shop owner whose ability at voice disguises always lands him in trouble. Backus was heard as Hartley Benson, the town's egomaniac Beau Brummell who was mostly in love with himself.

The art of mimicry continued to be used in the cartoons. Dave Barry reprised his fine Bogie imitation for Freleng's *Slick Hare* (1947). Young utility comedian Stan Freberg became another Warner semi-regular in early 1945, following a voice audition. Bob Clampett employed him to do the dog who spoke like President Roosevelt in *For He is a Jolly Good Fala* (Fala was the name of FDR's famous real-life pooch). That cartoon was abandoned following Roosevelt's death in April 1945, but Freberg was by then a new talent on call for small roles. He graduated to bigger parts like Junyer Bear, originated by the late Kent Rogers, and as one of the overly polite Goofy Gophers. In *Birth of a Notion* (1947), an underrated Daffy Duck begun by Clampett and finished by McKimson, Freberg did the best Peter Lorre imitation heard in cartoons. [189]

Treg Brown recalled, "[At one session] Stan and Mel got into a fight, because Stan was [then] like Milton Berle, stealing other guys' gags and voices." As Brown saw it, "Stan was only good for maybe four or five voices; I just didn't see him as in the same category as Mel." [190]

According to Chuck Jones and writer Lloyd Turner, Blanc was occasionally threatened by new kids on the vocal block, coming across as somewhat territorial. "He could be a tough guy" said Turner, who observed firsthand the recording date at which the physical altercation with Freberg took place. Apparently it was triggered when Freberg did a joking imitation of Bugs Bunny within earshot of Blanc, who blew his stack and began strong-arming the young vocal upstart. [191] And when story man and future voice artist Bill "Bullwinkle" Scott was with Warner Cartoons for a year, he sat in on a recording and "I made a couple of suggestions" regarding Blanc's delivery to director Art Davis, for whose unit he was writing; "I heard later that Mel adjured Artie not to bring 'Shakespeare' to any more sessions." [192]

Although Blanc remained a highly prized asset to Warner Cartoons as post-war budgets tightened, a few films seemed to suffer from his overuse. *The Windblown Hare* (1949), for instance, had Blanc performing all five characters and, while his acting was up to his usual high standard, several voices were simply too similar: one of the three pigs sounds almost identical to the cartoon's star Bugs Bunny.

Throughout the forties, the classy Robert Bruce remained the most frequently used "off-screen" commentator voice, in such films as *Of Thee I Sting* (1946) and *Fin 'n' Catty* (1943). Bruce continued to enjoy a twenty-year run in the Warner Bros. cartoons as their most distinctive narrator, from 1939-1958, happily anonymous all the way through his final call for *Bonanza Bunny*.

Warner Bros. Cartoon Voices in the Fifties

By the end of the forties, budget cutbacks were an inescapable reality due to rising production costs and union mandated post-war wage increases. These factors, and the inexorable encroachment of television, meant that the short cartoon was perceived to be facing imminent extinction; against all odds, though, they managed to survive. Exhibitors might have groused about the cost of cartoons but they couldn't deny their popularity with theatre patrons. Warner Bros. continued releasing cartoons all the way through 1969. But while Warner Cartoons scored with many outstanding classics in the new decade, the films were inevitably affected by the budget cuts over time.

Less money for the earlier luxuries of animation and design meant that the cartoons began to appropriate the streamlined look of UPA. As the story men and directors aged, a certain formulaic quality began affecting the films: by late in the decade the Tweety, Foghorn Leghorn and even Bugs Bunny series began to look a little shop-worn and by-the-numbers. Essentially, the great Warner characters had hit their peak in the late forties. Some cartoons seemed truly lightweight when compared with their classic progenitors from ten years previous: *High Diving Dare* released in 1949 is undeniably brilliant, while *Horse Hare*, again featuring Sam and Bugs, is a distinctly lesser effort.

One result of the smaller budgets meant that a large number of cartoons now centred around two-character adversarial comedy, Freleng's long series of Tweety and Sylvester being the prime example. Or there was McKimson's Sylvester and Hippety Hopper the kangaroo series, or Foghorn Leghorn and his canine nemesis, even Jones's Wolf and Sheepdog. And there were now single characters who could appear over and over, like Pepe Le Pew, the Tasmanian Devil and the tiny Martian. This large cast of recurring characters in a time of animation shortcuts required a lot of dialogue. Blanc, a master at making gabfests fascinating, was able to vocally dominate the fifties Warner output almost by default. It was obvious he would be indispensable to the cartoon makers for several years to come, and it was a source of much pride to the now veteran voice man who thrived on his work.

The years 1948-55 were some of Blanc's greatest. In those years he honed Warner's distinctive stable of post-war regulars like Foghorn Leghorn and Yosemite Sam to pinpoint vocal hilarity. He added eccentric new character voices like Chuck Jones's diminutive Commander X-2 from the planet Mars, later named Marvin the Martian for the inevitable merchandising. Indeed it is Blanc's voice acting in the fifties, even with long-established stars like Bugs, Porky and Daffy, that has entered the popular consciousness as the benchmark of how these famous characters should sound for all time. Blanc's work for Freleng was often spectacularly good, his manic readings of Warren Foster's sharp dialogue defining the art of acting for animation. His portrayals of blustery Yosemite Sam in *Ballot Box Bunny* (1951) and *Hare Trimmed* (1953), and the harried Sylvester in *Canned Feud* (1951), remain unequalled for energy and comic flair.

The directors looked to match Blanc's strong vocal presence by seeking talented casual voices for one-off supporting parts. By mid-decade fresh artists like Daws Butler and June Foray were being heard as extra characters in many of the cartoons. Despite the lowered budgets, other distinctive voices were auditioned and hired, many more than once.

Robert McKimson, who had been directing since late 1944, frequently tried new voices in his cartoons. These included slinky actress Grace Lenard as the nympho se-duck-tress of *The Super Snooper* (1952), Gladys Holland as Daffy's dizzy high-pitched girl-friend in *Muscle Tussle* (1953), and the great Runyonesque actor Sheldon Leonard who played the short-lived cat named Dodsworth. McKimson also used Leonard, sped up on the track, as the pugnacious bantam in *Sock-a-Doodle Do* (1952), recalling, "I believe it was [Leonard's] first cartoon voice." [193]

One of the most oddball Warner voices in any cartoon was for a strange little crow in *Corn Plastered* (1951), a bizarre McKimson one-shot experiment. Another mechanically sped character voice, the outré little bird was portrayed by entertainer Pat Patrick, who created the similarly eccentric character "Ercel Twing." Patrick was playing that part each week on radio's *Charlie McCarthy Show* in the same weird voice, but not sped.

A solid new Warner Cartoons regular in the early fifties was harsh-voiced comic actor John T. Smith, who played the bully-ing construction worker in Bugs Bunny films like *Homeless Hare* (1950), and who is most likely best remembered as the nasty dog who grouses, "What!!! No gravy????" in the typically dark Mike Maltese story *Chow Hound* (1951), directed by Chuck Jones. Smith was also funny as Crusher, the muscle-bound champion wrestler easily bested by Bugs in 1951's *Bunny Hugged* ("Yeah, well I was just passing through - duuuuhhhhhhhh"). A mad scientist voice he did for Jones's *Water, Water Every Hare* (1952) fooled many latter-day cartoon buffs into thinking it was Vincent Price's voice, although it wasn't even intended as an imitation of the actor (indeed the long horror film portion of Price's career hadn't begun when the cartoon's dialogue was recorded). A reliable, versatile supporting voice artist, Smith was also the fine Barry Fitzgerald-type leprechaun in *The Wearing of the Grin* (1951). For Bob McKimson he was one of the exceedingly dim mountain men outwitted by Bugs in *Hillbilly Hare* (1950).

McKimson said, "[Smith] was rather limited in his range, but had a very good deep voice which we used from time to time." Smith had already worked on Paramount's *Speaking of Animals* and UPA cartoons before breaking in at Warner Bros. Actress June Foray added that John T. Smith was limited for on-screen work due to a withered arm. In the late seventies Daws Butler, who worked with Smith on many commercial voice-overs, wistfully said, "I always wondered whatever happened to Smith." [194]

Chuck Jones and his comically gifted story man Mike Maltese are justly famous for producing several unique, rather experimental, cartoons in this decade, like *Duck Amuck* (1953), another fine Mel Blanc showcase for a Daffy who runs the emotional gamut from egotistical enthusiasm to near-nervous breakdown.

Among the best of the Jones-Maltese specialties were their musical parodies, particularly when it came to the rarefied world of grand opera, including the clever take-off *Rabbit of Seville* (1950), where Bugs via Blanc shone with his artful barbershop vocalizing of the mangled libretto. Another excellent operatic short was *Long-Haired Hare* (1949) in which the rabbit wreaks sweet revenge on an arrogant baritone by destroying the Hollywood Bowl. Jones recalled the singer they used: "His name was [Nicolai] Shutorov; he did the opera-singer's voice for *Long-Haired Hare* and died very shortly after that while on tour." [195]

However the most singularly enduring musical entry directed by Jones remains *One Froggy Evening* (1955), and it is particularly satisfying for your author that the frog's singing voice, forgotten by everyone involved for decades, was finally uncovered and verified during research at the USC Warner Bros. archive. The amphibian's joyous Gay nineties baritone ("Hello ma baby, Hello ma honey, Hello ma ragtime gal") belonged to popular veteran bandleader-singer Harry "Bill" Roberts.

The identification of Bill Roberts was the result of tenacious trawling through music department records, because Jones and others simply couldn't remember the man's name, no matter how abidingly memorable the cartoon itself.* In one interview Jones suggested a young baritone named Terrence Monck, [196] but, as is often the case, time had blurred memory: Monck, who sounded like a "straighter" Bill Roberts, in fact sang in a couple of Jones's later MGM Tom & Jerry cartoons like *Cat and Dupli-Cat* (1967).

*In fairness to Jones most industry veterans were forgetful on voices. The near-photographic memory of Bob Clampett notwithstanding, foggy recall is understandable. It is a big "ask" to expect a day-player's name to remain in a director's memory some forty five years after a two-hour recording session. Therefore, it's a pity that more payroll records and dialogue sheets weren't saved for posterity. Certainly, none of these cartoon makers expected anything like the longevity or attention that their films have enjoyed in the succeeding decades. Indeed, back in the day they were intended for just one or two theatrical screenings before the unforeseen advent of TV reruns, followed twenty years later by home video, that insured their perpetual afterlife.

The standard procedure was for Warner's choral director Dudley Chambers to contract a freelance singer like Bill Roberts, after consulting with Carl Stalling or music arrangers Milt Franklyn and Eugene Podanny. But in the case of *One Froggy Evening*, Jones noted that the cartoon took a long time to reach completion, because everything - including "searching for a fine singer" - took longer than normal. [197] Jones wasn't kidding: Roberts recorded the frog's vocals on 20 April 1954, and the cartoon reached theatres some twenty months later at the end of 1955. One of the frog's songs, the much quoted "Hello Ma Baby" was suggested by story man Mike Maltese who recalled the catchy tune from 1899 being sung in a tavern at the start of the 1941 Warners feature *The Sea Wolf.* [198]

Another immortal Warner "voice" didn't even belong to a performer. Background painter Paul Julian supplied the familiar "mheeep-mheeep" noise of the Road Runner. As Jones recounted, "Julian did the original 'beep-beeps' which are still used today. As he walked down the Warner Bros. hall carrying a load of backgrounds he couldn't see where he was going so he beep-beeped to get people out of the way. At that time Mike Maltese and I were completing the first Road Runner [story]. Upon hearing Julian's beep-beep we bowed deeply to the east and said, 'Ok God, we'll take it from here,' because it was so obviously the voice of a Road Runner." [199]

Treg Brown said, "The minute that Paul did that, we knew that was [the sound we wanted]. He was kidding, but Chuck heard him, and dragged him over to the recording stage [for *Fast and Furry-ous* (1949)]. We had a little trouble with the Actors' union, but they got over that, because Mel was the standby on that [Blanc recorded some noises for the Coyote in this first cartoon]." [200] As for Julian himself he remembered, "Treg took me across the lot to this recording set-up. I spent a happy, silly afternoon going 'Beep' into the microphone and listening to it played back [at a faster speed]." [201]

Incidentally, the noise of the Road-Runner's tongue, used from the second cartoon in the series, was supplied by assistant sound man Dale Pickett, from an effect Brown had made by tapping the top of a bottle. The speeding effect of the elusive bird's supersonic movement was achieved with a machine called "an inertia starter." The device was also used under the whirlwind approach of McKimson's maniacally voracious Tasmanian Devil. [202] Arguably the strangest voice assignment for which Blanc was ever tasked, "Taz" boasted a wildly garbled vocal pattern perfect for Blanc's "leather larynx," as McKimson once described it. [203]

The mid-fifties saw Blanc being partnered in some cartoons with the gifted actor Daws Butler, already well regarded for his unique character voices on Bob Clampett's cult TV puppet show *Time for Beany*. Blanc admitted to cartoon director-writer Mark Evanier that Butler was "the first voice-man he truly regarded as a competitor." [204]

An interesting insight into voice actor / director politics is found in a letter Chuck Jones wrote to his daughter in March 1955:

"I just returned from recording a new picture: *Barbary Coast Bunny*. I used a new actor, Daws Butler, in the role of the heavy. He's a very clever guy, hard-working, intelligent and refreshing. He's the one who worked with Stan Freberg on all those [Capitol comedy] records...

"I must say that I learned a great deal from him. He gave a splendid and new angle to this character, a sort of Marlon Brandoish mushy-mouthed delivery that seemed very funny to me... we rewrote the dialogue a little to fit [his Brando] conception and, as I say, it came off beautifully.

"Another thing I noticed is that Mel Blanc, who was there to record the rabbit, was well aware that he has some competition from Daws. He really worked today. I have never seen him evidence more interest in his work. I think I shall hire a sort of stand-by talent on recording days if this is what the goad of rivalry does for Mel. Like others, I suppose, he is likely to get a trifle smug occasionally." [205]

Daws Butler's own take on the difference in the two actors' styles was typically self-effacing: "When Chuck would have a character like a sympathetic father talking to a little boy [*Boyhood Daze*, 1957] - the type of thing that Mel couldn't do - he would always have me do them: sensitive, low key, naturalistic stuff. [Whereas] Friz used to like me, and McKimson [too], for broad things; they would call me over to the old studio on Sunset, and they would say, 'This is the [story board], and we've got this cat,' and I would come up with [a Frank Fontaine type of voice].

"They would have you read the line two or three ways. They'd say, 'Read it fast, read it slow.' Mel would read all his lines [separately] and they'd inter-cut them. They were directing you with what the character's attitude was, 'He's mad, he's this, he's that.' They would say, 'Do you do a Frank Fontaine type voice?; we think that voice would go with this character.' They were always going for impersonations. They've [already] got half the battle won [with a recognizable voice impression]." [206] Butler's Frank Fontaine voice was used for Sam the orange cat in cartoons like *Mouse and Garden* (1960) and in some of the period's weaker TV show parodies like *Stupor Duck* (1956), an ominous portent of lesser cartoons to come.

Around this same time, June Foray took over the Witch Hazel and Granny voices from Bea Benaderet who had committed herself full-time to on-camera television work: she played neighbor Blanche Morton weekly on the long-running *George Burns and Gracie Allen Show* and starred as Kate later in *Petticoat Junction*. Butler and Foray had both begun to earn their stripes as reliable voice actors by this time. Their character voices were highly prominent on Stan Freberg's 1953 Capitol record take-offs of *Dragnet*, and those comedy platters sold in the millions. They provided imitations of Art Carney and Audrey Meadows for a follow-up Freberg recording of "The Honey Earthers" which parodied the classic *Honeymooners* TV show. Soon after that they recorded McKimson's animated parodies *The Honey-Mousers* (1956) and *Cheese It, The Cat!* (1957). For those cartoons Butler also added his imitation of Jackie Gleason, which met with the TV comedian's hearty approval.

Still more voices began populating the Warner Bros. cartoons. Veteran radio actor Jack Edwards supplied some excellent and accurate Mexican dialect voices in *Speedy Gonzales* (1955). Other fifties talents included Dal McKennon, one of Walter Lantz's prominent voice actors, Lucille Bliss who had voiced television's first animated star "Crusader Rabbit," specialty child actor Dick Beals who played the Walter Mitty-ish schoolboy Ralph Phillips in *From A to Z-z-z-*

z-z (1954), and newscaster Norman Nesbitt whose solid, well-modulated commentary graced cartoons like *Goo Goo Goliath* (1954). Lloyd Perryman, a countrified musician-comic associated with the Sons of the Pioneers vocal ensemble, played the slow-drawling old dog in McKimson's *Weasel Stop* (1956). And Ed Prentiss, formerly radio's *Captain Midnight*, doubled as both narrator and show biz agent in *Nelly's Folly* (1961). Prentiss narrated some others, possibly on Blanc's recommendation as they were neighbors in Pacific Palisades.

But beyond these extra voice talents, the Warner Bros. star characters were now fully defined and Mel Blanc reigned supreme, often rising to inspired heights in cartoons featuring A-grade comic material tailor-made for his gifts. Notable ones included the western spoof *Drip-along Daffy* (1951), *Robin Hood Daffy* with its memorable "Yoicks, and away!!" (1958), *Birds Anonymous* and Sylvester's desperate "After all....I am a Pussy cat!!!" (1957) and the amusing fractured French and Gallic puns crafted by gag man Michael Maltese for the Pepe Le Pew films. According to Bob Clampett, it was Maltese who suggested that Blanc employ an exaggerated Charles Boyer voice for the amorous skunk's first appearance in the 1945 *Odor-Able Kitty*. [207]

The directors Jones, Freleng and McKimson were still at their peak in the early part of the fifties producing truly classic cartoons. Some of the lines Blanc delivered in those films became immortal on their own, quoted by a generation who grew up hearing them over and over on TV: "You're desthhhpicable," "Ah hates rabbits!!!," "Think, I say, think boy!!...I keep tossin' 'em and you keep side-steppin'!!," "Where's the ka-boom?" and "Hello, breakfathhhht!" being just a few among them.

As noted earlier, several of Blanc's famous character voices were pitch-changed mechanically. This was achieved via a variable speed oscillator when he was recording directly on film, and later electronically with audio tape which was introduced from 1947. Blanc's own vocal equipment, always a little naturally coarse, grew increasingly so with age, and speeding his voice was necessary, especially for the proliferation of small, cute characters in the fifties like Tweety, Sylvester Junior and Speedy Gonzales. Blanc and Stan Freberg were both sped-up for two sets of co-starring roles, the chronically OC-polite Goofy Gophers, and as the wiseacre mice duo of Hubie and Bert.

Of course the earliest star characters Porky Pig and Daffy Duck had been sped from the beginning, and Daffy was by this time basically a pitched-up Sylvester voice. But while the duck's and cat's actual voices may have been identical, their attitudes were totally different, and it was here that Blanc's awesome gift for character acting was truly apparent: both characters are eternal losers, but no one could ever mistake Daffy Duck for Sylvester.

Warner Bros. Cartoon Voices in the Sixties

The Warner Bros. cartoons of 1961-69 are now considered virtually negligible when compared with the sublime works of the preceding twenty years. Several factors contributed to the decline in quality, including spiralling labor costs and a shrinking world market for theatre shorts in the established age of television. But it was mainly due to the loss of several unique studio talents: writers Michael Maltese and Warren Foster defected to Hanna-Barbera, musical director Carl Stalling retired and actor Arthur Q. Bryan, the longtime voice of Elmer Fudd, died in November of 1959. These departures, and an overall sense that the theatrical short was now on life support, had the cartoon makers feeling like they had seen the best of it. From the late fifties onwards the directors - Jones, Freleng and McKimson - were making cartoons that seemed occasionally dull and repetitive. It was as if their greatest work was now behind them.

In 1960 David DePatie, head of Commercial and Industrial Films at Warner Bros., was asked by Jack Warner if he would also run the animation studio. DePatie agreed to take on the cartoon division. By this point the Warner cartoons were looking puny compared to the high quality shorts of ten years before. Times were changing in the amusement field, and sixties economics dictated that even theatrical animation adopt some of the cost-saving measures of TV cartoons. Everyone grudgingly accepted the reality: limited animation was the future and the glory days were over. But as the new decade began, no animation connoisseur could have predicted such ill-conceived abominations as the long series pairing Daffy with Speedy Gonzales, which lobotomized the duck's formerly complex character so dreadfully.

Voice-wise the sixties was still mostly Mel Blanc's turf, and for several years he remained on call to voice his well-established roster of Bugs, Daffy, Sam, Foghorn, Tweety, Sylvester, Speedy and Pepe Le Pew as well as material for the new *Bugs Bunny Show*. June Foray still scored an occasional role, although Julie Bennett was also doing some female parts. But poor Elmer Fudd was now being voiced by Hal Smith in a so-so sound-alike for truly lame cartoons like *What's My Lion?* (1961). Indeed, from around 1957 the studio had gradually come to resemble a shell of its old self. The Looney Warner Bros. magic was missing.

The top studio talents like Jones and Freleng were now devoting most of their time to television, with much new bridging material required for the ABC network's *Bugs Bunny Show*, material far superior to the concurrent theatrical cartoons.

Even Blanc sounded flat on occasion, a combination of lacklustre writing and the lingering results of a traumatic, near-fatal auto accident in January 1961 from which he eventually, and remarkably, recovered to full vocal strength. By 1962 his famously full-bodied yells could once again be heard in episodes of *The Flintstones*. Blanc's powerful vocal instrument was finally diminished by the aging process, starting from the mid-seventies.

It was in the 1961-62 theatrical season that Warner Bros. Cartoons finally commenced screen-crediting "additional voices," after thirty years of an industry policy that kept their names anonymous. Regrettably, the voice talents who worked alongside Blanc in this period - reliable old radio players like Herb Vigran and Tom Holland - were foisted with vastly inferior material. The mechanical early-sixties cartoons bearing the Warner logo basically resembled Hanna-Barbera's TV fare, although as animator Mark Kausler noted, H-B's cartoons of the period were often livelier.

Essentially the newest Looney Tunes completely lacked the one thing which made them so special in previous decades: the old Warner gag sensibility. The loss of Maltese, Foster and Ted Pierce was considerable. In 1960 Chuck Jones hired John Dunn, a gifted gag and storyboard artist with eight years of Disney experience working for Ward Kimball. He tried revitalizing the cartoons.

Dunn began with some bridges for the new *Bugs Bunny Show*, then wrote a theatrical cartoon for Freleng, *The Pied Piper of Guadalupe* (1961). He also wrote some Chuck Jones shorts that attempted something different, like the abstract experiment *Now Hear This* (1963). Another was *I Was a Teenage Thumb* (1963), strikingly designed in Ronald Searle style by Bob Givens. It featured seasoned radio artists like Julie Bennett and English actor Richard Peel as subtly written British characters. Dunn continued writing some of the better cartoons in the early sixties like *The Last Hungry Cat* (1961) and *Honey's Money* (1962), which at least capture some of the old Looney pace and attitude.

Other new writers were also on board. An occasional interesting one-shot like Chuck Jones's *Nelly's Folly*, a 1961 story by Dave Detiege, called for inventive voice-work. Jones always expressed "amazement at the strength" of diminutive session vocalist Gloria Wood's singing voice for Nelly. [208] The male giraffe was recorded by baritone John A. Ford, at one point the understudy to opera immortal Ezio Pinza.

But these were the exception: what challenge could such mind-numbing cartoons as *The Jet Cage* (1962) or *Nuts and Volts*

(1964) offer voice artists like Mel Blanc, apart from going through the motions? At least he was getting a pay-check and by then he was doing regular Hanna-Barbera TV cartoon gigs; his best work for that studio were his famous Barney Rubble and Mr. Spacely voices for *The Flintstones* and *The Jetsons*. They were roles that gave Blanc something well written and funny to interpret and bring to vocal life, as only he could.

In these final years, Blanc worked alongside some newer actors. Ralph James, later the voice of the intergalactic Orson on TV's *Mork and Mindy*, did a fine Walter Winchell in one of the period's livelier Bugs Bunny cartoons, *The Unmentionables* (1963). *Bartholomew Vs the Wheel* (1964) was unusual, a Thurber-influenced short narrated by thirteen-year old Canadian child actor Leslie Barringer, and visually resembling a lost Bobe Cannon UPA short from the fifties. June Foray was so busy in the mid-sixties that she was often unavailable. Granny was voiced by radio veteran Ge Ge Pearson and a Granny lookalike in *Corn on the Cop* (1965) was done by newer voice actress Joanie Gerber.

The times were certainly changing. Warner Bros. head office in New York met with DePatie in 1961 and gave him the news: an executive-mandated shutdown of the cartoon studio. Robert McKimson said the staff had been expecting this for years. Warner Bros. Cartoons closed shop in early 1963 following the completion of a few final shorts and the 1964 combination Don Knotts feature *The Incredible Mr. Limpet* (which cast Paul Frees as the voice of old Crusty the animated fish). The writing had been on the wall in any event: a year earlier, after being admonished for moonlighting on the UPA cartoon feature *Gay Purr'ee*, a film he had written, Chuck Jones departed to head up his own company.

Friz Freleng quickly entered into a new partnership with David H. DePatie. They had worked well together since the mid-fifties on commercials and they formed an independent company, DePatie-Freleng Enterprises. Soon enough, a great opportunity knocked. Freleng's crew created the striking and stylish cartoon titles for Blake Edwards's 1964 hit comedy feature *The Pink Panther*. That job proved so successful that producer Harold Mirisch offered DePatie-Freleng a theatrical series of short cartoons to star the sleekly inscrutable feline, for release through United Artists. As well, the outfit picked up work on commercials and more title sequences. Freleng was suddenly busier than he had been in ages.

Meanwhile the consistently high ratings for the successful *Bugs Bunny Show* reruns saw Jack L. Warner reconsider the fate of the animation studio. Hoping for some profits to flow from releasing brand new theatrical shorts, Warner initially commissioned a season of thirteen cartoons to be made by DePatie-Freleng. They would feature some of the old star characters. At the end of 1963, DFE was leasing Warner Cartoons' old Burbank studio for $500 a month.

After directing four new Warner cartoons and writing the story for *Corn on the Cop* (1965), Freleng became too busy with the Pink Panther series and other DFE commitments. He delegated the direction of the new Warner cartoons to veteran Bob McKimson. Freleng's involvement now required just the okaying of storyboards. By the mid-sixties the budgets were hopelessly tight, and consequently the animation suffered even more. To make things worse, the writing was consistently weak.

McKimson's limited resources produced cartoons that were often below mediocre. Lamentable entries like *Mucho Locos* (1966), *Well Worn Daffy* (1965) and *Swing Ding Amigo* (1966) are best avoided by discerning students of the Hollywood cartoon. Even Mel Blanc's delivery sounded bored at times. Mexican comedian Pedro Gonzales-Gonzales, discovered on Groucho Marx's TV quiz *You Bet Your Life*, managed to add some vocal spark to the ever-worsening cartoons starring a pitiful bastardisation of the once-great Daffy Duck.

To ease DePatie-Freleng's workload the final eleven Road Runner cartoons were farmed out to Format Films. These wretchedly vapid Rudy Larriva-directed versions of the once-great Chuck Jones series are truly sad to behold.

While DFE's crew of artists at least enjoyed steady employment in an eternally chancy industry, they were painfully aware that much of what they were making was drearily feeble. Someone should have pointed out to Mr. Warner that a Golden Age has only a finite lifespan. The downward artistic spiral continued unabated. DFE was now swamped with Pink Panther theatrical cartoons and commercial assignments. The last of its thirty seven Warner cartoon releases was *Daffy's Diner* (1967). By then DePatie-Freleng had relocated to the Union Bank building in Sherman Oaks.

It was then announced that Warner Bros. would officially re-open its own animation department under former public relations head Bill Hendricks, from 1966. While the studio was being re-organized, three interim 1967 Warner Cartoons (*Quacker Tracker, The Music Mice-Tro* and *The Spy Swatter*) were subcontracted to Herbert Klynn's studio Format, which had recently finished those awful Road Runner shorts for DFE.

When the re-opened Warner Cartoons commenced work on twenty three final theatricals, the budget was the lowest it had ever been. They were now interchangeable with the cheapest of TV cartoons because that was the intended medium for their future life in rerun heaven. Veteran director Alex Lovy handled the first sixteen cartoons, with the remainder made by Bob McKimson. New characters were introduced. The downright dreary Cool Cat series featured voice-work by the superb mimic and dialect expert Larry Storch. But an artist like Storch, known for decades as "the Rembrandt of Impressions," needed a much classier vehicle for his wide comic talents. Here he was reduced to voicing threadbare dialogue.

Cool Cat aside, the Hendricks era saw a slew of other characters vying for stardom, each relatively unsuccessful: Merlin the Magic Mouse was just Daws Butler, and later Larry Storch, doing a W. C. Fields. *Bunny and Claude* (1968) proved a limp nod to Warner's

1967 gangster megahit *Bonnie and Clyde*, with Blanc voicing Claude and Pat Woodell (aka Bobbie Jo in the first two seasons of *Petticoat Junction*) cast as Bunny. A unique "Special" cartoon, *Norman Normal* (1968), was produced as part of folk group Peter, Paul & Mary's deal with Warner Bros. Records, and was narrated by Paul (Noel P. Stookey) himself.

As for Mel Blanc, by now regarded as the Godfather of animation actors, his Warner Bros. theatrical days came to an ignominious end with blah 1968 cartoons like *Chimp & Zee* and *See Ya Later Gladiator*. His late sixties vocal range was mainly heard on various commercials like the "Frito Bandito" spots and in second-rate TV cartoons for Hanna-Barbera such as *Peter Potamus* and *Secret Squirrel*. Television did not prove the equal of even the dying theatricals as had been predicted, and it wasn't long before many TV cartoons began to resemble a formulaic sausage machine, as they took a twenty-year nose-dive into the unwatchable. Television animation wouldn't enjoy a new lease of creativity until the cable boom of the eighties.

In early 1969 the Warner Bros. studio closed for the last time when the Kinney Corporation took over and looked to cut costs. Fortuitously, DePatie-Freleng's studio afforded several more years employment for many of the old guard Warner layout and animation crew. These pioneers, some of whom went back to the era of silent film, were able to enjoy another decade working at the job they loved. The many new theatrical cartoons that emerged from DePatie-Freleng's long-running United Artists deal were frankly superior to the final Warner Bros. entries, and some of these shorts still play well today. *

* Sidebar: Voice actors in DePatie-Freleng cartoons

The cartoons produced by DFE and released between 1965 and 1976, are just beyond this book's Golden Age parameter, but it would be discourteous of me not to include a mention of them here, considering they were the very last American theatrical cartoon shorts. The often classy films were made by a team of creative veterans from the classic era. Chief among them were Friz Freleng, Hawley Pratt and Gerry Chiniquy and the incredibly prolific story-sketch man John W. Dunn. As well, the cartoons were made by legendary animation and layout names like Norm McCabe, Art Davis, Sid Marcus, Manny Gould, and Don Williams, whose roots went back to the earliest Warner and Screen Gems cartoons.

The Pink Panther series commenced in the 1964-65 theatrical season. They were virtually all pantomime shorts, although in two early entries Freleng experimented with a talking Panther. The then hot young impressionist Rich Little gave him a Rex Harrison type voice in *Sink Pink* (a one liner, with Paul Frees voicing the villains). *Pink Ice* featured Little as all the voices, including a Hitchcock impression for the bad guy. United Artists quickly ordered the return of the mute Panther. Once the Panther was off and running it was the turn of The Inspector. He was modelled as a squat version of the movie Clouseau character, and got his own off-shoot series of thirty four shorts in 1966. He was voiced by television comedy actor Pat Harrington, Jr. who also played loyal Sergeant Deux-Deux. His flustered superior, The Commissioner, was spoken firstly by Larry Storch and then, for a longer time, Paul Frees. Harrington's subtle underplaying contrasted well with the broader cartoony bombast of Frees. Other actors used in the Panther and Inspector shorts included familiar voices from UPA and Hanna-Barbera, including Marvin Miller, Lenny Weinrib, Don Messick, Hal Smith, Joan Gerber, Diana Maddox, Helen Gerald and June Foray.

After three years, some new characters appeared in the DFE stable at United Artists' request. Six theatrical series, each containing seventeen cartoons, emerged between 1965-75. These new creations, even allowing for individual shorts that were weak or repetitive, seemed fresh and amusing when compared with the anaemic late Warner Bros. cartoons of the period. If the animation got more limited as time went by, the design work on each short was often striking and the musical cues were classy.

The first new series was Roland and Rattfink which ran from 1968-71. It featured the voice artistry of Lennie Weinrib in the dual roles of a flower age pacifist constantly at odds with an out and out dastardly villain. For Roland and Rattfink Weinrib adopted an amusingly hammy delivery in the style of late 1800s moustache-twirling melodrama. Weinrib, whose creative talents extended to writing, was fast becoming one of the top multi-voice talents of the late sixties-early seventies. A favorite of producers Sid & Marty Krofft, he was the voice of *H. R. Pufnstuf* and worked on TV cartoons for Hanna-Barbera and Filmation. For Fred Wolf he did some outstanding characters in the Harry Nilsson feature *The Point* (1971). June Foray, Athena Lorde and Pete Halton voiced one cartoon each; for one short, *The Deadwood Thunderball* (1970), Weinrib was unavailable, so the leads were shared by mimics Dave Barry and John Byner.

Following this series was arguably the best loved DFE property from that period, The Ant and the Aardvark. These cartoons featured terrific voice work by the always funny impressionist-comedian John Byner. Byner was at the time a highly regarded television talk-variety guest, whose laid back and quirky style incorporated odd observations and a long list of uncanny impressions encompassing singers, actors and TV names like Ed Sullivan. By injecting the personalities of two contemporary comedy-variety stars into the leads (Dean Martin as a small red Ant vs. Jackie Mason as a large blue Aardvark), every utterance they spouted was laughable even when the dialogue wasn't. Radio old-timers Marvin Miller and Athena Lorde did an episode each, but this was definitively Byner's show.

The Tijuana Toads ran from 1969-72. Freleng cast the voices almost as soon as the contract was inked. He remembered the actors he hired fifteen years earlier to voice the loco stars of *Two Crows from Tacos*, released in 1956. They were radio veterans Don Diamond and Tom Holland. In the years since that cartoon Freleng used Holland as Speedy Gonzales's memorable sidekick Slowpoke Rodriguez, "the slowest mouse in all Mexico." Diamond was well regarded for his comic TV roles: on Disney's hit *Zorro* series he played Corporal Reyes, while his "Crazy Cat" character appeared in some fifty episodes of the frontier sitcom *F Troop*. For these cartoons, Diamond was El Toro and Holland did the voice of Pancho. A supporting character was Crazylegs Crane voiced by busy character actor, Larry D. Mann (the goofball bird popped up as support in three different DFE series before inheriting his own set of sixteen TV cartoons). Athena Lorde and Julie Bennett contributed occasional female voices.

The next series showcased a speedy serpent known as The Blue Racer, another successful DFE property. The Racer appeared in one Tijuana Toads entry, *A Snake in Gracias*, and was well received. His own series ran from 1972-74, and Larry D. Mann voiced the starring part, supported by Tom Holland as "Japanese Beetle." Mann was a Canadian actor, an ex-DJ from Toronto who like many radio talents of that time possessed a flexible range of good character voices. He was heard in TV cartoons and commercials for a raft of other production companies (Rankin-Bass, Hanna-Barbera, Ruby-Spears and Filmation). Occasional extra roles were voiced by Joan Gerber, Bob Holt, Athena Lorde, Paul Winchell and the Japanese actor known simply as Mako.

Hoot Kloot was the next DFE character in a modern-day Western parody series based around a small but loudmouthed lawman. He was voiced by Bob Holt. Holt, like Larry D. Mann, was another busy character actor who fell into voice-work early in his career and happily remained there. When he was cast as Kloot, Holt was well on the way to becoming a top seventies voice artist for both cartoons and a ton of animated commercials. Even the great Paul Frees was well aware that Holt was a new voice on the block to reckon with. Holt worked for Hanna-Barbera, Ralph Bakshi, Disney and others. He not only voiced the title role of Kloot, the squat and stocky Sheriff, but also his "hobblin' horse" Fester who talked like Walter Brennan. Sadly Holt died suddenly in 1985, aged just fifty six. Larry D. Mann spoke for the zany Crazywolf, a hillbilly canine semi-regular, and there were one-time appearances by TV cartoon voices Hazel Shermet, Joan Gerber and Allan Melvin.

The Dogfather was the final DePatie-Freleng theatrical series, cashing in on the huge popularity of the two hit gangster movies based on Mario Puzo's book *The Godfather*. Regular DFE voice Bob Holt gave the Dogfather the requisite Brando-esque whine, with Daws Butler voicing his off-sider Louie, the runt of the Dogfather's litter. In 1974 Butler, just starting the recording sessions for this series, said, "Louie is the loyal little henchman type, so I immediately thought of Edward G. Robinson's sidekick in *Little Caesar*, a small guy who was always buttering up the boss. That was an actor named George E. Stone, so I went for his toadying attitude." [209] Occasional support voices were Frank Welker, Larry Mann, Hazel Shermet and Joanie Gerber.

For full coverage of the DFE cartoon saga you can't do without Jerry Beck's fine book *Pink Panther: The Ultimate Guide to the Coolest Cat in Town* with its comprehensive DFE filmography, while Mark Arnold's historical work, *Think Pink! The DePatie-Freleng Story* gathers many interviews into one thick tome.

***

So winds down the Golden Age saga of Warner Bros. and its distinguished cartoon voice legacy. In the context of voice artistry it remains, indubitably, "the Mel Blanc story." With hindsight, it was not so much Blanc's vocal versatility: as great as that was, certain actors like Paul Frees had a longer "list" of distinct imitations and voices. Rather it was Blanc's splendid gift for crazily energized comic interpretation and endlessly funny characters that put him at the very top of the cartoon tree. His talent meshed perfectly with creatively gifted directors and story men who knew the precise comic inflections they wanted, and were able to supply Blanc with top-notch comic dialogue.

As Michael Barrier observed, "No other actor had [Blanc's] good fortune to speak for so many continuing characters in theatrical cartoons." [210] Extract Mel Blanc, and one wondered about the void, indeed a void still struggling to be fully filled, following his passing in 1989. At first it was assumed his son Noel would simply take over his starring roles. But although he recorded a few episodes of *Tiny Toons* in 1989, Noel openly admitted he wasn't the singularly gifted talent his Dad had been, telling one interviewer, "I never really wanted to do voices."

One of the finest Mel Blanc soundalikes is Jeff Bergman, first heard on TV's *Tiny Toons Adventures* and the 1991 revival short *Box Office Bunny* directed by Darrell Van Citters. In that cartoon his matching of Bugs, Daffy Duck and Elmer Fudd was astonishingly good. Jeff is a diligent and meticulous student of voices and a nonpareil impressionist. He enjoyed a brief flurry of recognition in the early nineties in two enjoyable Greg Ford-produced shorts *(Blooper) Bunny* and *Invasion of the Bunny Snatchers*. After those cartoons he became one of several vying for the Looney Tunes roles, as Warner Bros. began rotating actors, perhaps leery of having just one person as the new "voice of 'em all." After Bergman settled in Los Angeles in 2008 many of the voices at which he excelled slowly reverted to him.

Two more Mel Blanc replacements are, sadly, deceased: the late Greg Burson and Joe Alaskey, both accomplished "voice-matchers," were on call from 1990 for a range of characters. Burson, also the replacement for Jim Backus's Magoo voice, was heard in the mid-nineties revival short *Carrotblanca* as a good Bugs. In this show he worked alongside Alaskey who was both Daffy and Sylvester. Alaskey, a stage trained actor and standup impressionist from Boston, was also the hapless pussycat in the TV series *The Tweety and Sylvester Mysteries*. One of his more notable credits were the lead voices of Bugs, Daffy and Sylvester for the 2003 feature *Looney Tunes: Back in Action*.

The new millennium shorts, although made by talented people with vast respect for the classic heritage, had a decidedly mixed reception. The hardcore fans felt there was something just a tad off about each modern-day Looney Tunes revival. It might have been the story material, or perhaps gag timing choices by individual directors, but Warner animation buffs sensed something was intangibly askew with their beloved characters. It was often put down to the old saying, "You can't go home again."

For a comprehensive look at how the classic Warner Bros. cartoon stars have been handled in the modern age, including analyses of blockbusters like *Space Jam* and *Back in Action*, Jamie Weinman's book *Anvils, Mallets & Dynamite (The Unauthorized Biography of Looney Tunes)*, published in 2021, is well recommended.

As this book reaches completion in early 2022 there are encouraging signs from a new generation at Warner Bros. Animation. They appear up to the challenge of making cartoons which capture the sound and feel of vintage Looney Tunes, with authentic winks to Clampett, Avery, Freleng and Jones. Some productions from 2019 seemed to get the beats and the "energy" right. Only time will tell. But with expert voices and lifelong Looney Tunes students like Bergman, Billy West, Bob Bergen, Eric Bauza and others at the helm, it is looking - and certainly sounding - highly promising. Hopefully "Th-th-th-th-that's NOT all folks!!"

The Classic WB Canon today

As for the actual Golden Age Warner Bros. cartoons, they were once in regular cable rotation on Cartoon Network (they disappeared from free-to-air TV in 2000 after a marathon forty five year run). Various VHS collections appeared early in the life of that format, while lavish laserdisc sets lasted only a short while. Happily, the release of the cartoons on DVD began in late 2003 with the lovingly curated Looney Tunes *Golden Collection* series. The six volumes featured eye-popping restorations from original negatives, gloriously uncut and uncensored. The classic films hadn't looked this good in sixty years. Technology kept improving, and even sharper-looking copies appeared on Blu-ray collections. Finally in 2020 fans could enjoy HD restorations of many long-unseen Looney Tunes & Merrie Melodies, screening on MeTV, ensuring that the Looney canon finally looked and sounded as nature intended, for future generations to enjoy over and again.

Chapter 2

MGM Cartoon Voices, 1934-58

Virtually no information exists on the voices - minimal as they are - for Ub Iwerks's Flip the Frog cartoons, financed by Pat Powers and released by MGM from 1930-1933. The earliest Flip entries use staff voices, some of whom sound distinctly amateurish. Child movie star Jane Withers briefly played the title role of Willie Whopper, Iwerks's second series, but that character seemed to stump the creators who kept changing Willie's appearance, while his voice went from older boy to a poor adult reading. Young Ms Withers also plays the cute little bear in Jack Frost (1934), which highlights a hot Cab Calloway-type jazz number by popular Coast vocal group The Jones Boys. By the time of Willie Whopper, vocal quartets like The Uptowners and various session soloists were providing most of the professional voices.

The Willie Whopper series was released by Metro through the end of the 1933-34 season. Iwerks's next project, the Comicolor cartoons, was distributed independently via entrepreneur Pat Powers's Celebrity Productions. They featured some excellent musical scores by Art Turkisher and future Warner Bros. cartoon composer Carl Stalling. Stalling himself provided voices for some of the Comicolor shorts (he recalled an Amos & Andy take-off). These cartoons feature vocal groups and actors familiar from early Disney shorts, notably Billy Bletcher who plays the nasty Pincushion Man in Balloon Land (1935), and Purves Pullen, who plays lead in Simple Simon, while animator Norm Blackburn essayed the title role in The Little Red Hen (1934). Basso profundo Delos Jewkes is

heard as the king in The Queen of Hearts (1934), while pro-
lific tenor Bob Priester is in several entries, including the title
role of Humpty Dumpty (1935). Another smooth bass singer
heard often is Homer Hall, in cartoons like Sinbad the Sailor
(1935) and the 1936 Ali Baba ("Open Sesame"). The familiar
girl trio The Three Rhythmettes sing for Puss in Boots (1934),
while child actor Tommy Bupp was heard with other junior
performers in the final entry Happy Days (1936). Staff voices
were still being heard as late as another 1936 Comicolor, Dick
Whittington's Cat.

1934-38: The "Happy Harmonies"

In early 1934, almost one year after their break with Leon Schlesinger, Hugh Harman and Rudolf Ising were working, unpaid, on pre-production of a featurette-length cartoon of *The Nutcracker*. But by mid-February that project was abandoned when they firmed a deal for a new color theatrical series. Named Happy Harmonies from the second cartoon onwards, the series was released by Hollywood's most prestigious studio Metro-Goldwyn-Mayer. Harman and Ising would now enjoy higher budgets, if not quite as generous as Disney's, and many of their crew from the Schlesinger period made the move to Harman-Ising's new setup. Their earliest cartoons often looked like the old Warner releases although the soundtracks became more intricate.

The composer for the MGM cartoons was radio conductor Scott Bradley (1891-1977), who had notched up several years of experience as both a pianist for Disney shorts and an arranger for several Ub Iwerks cartoons. Bradley met Harman and Ising in late 1933 and agreed to write the music for a special animated sequence, "The Walrus and the Carpenter," for part of that year's Paramount all-star feature *Alice in Wonderland*. Harman-Ising made this sequence soon after their split with Schlesinger.

Bradley replaced Harman-Ising's original musical director Frank Marsales. After providing the scores for the subcontracted Cubby Bear cartoons, Marsales left animated cartoons in 1934 for the burgeoning radio industry with his own air-check recording business. He would later return to films, scoring Lantz cartoons at Universal in the late thirties. Another standby from the Schlesinger era was sound editor Fred MacAlpin who remained with Harman-Ising, becoming an important contributor to their Metro soundtracks.

At first, Harman and Ising engaged the same voice talent from their Warner-released Merrie Melodies and Looney Tunes, including the male quartet The King's Men in *The Calico Dragon* (1935), and local Los Angeles radio star Johnny Murray who plays radio announcer "Graham Cracker" in *The Old Plantation* (1935). During the first year, the cartoons resembled little more than color versions of the earlier Merrie Melodies: *Toyland Broadcast* (1934), which featured Murray as the falsetto-voiced MC, could easily have passed for a 1933 Warner Bros. entry. After completing three cartoons, Harman-Ising moved from their Hollywood Boulevard setup to new premises on N. Seward Street near Highland Avenue.

Always seeking improvements in the films, the restless Hugh Harman soon began overspending on their already generous budgets by headhunting established talent from the art world, like designers Maurice "Jake" Day and Corliss McGee, and the cartoons quickly made a leap in visual quality and animation techniques. Certainly, the draftsmanship improved dramatically just as 3-strip Technicolor became available in late 1935; Disney, ever ahead of the pack, held a two-year monopoly on the full spectrum color process from 1933-35. More than any other series, the Happy Harmonies would come to resemble Disney's Silly Symphonies, if not as satisfying story wise, at least visually.

When he broke with Schlesinger a year before, Harman retained the rights to the Bosko character he created. Bosko began appearing in the early MGM cartoons. He was voiced by a different actor in each film. At first his speaking was done by a child for *Bosko's Parlor Pranks* (1934) which used recycled animation from the Warner shorts (Rudy Ising spoke a couple of Bosko's gag lines in Jimmy Durante-esque tones). For his next appearance Bosko had both of his old Warner Bros. voices, Max Maxwell speaking and Johnny Murray singing, for *Hey-Hey Fever* (1935). Murray post-recorded the songs after the animation was completed.

From 1935 design artist Mel Schwartzman (later known as Mel Shaw) transformed Bosko into a realistic, sweet little boy. His voice was provided by a couple of Black performers, one being, in Harman's words, "a real cute little kid, about six years old at the time. I can't remember his name." [1] This was almost certainly one of the child actors seen in thirties feature pictures like *The Green Pastures*, possibly Donald Brown or Philip Hurlic. Another Bosko voice actor had a light teenage sound heard in *Bosko's Easter Eggs* (1937) and *Circus Daze* (1937). It was likely Eugene Jackson, but no information survives from this period in MGM music files. Still another child was, according to Harman, filmed as a reference model for the realistic Bosko's dance steps, seen for example in *Little Ol' Bosko and the Pirates* (1937). This child was possibly a dancer named Cullen Morris.

African American talents were the beneficiaries of a goodly chunk of work in the Harmonies. An excellent child performer voiced Bosko's young girlfriend, and her squeals of fear and delighted laughs were the result of diligent coaching by Hugh Harman. At least two actresses played Bosko's mother prior to the arrival of Lillian Randolph. I would dearly love to identify all these fine players but, alas, recording logs from the thirties have vanished.

The Happy Harmonies, like Disney's contemporaneous Silly Symphonies, often called on specialty bird and animal "barnyard mimics" like Dorothy Lloyd and Marion Darlington. Whistler Purves Pullen, who worked for all the major cartoon companies, did the title role trilling for *The Chinese Nightingale* (1935). In the forties Pullen became famous as a member of Spike Jones's novelty troupe using the stage name "Dr. Horatio Q. Birdbath." As well, Fred MacAlpin populated the cartoons with a raft of original sound effects, including a chromatic xylophone, and the pit-drum collection of a retired studio percussionist, containing a wide, cartoon-like assortment of slide whistles, Jews-harps and sirens. [2]

As was the norm in thirties cartoons, which continued to exploit music as their strong suit, virtually every Harman-Ising film featured vocal groups. The Rhythmettes trio, heard everywhere in West Coast animation from Walt Disney to Walter Lantz, provided their customary attractive close harmony in the 1935 cartoons *Honeyland* and *The Chinese Nightingale*. Later in the decade, when Harman and Ising were contract employees at MGM's new animation studio, the Rhythmettes sang in Ising's cartoons *The Little Goldfish* (1939) and *The Milky Way* (1940).

A second girl's trio, The Three Harmonettes, was virtually exclusive to the MGM cartoons; one of its members was married to an editor who worked with the sound department. [3] They provided a slightly more "little girl" sound in several Harman-Ising films, including the first release, *The Discontented Canary* (1934). They were also the three "see, hear & speak no evil" simians in Harman's *The Good Little Monkeys* (1935) and the trio of baby feeding flasks in his visually sumptuous cartoon *Bottles* (1936), both of which featured music and lyrics supplied by the young William Hanna. [4]

Perhaps the most interesting vocal groups were those featured in Harman's unique "jazz frog" cartoon musicals. Harman had been most impressed by RKO's 1935 musical feature *Hooray for Love* which showcased famous entertainers like Fats Waller and the great dancer Bill "Bojangles" Robinson. Harman and Jack Caldwell wrote the story for what was the template of the series, *The Old Mill Pond*. As Ising explained, "[Jack] 'Moe' Caldwell had as much to do with [those cartoons] as anyone. Caldwell was a tap dancer. He was originally hired to show the animators how to have Bosko tap-dance [during the Schlesinger era, as noted in Chapter One]. 'Moe' did the poses for [the jazz Frog cartoons], then Hugh became imbued with the idea; we also got a good bunch of [Black] imitators who could do [Louis] Armstrong and the others to perfection." [5]

The Four Blackbirds, The Jones Boys, The Basin Street Rhythm Boys and other African American close-harmony groups provided these impressionistic films with catchy vocals, while the amusing impersonations of Satchmo and Fats Waller were by mimic Harland Evans.

Among the striking shorts are *The Old Mill Pond* (1936) and *Swing Wedding* (1937), which boast funny and well-animated take-offs of jazz legends like Cab Calloway, Waller and "Bojangles" Robinson. Typical of the arbitrary and fragmented method of cartoon voice recording, white animator Norm Blackburn provided the imitation of Black comedian Stepin Fetchit for *The Old Mill Pond*. [6]

Hugh Harman recalled that most of the special lyrics for these cartoons were written by Moe Caldwell and young Bill Hanna, while Caldwell collaborated with Scott Bradley and the Black musicians on the intricate scores. Leroy Hurte's Blackbirds had first sung in Ising's *Toyland Broadcast* (1934), providing a hot rendition of "Jungle Fever" a 'la The Mills Brothers; the number had been sung by the genuine Mills quartet in that year's MGM feature *Operator 13*.

Musically the Happy Harmonies benefited mightily from the lively scores composed by Scott Bradley; they were as distinctive a feature of the MGM cartoons as Carl Stalling's music was at Warner Bros. Discussing his signature sound, Bradley opined, "I conducted the orchestra myself. I read about Stalling, that he used the big Warner orchestra, but [animated cartoons] didn't need it. I used twenty pieces - that's all I needed. You don't need a symphony orchestra for cartoons." [7]

Not surprisingly, Rudolf Ising continued to provide a few voices himself, including the villainous spider in *Honeyland*. The tradition of in-house voices lingered. Sound cutter Fred MacAlpin recalled,

"I had terrible laryngitis one day, and they were looking for some-one to recite the first few verses of 'The Shooting of Dan McGrew' [in *Barnyard Babies* (1935)]. Rudy heard my [croaky] voice and he said, 'That's what we want. Can we go over there today and get it?' And that's what we did." [8] That voice was for a little pony dressed in a cowboy outfit. MacAlpin, Harman and Ising continued to provide miscellaneous vocal bits and effects.

Distinctive freelance voice pros in the early years included the reliable Billy Bletcher in *Hey-Hey Fever* (1935) and Charlie Lung, radio's "Man of One Hundred Voices," who did the Oriental dialects in *The Chinese Nightingale* (1935). Lung was accomplished at a wide range of foreign accents and character voices. Although he seemed a natural for vintage cartoons he appeared in just a handful over the years.

L.A. Times entertainment columnist Philip Scheuer wrote a lengthy article about film voice dubbing in April 1935. In mention-ing the MGM cartoons, he wrote, "Harman-Ising ('Happy Har-monies') draws 75 per cent of their [voice] people from radio, the balance from stage and film. Ian Wolfe, an actor in '*David Copper-field*'; Johnny Murray, KFWB m. c.; the Four Blackbirds (KFI radio); the Californians and the Rhythmettes (said to have been the origi-nal 'Three Little Pigs') are a few of them. A reel will [require] only about thirty minutes' work for a capable artist, Harman-Ising state, with salary ranging from $10 to $50." [9]

Baby-voiced Berniece Hansell, ubiquitous in Hollywood car-toons from 1934, was heard as the title character in Ising's hand-some Little Cheeser cartoons. Ising said, "Bernice Hansen [sic] was, I would say, between twenty five and thirty years old, but when she was a child, she had had a throat injury, and her throat never devel-oped, and she actually talked like a little six-year-old kid. She was the Cheeser voice and any squeaky little voice you'd want. I had a lisp on Cheeser, and I used to write the [dialogue] lisped, and she one time told me, 'You don't have to do that, just tell me where you want him to lisp, and I'll lisp it for you.'" [10] A second "tiny" voice, heard often with Hansell, remains unidentified. Ising could not recall her name, but when discussing voices he referred to "the girls." [11]

"Berniece couldn't sing," added Ising. "For [*When the Cat's Away* (1935)] she was supposed to sing words we'd written to the tune of 'Little Brown Jug,' and Scott had written the music too high, and her voice broke completely. He was going to rewrite it, and I said, 'No, that's good just as it is.' It really got a terrific [audience reaction] in the theatres, because you knew that little mouse was really stretching." [12]

The visually stunning *Bottles* (1936) also contains a performance by Berneice Hansell voicing, naturally, a baby's bottle. This cartoon was inspired by the radio horror program *The Witch's Tale*, and they used Martha Wentworth, often billed as radio's "woman of a thousand voices" as the witch. [13] She hosted the actual radio show as Old Nancy, a shrill, cackling crone who related the eerie stories. Ms Wentworth performed in various Happy Harmonies, including *Barnyard Babies* (1935) and *The Old House* (1936) and continued in various MGM cartoons into the forties.

Bottles also showcases some of the busy but anonymous professional singers who populated the choruses of countless thirties Hollywood cartoons and live action shorts. These include baritone Allan Watson singing as the Scots jug, and two striking basso voices: Delos Jewkes as the hot water bottle who drones "Rocked in the Cradle of the Deep," and Dudley Kuzelle of the excellent Guardsmen quartet who sonorously warbles "When Yuba Plays the Rumba on the Tuba."

Delos Jewkes also sings bass for the nasty winter wind in *To Spring* (1936), with radio actor J. Donald Wilson doing the voice of the industrious elf boss ("Time for spring I say!"). That cartoon boasts eye-popping color styling by water-colorist Lee Blair, who assisted the new co-directing team of young William Hanna and Paul Fennell, under Harman's supervision.

But all this color and movement was for naught. Increasingly, the sinfully lush Technicolor shorts like *To Spring* had become the Harman-Ising norm, and the Happy Harmonies routinely went over budget; indeed, the contrary Harman saw to that. It was no surprise when MGM decided to terminate its agreement with Harman-Ising in mid-1937. In any event, Metro, who had always wanted the independent Harman-Ising team as contract employees, was planning to open its own animation studio. The new cartoon shop would be headed by MGM shorts department sales-executive Fred Quimby (1886-1965) who had earned an excellent corporate reputation, even if his knowledge of the creative aspects of animation remained ever minimal.

When sound man Fred MacAlpin moved to MGM's new studio, he left Harman and Ising his sound effects library, along with some bruised feelings ("Hugh didn't speak to me again"). [14] Bill Hanna, Max Maxwell and top ranked character animator Robert Allen also defected, while Quimby asked Disney's story chief Ted Sears, who was due to visit New York, to help poach some top East Coast artists. Maxwell meanwhile phoned Sears's animator pal Jack Zander in New York. Zander recalled, "Max was sort of in charge of production for the new group at MGM. He asked if I would like to come back and bring some talent with me and I agreed."[15] Zander recruited several top artists from the Terrytoons studio, including outstanding character layout men Dan Gordon and Joe Barbera.

The main item on MGM's new cartoon agenda was for a leading character with which to compete with Disney and other animation houses. Bosko was quietly retired in 1937, and MGM still had virtually no animated "stars." Even Ising's winsome leading mouse Little Cheeser lasted for just three cartoons.

It was no surprise when Harman-Ising were let go. Harman, by temperament, was not predisposed to working on an equivalent to Donald Duck or Porky Pig simply to appease Quimby and the Metro board. Besides which he was chafing at the cartoon gag conventions then in place, and keenly desired to make a more "serious" use of animation's potential. He even expressed an artistic ambition to do for animation what Orson Welles was then doing in live theatre.

The upshot was that Harman and Ising, gone from Metro, suddenly needed work. For the next several months, they took on a subcontract job, making the Disney Silly Symphony *Merbabies* (1938). It was directed by Ising in exchange for the loan of their ink and paint staff to Disney who was falling behind schedule on his mammoth feature project *Snow White and the Seven Dwarfs*. Soon enough, however, Hugh Harman and Rudolf Ising would return to the new MGM cartoon studio as will be seen in Part Two.

Frustratingly, there are still various unidentified voice artists in the Happy Harmonies cartoons, including several elusive child actors, particularly those heard in the later Bosko shorts. It is fervently hoped that at least some names will become known to the author for a future edition of this book.

Part Two: Voices in MGM Cartoons, 1938-57

In 1937, MGM commenced construction of its own cartoon department on Culver City's Lot Two. The two-storey studio, designed under Fred MacAlpin's technical direction, boasted state-of-the-art animation equipment custom ordered by "Max" Maxwell and was ready by August. Thanks to an ill-conceived front-office decision, the facility's first series would be an adaptation of the Germanic characters from Rudolf Dirks's comic strip for United Feature Syndicate-Joseph Pulitzer, "The Captain and the Kids." These unprepossessing Teutonic caricatures proved a poorly advised move just as war clouds were gathering in Europe.

MGM, of course, was regarded as the most lavish studio in Hollywood. As MacAlpin noted, "The set-up was much better, technically, and being a part of MGM made a big difference. We could hire talent and pay them better. We had a raft of people coming in whenever we wanted a voice, and we went through dozens and dozens of them. We [hired] Billy Bletcher, and Mel Blanc, and Sara Berner, and Martha Wentworth, and Lillian Randolph." [16]

Indeed, several familiar Hollywood cartoon voice actors began appearing in this era. Mel Blanc's first cartoon for MGM was the Captain and the Kids entry *A Day at the Beach* (1938), directed by Friz Freleng, who had been poached from Schlesinger's by Quimby during the nationwide talent raid for MGM's new animation setup. "Quimby made a bunch of promises to me, none of which he stuck to," groused Freleng, still bitter about his time at MGM forty years later. [17]

Blanc voiced several more Metro cartoons, including the gobbling title lead in *Tom Turkey and His Harmonica Humdingers* (1940), which featured the famous Harmonica Rascals on the track. Blanc also played the boorish con-artist in *The Little Mole* (1941) before his exclusive Schlesinger-Warner contract took effect in the spring of 1941. His most famous MGM cartoon role was his uncharacteristically subdued performance as grandfather squirrel in Harman's effective but rather sombre *Peace on Earth*, released in 1939.

In contrast, Blanc's wildest performance at Metro was for the western parody *The Lonesome Stranger* (1940), Harman's deliberate attempt at the Schlesinger style. Sadly that style, zany and satirical by 1940, was one for which Harman was temperamentally ill-equipped, and the cartoon never captures the zip and pace of the Warner parodies. In trying too hard the cartoon feels like a lesson in overkill. Even voice-wise, Blanc was directed to overplay already over the top characters, with his haplessly nerdish title character doing battle with by far his loudest and most endlessly chortling villain ever!

MacAlpin recalled urging Fred Quimby to put Blanc under contract. "I said, 'He has such a variety, none of the rest of them has this.'[Quimby] said, 'You've got Billy Bletcher.' I said, 'Billy Bletcher can only talk the way Billy Bletcher talks, but Mel has a lot of different ones.' Well, a month or two later [Blanc] was under an exclusive contract to Schlesinger." [18]

Meanwhile, Bletcher and Martha Wentworth made a fine "Dutch dialect" team in the sepia-toned "Captain and the Kids" films, as Der Captain and his harried hausfrau. One trade item revealed, "The studio had considerable trouble finding the proper voices for these characters, but finally selected Shirley Reed and Jeannie Dunne to impersonate Hans and Fritz. The head men decided that eventually [small] boys would turn into baritones [but] Misses Reed and Dunne won't..." [19] An *Associated Press* item noted that Billy Bletcher was put to a contract to speak for the Captain "and he cannot use that voice for any other purpose. But he is still free to use the other 999 voices in his repertoire. He calls it the ideal contract." [20]

In these cartoons, directed by Bill Hanna and Robert Allen, Blanc played Pirate John Silver in all but *The Captain's Christmas* (1938), a charming color episode directed by Friz Freleng. This cartoon featured Billy Bletcher at his Bow Bells Cockney best as Pirate John, and musician Bert Lewis hired Charles Bennett's Comedy Quartet as the back-up crew of singing pirates who warble "'Ang Up the 'Olly in the Window."

Pinto Colvig, famous as Disney's Goofy voice, also enjoyed a brief tour of duty at MGM's new plant, as both story man and voice talent, and can be heard in a couple of the 1938 Captain and the Kids entries like *The Pygmy Hunt*, before his 1939 departure for the new Max Fleischer studio in Miami. The memorable opening music for this series was composed by Lewis, a Disney veteran, who provided a catchy German "oom-pah band" title theme.

The Captain and the Kids films occasionally boasted humorous gags, like the funny comic action drawings of a clumsy horse in *Mama's New Hat* (1939). But the series proved less than successful with both audiences and exhibitors. To be fair the cartoons boasted some fine animation sequences that remain memorable. Walter

Lantz's ex-partner Bill Nolan animated a monster rooster fighting the Captain in *Poultry Pirates* (1938). The series seemed to be hitting its stride just as it was cancelled. Animator Mark Kausler noted two striking moments: a hilarious rooster battle animated by Emery Hawkins in *Honduras Hurricane* (1938) and Hawkins's and Irv Spence's fine seagull cycle and seal chase around the decks in *Seal Skinners* (1939). But some of the MGM cartoon staff frankly hated the series from its inception. Maxwell noted, "MGM made a big mistake in trying to start a cartoon series in black and white, in the first place." [21]

The series' resounding failure was one of several hiccups in the first year of operations. "There was this worry all the time," [22] recalled Maxwell. That "worry" resulted in two brief, unhappy production stints under famed newspaper cartoonists Harry Hershfield and Milt Gross, neither of whom had much familiarity with the modern animation process: although Gross had worked on many silent cartoons for Goldwyn-Bray from 1919-21 including *Mutt and Jeff*, the realities of making sound cartoons were a whole new ball game. The MGM board apparently assumed, more than once, that "cartoonists" meant those of the newspaper variety.

Both Hershfield and Gross were proven story tellers and "ideas" men. But Harry Hershfield's short reign proved costly and constrained by impractical suggestions, and he didn't last long. Milt Gross produced just two cartoons featuring his Count Screwloose character. They proved far too roughhouse for Quimby's conservative tastes. One of them was the amusing *Jitterbug Follies* (1939), featuring wild gags, funny Bill Littlejohn animation, and high-decibel, caffeine-energized voice-work by radio comic talents like Mel Blanc and Harry Lang that seemed to belong more in a zany Schlesinger cartoon made by Bob Clampett.

Quimby eventually admitted the cartoon studio was in trouble. Desiring a return to the lavishly produced cartoons of a season earlier, MGM contracted the recently bankrupt Harman and Ising.

And so, in October 1938, the veteran duo returned to making Metro cartoons in glorious Technicolor, but this time as employees on the MGM lot. According to Maxwell, it was felt that "[Harman and Ising] could save the day. But they didn't save the day either. They made some good pictures out there, as good as they'd been doing, or better. But [as before] they cost too much to suit MGM." [23] Scott Bradley, at the insistence of Harman and Ising, returned to compose Metro cartoon scores for the next eighteen years, displacing Bert Lewis.

Harman and Ising began with three cartoons they had commenced while finishing up their subcontract direction of the Disney short *Merbabies*. These were *The Art Gallery* and *Goldilocks and The Three Bears*, both by Harman, and Ising's *The Little Goldfish*. They were released in 1939. During work on *Merbabies* they had pitched these cartoons to Disney on the basis that if they could make them, he would release them. But Disney finally turned them down. This infuriated Harman who strongly felt that after *Merbabies* Disney owed them. [24]

Harman and Ising now ran separate units, with Friz Freleng working as a director under Harman. But not for long: in April 1939 Freleng, disgusted by what he interpreted as "the office politics" rife in the MGM studio, returned to the easy familiarity of Schlesinger's looser setup, where he felt much more at home. [25] Quimby, meantime, commissioned a third unit, headed by the team of story timing expert Bill Hanna and character layout man Joe Barbera, both of whom had been working in Ising's unit. Their first cartoon as directors was *Puss Gets the Boot* (1940) and it was overseen by Ising. Barbera maintained that Ising essentially contributed nothing.* The short featured a winning cat and mouse combo who would very quickly become MGM's top animation stars, Tom and Jerry.

* Historian Michael Barrier noted that two animators, Jim Pabian and Bob Allen, gave Ising credit for helping develop this cat and mouse story. [26]

The MGM cartoon voice stable featured a combination of veterans from the old Happy Harmonies along with several new freelance players. Harman and Ising were always after new talent and one feature article about the team noted that "the two men listen to the radio, mostly to study voices because voices are important in their work." [27] Female radio talent provided a large percentage of that voice work. The Hanna-Barbera unit used them just as often.

Radio's top character comediennes Sara Berner, Blanche Stewart and Elvia Allman were heard to fine advantage in cartoons like Hanna and Barbera's *Gallopin' Gals* (1940) as all of the gossipy racehorses, while the fine character actress Martha Wentworth revived her famous "Witch's Tale" radio voice for *The Fraidy Cat* (1942). She also played Mama Bear in Harman's Bear Family shorts. Ising ended up voicing both Papa Bear for Harman and his own offshoot character Barney Bear. Both were slow moving, lazy types who resembled a cross between comic actors Edgar Kennedy and Oliver Hardy. Both bears spoke in a laid-back, gruff Wallace Beery voice resulting in a sleepy character which many say was close to the real Rudolf Ising himself. [28] Your author would love to confirm the identity of the small child who was the voice of Wilbur the baby bear, as well as playing the title character in *The Bookworm* (1939).

The prolific Sara Berner also spoke for the normally speechless Jerry Mouse in the animated "Worry Song" combination sequence with Gene Kelly for the 1945 feature musical *Anchors Aweigh*. [29] Another distinctive female voice was radio dependable Paula Winslowe who played concerned mothers in cartoons like *The Little Mole* (1941). The talented African American vocal artist Lillian Randolph was heard throughout the forties as the flustered house maid in the Tom and Jerry cartoons, a character first seen in a 1935 Disney Silly Symphony, *Three Orphan Kittens*. The maid had been dubbed "Mammy Two Shoes" by Disney's animators, due to the fact she was mostly unseen above the hemline.* Even that voice changed on occasion at MGM: while Ms Randolph was a fine contralto singer, as is obvious in Disney's 1943 *Figaro and Cleo*, when the MGM housekeeper sings "I've Got It Bad and That Ain't Good" in *The Mouse Comes to Dinner* (1945), it was with the voice of vocalist Anita Brown. [30]

* The maid's MGM name was in fact "Dinah," used in Dell comic books and Whitman story books in the forties. Twenty years later, reflecting a changing world, the maid was suddenly speaking in an Irish brogue on *Tom & Jerry* TV prints: a mid-sixties re-dubbing job for busy voice actress June Foray. Apparently, the television watchdogs decided that Irish was deemed a safe stereotype.

Other Black performers enjoyed good voice-roles in MGM cartoons: Central Avenue nightclub comic Billy Mitchell gave musical life to the love-starved crow in Ising's enjoyable *Romeo in Rhythm* (1940), while trumpeter-vocalist Ira "Buck" Woods belts out a great "Is You Is or Is You Ain't My Baby?" in the Tom and Jerry entry *Solid Serenade* (1946). [31] Mitchell, Ben Carter, Lillian Randolph and others provided the talking undersea creatures in Hanna & Barbera's musically exuberant *Swing Social* (1940). Barbera recalled that the cast of players came from "an all-Black musical in town–with a terrific cast–whom we hired for the voices. Unfortunately, Bill [Hanna] wrote the Black dialect [on dialogue sheets] in the way a white man thinks a Black man talks, and the actors strained to read and sing the lines in that stilted manner." [32]

Some MGM cartoons featured actors who were called on because of their distinctive motion picture work. Diminutive Russian actor-musician Leon Belasco played Ivan Skavinsky Scavar in Harman's *Abdul the Bulbul-Ameer* (1941). Harman gave this cartoon to animator Tony Pabian to direct. Based on Frank Crumit's famous 1927 adaptation of a British novelty song from 1877, it was narrated musically by the sonorous bass baritone Harry Stanton, accompanied by Scott Bradley's fine Cossack-flavored arrangement. [33] Interestingly, Harman re-employed his early voice man Johnny Murray as the fight commentator, a voice Murray had first used a decade earlier in the Warner release *Battling Bosko* (1932). Another film, *The First Swallow* (1942), directed by Jerry (later Jameson) Brewer for Ising's unit, featured the distinguished Spanish-American character actor Pedro De Cordoba as the aged Franciscan padre who relates the story. [34] Schlesinger story man Mike Maltese, an inveterate movie buff, aptly described De Cordoba's voice as "all tone and diction: smooth." [35]

Several MGM cartoons boasted distinctive narration by leading radio voices. They included newsreader-announcer John Wald, who did announcing for *What's Buzzin, Buzzard?* (1943) and superfast play by play in *Batty Baseball* (1944). Truman Bradley narrated *Gallopin' Gals* (1940), and, most often, the mellifluous Franklin Bingman, an NBC staff announcer, added fine descriptive color and a mock pomposity to entries like *The Goose Goes South* (1941) and *War Dogs* (1943).

Another under-used performer was rustic banquet entertainer and radio character voice Elmore Vincent, who played excellent old codgers. Vincent, well-known on radio for his clueless political windbag "Senator Fishface," did a couple of Harman and Ising shorts, returning a few years later to play the venerable choir master in Hanna-Barbera's 1955 CinemaScope release *Good Will to Men*. This was a remake of Harman's *Peace on Earth* from fifteen years earlier, which featured Mel Blanc in the grandfather role which Vincent enacted for the new version. [36]

Once the Tom and Jerry series was a solid hit, it became the Hanna & Barbera unit's sole output. Voice talents were used less frequently for the simple reason that the brilliantly animated cat and mouse films were mostly mute. On odd occasions when Tom spoke it was with the voices of radio artists like Harry Lang who provided cat squawls and other effects, or vaudeville mimic

Jerry Mann who did Tom's Charles Boyer Gallic accent, as well as the Walter Winchell radio voice, in *The Zoot Cat* (1944). Mann, nephew of stage comedian Joe Weber of the legendary Weber and Fields vaudeville team, signed a six-month contract with MGM but ended up not being used on camera. Worried about his option, he took a stroll around the lot in search of a job and made himself known to the animation department. Mann ended up with a short-lived role working at MGM Cartoons, on call for both vocal effects and gags while between live engagements. [37] Mainly a stage performer, Mann enjoyed a long run as the Peddler in the musical *Oklahoma!* But he continued to be used by Hanna and Barbera whenever he was in town, and his voice is heard in a few fifties cartoons like *Casanova Cat* (1951) and *Slicked-Up Pup* (1951). By 1960 he ended up doing some fine character voices in the first season of Hanna-Barbera's *The Flintstones*, including the Phil Silvers-like Snorkasaurus.

The versatile King's Men, the original group from Ising's old Warner Merrie Melodies, was the most prolific vocal quartet heard in MGM cartoons. They sang in films like *Home on the Range* (1940), and in *Baby Puss* (1943) they were funny as Tom's sarcastic feline pals. [38] They were heard through the fifties, in Tom and Jerry cartoons like *The Two Mousketeers.* (1952). In *Texas Tom* (1950) leader Ken Darby provided Tom's basso singing voice ("If you're ever down in Texas, look me up").

Metro's cartoons kept hiring radio and movie character actors to keep the voices fresh. Some were prolific in cartoons, others only did a few animation jobs but should have done more. Veteran vaudeville comic Harry Lang was the delightfully unctuous kiddie-show host Uncle Dudley in *Jerry's Diary* (1949), while New York radio veteran Luis Van Rooten - later heard as the King in Disney's 1950 feature *Cinderella* - played the celestial express clerk in *Heavenly Puss* (1949). The always distinctive Hans Conried narrated *Johann Mouse* (1953). Conried's agent successfully wangled on-screen voice credit for his client, a first for MGM Cartoons. That cartoon also boasted the musical talents of concert pianist Jakob Gimpel, who had "doubled" for Spencer Tracy's on-screen piano playing in *Without Love* (1945).

Certain vocal effects for Tom, including his familiar long, agonized one-note yells, were performed by director Bill Hanna who recalled, "Whatever verbal effects were employed were basically yowls, ouches, screams, roars or sobs that we thought were just as universally understood as the animation itself. Joe and I would schedule a session about every two months to record these vocal effects. Joe would be up in the booth along with the sound engineer and would direct me as I did the vocals for Tom and occasionally Jerry." [39]

These eccentric noises were filed as numbered stock on blank film in Fred MacAlpin's sound library. According to MacAlpin, "Whenever Tom gets slammed and he yowls, that's mostly Bill Hanna. He always wanted it louder and louder. Well, I could record it loud, but the question was putting it into the theatre. There was a certain [audio] limit that was given, both on the bottom and the top [of the frequency spectrum], to satisfy the front seats and the back seats in a theatre. It amounted to a spread of about forty nine [decibels]. In those days you could break film valves if you recorded too loudly." [40]

***

The comically brilliant director Tex Avery arrived at MGM in late 1941, following six productive years at the Schlesinger studio. He took over Hugh Harman's unit. Harman, characteristically unhappy at MGM, finally departed in the spring of 1941 to set up as an independent in Beverly Hills. He was soon busy making wartime training films. Then, a month after Avery's arrival, Ising left for Officer Training school in Florida before taking up a post at the Army's

First Motion Picture Unit at Fort Roach (Hal Roach's film studio, close to MGM in Culver City).

As with his Warner Bros. cartoons, gags and laughter were always uppermost in Avery's "modus operandi," and he continued to populate his films with voices from top-ranking radio comedies. One of the early artists he used at MGM was Bill Thompson who played the bumbling Nazi title character in Avery's first release, *The Blitz Wolf* (1942). Thompson was one of the top anonymous pioneer voices in Golden Age cartoons. For Avery he would next speak for the mush-mouthed little dog Droopy (so named on a 1942 model sheet, though not actually identified as Droopy in any of the opening titles until 1949).*

*The famous mutt was first called "Happy Hound," a name used by Carl Barks in forties *Our Gang* comic books.

Bill Thompson hailed from Indiana where his parents were stage performers. During his years as a young vaudeville actor-dancer, he discovered his gift for funny accents. In 1934 when he was twenty-one he appeared at the Century of Progress show in Chicago. There he won an NBC audition after wowing the judges with a routine involving ten different characters with varying dialects. He was soon appearing on Midwest radio comedies including *The Hoffinghams* on which he played Count Foronicholas Drinkalotapop with a heavy Greek accent. The *Fibber McGee and Molly* program hired him to play a variation of that role. Thompson had the studio audience in hysterics and was on his way to national fame. In 1939 he relocated to Hollywood with the *Fibber McGee* company. That program showcased his weekly array of funny, original characters like Horatio K. Boomer, Nick DePopolous, the Scotsman Angus MacPherson, Irish cop Clancy and his garrulous Old Timer. Thompson's elastic, fizzy voice was soon heard in cartoons for Lantz and Schlesinger.

As Avery told his biographer Joe Adamson, the low-key bas-set hound was adapted from Bill Thompson's famous henpecked cream-puff voice "Wallace Wimple," heard weekly on NBC's top-rating *Fibber McGee and Molly*. [41] Thompson had introduced that character, his most popular voice creation, in April 1941 on the radio show. Droopy, the unflappable little hound who spoke in a slower version of the Wimple voice, became one of Tex Avery's top cartoon characters. He was first seen in *Dumb Hounded* (1943).

According to Avery's long-time story man Heck Allen, the director himself filled in for Droopy's voice during the war, when Thompson was serving in the Navy. There is a noticeably different Droopy voice in cartoons like *Jerky Turkey* (1945) and *Northwest Hounded Police* (1946). [42]

Recalling the vocal auditions that were a weekly occurrence, Avery remarked, "I think [voice actors were paid] $75, plus $5 if you did more than one character's voice. Sometimes they would do two, especially the girls, like Sara Berner. Of course, they were just starving, they were knocking on our door [auditioning] every day; things were bad." Sara Berner had done several cartoons for Avery when he was at Schlesinger. Avery told Milt Gray, "We had voices in mind for all of our cartoons, and when the time came, we called in a voice talent." [43]

Avery also called on veteran Disney voice-man Pinto Colvig, whom he had known since 1929 at Universal. Colvig satirized his own Practical Pig character for Avery's *Three Little Pigs* parody *The Blitz Wolf*. Some of Avery's ex-Warner cartoon voices, like Billy Bletcher, Sara Berner and Kent Rogers, turn up in his funny gothic mystery spoof, *Who Killed Who?* (1943) which features a vet-eran character actor, Robert Emmett O'Connor, as the on-camera host. Avery was always seeking fresh voices at Metro. "We gradu-ally stopped using the gruff, Bluto type of voice; and the old Billy Bletcher tough voice too," he explained. [44]

Radio was the source for home entertainment in that era and cartoon people, ever aware of comedy trends, took the medium seriously. Avery acknowledged that many cartoon characters, including some of his own, began life simply as a distinctive voice that suggested a character. One of his creations that demonstrates this perfectly was the truly oddball Screwy Squirrel, again based on a then-famous radio character, Wilbur Hutch, the idiotic boyfriend of Betty Lou on the NBC comedy program *The Tommy Riggs & Betty Lou Show.* [45]

Wilbur was created by prolific radio actor Wally Maher, as a nasal-voiced imbecile with an annoying sniff. Avery basically built Screwy around this voice, then added his savagely anarchic cartoon personality to the blend; the screwball Squirrel finally proved too strangely zany to be successful, and he was "killed off" in his fifth cartoon, *Lonesome Lenny* (1946). That cartoon also featured Sara Berner as dopey dog Lenny's rich owner whose voice is an uncanny imitation of fluttery comedienne Mary Boland, who specialized in slightly dizzy society matrons. In later years, Avery blamed his choice of the voice for Screwy Squirrel's demise, saying, "The voice * was not good; I think it hurt the character. But, at the time, I thought it was funny. He had adenoids and he sniffed, which was very bad [a direct lift from the radio character]. I think if we'd had a better voice on Screwy Squirrel, he would have been a better character." [46]

*Four decades later, stand-up comic Charles Fleischer was inspired to lift a smidgen of Screwy's delivery for his title-role voice in the 1988 feature *Who Framed Roger Rabbit.*

Avery's sounding board on story and gags was Heck Allen, who told biographer Joe Adamson, "[Tex] did everything, including some of the voices. If talent weren't available, hell, he'd go and do the voice himself. Tex was a bearcat for dialogue. God, he would have twenty or thirty takes on a line. We would sit in that projection room and run those [takes] over and over and over again. I couldn't tell one from the other. But Tex would eventually pick one, and I'd say, 'Yeah! Just the one.'" [47]

Allen elaborated further in the 1988 Avery TV documentary, *The King of Cartoons*: "[Tex] was a hellion on sound: he'd get up there in the damned recording booth. And I remember one [dialogue] line on a picture [*Jerky Turkey*] was [Allen imitates the replacement Droopy voice] 'Well, I don't know.' We ran that line twenty-seven times; I stopped counting after he'd trashed a couple, like [takes] ten and fourteen. And he took all of 'em, and still wasn't satisfied. And so, he said, 'I'm gonna pick one, you pick one, and then we'll toss and see which one goes.' Which we did, and I won, and he lost. And he sat there a minute and he said [to the sound man], 'Let's try that one more time, Max.'" [48] This anecdote lends credence to the speculation that Avery himself was Droopy's mid-forties stand-in voice while actor Bill Thompson was in uniform.

The diminutive Frank Graham was known on radio as a "man of a thousand voices," albeit in a dramatic, rather than comic, context. He was heard in nightly fifteen-minute radio fare like *Nightcap Yarns* where he played all the parts as a one-man theatre, eventually notching up over four hundred instalments. Graham became a utility voice at Metro and other cartoon studios in the early forties. An excellent, mellifluous narrator in Avery's *Big Heel-Watha* (1944), *The Shooting of Dan McGoo* (1945) and others, his most famous cartoon voices were the dual roles of The Fox and the Crow for Screen Gems Cartoons. He varied his guttural Crow voice for the lecherous wolf in Avery's famous Red Hot Riding Hood series. Avery recalled, "Graham had class, and he was easy to coach. He really put more into it than we had in our dialogue." [49]

As for the sexy Red, superbly animated by Preston Blair virtually without the aid of reference footage, she was spoken by Sara Berner while her singing voice was dubbed by some professional big band chanteuses. These included Connie Russell in *Red Hot*

Riding Hood (1943) and Imogene Lynn in *Swing Shift Cinderella* (1945). Ms Lynn, a featured soloist with the Artie Shaw orchestra, did the vocalizing in three cartoons singing numbers like "Put Your Arms Around Me, Wolfie [i.e. Honey]." A lookalike diva in *Wild and Woolfy* (1945) sang authentic country & western, so she was given voice by Ann Pickard from the rural Pickard Family musical aggregation.

Dick Nelson, a versatile radio man with a flair for mimicry, supplied the voice of the smaller bear George for the George and Junior cartoons. His voice was inspired by the Flatbush dialect of Ed Gardner's famous "Archie" character on radio's *Duffy's Tavern.* Nelson's major animation work was for the Lantz cartoons at Universal. Avery himself owned up to speaking for the big and decidedly dumb Junior, continuing his long fascination with John Steinbeck's Lenny character from the 1939 feature *Of Mice and Men.* [50]

Another young mimic working in forties cartoons was Walter Craig, who did a Charles Boyer voice in *Little 'Tinker* (1948). In an interview with Milt Gray, Avery recalled, "For *Uncle Tom's Cabana* [1947],we wanted an Andy [i.e., an imitation of Charles Correll from *The Amos & Andy Show*] for the role of Uncle Tom, and the guy - I can't think of his name - gave us a perfect Andy; he was a white guy." [51] This mimic is unconfirmed: it was possibly an obscure but accomplished talent named Bert Henderson who had been appearing on the Al Pearce radio show for Camel cigarettes, specializing in matching radio voices like Pearce himself and both *Amos & Andy.* Another theory is that actor Will Wright, who worked on air with the real Amos & Andy cast and was known to affect a good Andy voice himself, is playing Uncle Tom. I lean towards Wright because the role was a particularly talkative one and it is delivered by an obviously skilled radio artist.

New voices kept appearing in the Avery cartoons. He hired movie actor Nestor Paiva, who specialized in ethnic roles, as the rotund Mexican bullfight announcer in *Senor Droopy* (1949). And one of radio's finest comic supports, John Brown, best known as the eternally-gloomy undertaker "Digger O'Dell" on *The Life of Riley*, read the pun-filled script of Avery's *Symphony in Slang* (1951). He was rehired by the director to read the narration for *Dixieland Droopy* (1954).[52]

Daws Butler, one of the most famous voice artists in the TV cartoon era, was given one of his earliest animation assignments by Avery. John Burton, the long-time production manager at Warner Bros. Cartoons, had no immediate work for the young radio actor in 1947 but put in a word for him with Avery who was ready to record another of his Wolf & Red Riding Hood cartoons, *Little Rural Riding Hood* (1949). Butler auditioned for Avery and won the role of the unflappably urbane city wolf by deploying his dryly amusing George Sanders imitation. Butler also recorded a subtle Ronald Colman impression for the English fox in *Out-Foxed*, a concurrent Avery project.

This put Butler in solid with MGM Cartoons, where he began supplying incidental voices for various Avery and Tom & Jerry entries, ensuring his future when, several years later, Hanna and Barbera moved to television. Butler's TV co-star, ventriloquist Don Messick, was also started in cartoons via Avery, in fact upon Butler's recommendation: for *Wags to Riches* (1949) Messick voice-matched Droopy when Bill Thompson was unavailable. Messick also played Droopy in *The Chump Champ* (1950).

Butler recalled, "Tex said, 'Do you know anybody who can do a voice like [Droopy]? Can you do it?'" Butler replied, "'I could approximate it, but I do know a guy who can do it very well, and his name is Don Messick.' I'd met Don at one of the radio schools. Don went out and did Droopy's voice and they liked it. [Then] I think Bill and Joe used him. When it came time for Hanna and Barbera to leave MGM, they called me, and they called Don Messick, because we were what I call thinking, inventive actors. They called us in to do a show they were planning called *Ruff and Reddy*."[53]

Butler was one of the most prolific of the MGM voice artists of the fifties, working alongside Thompson who continued playing Droopy right up to the demise of MGM Cartoons in 1957. Butler was one of several actors who played Spike the bulldog in the Tom & Jerry series; the tough-guy hound was originated by Billy Bletcher in the 1945 entry *Quiet Please.*

Most notably, Avery gave Daws Butler's South Carolina comic accent its first good exposure in theatrical cartoons, as the slow-moving wolf in *The Three Little Pups* (1953) and *Billy Boy* (1954). This voice was modified, eventually becoming Butler's first famous TV character, *Huckleberry Hound.* Avery recalled, "He did a great voice that we were going to build a series on - the South Carolina wolf. We just flipped over [Butler's reading of] the lines." [54] So did theatre audiences; Avery recalled the normally humourless Quimby insisting that Daws Butler be used again.

Butler provided an insight into Avery's direction of voice talent, telling Milt Gray: "I went out to see Tex on the big recording stage at MGM. Tex was a marvellous guy to learn the business with. He was the first brilliant director I ever worked for and [he was] such a fussy man. This was before they had tape, and everybody was afraid of wasting film, so he would rehearse me, and rehearse me, and rehearse me, until I wouldn't have any voice left. There would be yells - he loved yells. A yell is a yell, and I do pretty good yells, but he would have me do about eight of these, then he would say, 'Gee, that's close.' Then he would say, 'Well, let's lay one down,' then we'd do it on the film. Then he would always throw in a couple himself, just for protection."

"Tex would always rehearse, rehearse, rehearse. [He] would call me out, and he'd say, 'This is the character,' then you'd go over and do it. You didn't have thirty people to audition with, to get the part [as was common practice in later years]." [55]

As Heck Allen noted, Avery himself provided occasional voices for his cartoons, just as he had in his earlier tours of duty with Lantz and Schlesinger. Avery's familiar chortle, for instance, is heard as the bullying dog in *Bad Luck Blackie* (1949), and he contributes several others like the villainous wolf in two 1954 western parodies, *Drag-a-Long Droopy* and *Homesteader Droopy* ("It's the laaaaaaw of the west"). Avery explained, "I did some western heavies, due to [story man] Heck Allen. We'd check talent, and they couldn't get the inflection I wanted, and a number of times Heck said, 'What the hell, do it yourself.' We'd come back after an audition when we'd listened to maybe four voices, and I'd say, 'I didn't like any of them.' So, with his encouragement I'd do them." [56]

Animator Mike Lah added, "[Tex] could do voices, and he did quite a few voices. As a matter of fact one of the voices he did came up because he corrected somebody else, and that somebody else said, 'Well why don't you do it - you're doin' it better than I can do it.' Tex said, 'Okay, I'll give you another voice to do.'" [57]

***

MGM continued to hire top broadcasting talents. One noted voice artist who worked several cartoon studios in Hollywood was youthful satirist Stan Freberg. At the time he was Daws Butler's vocal co-star in Bob Clampett's successful TV puppet show *Time for Beany*. After breaking in with Schlesinger cartoons, Freberg did voices for Screen Gems, UPA and Disney. For MGM in the early fifties, he was in cartoons like *Posse Cat* (1954). Avery recalled Freberg coming in for several auditions, "but I'm darned if I can recall actually using him." [58] Prolific radio comic Harry Lang, most of whose cartoon career transpired at Screen Gems, has already been noted in this chapter as an early "noise" for Tom. Lang had a trick voice which he used for whistling effects, Donald Duck imitations, and gruff voices. One of his gimmicks was an infectious belly-laugh. His track for *Mouse Trouble* (1944) was so memorable it was filed in the sound library and re-used in later cartoons, whenever Tom was doubled-up laughing at one of the sadistic tricks he played on Jerry.

Certain MGM titles required specialty talents. The Tom and Jerry entry *Pecos Pest* (1955) utilized George "Shug" Fisher & His Hillbillies. Fisher was a stammering gimmick-voice comic from the Sons of the Pioneers country vocal group. He sang his novelty tune "Froggie Went A-Courtin'" as Jerry's talented uncle. [59] If you are interested in what Fisher looks like, he has a good role in John Ford's 1962 classic *The Man Who Shot Liberty Valance.*

Avery's sublime opera parody *The Magical Maestro* (1952) needed a classical artist, and a vocal track featuring MGM musical contractee Carlos Ramirez, [60] originally recorded for the 1945 musical *Anchors Aweigh*, proved perfect for the cartoon's operatic bulldog. As well, Columbia Records' novelty group The Mary Kaye Trio, a pioneering and hugely popular Las Vegas lounge act from 1952, provided most of the odd vocal transformations suffered by the hapless baritone Poochini [61] as he valiantly attempts to make it thorough Rossini's "Largo al Factotum." The cartoon even featured a caricature of maestro Scott Bradley.

Avery's fellow hometown boy Woodward "Tex" Ritter, country singer, western film star and father of the late TV comic actor John Ritter, did deadpan narration for the stone age cartoon *The First Bad Man* (1955). Gag-wise this was a precursor to TV's *The Flintstones*. Indeed, both Avery's cartoon and the later television show featured striking character layouts by Ed Benedict.

Still another specialist was hired in 1952: a professional laugher named Fred Karbo had to do a crowd of cats giggling. He ended up doing eighty seven different laugh takes which were combined in *Life with Tom*. [62] And the famous "Mr. Sound Effects," Wes Harrison, performed such vocal noises as "a tree falling for a Tom & Jerry cartoon," a role he got after he paid a cold call to MGM while in his Navy uniform. [63] Harrison's amazing ability to reproduce all manner of sounds with just his throat and a microphone was immortalized on his LP recording of the great duck hunt.

Prominent in voice-overs during the early fifties was the gifted actor-mimic Paul Frees, who did his first MGM cartoon for Hanna & Barbera as the Bogart-inspired title character in *Jerry's Cousin* (1951).[64] Director Dick Lundy also took advantage of Frees's mimetic talents, employing him as the final Wallace Beery-inspired voice of Barney Bear. Avery used Frees as the resonant narrator of his hit-and-miss spot gag cartoons like *T.V. of Tomorrow* (1953) and *The Farm of Tomorrow* (1954). Frank Graham, who had done similarly sepulchral narration for some of Avery's forties cartoons, committed suicide in September 1950. Frees effectively became Graham's replacement. He was the lone voice of every character in *Cellbound* (1955), Avery's final MGM cartoon (assisted on the soundtrack by well-known Los Angeles session harmonica blower Gus Bivona).

June Foray, the most famous 20th century female animation voice artist, first worked for Tex Avery in 1950 in *Car of Tomorrow*. She and Daws Butler were teamed in *One Cab's Family* (1952), and she did her patented cackling witch for a Tom and Jerry, *The Flying Sorceress* (1956). Another female voice talent, and a fine impressionist, was Colleen Collins who was not used enough in animation. Avery hired her as the gawky Judy Canova sound-alike, Country Red, for 1949's *Little Rural Riding Hood*. [65]

One of the most distinctive MGM voice artists was radio veteran Patrick McGeehan, well-known as the one-man stock company on Red Skelton's long-running radio show. For Avery, the flexible McGeehan was heard as the Southern-accented hunter in *Doggone Tired* (1949), doubling as both Droopy's pompous lawyer and an Irish dog catcher in *Wags to Riches* (1949). McGeehan's most memorable role was in *Rock-a-Bye Bear* (1952), for which he played the hapless hibernating title character who endlessly bellows, "Ah hates NOISE!!! Can't Stand NOISE!!!!!!"

A fifty-year mystery was finally solved in 2005 when, out of the blue, a woman joined an internet cartoon forum and identified herself as the little girl who used to do the tiny French mouse in Tom & Jerrys like *The Two Mousketeers* (1952) and *Tom and Cherie* (1955). Her name is Francoise Brun-Cottan. She wrote, "Yes, I voiced Nibbles a.k.a. Tuffy when I was five or six years old. Hanna and Barbera wanted a high voice with a French accent. Having newly immigrated to the United States I fit that bill. As I could not read English, I had to memorize my lines. I remember having to stand on a high stool, so I was the same distance from the mic as the man (whose name I do not recall, sadly) who voiced Tom. It was a lot of fun. I spent some time on the Metro lot and did bit parts in films. After my mother re-married [the screenwriter Franklin Coen], my career - such as it was - ended." [66]

Following Avery's 1953 departure to the Lantz studio, animator Michael Lah directed some final Droopy cartoons. Hanna and Barbera, signed to a five-year contract in 1952 following Quimby's retirement, were already sensing trouble brewing. They began planning for a future in made-for-television animation.

As MGM's cartoon department wound down, the final films began looking more and more like a hybrid of UPA and the Hanna-Barbera TV style to come. The main voices were still the proven stalwarts Daws Butler and Bill Thompson. They were supported by a handful of seasoned radio players including Julie Bennett, who specialized in teenagers like the babysitter in *Tot Watchers* (1958). Others included Vic Perrin and Lucille Bliss, while child actress Danielle Baiu was heard warbling off-key in *Neapolitan Mouse* (1954). For *The Vanishing Duck* (1958) Joe Barbera auditioned and used actor Richard Anderson as hubby George; Anderson later turned up as Oscar Goldman in TV's *Six Million Dollar Man*. The little quacker was voiced by nightclub entertainer Merle Coffman, whose stage name was "Red Coffey." He did the cute duck voice for both cartoon units and ended up in Hanna-Barbera TV cartoons as *Yakky Doodle*.

Daws Butler sure sounded like he was being groomed to be Hanna-Barbera's top TV voice: for some 1957 Metro releases featuring Spike and his kid Tyke (*Give and Tyke* and *Scat Cats*) he did a fine Art Carney "Norton" voice which would soon be modified to fit a certain Yogi Bear. The crunch came in the spring of 1957, when Metro closed its cartoon division. Most of the animation staff went with either Hanna-Barbera Productions or the commercial studio Quartet Films, named for its four founders, Mike Lah, Art Babbitt, Stan Walsh and A. Arnold Gillespie. Bill Hanna and Joe Barbera made their mark in television in late 1957 with *Ruff and Reddy*, the first vehicle to team the great voice duo of Daws Butler and Don Messick. A year later the two actors were off and running as TV's top cartoon voices when Hanna-Barbera launched *The Huckleberry Hound Show.*

As for that backyard bulldog Spike, he had the honor of being the MGM character who was voiced by more actors than any other: at least six provided his paternally protective patter, depending on who was available for a session. Pat McGeehan, Bob Shannon, Daws Butler, Jerry Mann, John Brown and Stan Freberg all spoke for the father mutt, and all of them did it a 'la Jimmy Durante, proving that the old Schnozzola was likely the most mimicked celebrity voice ever to grace the cartoon world.

***

In 1961 Metro revived Tom and Jerry for two series of subcontracted cartoons that captured none of the spirit of the originals. Gene Deitch's low-budget cartoons are best ignored by all but Tom & Jerry completists, while Chuck Jones's series was, at least, handsomely designed and animated. The Jones cartoons were mostly voiceless stories. The relatively sparse dialogue was handled by veterans Mel Blanc and June Foray (and yes, even Bill Hanna's recorded yowls of agony turn up).

In hindsight, voices were less important overall to MGM Cartoons than they were to Warner Bros. which boasted the strongest array of characters in all the Hollywood based studios. Metro's biggest drawcards, Tom and Jerry, were essentially pantomime stars, as compared with Warner's large array of hip zanies who were prone to spout reams of wise-guy wordplay. Mike Lah noted that the relative lack of voices was partly Quimby's policy: the studio manager's long-held belief that too much American dialogue impaired a cartoon's chances for foreign release. [67] Despite this, the MGM cartoons provided employment for many interesting voice talents over its twenty-three year run, while as an animation studio the Metro team produced some of the most visually sumptuous, and finely animated, cartoons of all time.

Chapter 3:

COLUMBIA-SCREEN GEMS
Cartoon Voices, 1930-49

The hundreds of theatrical cartoons made at the Charles Mintz Studio (later known as Screen Gems) and released by Columbia Pictures, are still virtually unknown today, despite scores of Golden Age cartoons being uploaded to YouTube. Yet they deserve to be known. Although wildly inconsistent, some of them remain undeniably interesting.

At various times, the Columbia cartoon shop saw many of the best animation and design talents, from studios as diverse as Disney and Lantz, doing tours of duty. Regrettably though, Screen Gems was forever incapable of attracting story men the calibre of those at Schlesinger's, and its range of lead characters was in the end woefully limited. Its few viable "stars," headed in the thirties by Krazy Kat and Scrappy, don't revive well. Columbia's Krazy was more a simple Mickey Mouse clone than anything resembling George Herriman's famous comic-strip feline, save for one unsuccessful attempt at aping the original in 1935's Li'l Ainjil. And that inconsistency was typical of Columbia cartoons from beginning to end.

The Columbias at least benefitted from a range of excellent voice talents, including most of the top names - Mel Blanc, Dave Weber, Billy Bletcher - from Hollywood's other animation setups. This situation underlines the essentially small size of the Hollywood cartoon fraternity with its regular cross-pollination of animators, story men and executives, along with a shared pool of reliable vocal artists.

In February 1930, producer-distributor Charles Mintz moved his small animation outfit, then known as the Harrison-Gould "Krazy Kat" studio, cross-country via rail, from its 45th Street location in Manhattan to the Winkler Productions cartoon studio on Western Avenue in Hollywood. One year earlier the Winkler plant had lost its Oswald the Lucky Rabbit contract to Universal Pictures. After setting up in Los Angeles, Mintz signed a deal with RKO for a cartoon series, the star of which had yet to be created. Already in place was a new Columbia Pictures release deal for the sound Krazy Kat cartoons. When the New York boys arrived on the Coast, Winkler's was renamed the Charles B. Mintz Studio; it became known as Screen Gems only when Columbia became half owner, starting in 1933.

Mintz's chief artistic talents were his senior animators Ben Harrison and Manny Gould, who continued supervising the Krazy Kat cartoon series which they originally made in New York as silent cartoons released by Paramount. Now they were adjusting to the new disciplines of making cartoons with sound. Other staff members who made the move West included the gifted pianist and musical director Joe DeNat, production manager James Bronis, and the youngest recruit, a talented teenage inker and assistant animator named Harry Love.

Once the West Coast operation was underway, Charles Mintz phoned the veteran *Koko the Clown* animator Dick Huemer and persuaded him to relocate. Mintz promised Heumer he would be appointed the director of a new cartoon series for release by RKO-Radio Pictures. Huemer, in turn, convinced his New York animator pals Sid Marcus and, a few weeks later, Arthur Davis to make the transcontinental hop. The new RKO series starred *Toby the Pup*, a character created by Marcus who served as the chief gag man, with Dick Huemer supervising the stories and animation. Huemer also supplied Toby's voice. The Toby cartoons, some of which remain unavailable for evaluation, lasted just one season

144 • KEITH SCOTT

(eleven shorts released in 1930-31), by which time Mintz had cut a deal for a second Columbia series. This opportunity occurred when Mintz's competitor and old adversary Walt Disney cancelled his own Columbia release for a financially better deal with United Artists.

For Mintz's second Columbia slot, Dick Huemer created a character called Scrappy, a mischievous young boy, and as with the Toby the Pup cartoons he supervised the series alongside Marcus and Davis. As Huemer recalled, "On Scrappy and all those other dopey Mintz cartoons, there were no animators credited; it was always *by* Dick Huemer." [1] After directing twenty-three Scrappy entries, Huemer balked at the salary cuts being proffered by Mintz. At Ben Sharpsteen's invitation he moved on to a fruitful career at the Disney studio in 1933. The other Scrappy crew members, however, remained at the Mintz studio for the rest of the decade.

In this early Mintz period, in-house personnel - story men who were essentially their own directors - supplied what little voice-work there was. As the comically gifted story man Sid Marcus recalled, "Columbia restricted dialogue; their foreign revenue was high, and they didn't want to spoil that by putting American dialogue in our pictures. We were restricted to lines of dialogue that were one or two words. So at the recordings, whoever was there pitched in; we had no professionals [in the early thirties]." [2]

The Mintz studio's own vocal talent for these early cartoons ranged from reasonably competent to frankly amateurish. Marcus said, "Everybody did voices: Jack Carr; Manny [Gould] did some; Artie [Davis]." [3] Bob Clampett identified animator Carr, who later joined the Schlesinger studio, as the early voice of Mintz's first star character Krazy Kat, a falsetto distinguished by a Mickey Mouse type of nervous laugh. [4] The use of staff voices lasted longer at Mintz than at competing studios, and outside talent bookings were the exception for the first five years. By late 1932 an occasional vocal quartet was hired, while show-biz themed cartoons like the Krazy

Kat entry *Minstrel Show* featured Bing Crosby mimic Henry Taylor of the Radio Rogues impersonator-trio. There was also a warbler who sounds suspiciously like Cliff Edwards. *The Crystal Gazebo*, a 1932 parody of radio's popular mystery serial *Chandu the Magician*, used suave British-born announcer Thomas Freebairn-Smith, later a top Hollywood radio executive.

In the early years Joe DeNat's scores were competent but somewhat lifeless, as if a half-decent dance band was backing the cartoons with their "book," consisting of a raft of familiar public domain tunes like "Turkey in the Straw."

Sid Marcus recalled a specific recording anecdote to historian Milton Gray: "I remember one time there was a cat singing 'Oh, How I Miss You Tonight' on a fence, and I figured I would do that [voice]. I got in front of the microphone, and Joe DeNat was the conductor, and we had our 15-piece orchestra; men that DeNat hired. We recorded at Columbia...we used their [recording] stage. I was supposed to do this cat, and I got up in front of the microphone, and Joe DeNat, with the baton, went one, two, three -- and instead of getting music, I got fifteen razzberries from the orchestra. That was the general feeling of making cartoons in those days." [5]

The cartoon to which Marcus refers is *Sassy Cats* (1933) from the Scrappy series. It was a precursor, plot-wise, to the popular Warner Bros. cartoon, *Back Alley Oproar* (1948). This amusing, whiny cat vocal by Marcus was re-used for a 1937 Scrappy entry, *Puttin' Out the Kitten*. The Mintz recording sessions were held, recalled Harry Love, "at Columbia Pictures on Gower Street, and at RKO Radio Pictures [presumably Love meant where the long-lost Toby the Pup tracks were made]." [6]

The now obscure Scrappy series runs to almost ninety cartoons. They are a mixed bag indeed, containing moments of inspired cinematic invention, along with as many low-lights. Several Scrappy cartoons boast creative gags, a high level of animation for the period, and fine background art. But they would be virtually impossible to revive for mass audience consumption in today's totally changed society. This is due to their succession of often jaw-dropping gags involving children at gunplay in *Dizzy Ducks* (1936), sadistic revenge in *The Puppet Murder Case* (1935), and shockingly hideous and unpleasant villains in cartoons like *The Wolf at the Door* (1932) and *Scrappy's Ghost Story* (1935) who would undoubtedly be blamed with inducing nightmares in impressionable minds.

The rampant exaggeration and strange character designs reflect the East Coast background of the staff; indeed, only the pre-code Max Fleischer cartoons can compare with the early Columbia output in their relentlessly surreal qualities. Various Scrappy cartoons have non-existent stories but boast dreamlike narrative structures; in *Let's Ring Doorbells* (1935) the kids gleefully torment an overweight man and are later trapped in a madman's mansion where they suffer a nightmarish punishment. The often topical Depression plots, like *The Flop House* (1932) and celebrity caricature entries like *Scrappy's Party* (1933) or *Movie Struck* (1933), would be virtually impenetrable on home video without some linking explanations to put these often peculiar cartoons in context. That hasn't stopped most of the eighty five or so Scrappy cartoons from being uploaded to YouTube, by and for a growing band of vintage cartoon buffs.

Likewise, the Krazy Kat cartoons display the same absurd stream-of-subconsciousness apparent in the Scrappy shorts, along with striking character models and often painstakingly detailed animation, noticeable in films like *Lighthouse Keeping* dating from 1932. They are certainly the equal of the Harman-Ising Bosko cartoons in smoothly choreographed synchronization with the music. The weak point with Krazy Kat was story construction, which remained rooted in Mintz's early style for almost its full run, long after other cartoon studios had begun refining areas like story and dialogue. Late in the series, some Krazy entries employed the Warner Bros. spot-gag formula in 1938 films like *Krazy's Travel Squawks* and *The Auto Clinic* to no great effect.

And yet, coming from the depths of the Great Depression, certain titles are worth seeking out: some of the early Krazy Kats are startling social records, with the almost motivational *Prosperity Blues* (1932) appearing one year before Lantz's better-known and similarly morale-building Oswald the Rabbit cartoon, *Confidence.*

Once full 3-strip color became available to all the animation studios in the Fall of 1935, a spate of musical cartoon series attempted to compete with Disney's visually sumptuous Silly Symphonies, which had proved huge crowd pleasers in the burgeoning short subject field. Earlier, while on full-color standby, each studio experimented with the lesser 2-color Cinecolor process until the releases of early 1936, when Technicolor's full spectrum became available to all producers. Lantz unfurled his CarTune Classics, Iwerks made the independently released Comicolor series and, back East, Fleischer produced the Color Classics shorts. Although all these series boasted creative and catchy musical content, and sincerely aimed for improved animation, none of them managed to topple the Silly Symphonies.

For Columbia, Mintz unveiled a new series called Color Rhapsodies with *Holiday Land* (1934), featuring an appearance by his normally monochrome star Scrappy. This series was handled by two units: one was supervised by Manny Gould and Ben Harrison, and the second by Art Davis and Sid Marcus. They featured higher budgeted cartoons, eventually in full and gorgeous Technicolor. How times had changed in just one decade: ironically Mintz was now attempting to compete with Disney, the man who once took distributor Mintz's often pedantic orders during the four years of production on the silent Alice Comedies.

An article in the *LA Times* from April 1935 covered voice dubbing in the movies and mentioned the Mintz cartoons. Some valuable uncredited names were disclosed: "Charles Mintz, who produces shorts for Columbia, acknowledges the services of Leone Ledoux as 'Scrappy' and George Winkler as 'Krazy Kat.' One Allan

Watson sings bass when bass is required, and there is a useful lady named Celeste Rush, and a Paul Taylor chorus." [7]

As this item disclosed, some excellent vocal groups and soloists began to be heard in the charming Rhapsody cartoons. Paul Taylor, a singer who graduated to chorus master on Bing Crosby's prestigious *Kraft Music Hall* radio show contracted many vocal groups for the movie industry. Often on call was a male quartet named The Uptowners, whose leader was resonant bass singer Homer Hall, prominent on the soundtracks of visually lavish Technicolor Mintz titles like *Bon Bon Parade* (1935) and *Merry Mannequins* (1937). This vocal group had previously worked for Iwerks in various Comic-Color musical cartoons like *Sinbad the Sailor* (1935) and of course in Disney's Silly Symphonies.

Frustratingly, the identity of one female vocal trio has not been confirmed, with The Three Harmonettes being the best guess. Suffice to say they were heard in several thirties Mintz-Screen Gems cartoons, with the producer saving on talent fees by having the most vocally distinctive member of this group playing various speaking parts, including, briefly, both Krazy Kat and Scrappy for the studio's black and white releases; she even pops up in a few forties cartoons.

Another of Hollywood's accomplished female trios, The Rhythmettes, was also heard in the Color Rhapsodies, including the attractively animated *The Untrained Seal* (1936). The *Los Angeles Times* column revealed that the Norman Bennett Agency was the go-to place for all these "disembodied" voices constantly needed by film companies, with "more than 200 singers on its list." The talent agency could supply anything from "a soloist to an ensemble 'background' for a musical scene." [8]

Marcus recalled cowboy star comic Smiley Burnette doing his trick "froggy" voice for a couple of titles. [9] A likely one was the gravel-voiced singer heard behind the Three "Cupid Stooges" creature in *Bon Bon Parade*. Burnette may even have contributed to a brief color series based on Billy DeBeck's famous *Barney Google* comic strip, but these cartoons have not survived intact, the soundtrack elements being lost to the ages. Two names are probable voice suspects: mimic Sid Raymond, while in Los Angeles in 1935 with a Major Bowes travelling radio unit, claimed to have done a Columbia cartoon or two, while diminutive actor Bud Duncan, the distinctive Irish voice of radio's *Cinnamon Bear,* also mentioned cartoons in his publicity. But without the audio these names are impossible to confirm.

The Color Rhapsodies featured some intricately animated musical scenes. Animator Harry Love recalled, "Ben Harrison always had to have a march, a parade. If it was a clothesline [the laundry items] were all marching. And [he] always gave me those perspective parades to do. He tried to keep 'em in sync [with the] music." [10] Love also spoke admiringly about the chief Color Rhapsodies animator Manny Gould for the next forty years. "This guy was a Disney animator without ever having worked for Disney. He was always for good drawing and quality, and he had a sense of timing. Manny was the one who checked the animation...he was a much better artist and much better animator than Ben." [11]

It is apparent to modern viewers that the intricate musical tracks for the Color Rhapsodies are the product of excellent arrangers and sound technicians. Certainly, it is from this point that the prolific and virtually forgotten Screen Gems composer Joe DeNat, a former Tin Pan Alley pianist in New York, deserves to be better known for his work on these films. DeNat and veteran lyricist Bernie Grossman, occasionally assisted by Columbia contract tune-smith Nico Grigor, fashioned many excellent cartoon scores. They range from Broadway-influenced as in *Merry Mannequins* (1937) through comic-opera for *Glee Worms* (1936), to Central Avenue jazz, with *Swing Monkey Swing* (1937). Virtually all the scores were originals, without the luxury of a raft of popular tunes like those owned by Warner Bros. or Paramount. Only occasionally did a Mintz cartoon boast a song from a Columbia feature film such as the infectious

Let's Go (1937) which took its title from the hit number warbled by nightclub headliner Harry Richman in his popular starring vehicle *The Music Goes 'Round* (1936). This was an example of early cross-promotion as the cartoon was released to coincide with the Columbia feature.

Indeed, from the mid-thirties Mintz's musical soundtracks were often the equal of those from better known cartoon studios. Columbia's sound department was already well regarded: in 1936 they won an Academy Award for recording the operatic feature *One Night of Love* (1935). Its title song was parodied in Mintz cartoons like *Birds in Love* (1936) which relied on the excellent whistling talents of sound mimic Marion Darlington. Columbia even received a scientific achievement Oscar for introducing "the application of the vertical cut [or 'hill-and-dale'] recording method to studio production." Mintz was the beneficiary of this audio advance, ensuring his cartoon vocals and scores, cut on discs then transferred to film, sounded vibrant.

From the 1936-37 season, the newer breed of freelance radio-cartoon voice specialists began working for Screen Gems, by now the official name for Mintz's cartoon studio. Mel Blanc's first Columbia credit was the strikingly storybook-designed *The Foxy Pup* (1937) for sub-contract producer Ub Iwerks. Blanc, willing to work hard on any dialect he was asked to reproduce, was also heard in *Spring Festival* (1937) in which he gives a neat imitation of famous Scottish music-hall legend Sir Harry Lauder. Also in this period the growly Billy Bletcher was giving his usual sterling performances in cartoons like *Two Lazy Crows* (1936) for which he plays an Oliver Hardy-style crow, alongside British "silly ass" comic Val Stanton who voices the other crow in matching Stan Laurel-esque tones.

Two Lazy Crows was the first of the several cartoons produced for Mintz by animation pioneer Iwerks, following his split with distributor Pat Powers when his Comicolor contract terminated in 1936. Bletcher had done voices for Iwerks on some of those cartoons, including the role of the memorably mean-spirited pin-cushion villain of *Balloon Land* (1935). The Iwerks studio, based in Beverly Hills at 1749 Santa Monica Boulevard, subcontracted on fifteen distinctive Color Rhapsody cartoons released by Columbia between 1937 and 1940, several of which were directed by Paul Fen-nell.

Bletcher and fellow Disney voice veteran Pinto Colvig appeared in a typical Iwerks produced cartoon, *The Frog Pond* (1938). Bletch-er's belligerent basso was amusing as the bullying, horny amphib-ian who lecherously orders, "We'll have a party ... and I want d' feminine touch!" Blanc also continued acting for Iwerks in vari-ous Color Rhapsodies. His voices were heard in *Blackboard Revue* (1940), another uniquely designed cartoon in which chalk figures cavort and the gothic ghost story *Midnight Frolics* (1938). Iwerks quit cartoon production in early 1940, returning to work on techni-cal development for the Disney studio that fall.

Movie and radio star imitations, so common in thirties car-toons, were at first handled by the excellent Three Radio Rogues, consisting of impressionists Henry Taylor, Jimmy Hollywood and Eddie Bartell. Their clever voice imitations brought various broad-casting and film personalities to caricatured life in Color Rhap-sodies like *Merry Mutineers* (1936) and *Gifts From the Air* (1937). The Radio Rogues were under contract to Columbia at the time, appearing in three live-action shorts directed by vaudeville comic Benny Rubin. [12]

The prolific Dave Weber, another specialist in celebrity voice impressions, also began working for Mintz in the 1936-37 season, and his Joe Penner and "froggy" voices were heard as often here as in the contemporaneous Warner Bros. and Lantz cartoons. [13] One Mintz Color Rhapsody was a virtual showcase of his abilities as Weber supplied a huge array of radio star impressions, caricatured as birds. The short, a satirical take on the *Community Sing* radio program, was called *The Big Birdcast* (1938). Weber regarded the art of mimicry as an offshoot of dialect and speech analysis, and he produced voice imitations of long-forgotten radio names doing long-forgotten topical gags. These include an allusion to Jack Benny and Fred Allen and their comic on-air feud as to who was the best radio comedian. The catchy 1936 hit song "Sing, Baby, Sing" links spoofs of top broadcast stars like crooner Rudy Vallee, newscaster Walter Winchell and comedians Milton Berle, Ed Wynn, Joe Penner and Eddie Cantor.

Amazingly, Weber contributes seventeen voices in *The Big Bird-cast*, aided by two other mimics: Lind Hayes imitates orchestra leader Ben Bernie, and double talk comedy-vocalist Cliff Nazarro does the singing voices for Bing Crosby and Eddie Cantor. The cartoon even manages to capture visual characteristics of each celebrity even though they are drawn as birds. From 1938 to 1940, Weber and Blanc virtually dominated the Columbia and Lantz voice work in Hollywood. Indeed, the only established voice not used in Columbia cartoons was, surprisingly, baby voiced Berneice Hansell who was heard everywhere else.

Unfortunately, the hapless Krazy Kat remained stuck in the early Bosko-Oswald-Mickey Mouse style and was vocally inconsistent to the end. As noted, his early falsetto was provided at first by animator Jack Carr. After Carr left the Mintz studio, Krazy was spoken by producer George Winkler. But by late in the decade Krazy's voice was virtually different from cartoon to cartoon, reflecting the Mintz staff's total inability to find a handle on his character. If he wasn't mute, then actors Billy Bletcher in *The Merry Café* (1936), Dave Weber in *Krazy's Travel Squawks* (1938) and finally Mel Blanc for *The Lone Mountie* (1938) spoke his lines. Krazy finally died from a terminal lack of charisma in 1939, with one final exhumation in the Harry Love-directed entry *Mouse Exterminator* (1940).

Likewise, the eternally youthful Scrappy was played by various people. They included a poorly acted staff falsetto in cartoons like 1934's *Holiday Land*, then a long run by radio actress Leone Ledoux, a Texas born girl who specialized in baby and child voices on radio and who was a Columbia cartoon mainstay. Finally, child actor Robert Winkler * took the Scrappy role in 1937. Bobby Winkler, much heard on radio and a minor member of Hal Roach's "Our Gang" comedy shorts, also voiced Columbia cartoons like Art Davis's *The Foolish Bunny* (1938) in which he played the title character, and *Mountain Ears* (1939), where he voiced a cheeky backwoods boy. Fifty years later Winkler recalled that, "Mr. Mintz was trying to see if both characters had potential for an ongoing series." [14]

* No relation to studio manager George Winkler or his sister Margaret, alias Mrs. Charles Mintz.

Bobby Winkler noted that all the child actors in town mandatorily attended Hollywood Professional School each day from 9.30 until midday. Via his meticulously maintained scrapbooks, he remembered, "Those kids that worked in radio were almost invariably involved in cartoons. Some of the kids I worked with who I admired so much were Conrad Binyon and Bernice Kamiat. She was later called Cara Williams, but in those days, she was, I guess, the finest young girl actress in radio and dubbing in animation that I knew." [15]

As the cartoons at Warner Bros. and MGM began making enormous strides in humor and animation from 1938, a feeling of stultifying sameness became ever-more apparent at Screen Gems. By the end of the thirties, the Krazy and Scrappy cartoons were phased out and replaced by two new black & white series, dubbed Phantasies and Fables. These were hit-and-miss one-shot cartoons, forever in search of a new potential star character, and made on limited budgets; recycled animation footage became common. The expensive Color Rhapsodies remained the studio's biggest draw card, often eliciting favourable exhibitor comment. By mid-1942 the Fables had expired, leaving the Color Rhapsodies and Phantasies as the studio's two umbrella series though the final releases of 1949.

Producer Charles Mintz is often painted as a villain in animation histories following his famous falling out with Walt Disney over the Oswald Rabbit silent cartoons in early 1928. But Mintz comes across in various recollections as a man who was well liked by the Screen Gems crew. Sid Marcus noted that Mintz, like Leon Schlesinger, always steered clear from the production side of the cartoons, allowing his appreciative staff a degree of creative freedom. [16] Harry Love described Mintz as "a man of great integrity whom everyone loved." [17] Arthur Davis also spoke highly of him, and even the contentious Hugh Harman, very unforgiving of certain people, liked Charles Mintz as a person very much. In fact, Mintz's studio nickname was "Good-time Charlie." [18] Ironically, his hands-off approach, his non-interference and seeming lack of leadership could help explain the proliferation of misfired comic ideas and often poor timing in many of the films.

Sadly, Mintz's health began to fail in his last two years. Before his death he had been taking heat from Columbia's board of directors about the increasing cost overruns on often-lavish Color Rhapsodies like *Spring Festival* (1937), *Animal Cracker Circus* (1938) and other richly detailed films. When these debts continued to mount, Mintz was relieved of his duties by Columbia, who put James Bronis in charge. Bronis was billed as the studio's production manager but, according to Harry Love, "[Bronis] was essentially Mintz's drinking buddy." [19] Charles Mintz, likely further stressed by his dismissal, suffered a fatal stroke at the end of 1939 and passed on January 4, 1940. According to Love, "When [Mintz] died the whole thing went to pot." [20]

In short order big changes occurred at Screen Gems. Ben Harrison and Manny Gould departed to other studios. Long-time story man Allen Rose was let go. The reliable music director Joe DeNat remained for a couple more years before being replaced by his associate and arranger Eddie Kilfeather through most of the new decade; staff musician Paul Worth shared composing duties with Kilfeather on several of the forties scores.

The cartoons produced in the eighteen months following Mintz's demise were among the drabbest and most technically inept in the studio's history. Mintz's brother-in-law George Winkler was appointed the new producer. Winkler's previous claim to fame was taking over the production reins of the Oswald cartoons after Mintz poached most of Disney's staff in 1928. Winkler was, noted Rudolf Ising, a "highly nervous man" who was essentially just "a film editor." [21] Creatively out of his depth, Winkler began slashing budgets, salaries and schedules in a ham-fisted manner intended to appease Columbia's board, but which inevitably led to staff resentments. Directors Arthur Davis and Sid Marcus continued making competent but listlessly uninspired films: Davis caricatured himself in mild cartoons like *The Way of All Pests* (1941). These two veterans, stuck in the old ways, were on borrowed time, and would be eased out via studio politics.

Voice-wise, Mel Blanc dominated the Columbia cartoons at this point. But Blanc's voice acting was essentially unmemorable because of the studio's lack of animated stars and its often embarrassingly poor stories and dialogue. In some cartoons, like *Tangled Television* (1940) and *The Cuckoo I.Q.* (1941), Blanc is directed to yell unfunny lines, becoming positively strident. In his four years as a voice for Screen Gems cartoons Blanc did virtually nothing to match his sterling work at Warner Bros. Other animation voice "regulars" including Billy Bletcher, Danny Webb (formerly Dave Weber), Sara Berner, child actor Robert Winkler and narrators like the resonant Franklin Bingman, often co-starred with Blanc in this transitional period.

Several of that era's Columbia cartoons look and sound downright bizarre, but closer scrutiny reveals that the fault lies squarely with the severely inadequate story department. A general feeling of anything goes in the cartoons was an indication of chronic Screen Gems burnout. A prime example is the 1941 release *It Happened to Crusoe*. This short is simply an excuse for using the convenient mimicry of voice talents Jack Lescoulie and Danny Webb. Lescoulie imitates Jack Benny and Webb does both Fred Allen and Benny's radio valet Rochester. But the cartoon does nothing with those comedians' richly developed radio personalities, and completely squanders Benny and Allen's then famous mock-feud. The film merely deploys poorly directed "radio voice imitations" speaking as badly drawn cannibals with no attempt at facial or physical caricatures to match the well-known voices. It was mimicry for no reason and the resulting story, already very weak in conception, is a total mess: native chief's son hates meat, prefers vegetables. The use of Jack Benny's and Fred Allen's voices was totally pointless, and the cartoon was also unforgivably unfunny.

George Winkler continued hacking the budgets on the black & white cartoons, while Columbia's management expressed concern about the ongoing lack of star characters. There was negative feedback from unimpressed exhibitors, who reflected in turn unimpressed theatre patrons. Bigger change was in the air at Screen Gems, and behind the scenes machinations were underway.

***

The singularly talented Frank Tashlin, fresh from two years in Disney's story department, joined Screen Gems around Easter of 1941, as head of its story division. This was a new department the studio had never enjoyed, keeping it years out-of-step with other Hollywood cartoon factories. Tashlin began by writing a successful story, *The Great Cheese Mystery*, directed by Art Davis, with the mice voices handled by Mel Blanc. Six months after Tashlin signed on, a shakeup saw veteran staffer George Winkler ousted: he ended up at the Schlesinger studio for a time as overseer of the Ink and Paint department. Tashlin was promoted to the role of production supervisor, with Columbia executive Ben Schwalb named Screen Gems studio manager. [22]

Art Davis recalled Tashlin being specifically brought in "to compete with the Warner Bros. cartoons,"[23] by now perceived to be challenging and often out-doing Disney's supremacy in the animated shorts field. Tashlin, always a restlessly original talent, effectively revitalized the tired animation shop by hiring various young Disney-trained artists like John Hubley and Zack Schwartz, who had been on the picket lines in that year's rancorous Disney studio labor strike. There were early rumblings of a new artistic approach. Suddenly, there was a shared feeling of excitement and creative hope about this "new" cartoon shop: it felt as if old boundaries were crumbling with graphic experimentation being openly encouraged.

The Columbia cartoons which followed were, if nothing else, far more daring and hence more interesting than anything the Screen Gems crew had been making, excepting a few inventive Color Rhapsodies. Certainly, a few excellent cartoons appeared at this time, the equal of any of the Hollywood competition, along with as many that were complete misfires.

Various flexible radio actors became semi-regular voices in the Columbia cartoons, with the gifted Frank Graham being the most prominent. Essentially, Graham became the studio's main voice talent by replacing Mel Blanc.

Screen Gems's first Fox and Crow cartoon, *The Fox and the Grapes* (1941), was a most inventive Tashlin classic, and obviously influential on later adversarial cartoon series like the Roadrunner v. Coyote or Tweety v. Sylvester. It featured Mel Blanc as the voice of both starring characters and he gave a fine performance. But it proved to be Blanc's last Columbia cartoon, recorded just before his exclusive contract with Schlesinger-Warner Bros. took effect in April 1941. [24] The same month saw the release of versatile voice-man Danny Webb's last Columbia cartoon, *The Merry Mouse Café*, before he enlisted for military service.

With the sudden loss of two of the most established and capable voice talents in animation, the path was clear in the spring of 1941 for Frank Graham to step into the role of multiple voice expert at both MGM and Screen Gems. Graham, known on radio as "The One-Man Theatre" in the series *Nightcap Yarns*, made his first appearance at Columbia narrating Tashlin's spot gag entry, *A Hollywood Detour* (1942). He went on to be the voices of both the Fox and the Crow for Columbia's most successful cartoon series, starting with the second entry *Woodman, Spare That Tree* (1942).

Expanding on Mel Blanc's original brief - milquetoast fox vs. gruff Bronx crow - Graham adopted comic actor Franklin Pangborn's mannerisms for the prissy, effeminate fox, and gave a close voice imitation of vulgar Broadway comic B. S. Pully for the cigar chomping crow. This was almost the same gravel voice he used for Avery's "horny Hollywood wolf" character at MGM. The vocal contrast worked well, and the two protagonists became the leading lights of Columbia's animated output during the forties in several excellent cartoons like *Room and Bored* (1943). Of all the cartoons that Screen Gems produced, the Fox and Crow entries are the ones that still hold up decades later.

Other reliable cartoon vocal standbys Billy Bletcher and comedienne Sara Berner contributed some excellent voice acting during the transitional period of 1941-42. Bletcher, one of Tashlin's regular hires at Warner Bros. in the late thirties, lent his funny thunder-basso to parody-based cartoons in 1942 like *Wolf Chases Pigs* and *The Wild and Woozy West*, while he and Ms Berner starred in a beautifully animated fairy tale take-off, *Red Riding Hood Rides Again* (1941). This cartoon was director Sid Marcus's answer to Tex Avery's Warner bedtime story parodies like *A Bear's Tale* (1940).

Other voices auditioned for Columbia. Kent Rogers, the young radio actor and fine mimic heard in several Schlesinger and Lantz cartoons, appeared in Paul Sommer & John Hubley's *The Vitamin G-Man* (1943); some might argue that Rogers was the only good thing about it. And the great Pinto "Goofy" Colvig, with a previous late thirties stint as story-and-voice-man at Columbia under his belt, returned from his two-year jaunt at the Fleischer Studios' Miami setup just in time to voice a new character, Punchy the Pelican, for Tashlin's *The Tangled Angler* (1941) and *Under the Shedding Chestnut Tree* (1942).

Colvig wasn't the only ex-Florida emigre. In April 1942, following Paramount's takeover of his cartoon studio, Dave Fleischer relocated to the West Coast and became executive producer at Screen Gems per the request of New York-based Columbia boss Jack Cohn (older brother of West Coast production chief Harry Cohn). The elder Cohn had smelled trouble with the bright young "new guard" of Columbia animators and designers. Cohn was no doubt aware of their active roles in the previous year's Disney strike, and their memberships in the Screen Cartoonists' local. That union's bargaining agent was Bill Pomerance, perceived by Cohn to be progressive, i.e., left-leaning. Cohn felt that a hard-nosed veteran like Fleischer was needed to pull the studio into line. Fleischer recalled arriving in the middle of a sit-down strike that had already become costly, and he decided to call the organizers' bluff by threatening to close the place down. [25]

Fleischer told historian Joe Adamson, "I called all the [Screen Gems staff] people into the projection room and said, 'Now boys and girls, I'm very sorry that I can't raise your salaries. I don't know your abilities. But I will raise salaries when I find out you're [each] worth it. But you have to work here at least a few weeks.'"

According to Fleischer, it wasn't long before Pomerance arrived at the studio and was speaking in a threatening manner. Fleischer recalled him asking, "'Well, what are you going to do?' I said, 'I'm going to tell you to keep your mouth shut. And if you use any more language like that, I'm going to call the police,' and I reached for the phone." Pomerance backed down once he realized the Cohn brothers were sticking by Fleischer. "The next day [the staff] came in and everybody went to work." [26] Fleischer refused to kowtow, having lived through one long and ugly strike in Manhattan five years earlier.

Fleischer's reign at Screen Gems produced various odd one-shot cartoons including at least one close remake of a Fleischer Studio title: *Imagination* (1943) resembled *Raggedy Ann and Raggedy Andy* (1941). Unfortunately there was a marked clash between Fleischer's earthy East Coast gag sensibility, rusted on since the twenties, and the more cerebral approach of the artistically hungry team who desired the same creative freedom they had enjoyed under Tashlin. It was a classic example of a generation gap, and stylistically these young turks spoke a different language to a pioneer like Fleischer. Both sides would have to get used to each other.

During the Fleischer-Screen Gems era, some new voice artists were added to the talent pool. Another radio heavyweight began working in Columbia cartoons around the time of Frank Graham's ascendancy. Vaudeville veteran Harry Lang was, like Mel Blanc, a top choice of radio producers for zany stooge-comedy roles. Lang was heard in various Phantasy cartoons like two 1942 releases, *A Battle for a Bottle* and *Old Blackout Joe*. Lang remained at Columbia through Fleischer's reign and beyond; like Bletcher, Lang was also heard in MGM, Lantz, and Disney cartoons during the World War II years.

Harry Lang possessed an unusual trick voice, enabling him to do Donald Duck and various animal sound effects including a range of mewling felines: he had performed these voices in Hugh Harman's 1941 MGM cartoon *The Alley Cat*. Lang was a vocal ringer for Clarence Nash who was not only the genuine voice of Donald but who also excelled at feline sounds like those in *Donald's Lucky Day* (1939). In his twenties vaudeville heyday, Lang was most renowned as a dextrous specialty whistler, and he trilled musically for Screen Gems's later, short-lived canary star Flippy, who first appeared in 1945.

An expert dialectician, Lang's most distinguished performance for Screen Gems was in Hubley's serious anti-fascist cartoon *Song of Victory* (1942), in which he played the Hitleresque vulture. His Hitler imitation was also used in Disney's *Reason and Emotion* (1943), and, far more realistically, in the Treasury Department's powerful radio drama *Return to Berchtesgaden*. Lang had his share of Columbia clinkers however, including various dreary duds in the black and white Phantasy cartoons. One of these was the dire Fleischer story *As the Fly Flies* (1944), in which Lang played Professor Puzzlewitz, another doomed Screen Gems attempt at developing a starring character.

One singularly odd cartoon featuring Lang's voices was *Mr. Fore by Fore* (1944), a golfing story burdened by Screen Gems's two abiding problems: weak story structure and woeful comic timing. Sometimes a frantic chase in a Columbia cartoon would end with, say, a destructive crash gag which required zany Treg Brown-like audio effects. But more than once the accompanying Screen Gems sound effect was either inadequate or virtually non-existent, with the result that the animated gag limped to nothing. This left the audience cheated of comic impact; it was akin to a sneeze that didn't arrive.

Soon after Tashlin's brief but eventful reign ended in the summer of 1942, the talented story sketch artist John Fraser McLeish, another Disney striker who defected to Columbia as a story man, began acting in 1943 Screen Gems titles like *Professor Small and Mr. Tall* and *Willoughby's Magic Hat*. Beyond his revered artistic talents, McLeish, stagestruck since childhood, was blessed with a magnificently stentorian voice already recognizable from his time at Disney as the narrator of Jack Kinney's fine "How-To" sports cartoons featuring Goofy. Just twenty-six years old at this stage, the resonant McLeish sounded like a hammy, gin-soaked theatrical twice his age.

For Screen Gems McLeish wrote a Horatio Alger parody called "From Rags to Rags," which Hubley fashioned into a melodrama sendup, its final title being *The Rocky Road to Ruin* (1943). McLeish also narrated the cartoon in the John Barrymore-esque tones he deployed two years before at Warner Bros. for Chuck Jones's *The Dover Boys* (1942), a notable cartoon for which McLeish had toiled in character design and story. His involvement in that cartoon was undoubtedly why the Columbia entry seemed almost a so-so remake. McLeish voiced several other cartoons with Harry Lang, one of which, *The Herring Murder Mystery* (1943), directed by Dun Roman, remains a little known but bona fide absurdist classic and a parody of radio's *Information, Please.* We will meet the singular John McLeish again in the Disney studio chapter.

The Screen Gems directors, like their contemporaries at Schlesinger and MGM, occasionally hired extra radio actors to augment the voices of semi-regulars like Frank Graham, Harry Lang and John McLeish. Several female voices were supplied by preeminent radio actresses Lurene Tuttle and Ge Ge Pearson. Other versatile radio talents who enhanced the soundtracks of mid-forties Columbias included Patrick McGeehan in *Nursery Crimes* (1943), child actor Joey Pennario in *Wolf Chases Pigs* (1942), Byron Kane, the narrator of *Polly Wants a Doctor* (1944), Hanley Stafford, the voice of radio's Daddy Snooks and using the same flustered tones for a famished spider in *The Fly in the Ointment* (1943), and Grace Lenard as a slinky voice in *The Dream Kids* (1944). [27]

Talents from other fields were also employed for voices: nightclub mimic Dave Barry moved to the West Coast in December 1943 and signed with Columbia for cartoons. [28] Barry had recently worked for Fleischer Studios in Miami as one of the better Bluto voices, and was aware that Dave Fleischer was heading to Screen Gems. Barry was cast as all the crazy voices in *Tangled Travels* (1944). Another mimic with extensive stage and radio experience was Jerry Mann who in the early forties lived in Los Angeles before joining the touring company of *Oklahoma!* for a long stage run. Mann did several shorts for Columbia, including the parrot star of *Cholly Polly* (1942) and *Polly Wants a Doctor* (1944).

The fine thirties female vocal group The Rhythmettes, now named The Betty Allen Trio, improved two poor cartoons, *Nursery Crimes* (1943) and *Hot Foot Lights* (1945). The noted Calypso singer

Lance Pinard achieved minor celebrity as "Sir Lancelot" during the Latin "good neighbor" influx of World War II and appeared in some classic Val Lewton horror mysteries at RKO. He arranged and vocalized the catchy music for the decidedly bizarre pacifist cartoon *The Disillusioned Bluebird* (1944), the final Screen Gems cartoon produced by Fleischer.

Director Howard Swift was responsible for a short-lived, and rather lame, Li'l Abner series during Fleischer's stint as production head. In 1944, five cartoons based on Al Capp's then ten-year-old comic strip were released to very little enthusiasm. Swift spoke of the difficulty of animating this well-known newspaper character: "If you kept him the way Capp drew him, it was perfect. But the minute you got onto some strange pose he ceased to be Li'l Abner." Swift added, "I had the best voices I could get. I recorded them all over at Columbia's main lot. Lurene Tuttle was Mammy Yokum and Daisy Mae, and I forget the guy's name - he was called 'the Man of a Thousand Voices' in radio in those days - he did the voices of Abner and Pappy Yokum." [Swift was trying to recall Frank Graham's name; in fact Abner's vocal delivery seemed to differ from cartoon to cartoon, highlighting the director's palpably uncomfortable take on the character.] [29]

The end of a cartoon studio

During this period the Screen Gems management problems continued, with parent Columbia Pictures still justifiably concerned about the overall quality of the cartoon division's output. In weekly exhibitor reviews the Disney, MGM and Warner Bros. cartoons often received raves, but the Screen Gems product rarely achieved more than a rating of "fair." Fleischer recalled running Screen Gems for two years as a "pretty good" operation. "We made a series of the Fox and Crow, which was very successful. We tried a series with Li'l Abner, and that didn't seem to go." But Fleischer became a victim of studio politics when Leonard Picker was suddenly put in charge over him. [30]

As Fleischer told Joe Adamson, "According to my contract I was responsible [for Screen Gems], but [Len Picker] came in and started firing people as brazen as could be." It did Fleischer no good when he complained to Ben Kahane, "Jack Cohn's assistant," who revealed that Picker was the brother of the man who owned the powerful Loew's theatre circuit. That kind of fraternal nepotism no doubt reminded Dave of his old Fleischer Studio and familial battles with brother Max. "I said, okay I want out. So I got my royalties and signed out. Universal wanted to know if I could make a series of pictures." [31]

When Fleischer departed for Universal towards the end of 1943, following the clash with Picker, the Screen Gems cartoon studio experienced a revolving door of new producers. Beginning briefly under executive Albert Spar, the studio was next managed by live action shorts producer Hugh McCollum, a name familiar from the credits on *The Three Stooges* films. Finally, musical conductor Paul Worth took interim charge. All these Columbia-appointed executives were simply administrative heads, with no actual animation, story, timing or layout experience between any of them.

Howard Swift and Bob Wickersham, top animators who were appointed heads of creative control under McCollum, strove hard to improve the cartoons but the studio was just not in the same league as Disney, where these two men were first trained. The talent pool of story and gag specialists was emphatically below par when compared with the Warner Bros. scribes. None of the Disney studio luxuries of time spent revising weak stories or money spent on retakes was even considered. Swift noted, "If you rejected a story you were behind schedule. We were always running over the $25,000 per picture budget. Compared to Disney you couldn't shoot many tests. But the biggest problem we had at Screen Gems was stories." He recalled being assigned Fleischer's story idea *As The*

Fly Flies (1944): "[For that cartoon] I got a terrible story that wasn't funny." [32] And this happened with increasing regularity.

Finally, Swift noted, "Columbia wanted to get out of cartoons as producers, so they called Bob [Wickersham] and myself over to the main lot one day for a meeting, and they told us they were going to close the studio. They offered us a contract; we could form our own studio and they would do certain [distribution] things." [33] The animators, well aware that the budget they were being proffered was too low to do the job justice, declined the offer.

***

Some of the most interesting, albeit flawed, Columbia cartoons emerged in the final two years of operations. With Fleischer gone by early 1944, and abreast of the scuttlebutt regarding Columbia's plans, top Warner Bros. cartoon director Bob Clampett and his lay-out and story assistant Mike Sasanoff lobbied to take over Screen Gems. [34] Always creatively restless and ambitious, Clampett had already set up his own office on Sunset Boulevard. He claimed to have financing ready for future cartoons and, with television almost a reality, various concepts for that medium.

Clampett and Sasanoff met with Columbia's president Harry Cohn. But unbeknownst to Clampett, the hard-nosed Cohn had already checked their credentials with Leon Schlesinger. Clampett later learned that savvy old Schlesinger had plans of his own. Schlesinger informed Cohn, via Leonard Picker, that Clampett was still under exclusive contract to him. He effectively pulled the rug out from Clampett's lofty producer-director ambitions. [35]

As events transpired, on 1 July 1944 Schlesinger sold his cartoon studio to Warner Bros. on the proviso that all its top creative talents - including, of course, Bob Clampett - would remain working there. Another stipulation stated that Schlesinger could not produce any competing cartoons for a period of five years.

Soon afterwards, though, with former head-of-trailers Edward Selzer ensconced as the Warner Bros. Cartoons' executive in charge, Schlesinger's right-hand man Raymond Katz took over at Screen Gems. The now retired Schlesinger was almost certainly a silent partner: Katz was, after all, Schlesinger's long-time head of business affairs as well as, conveniently, being his brother-in-law.

Meanwhile Clampett, restless about his future and as driven as ever, obtained a release from his Warner Bros. contract in the spring of 1945. Arthur Davis, who would take over Clampett's unit at Warners, saw this move as inevitable, noting that Clampett and Selzer, the new Warner Cartoons boss, had constantly clashed since the take-over the previous year. [36] Their battle of wills was also noted by director Friz Freleng and former Clampett animator Bill Melendez, the latter stating, "When Eddie took over, Bob's days were numbered." [37]

Katz now sensed an opportunity to both mollify Clampett and ensure that his new Screen Gems setup had a proven talent with whom he was familiar. So he asked the now-at-liberty Clampett aboard. Clampett's position would be overall "creative head" in charge of story, at double his old Warner Bros. salary. Clampett, in the process of setting up his own shop for the coming of television, took the Screen Gems job. It was, as he saw it, an "interim thing…a stopgap," and he brought veteran gag man Cal Howard into Columbia's animation setup. Clampett supervised four cartoons and was, as he put it, "all over all the stories and units." [38]

The Katz cartoons, described by Leonard Maltin as "pale carbons of the Warner Bros. shorts," [39] are filled with violent and bizarre slapstick gags and furious chases. They were - far more so than Tex Avery's MGM titles - virtual parodies of the Hollywood cartoon, reflecting the wild comedy minds of head story man Howard, director Marcus and Clampett himself. But there was an intangible weakness to the films. The studio obviously lacked an overall "crap detector," with Katz apparently holding no sway. It was as though a lack of artistic discipline had infected the filmmakers en masse. A budgetary measure had Cal Howard supplying some voices, with most others by radio man Bill Shaw and mimics like Dave Barry or Walter Craig. A further budget constraint meant that the final titles released under the Phantasy banner, while finally abandoning black-and-white, were filmed in the noticeably cheaper Cinecolor process.

Katz poached gagman Dave Monahan from Warner Bros. while former Lantz director Alex Lovy replaced Swift as head of one Screen Gems unit. The cartoons remained childishly silly, wildly inconsistent, eccentrically timed, and occasionally funny, with titles like *Up n'Atom, Cockatoos for Two, Swiss Tease* and *Boston Beanie*. [40] Those cartoons, released in 1947, were the four personally overseen by Clampett during his brief stay, and the voices he used occasionally echoed the zany qualities of his recent Warner cartoons. They included his protégé Stan Freberg who was prominent in a few, even reprising his fine Peter Lorre imitation for *Cockatoos*. [41]

Clampett didn't last long: once he was set up at Screen Gems he instantly felt frustrated. He sensed that the studio lacked the free-wheeling atmosphere of Schlesinger's old plant. He recalled, "Even the building seemed confining; all the rooms seemed small, with low ceilings. You felt hemmed in." [42] He pined for the freedom of his old Schlesinger gig, finding communication difficult in the new surroundings: "Their whole approach to animation, and gags, and stories, everything was so different." Certainly, some eccentric entries like *Kongo Roo* (1946) and *Loco Lobo* (1947) simply don't work, with clunky gag timing and very weak comedy. Clampett noted that some of the choices for voice artists were not the type of casting decisions he would have made. He left Screen Gems, dissatisfied, after several months,* just as Schlesinger's old secretarial assistant Henry Binder returned from war service. Binder, who possessed story and comedic talent himself, took over Clampett's supervisory role. [43]

* Clampett next freelanced, producing one final theatrical cartoon in late 1946 before achieving early TV renown via his famous puppet series *Time for Beany* on station KTLA. Republic Pictures president Herbert J. Yates invited Clampett to make a cartoon to demonstrate his studio's new Trucolor process. But Yates, who lacked the distribution clout of the majors, held little hope for an ongoing animated series. Clampett produced a typically quirky one-shot, *It's a Grand Old Nag*, released in 1947. It was budgeted at $20,000. He received uncredited story help from old Warner Bros. gag men Mike Maltese and Ted Pierce, who moonlighted for Clampett. [44] Stan Freberg receives a "Voice Characterization" credit, most unusual for that period. He played the lead character Charley Horse; uncredited performers Dave Barry, as Russian movie director "Gregory Retake," and the Betty Allen vocal trio, completed the film's voice cast. Although he was contracted to produce three more cartoons for Yates, Clampett chose to bow out.

Always a low budget film studio, Republic had one final stab at animation with the release of four *Jerky Journeys*, made with a team of moonlighting animation veterans. These were cheaply drawn but witty sendups of the short travelogue genre. Released between 1948-49, they were the brainchild of radio comedy writer Leonard L. Levinson who originated *The Great Gildersleeve* on NBC in 1941. To narrate these novelties he hired a radio talent he knew could deliver. Frank Nelson, the hilariously sarcastic floorwalker on Jack Benny's radio show, was a potent scene stealer and did his usual standout job. One of the Jerky Journeys, *Bungle in the Jungle*, is said to feature the voice of New York actor Kenny Delmar who created the classic radio character Senator Claghorn. This would indicate that Delmar recorded Levinson's cartoon either from New York or while in Hollywood shooting the Claghorn comedy feature *It's a Joke Son!* Of the four Jerky Journeys, only one, *The Three Minnies*, is known to survive.

An occasional Screen Gems one-off by directors Alex Lovy or Sid Marcus attempted to be different. *Flora* (1948) was a unique if lacklustre take-off of 20th Century-Fox's moody 1944 detective thriller *Laura*. But while the Screen Gems staff revelled in their relative freedom to once again experiment, many of these odder cartoons simply appeared self-indulgent to the audience: story man Dave Monahan recalled, "We did a couple of things that weren't zany, they were more cerebral. [*Flora*] was way ahead of its time, actually; it went over everybody's head. It laid a bomb. [But] we thought it was funny as hell."[45] The cartoon was narrated by the distinctive baritone voice of Gerald Mohr, later CBS radio's Philip Marlowe, in doom-laden film noir style. Mohr was starring in Columbia's B-unit *Lone Wolf* crime film series at the time.

The regular voices changed in the final Columbia cartoons. Regrettably, Frank Graham was unable to voice the last two Fox and Crow entries, *Tooth or Consequences* (1947) and *Grape Nutty* (1949) and the roles were handled by two others. These two cartoons suffered from a distilling of the Fox and Crow's personalities, and the lack of Graham's deeper acting talent: the effete Fox became a simple "dolt" voice, while the Crow was now just another gruff "mug."

Jack Mather, long-time voice of *The Cisco Kid* on the Mutual network, was another of several unsung but versatile actors in Hollywood cartoons of the forties. A prime contributor to Paramount's *Speaking of Animals* shorts, he also worked for Disney and Lantz, notably as the voice of Wally Walrus. In these late Screen Gems entries, Mather provided voices for cartoons like the lame Western spoof *Lo, the Poor Buffal* (1948) and a final spot gag entry *Short Snorts on Sports* (1948) featuring narration by Bing Crosby's long-time radio announcer Ken Carpenter. It was the first and only Columbia cartoon with future voice-giant Daws Butler.

The Katz-Binder cartoons went through the production mill rapidly. The animation staff had begun departing in late 1946, and the soundtrack dubbing and orchestra scoring were finished early the next year. The backlog meant that Columbia was still releasing these strange cartoons through mid-1949, some three years after the Screen Gems artists had disbanded upon completion of the contract. By that point Columbia Pictures sold its Seward Street animation building to Walter Lantz. Columbia's management firmed a new deal to release Stephen Bosustow's UPA-produced cartoons in a series to be branded "Jolly Frolics," starting with a revamped John Hubley rendering of old Screen Gems standbys, the Fox and the Crow.

PHOTOS

Alan Reed 1950s, voices for Disney, UPA

Cookie Bowers, many Fleischer characters, 1930s

COMEDY COMMANDO
Danny Webb (to give him the
nickname which General
Eisenhower himself conferred
upon him) bows a week from
today as emcee of WG⁻ ˙
"Guess Who?" His Pop and
Mom, Mr. and Mrs. Herman
Weberman, reside at 474
Brooklyn Ave.

DANNY WEBB, countless voices 1937-41 for Warner Bros.,
Screen Gems, Lantz, Disney, MGM

Dick Nelson, voices for Lantz, MGM, Warner Bros., 1939-55

Elvia Allman (Grandma in Red Hot Riding Hood),
also Disney, Warners, MGM, Columbia

Gil Warren, narrator Warner Bros., MGM

Gus Wicke voice of Bluto 1935-38, Fleischer

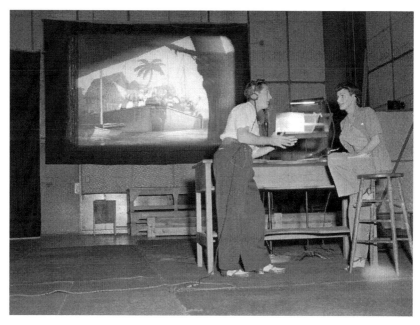

Jack Mercer & Margie Hines, post-dubbing, 1939, Fleischer Studios, Miami
(Courtesy, Jerry Beck)

Jack Mercer (Popeye), Mae Questel (Olive),
Jackson Beck (Bluto), Famous Studios

Jerry Mann, voices for MGM, Screen Gems

June Foray memorial art (Courtesy, ASIFA 2017)

June Foray, voices for Warner Bros., Disney, MGM, Lantz

Kent Rogers, voices and impressions for Warner Bros.,
Lantz, Screen Gems, MGM, Speaking of Animals

Marcellite Garner, the voice of Minnie Mouse for Disney

Mel Blanc , Warner Bros. publicity, 1940s

Mel Blanc photo, c.1960

Pat McGeehan, Doggone Tired, The Cat That Hated People, MGM, 1943-52

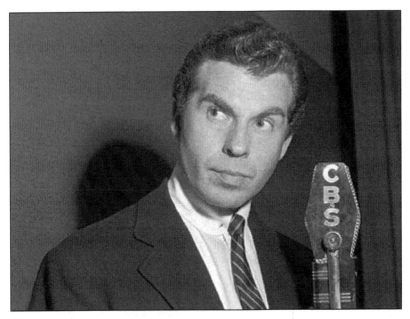

Paul Frees, narration for TV of Tomorrow, The Farm of Tomorrow,
Homesteader Droopy, MGM

Pinto Colvig - Disney Legend. Voice of Goofy for Disney, also Warner
Bros., Columbia, MGM, Fleischer Studios, Lantz, 1930-67

Sara Berner, voices for Warner Bros., MGM, Screen Gems, Lantz, Disney,
Speaking of Animals, Puppetoons

FRED (TEX) AVERY has joined Metro as director of a new
cartoon unit. Avery created the character, "Bugs Bunny," and
was the first to use off-screen narration in cartoons. Some of his
cartoons are "The Wild Hare" and "Cross-Country Detours."

Tex Avery in 1941 at MGM, many voices in his and
other's cartoons (Lantz, Warner Bros., MGM)

The Mary Kaye Trio, voices in Magical Maestro for MGM, 1952

ALLAN WATSON
BARITONE

CREDITS: Inglewood Park Concert, Hollywood Bowl, Forest Lawn, Featured with Choir of 500 in World Wide Broadcast, Soloist with Vancouver Symphony, 6 YEARS RADIO EXPERIENCE—10 YEARS SCREEN.

VOICE RANGE 2½ Octaves E to A

FOREIGN LANGUAGES: German, Italian, French. OPERA — CLASSICAL — BALLADS — LIEDER — ORATORIO.

DIALECTS: English, Scotch.

GILBERT & SULLIVAN OPERA—CHARACTER & COMEDY

ALLAN WATSON

Allan Watson, baritone in Silly Symphonies, Mintz, MGM, Lantz

ARTHUR Q. BRYAN
•

RADIO: Fibber McGee and Molly, Richard Diamond.

VIDEO: Hank McCune.

MANAGEMENT

Mel Shauer   •   CR-1-1103

Height: 5'7", Weight: 20 lbs. Age: 51. Hair: Blonde Complexion: Fair. Eyes Brown.

Arthur Q. Bryan, alias Elmer Fudd

Bea Benaderet, voices for Warner Bros., 1940s-50s

Ben (Bugs) Hardaway, Woody Woodpecker's voice 1943-49

Bernard Brown, the early voices of Bosko and Buddy, Warner Bros.

Bill Roberts, amphibian singer in Warner Bros.'
One Froggy Evening (Hello Ma Baby) (Courtesy, Jerry Beck)

Bill Thompson, Voice of Droopy, MGM, also Disney, Warner, Lantz

Billy Bletcher, Voices for Disney, MGM,
Warner, Screen Gems, UPA, Lantz, Puppetoons

COLLEEN COLLINS
●

RADIO: Jimmy Durante, Baby Snooks, Life of Riley, Stars Over Holly-
         wood, Commercials and spots (by the carload!), Suspense,
         Escape, Cisco.

SCREEN: Voices: for Universal, 20th Century-Fox, MGM, Disney, Gold-
         wyn, etc.

STAGE: Four years in clubs and theatres as Impressionist.

VIDEO: Those Housewife Commercials, "Gigi," in Gigi and Jock,
         United TV.

AFRA-SAG   HI 0101

Voice range: 7-50

Colleen Collins, voices for MGM, Lantz cartoons

DANNY WEBB

•

```
KEEP 'EM ALIVE, Columbia
LAUGH IT OFF, Universal
Lead in A STAR IS SHORN
    Columbia Short
```

Artists Bureau, Inc.
Lou Weber, Associate
HO-6951

Danny Webb, 1939, prolific cartoon voice, 1937-41

Danny Webb

DAVE WEBER
WO-62992   HE-5631
•

Dialect Voices on
Mintz and Schlessinger Cartoons
Featured Radio Comedian on:
"Burns and Allen", "Ken Murray",
"Milton Berle", "Funfare"
Political Voices on "March of Time"

**M. D. Howe Booking
Agency, Inc.**
Howard Bruce, Associate

Dave Weber, April 1937, before he became Danny Webb.

DAWS BUTLER
•

RADIO: Suspense, The Whistler, Dr. Christian,

FILM   MGM, UPA, APEX. Courtney Prods., Disney, Warner Bros.,
DUBBING: Columbia, 5 Star Prods.

VIDEO: "Beany" on Time for Beany (KTLA), Yer Ole Buddy (KTLA),
Featured on recordings: Belda, Talking Komics, Standard Radio
Transcriptions.

Voice range: 6-80

AFRA-SAG
AGVA
HI 0101

Height: 5'2", Weight: 150
lbs. Age: 33. Complexion:
Ruddy. Eyes: Grey.

Daws Butler 1949 photo, casting book. Voices for MGM,
Warner Bros., UPA, Lantz, Speaking of Animals.

Daws Butler and June Foray about to
enter a studio (Courtesy, Corey Burton)

Daws Butler, June Foray and Stan Freberg, Capitol Records

Daws Butler, voices for MGM, Warner, Lantz,
UPA, Hanna-Barbera, Jay Ward

Hair Bear · Quisp · The Sun · Funky Phantom · Capt. Skyhook · Bumble · Lambsy
Chilly Willy · Cap'n Crunch · Loopy-de-Loop · Baba Looey · Quick-Draw McGraw
Mr. Jinks · Snagglepuss · Dixie · Yogi Bear · Fibber Fox · Augie Doggie
Henry Orbit · Huckleberry Hound · Hokey Wolf · Blabber Mouse · Super Snooper
Lippy the Lion · Elroy · Cogswell · Wally Gator · Peter Potamus

Daws Butler's calling card 1970 (Courtesy, Daws Butler)

DICK NELSON

CREDITS: "Lead" in Your Neighbors—the Haines, Brenthouse, Signal Carnival, Dr. Christian, Irene Rich, Those We Love, Hedda Hopper's Hollywood, This Is the Show, Our Half Hour.

VOICE RANGE 15 - 45

DIALECTS: Irish, English, Scotch, Southern, Rural, Tough.

SPECIALTIES: Leads, juveniles, professionals, mugs.

DICK NELSON
HOllywood 6211 (Call Club)

Dick Nelson, voices for Lantz, MGM, Warner Bros., 1939-55

Earle Hodgins, Warner cartoons, 1935-37

Eddie Beal, vocal coach, arranger, accompanist.

Eddie Beal, arranged music for Warner cartoons Coal Black, Tin Pan Alley
Cats, Goldliocks and the Jivin' Bears, 1941-44

ELMORE VINCENT
•

RADIO: Lum and Abner, Maisie, Hopalong Cassidy, Smilin' Ed, "Fish-face" on NBC for five years.

STAGE: Busiest banquet entertainer in California. Lots of vaude and legit.

VIDEO: Smilin' Ed Gang, Spade Cooley, others.

AFRA-AEA
AGVA
•
HI 0101

Voice range: Middle age to old man.
Sing popular and western
MANAGEMENT
Lee Stewart (Pictures)   •   CR.-4-6123

Height: 5'11".
lbs. Age: 42.
Complexion: T.
Grey.

Elmore Vincent, MGM Cartoons

Fleischer Studios voices Jack Mercer, Margie Hines and
Pinto Colvig in Miami, 1939

The Four Blackbirds (CIRCA 1934) (L-R) David Patillo, Geraldine Harris, Leroy Hurte w/guitar (sitting) Richard Davis.

Four Blackbirds quartet, MGM, Warner Bros., Disney, Mintz cartoons

FRANK GRAHAM

THE CBS "ONE MAN THEATRE"

Over 400 Broadcasts of "Nightcap Yarns"

FRANK GRAHAM
HI. 0705—HO. 1212

Frank Graham, multiple voices for MGM, Disney,
Screen Gems, Warner Bros.

Hans Conried, voices for MGM, Disney,
Lantz, UPA (Courtesy, Trilby Conried)

HARRY LANG

CREDITS: Good News, Abbott & Costello, Big Town, I Want A Divorce, Joe Penner, Bob Benchley, Al Pearce, Irene Rich, Signal Carnival, Texaco Star Theatre, Jack Haley, Al Jolson, Grouch Club, True Story, Hall of Fun, Arch Oboler, Burns & Allen, Hedda Hopper's Hollywood.

DIALECTS: Mexican, Italian, French, Greek, Dutch, English, Swedish, Negro, Southern, Irish, Eskimo, Hillbilly, Russian, German, Scotch, Rural, Bronx, Western, Mid Western, Cockney, Chinese, Tough, Brooklyn, Canuck, Japanese, Jewish, Polish, Indian, Continental, New England.

SPECIALTIES: Professionals, old men, mugs, barkers, all types comedy and character dialects, Donald Duck and whistling.

Harry Lang, voices for MGM, Disney, Lantz

HARRY STANTON

SINGER • ACTOR

BASSO

CREDITS: SIGNATURE ANNOUNCER ON RUDY VALLEE SEALTEST SHOW. SINGING: Signaleers Quartette-Signal Carnival, Good News Choir—3 years, Soloist with Meredith Wilson 6 months on Signal Carnival, also with Gordon Jenkins. Solo Guest Artist 4 appearances Inglewood Park Concert. Basso with King's Men on Rudy Vallee Sealtest Show, 6 weeks with Kostelanetz—Tune Up Time. ACTING: Good News, Sealtest, Tune Up Time.

DIALECTS: Hillbilly, Western, Rural, Southern.

SPECIALTIES: Romantic leads, popular songs to grand opera. Professionals, heavies, goofy heavies. SING IN FRENCH, ITALIAN, GERMAN.

HARRY STANTON
HOllywood 6211

Harry Stanton, bass baritone voice in many cartoons, narration sung in Abdul the Bulbul Ameer

Jack Mather and Harry Lang - radio co-stars. Both did cartoons for Lantz, MGM, Disney (Courtesy, Jerry Haendiges)

Jack Mather, voice of Wally Walrus, also MGM, Disney,
UPA, Speaking of Animals, Puppetoons

JACK MATHER

RADIO—STAGE—SCREEN

JACK MATHER
HOllywood 6211 (Call Club)

Jack Mather, voices for Disney, Lantz, Screen Gems,
Speaking of Animals, Puppetoons

JACKIE MORROW
Height 5½ Inches

STAGE   SCREEN   RADIO
Rides   Dances   Sings   Bug
Bit with lines in "DINKY," Warners
"THE LITTLE MINISTER," R.K.O.; "RECKLESS," M.G.M.
"FATHER BROWN DETECTIVE," Paramount
Winner over Fifty Entrants in Joe Penner Impersonation Contest, Paramount Theatre
Synchronizes for "BUDDY" in the Animated Cartoons of "Buddy and Cookie" Series, Warner Relea
Official Master of Ceremonies for District No. 17, American Legion

Jackie Morrow, the final voice of Buddy, Warner Bros. 1934-35

JACKSON BECK

JACKSON BECK, voice of Bluto for Famous Studios, 1943-63

James Macdonald, Disney studio sound effects,
A voice for Mickey Mouse from 1946

Joe Dougherty, the original Porky Pig voice, 1934-37

John McLeish, Voices for Disney, Warner Bros., Screen Gems

JOHN T. SMITH

●

RADIO: Suspense, Whistler, Cisco. Red Ryder, Dick Haymes, Hollywood Calling, Phillip Marlowe, Hour of St. Francis. All Star Western Theatre, Conquest. News Commenator five years.

SCREEN: George O'Hanlon's Behind the 8 Ball (Warner Bros.), Bugs Bunny Cartoons (Warner Bros.), Jerry Fairbank's Speaking of Animals two years voices (Apex Films).

STAGE: Stock, Bainbridge Players, Vaudeville, MC and Comedian, My God!

VIDEO: Armchair Detective, Yer Ol' Buddy, Clyde McCoy Show.

Voice range: 35-60
MANAGEMENT
Douglas Aylesworth   ●   CR-5-8295

AFRA-SAG

Height: 6'1". Weight: 2
lbs. Age: 33. Hair: Brow
Complexion: Fair. Eyes: Blu

John T. Smith, voices for Speaking of Animals,
UPA, Warner Bros. (1948-54)

Johnny Murray, voice of Merrie Melodies
and Bosko, 1931-33, also MGM

June Foray 1960s calling card (Courtesy, June Foray 1973)

KENT ROGERS
GL. 6966

KENT ROGERS

ACTOR - SINGER

CREDITS: Silver Theatre, Dr. Christian, Rudy Vallee, Signal Carnival, Your Neighbors—The Haines, Hedda Hopper's Hollywood. **Five years of Network Shows. Lead opposite Linda Darnell on Silver Theatre.** Tenor.

VOICE RANGE 16 - 60 (Characters)

DIALECTS: Brooklyn, Hillbilly, Mid-western, Southern, Tough, Western, English, Cockney, Irish, Scotch, French, German, Italian, Jewish, Spanish, Chinese.

TYPES: Adolescents, Juveniles, Leads, Professionals, Old Men, Mugs, Neurotics, Fast Talkers, Impersonators, Comedy and Incidental Songs.

SPECIALTIES: Semi-classic to Popular Songs, Double Talk, Impersonations of 35 Stars and other Celebrities.

Kent Rogers, voices and impressions for Lantz,
MGM, Warner Bros., Screen Gems, 1939-44

DIALOGUE FOR PETERKIN   *SCRAMBLED EGGS*

Production #984

P 1   Boo!

P 2   Ad Lib Laughter. About 30 ft.

P 3   (Sore) Listen to all that Bragging! Counting their chickens before they're hatched! I wonder what they'd say if it all turned out different. Gee! Would their faces be red . . . if it didn't turn out as they expect . . . . if . . . if the eggs were changed (Giggle) I got an idea!

P 4   Ho Ho Ho And now I can play my flute!

P 5   Whassamatter, babies?

P 6   If I take care of you, will you be quiet?

P 7   (Exhausted) Alright! Alright! I'll get your mamas back, and let them take care of you. This is too much for me.

P 8   (Excitedly) It's a mistake! It's a mistake! You'd better get your wives and hurry home! Somebody mixed the eggs up and *THATS WHY YOU GOT THE* wrong children! (Pause)

But I fixed everything. I straightened it all out by myself.

P 9   Oh, some practical joker, I guess . . mebbe it was the squirrels!

OWL   DAVE   Whoooo?

Pete   Er. . ah .. well, maybe the chipmunks!

OWL   DAVE   Whooooo?

Pete   Well, it er ah it, it, . . .

P 10   It. . er . . it . . it was . . .

1st Bird   IT WAS YOU!

2nd Bird   Yeah, it was Peterkin! Let's teach him a lesson!

Crowd   Let's get him! Don't let him get away! The Rascal! After him, boys, etc.

P 11 (Pete)   That's positively the last prank I'm gonna play . . . Until the next time!

Lantz cartoon dialogue 1939, Scrambled Eggs page 1

DIALOGUE FOR BABY BIRDS

Production #994

C 1	VIC	(Baby Parrot)	Well, shiver me timbers! Polly wants a cracker! Auk!
C 2	VIC	(Parrot)	Auk! Pirates on the port bow. Au
C 3	DAVE	(Blackbird)	Hungry! Dear old Dixie! O'man seben! Right from Hebben!
C 4	CROWD	Crowd together start ad lib crying and yelling.	
C 5	MARGE	(Sissy Bird)	I'm hungry (extra print)
	SARA	(Mocking)	I'm thirsty! (extra print)
	TOGETHER	3 Birds	We're sleepy!
C 6	TOGETHER	(Crowd)	Yes!
C 7	MARGE	(Sissy)	Peterkin, I'm still hungry!
C 8	SARAH (2 extra prints)	(Sparrow)	Help, Help! Somebody save me! Help!
C 9	SARA	(Sparrow)	I want an ice cream cone!
C 10	SARA	(Sparrow)	I don't like vanilla . . Phooey!
C 11		(3 birds)	We want food! We want food! We want food! We want food!
C 12	MARGE	(Sissy bird)	I want a bath! I WANT SOME JELLYBEANS
C 13	DAVE	(Tough bird)	Hey, how about my diaper!
C 14	(extra print)	(3 birds)	We want better conditions! We want better conditions! We want better conditions!
C 15	(2 extra prints)	(3 birds)	Food! Food! We want food!
C 16	DAVE	(Tough Bird)	I repeat! Not about my diaper!
C 17	DAVE	(Tough bird, excited)	I want my diaper!
C 18	MARGE & DAVE	(Sissy) (Loud bellow)	Peterkin! I'm hungry. Peterkin, I'm hungry. Peterkin, I'm hungry. Do somet ing!

Lantz cartoon dialogue page 2, Scrambled Eggs, 1939

DIALOGUE FOR AD LIB CHARACTERS
Production #984

D1   Owl   Yawn . . . Humph! Peterkin!

D 2   Owl   I wonder what mischief he'll get

                     in today!

D 3   (Doc Stork
      Fred Allen) All the eggs will hatch in one hour.

Lantz cartoon dialogue page 3, Scrambled Eggs,
1939 (Courtesy, UCLA SC: Walter Lantz Collection)

LEONE LEDOUX

CREDITS: "Baby Dumpling" on The Blondie Show from beginning, Lux Radio Theatre, Texaco Star Theatre, Rudy Vallee, Lucky Strike. Transcriptions——Dubbing——Cartoons.

VOICE RANGE: From Baby Cries to 55

DIALECTS: Southern, Mexican, Spanish, Hillbilly, Rural, Western.

SPECIALTIES: Situation and gag comedy. Ingenues, leads, little boys, little girls, babies, baby cries, old women, doubles. SINGS IN CHARACTER VOICES OF ALL AGES. ALSO STRAIGHT LYRIC SOPRANO.

LEONE LEDOUX
CRestview 19682

Leone Ledoux, voices for Mintz, MGM, Disney, a voice for Scrappy,

Margaret Talbot, the original voice of Sniffles
(Courtesy, Jerry Beck via Rhys Talbot)

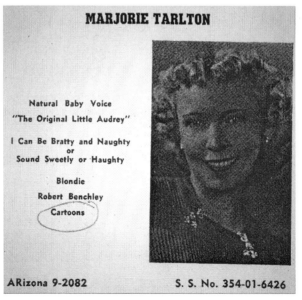

Marjorie Tarlton, voices for Warner Bros., Screen Gems,
Lantz, 1939-The second voice of Sniffles

Martha Wentworth (in The Witch's Tale)
voices for Disney, Warner Bros. MGM, UPA

MARTHA WENTWORTH

CREDITS: Lux Radio Theatre, Big Town, Joe Penner (3 years), Fibber McGee and Molly, Dr. Christian, First Nighter (13 weeks), Olsen and Johnson (13 weeks), Burns and Allen, Good News, Joe E. Brown.

ALL DIALECTS

SPECIALTIES: Old Women, Voice Matcher.

Martha Wentworth, voices for Disney, MGM, Warner Bros., UPA

Marvin_Miller, voices for UPA, Disney (1958 photo)

Mel Blanc recording a Bugs Bunny soundtrack

Mel Blanc 1940s

Mel Blanc as Bugs Bunny, 1940s

Mel Blanc as Pedro, NBC radio, 1940s
(Courtesy, Eddie Brandt's Saturday Matinee)

Mel Blanc publicity

Mel Blanc with author Keith Scott in Sydney, 1985

Mel Blanc's calling card (Courtesy, Mel Blanc, 1985)

MGM Cartoon scoring, 1939 for Swing Social, page 1

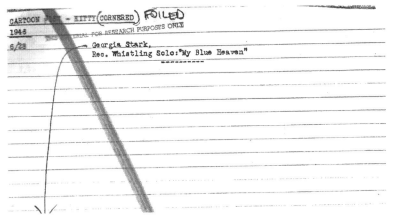

MGM Cartoon scoring, 1939 for Swing Social, page 2

MGM Music department talent req. for KITTY FOILED
(USC Cinema-TV Archives documents courtesy, Ned Comstock)

Paul Frees and June Foray outside studio (Courtesy, Corey Burton)

Paul Frees, 1970 voices for Disney,
MGM, UPA, Lantz, (Courtesy, Paul Frees)

PHIL KRAMER
HO. 1911

PHIL KRAMER

CREDITS: "Joe" in Ann of the Airlanes. Texaco Star Theatre,' Gulf Screen Guild Theatre. **Featured with Joe Penner,** "Hello Joe," **1936-38.** Featured Grouch Club, **as Willoughby,** 1938-1939, Burns and Allen, Al Pearce.

"Quote and Unquote"

DIALECTS: Bronx, Brooklyn, Hillbilly, Tough, Western, English, Cockney, Jewish.

TYPES: Mugs, Comedians.

Phil Kramer, voices for Warner Bros., Lantz, Famous Studios

Pinto Colvig and Goofy, his most famous voice

Robert Bruce, narrator Warner, Lantz cartoons,
1939-59 (Courtesy, Robert Bruce 1995)

ROBERT C. BRUCE JR.

ACTOR - ANNOUNCER

CREDITS: Dr. Christian, Hedda Hopper's Hollywood, Woodbury Playhouse, When Presses Roar, Second Wife,' Radic SCRIPTIONS: "Lead" in Ann of The Airlanes. Schlesinger, Katz and Universal cartoons. Commercial pictures and trailers.

VOICE RANGE 21 - 90

DIALECTS: Hillbilly, Mid Western, New England, Rural, Southern, Western, English, Cockney.

TYPES: Leads, professionals, old men, barkers, heavies, fast talkers.

SPECIALTIES: Old men, cartoon voices, narrations—commercial pictures and trailers.

ROBERT C. BRUCE, JR.
HOllywood 6211 (Call Club)

Robert Bruce, voices for Warner Bros., Lantz

ROBERT WINKLER

CREDITS: 3 Years signature voice and parts on Big Town, Lux Radio Theatre Screen Guild, Bob Hope Pepsodent Show, Al Jolson, Lifebuoy, Lucky Strike, Gene Autry, Amos & Andy, Hundreds of local broadcasts, radio transcriptions and recordings, Hollywood and Chicago. CARTOONS: Walt Disney, Voice of "Scrappy" (Charles Mintz), "Pete Parrot" (Schlesinger), "Hans and Fritz" (MGM). SCREEN: Established motion picture "Part" and "FEATURED" player.

VOICE RANGE 10 - 14

DIALECTS: Tough, Eastside, Rural, Hillbilly, Comedy English, Southern, Western.

Robert Winkler, a voice for Scrappy,
voices for Screen Gems, Warner Bros., MGM

SARA BERNER
●

RADIO: Star of Sara's Private Caper (NBC), "Mabel Flapsaddle" and "Gladys Zybisco" (Jack Benny), "Ingrid Mataratza" (Jimmy Durante), "Helen Wilson" (Amos 'n' Andy), "Crystalbelle," "Geneva Hafter" and "Aunt Nellie" (Beulah Show).

SCREEN: The Story of Molly X (U-I), City Across the River (U-I).

Voice Dubs—"Dancing Mouse" (Anchors Aweigh); "Talking Camel" (Road to Morocco), George Pal Puppetoons.

VIDEO: Ed Sullivan's Toast of the Town, Ted Mack's Original Amateur Hour (graduate guest), Buster Keaton Show, Tex Williams' Western Caravan.

MANAGEMENT

Milt Rosner   ●   CR-5-4042

AFRA-SAG
●

Sara Berner 1948 casting book

SARA BERNER

CREDITS: Eddie Cantor Texaco Show, Eddie Cantor Camel Show, Fibber McGee & Molly, Burns & Allen, Hedda Hopper's Hollywood, Joe Penner, Bob Benchley, Don Ameche Old Gold, It Happened in Hollywood.

VOICE RANGE Baby Cries to 60

DIALECTS: Hillbilly, Bronx, Brooklyn, Southern, Negro, Mid Western, Western, Mexican, English, Cockney, Irish, Scotch, Russian, Swedish, French, German, Viennese, Greek, Italian, Spanish, Japanese, Chinese.

SPECIALTIES: Telephone operator, Jewish women and children, impersonations, "Gloria Gluck" voices for Disney and Schlessinger. Impersonations, comedy, drama.

SARA BERNER
HOllywood 2686

Sara Berner, 1939 casting book

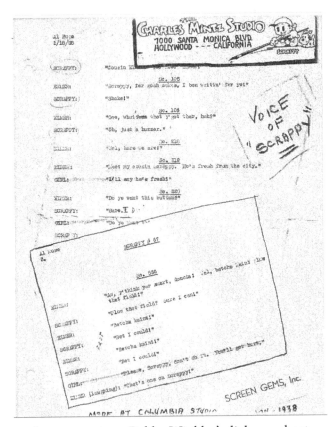

Scrappy cartoon Bobby Winkler's dialogue sheet
from 1938 (Courtesy, Bill Winkler)

Tex Avery, classic director (and voice of)
funny cartoons (Lantz, Warner Bros. MGM)

THE SPORTSMEN

CREDITS: (Current) Too Many Girls, RKO Radio; Melody Ranch,
Republic.

RADIO: Al Pearce Show, CBS; Don Ameche Variety Show,
NBC; Union Oil Show, NBC.

The Sportsmen Quartet - sang in many Warner Bros.
cartoons, also for MGM, Disney, Lantz

Thurl Ravenscroft (bass singer with Sportsmen Quartet and
The Mello Men quartet), voices for MGM, Warner Bros., Disney
(Courtesy, Thurl Ravenscroft 1995)

Verna Felton, Voices for Disney features

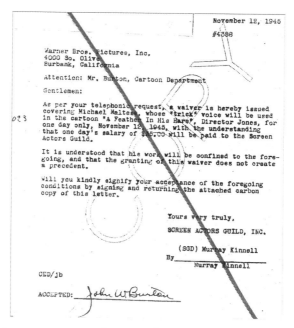

Warner Cartoons, correspondence with actor union SAG, 1945, regarding
A FEATHER IN HIS HARE

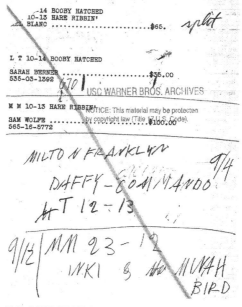

WB talent req. BOOBY HATCHED, HARE RIBBIN' dialogue, DAFFY
THE COMMANDO, INKI AND THE MYNAH BIRD, scoring

WARNER BROTHERS PICTURES, INC.
REQUISITION FOR EXTRA TALENT

FEBRUARY 14, 1942 ___193___

NUMBER OF PEOPLE	DESCRIPTION	DAY RATE
	WILLIAM DAYS	18.00
	MAXWELL SMITH	18.00
	JOHN RARIG	18.00
	THURL RAVINSCROFT	18.00
	PAUL TAYLOR	28.00
	"LOONEY TUNES" No. 778	
		65.00
	MEL BLANC	50.00
	PINTO COLVIG	25.00
	SARA BERNNER	
	"MERRIE MELODIE" No. 723	

WB talent req. for WACKY BLACKOUT
(singing chorus), DING DOG DADDY dialogue

WARNER BROTHERS PICTURES, INC.
REQUISITION FOR EXTRA TALENT

MAY 23, 1942 ___193___

NUMBER OF PEOPLE	DESCRIPTION	DAY RATE
	MEL BLANC	65.00
	MERRIE MELODIE No. 993	
	KENT ROGERS	35.00
	MERRIE MELODIE No. 915	

WB talent req. JACK WABBIT AND THE BEANSTALK (Blanc),
TORTOISE WINS BY A HARE (Rogers), dialogue

WARNER BROTHERS PICTURES, INC.		
REQUISITION FOR EXTRA TALENT		
1942		
WEEK ENDING DECEMBER 26TH		193

NUMBER OF PEOPLE	DESCRIPTION	DAY RATE
	MEL BLANC	$65.00
	CYRUS KENDALL	$50.00
	MERRIE MELODY #1-13	

WB talent req. MEATLESS FLYDAY dialogue

MAY 30, 1942		193

DESCRIPTION	DAY RATE	
MEL BLANC	65	00
EDWARD BEALE	30	00
VIVIANE DANDRIDGE	25	00
MILTON FRANKLYN	247	46
COLD BLACK & THE SEVEN DWARFS Merrie Melodie No. 827		
MILTON FRANKLYN	247	46
DOUBLE CHASER Merrie Melodie No. 607		

RNER BROS. ARCHIVES

WB talent req. Orchestra scoring and actor pickup lines, for COAL BLACK and scoring DOUBLE CHASER

October 28 _____ 19 44

NUMBER OF PEOPLE	DESCRIPTION	DAY RATE
	Richard Nelson	100.00
	Mel Blanc	75.00
		175.00
	MM 5-15 Racketeer Rabbit	

WB talent req. RACKETEER RABBIT dialogue

WILL WRIGHT
Citrus 12735

WILL WRIGHT

CREDITS: 12 YEARS ON THE MAJOR NETWORKS—40 WEEKS GANGBUSTERS—3 Seasons on Big Town, "Zeb" of Eb and Zeb—worked with Allen, Benny, Baker, Cantor, Pearce, Penner and Jolson.

VOICE RANGE 35 - 70

DIALECTS: Irish, Scotch, German, Italian, Spanish, Mexican, Rural, Southern, Mid Western, Negro, Cowboy Western, Mug, Chinese.

SPECIALTIES: Professionals, old men, leads, mugs, character and comedy dialects.

Will Wright, voices for Lantz, Disney

Chapter 4:

UPA Cartoon Voices, 1948-59

Far and away, the relatively small output of UPA theatrical cartoons was dominated by the voice of prominent comedy actor Jim Backus. He provided the bulk of the spoken dialogue over the studio's eleven-year theatrical run, most famously as their top star, "The Nearsighted Mister Magoo." But for the first few years the studio itself was the star, heralding a startling new wave of exciting design and visual inventiveness. UPA was embraced by a raft of film critics as representing a new cutting edge in the medium of animation, a stylistic break-through that momentarily seemed to infer that the previous decades of funny cartoons were now completely old hat and irrelevant. As with all new movements the studio's flame soon flickered, but the experimentation itself was a healthy trend in an industry that was always prone to safely repeating itself, which in fact UPA ended up doing.

BACKGROUND: Industrial Film & Poster Service and *Hell-bent for Election*

In 1943 with World War Two nearing the mid-point, Stephen Bosustow, formerly an artist at Disney and other cartoon studios, was approached at one of his sketching classes by a student look-ing to make a slide film on safety in shipyards. Bosustow agreed to produce the film with two ex-Disney design specialists, Zachary Schwartz and Dave Hilberman. The result was a filmstrip, *Sparks and Chips Get the Blitz*, and it led to the three associates forming

Industrial Film & Poster Service later that year. They quickly got a job offer in early 1944.

The United Auto Workers wanted a film to aid President Franklin D. Roosevelt's re-election campaign for an unprecedented fourth term. Art director Schwartz enticed the noted Warner Bros. cartoon director Chuck Jones to supervise the project at night, after his workdays at the Leon Schlesinger studio. Jones had recently been singled out for his use of striking designs and backgrounds in his Warner cartoons like *The Dover Boys* (1942) and *The Aristo Cat* (1943).

The film that resulted was *Hell-bent for Election* (1944) and while it resembled a Hollywood cartoon of the period, it had some unique streamlining qualities which hinted at what was to come. The more adult and overtly political nature of the material was certainly a change from zany animals. The soundtrack featured vocals by radio's Sportsmen quartet with narration by prominent actor-announcer Frank Graham, already well regarded in animation circles for his commentary work in both training and entertainment films for Disney, MGM and elsewhere.

Hell-bent was a success for the small company, and the artists quickly received projects for both the U.S. Army, including the series *A Few Quick Facts*, and the U.S. Navy which commissioned sixteen short films on aspects of flight safety between 1945-47. Now feeling more confident, the artists became bolder in design and layout, experimenting visually with each new assignment, including the various training films.

Bosustow was essentially the business head for Industrial Film and from the start he left the creative decisions to his talented staff. John Hubley was the earliest director. An unusually strong personality, "Hub" was the prime mover in the push to expand and experiment away from the accepted mode of theatrical cartoons. He was assisted by layout artist Zack Schwartz, animator Bill Hurtz and background painter Paul Julian. For Hubley this was like revisiting

Screen Gems in its brief moment of artistic freedom under Frank Tashlin's reign.

According to design artist Al Shean, Hubley also desired a new approach to voices, with a vastly more subtle style of dialogue for these cartoons. As Shean recalled, "He adamantly didn't want Mel Blanc, that was for sure!" [1] The navy cartoons were a potpourri of modern graphic techniques and animation stylings, and the voices hired included a blend of radio and theatre names like Morris Carnovsky, Herman Waldman, Charles Tannen, Howard Duff (radio's "Sam Spade") and Bill Conrad, later famous in TV cartoons for narrating the adventures of *Rocky & Bullwinkle.* [2]

From 1946 Industrial Film & Poster was renamed United Productions of America, shortened evermore to UPA, and Bosustow soon bought out the other partners. Hilberman and Schwartz relocated to New York. Hubley was appointed creative director. That year, their old client United Auto Workers commissioned a film to promote racial harmony and the result was *Brotherhood of Man*, directed by Bobe Cannon and designed by Hubley. This too proved a notable success.

But by 1947, with the House Un-American Activities Committee (HUAC) hearings into subversive communist influence in the movie industry, things began changing. Increasing post-war production costs and the real fears of red-baiting and blacklisting by conservative industry forces were felt as UPA's work offers quickly dwindled and the government projects began to dry up. The freedoms the young team of rebellious artists had enjoyed would now have to be tempered by the reality of putting food on the table.

The UPA Cartoons

In early 1948 Bosustow cut a deal to produce theatrical shorts for Columbia Pictures release. Columbia had recently seen its old Screen Gems cartoon factory shut down for good. Hubley and his like-minded artists were, as ever, eager to get away from old-school cartoon animals which they had long disparaged. But to avoid instantly rocking the boat with their new distributor, they agreed to do three films starring old Columbia perennials the Fox and the Crow as the initial productions. Visually, the characters, still appearing in comic books, underwent a Hubley overhaul with animator Bobe Cannon drawing the model sheets. The first "UPA" cartoon, *Robin Hoodlum* (1948), was all wry understatement, a subtle air of British restraint, with theatre actors Arthur O'Connell, Peter Virgo and James O'Rear emoting in a new, deadpan style of cartoon voice for the Sherwood Forest outlaw band. ³

Hubley's open disdain for traditional types of theatrical cartoons notwithstanding, he panicked during production of his first Fox and Crow entry, when it was still known as "Nottingham on Rye." Simply put, it wasn't funny, and he knew it. He had to eat humble artistic pie as he requested advice and moonlight assistance from top practitioners of the zany cartoons he purported to despise. Those who pitched in to help included Warner Bros. directors Friz Freleng and Chuck Jones, and their great gag men Michael Maltese and Ted Pierce.

With the Columbia deal in place and steady work at last a reality, UPA moved into small but spacious modern headquarters in a specially designed and architecturally striking studio in Toluca Lake, just opposite the big Warner Bros. Burbank studio lot. Work continued on the new look Fox and Crow cartoons. A new animation writer, hired to assist Phil Eastman, was the multi-talented Bill Scott. Most of the crew knew him since the wartime era at the First Motion Picture Unit. Scott had recently completed a year at the Warner cartoon studio. As he saw it, "You didn't dare mention the work you did at Warner Bros." ⁴

The next film, *The Magic Fluke* (1949), resembled the older Screen Gems Fox and Crow, with John T. Smith replicating Frank Graham's gruff Crow character. Smith, whose first animation work was for the *Speaking of Animals* novelty shorts at Paramount, was an excellent voice actor. He would soon be a familiar presence in early fifties Warner Bros. cartoons playing a rich gallery of gravel-voiced bully boy losers. Around the time he recorded *Magic Fluke*, Smith also played the lead sailor McGinty in one of the UPA studio's last sponsored films for the U.S. Navy, *The Sailor and the Seagull*.

It was UPA's third commercial release, and the first made under the Jolly Frolics umbrella title, that changed everything for the brand-new studio. *The Ragtime Bear* (1949) was meant to kickstart the career of the titular banjo strumming grizzly, but a supporting character stole the picture, a crotchety and sight-impaired senior citizen named Magoo.

At first the character was envisioned as an irritating grouch, with a dash of W. C. Fieldsian obstinance. Hubley immediately knew that this character would require a highly distinctive voice. He turned to an old Army acquaintance, an actor named Jerry Hausner.

Hausner was a show biz veteran who was one of those jack-of-all-trades types, adaptable in many areas. After an early career in vaudeville, where he learned to do trick voices and noises from a ventriloquist, he was gainfully employed in Hollywood's booming radio industry. From 1937 Hausner had been a mainstay of countless dramatic shows, playing all manner of utility parts like elevator operators, clerks and crooks. He also featured in hundreds of comedy programs as wise-guys, comic whiners, and doing his famous schtick of accurately imitating a baby's cry which always garnered a huge studio audience laugh. He ended up performing these baby noises in a 1951 UPA cartoon, *Family Circus*.

Hausner enlisted in the Army in 1942, and his duties at Armed Forces Radio Service brought him into contact with the large band of cartoonists at the First Motion Picture Unit, the wartime animation shop housed at the Culver City studio of veteran comedy producer Hal Roach. This set up was formed to make effective Government training films, and it was where Hubley, Bill Hurtz and other future UPA staffers were toiling soon after war was declared.

In 1945 Hubley asked Hausner to be the lead voice in the second sponsored film for the Auto Workers union, *Brotherhood of Man*. Hubley and his actor friend remained in touch after that project. With the latest Columbia title ready for dialogue recording, Hubley phoned Hausner and arranged a meeting. From that point Hausner became a prized studio contact, noting "[Hubley] frequently consulted me about the casting of voices at UPA." Hausner's knowledge of the leading radio talent in Los Angeles would prove invaluable. [5]

For *The Ragtime Bear* project Hausner recalled Hubley asking him who he could recommend for the codger's voice, and who could, "above all, not sound like W. C. Fields! Jim Backus was my immediate choice. I played Waldo, Magoo's stupid nephew, so I was present at all the early recording sessions." [6] In mid-1946, Backus, a regular on Alan Young's network comedy program, had moved west from Manhattan when the series transplanted to Hollywood.

Jim Backus and Jerry Hausner were soon being booked together on various Pacific Coast comedy radio series. They were even regulars on *The Mel Blanc Show* at CBS in the 1946-47 radio season. Both Cleveland natives, they hit it off and enjoyed each other's company. Hausner considered Backus a charismatic and inventive actor with a finely honed comic sense. Even Hubley was a little intimidated at first by the confidently garrulous Backus.

Hubley quickly realized that actors preferred playing off one another, rather than emoting alone in an empty sound booth. Backus was a specialist comic actor, so he naturally improvised. Hausner noted, "I was his best audience, so after Hub showed us the storyboard and explained the action, we'd spend an hour enjoying ourselves, elaborating the simple lines that were written." He added that all the silly little song asides, mumbles and muttering that we now know as the essence of the Magoo character were ad-libbed by Backus on the spot. Hausner recalled Hubley doing something no other director had done in his experience: after the voice takes were completed, he encouraged them to do an improv version of the script, and Backus went creatively wild. [7]

The Ragtime Bear cartoon was a hit and inevitably Columbia pushed for a new series of Mister Magoo shorts. Hausner: "We were paid $50 each for the [first] session. It was announced there were to be five more to do that year. Naturally, Backus wanted more money. Hubley called me in despair. 'Backus is threatening to quit unless we give him more money.'" Hausner had to convince his colleague that there was no hidden pot of gold for these low-budget theatricals.

Instead, Backus settled for a screen credit - "Magoo's Voice, Jim Backus" - starting with the fourth cartoon in the series, *Trouble Indemnity* (1950). Hausner noted, "[That] appealed to him. His instinct was right. In the long run, it helped his career considerably." [8] The screen billing quickly gave Backus as much recognition as Mel Blanc. Audiences would soon begin to associate Backus, the distinctive actor they saw on TV in the sitcom *I Married Joan* and in serious movies like *Rebel Without a Cause* (1955) with the myopic little cartoon bumbler, but far from being a curse it actually served to stress his versatility. Twenty years later as a guest on TV's *Laugh-In* Backus was still doing the Magoo voice in a blackout skit.

Both actors were heard in virtually all the early Magoo cartoons. As seasoned actors, they soon sensed that Hubley was unique among directors. Hausner said, "We all felt that Hubley was a true genius with a clear vision of what he wanted on the screen." He described the director's recording sessions as "short. Everyone worked hard. No tedious, humiliating auditions for the actors. One of the early TV commercials Jim Backus and I voiced for Hub was 'It's a FOOR-RDDD!!' But no residuals in those days, and we wound up [again] with fifty bucks." [9]

Hausner and Backus even sold UPA a story which became the cartoon *Destination Magoo* (1954) after Warner Bros. gag veteran Ted Pierce did a polish. For this cartoon Backus also supplied an imitation of that grand old actor Lionel Barrymore. Following their early success, the Magoo theatrical cartoons were a Columbia staple, running for a decade.

When the restless Hubley left UPA in 1952, the Magoo series was already being directed by Pete Burness, a fine veteran animator who had been promoted. Hausner said Burness was "a kindly, quiet, patient man, and while he didn't have Hubley's flair, it was a pleasure to work with him." [10]

Burness's Magoo entries were attractively designed and often amusing, but Mister Magoo the character inevitably became over-exposed. His personality slowly shifted from the humorously cantankerous old coot to a far milder, good-humoured codger, and finally to an annoying senior citizen, with a too-repetitious series of predictable "near-sighted" gags. Film by film, the character morphed into one-dimensionality, and the old man became rather irritating. Those muttered asides, so unique in the early films, started to sound mechanical, essentially Magoo on autopilot. In today's much changed world, Magoo would have little chance of a revival: gags about visual impairment are perceived by some viewers as making light of a serious disability.

From the beginning, there was one unique quality to the studio's output, and that was the music for each cartoon. UPA was the only animation studio in the entire theatrical era without a contract musical director on staff. Instead, individual musicians were called in on a for-hire basis to compose the score for each cartoon. This ensured there was always a different feel to each short, and there were contributions from a wide range of musical talents. Everyone, from jazz names like Shorty Rogers to leading radio musicians like Lyn Murray to well-known film composers like David Raksin, undertook composing gigs for this suddenly prestigious cartoon studio. Various novelty music specialists who worked for UPA would graduate to long careers in television cartoons: Hoyt Curtin contributed mightily to Hanna-Barbera, while Dennis Farnon and Frank Comstock were later hired by Bill Scott for Jay Ward TV themes.

One interesting score came from jazz great Phil Moore, chosen to do the music for Hubley's final and greatest UPA cartoon, *Rooty Toot Toot* (1952). The idea had been suggested by Bill Scott who caught a performance of a new interpretive dance production while on a trip back East. [11] The show he attended was an adaptation of the famous folk song about the doomed romantic couple Frankie and Johnny.

The eventual cartoon would become a witty animated ballet against striking modern art, with solid but quirky animation that matched the unique design and score effectively. The soundtrack featured two singers from the fine vocal quartet The Mello Men singing special lyrics by Allen Alch, and band singer Annette Warren warbling three roles: as the narrator, Frankie and Nellie Bly, the vamp of the tale. The male group's leader was basso profundo Thurl Ravenscroft, who played Honest John the attorney, visually modelled by Hubley on vintage character actor Porter Hall. The quartet's excellent baritone Bill Lee was both Johnny and the closing singer. [12] This was a fine adult cartoon boasting wonderful design work by Paul Julian. It also benefited from the hiring of dancer Olga Lunick as the cartoon's "choreographer," performing Frankie's and other characters' movements for the animators' reference.

In all, some twenty-five well known musicians wrote scores for UPA. In its last year, as the studio wound down in 1959, Bosustow could only afford so much with the shrinking budgets so one late entry, *Gumshoe Magoo* (1958), was scored with licensed library cues (it also skimped on an extra actor by having Jim Backus perform the three male voices). Then, when AFM, the musicians' local union, went on strike, *Bwana Magoo* (1959) boasted a non-musical soundtrack fashioned by the three ex-Spike Jones band musicians who had taken jobs in UPA's editing room. Joe Siracusa, Earl Bennett and Roger Donley created from scratch a sound pattern of animal imitations and rhythmic jungle effects. [13]

In the early years as Mister Magoo was becoming an established star attraction, Backus performed more characters for UPA than is realized. He was the speaking voice of hero John Harvard in the melodrama parody *The Miner's Daughter* (1950) while John's singing was supplied by veteran basso Harry Stanton. That year Backus also played the lead politician in *The Popcorn Story*. In 1953 he voiced the main role in one of the studio's sponsored films, *Look Who's Driving*, commissioned by Aetna for the Drive Safely campaign.

Backus even provided some supporting voices in the minor series Pete Hothead for which Jerry Hausner voiced the lead role. One of the voices Backus contributed was a snooty floorwalker using his funny millionaire snob character, familiar as Hubert Updyke on radio's *Alan Young Show*, a character already used by Warner Bros. for Backus's first cartoon role of the extrovert Genie in a 1948 Bugs Bunny short, *A Lad in His Lamp*. He revived the voice yet again for UPA in *Magoo Slept Here* (1953). *

* Backus reprised the character in the sixties for the long-running *Gilligan's Island* TV sitcom. There, the hilariously upper-crust Hubert Updyke became, for a new generation, Thurston Howell the Third.

UPA also made various non-Magoo cartoons during the first several years of its Columbia deal. They were released under the Jolly Frolics banner through 1953 and continued to explore the newer type of representational animation, design stylization, the revolutionary use of screen space and other experiments. Some of these cartoons, beyond their always inventive visuals, do not revive well as entertainment, particularly the gentler ones directed by Bobe Cannon which at their worst can be dull and twee. Today they are best looked back on as products of an experimental interlude that mostly succeeded respectably, a well-intended achievement in what remained a commercial entertainment industry first and foremost.

The most famous of Cannon's UPA cartoons was *Gerald McBoing Boing* (1951), adapted from the best-selling children's record. This fine cartoon, which still appears visually striking in both animation movement and design, was narrated in rhyme by prominent radio actor-announcer Marvin Miller, who would become famous on television as Michael Anthony in the long-running anthology *The Millionaire*. A Chicago radio pioneer who moved to Hollywood in 1944, Miller's rich and flexible baritone voice was being heard in the fifties on weekly radio fare like *The Whistler* and *The Railroad Hour*, and his fine delivery fit well with the storytelling approach of many UPA entries.

Remarkably for a cartoon shop with just one viable star character in Mister Magoo, UPA was the first animation studio - aside from the uniquely one-off case of Mel Blanc at Warner Bros. - to begin giving on-screen credit to a range of voice talents, and Bosustow and directors like Bobe Cannon and Ted Parmelee deserve kudos for this policy shift.

Some examples: early on, Miller was afforded billing for *Gerald McBoing Boing* ("Story Told by Marvin Miller"), *The Oompahs* ("Narration, Marvin Miller," 1952) and *Willie the Kid* ("Voices by Marvin Miller, Marian Richman, Martha Wentworth,"1952). Also in 1952, the cartoon *Madeline* gave credit for "Narration, Gladys Holland" and the following year *The Emperor's New Clothes* lists "Voices, Hans Conried." *Little Boy with a Big Horn* (1953) proudly billed "Character Voices, John T. Smith and Marian Richman." Smith must have been delighted. He did several now-famous voices at Warner Bros. in this period with zero name credit. It was no wonder that actors respected the little studio "just by The Smokehouse restaurant."[14]

Miller continued to receive screen credit in entries like *Gerald McBoing Boing's Symphony* (1954) and *The Rise of Duton Lang* ("Narration and Voices, Marvin Miller," 1955), while *Ballet-Oop* (1954) and the two Christopher Crumpet entries each carry the credit, "Voices, Marvin Miller & Marian Richman" (1953 & 1955). By far the most famous voice UPA employed was accorded big billing in their serious animated adaptation of Edgar Allan Poe's *The Tell-Tale Heart* (1953): "As Narrated by James Mason." Bill Scott, who adapted the story with animator Fred Grable, recommended the choice of Mason, one of the most huskily distinctive voices ever heard in movies. [15] The saturnine British actor supplied a moody reading that was the perfect complement for the film's eerily gothic atmosphere.

Another famous voice, Harold Peary, was famous for his ten year run as radio's blustery windbag *The Great Gildersleeve*. For UPA his distinctive tones were heard in *Spare the Child* (1955) for which he received the billing "Narrator, Hal Peary." Jerry Hausner, the studio's long-time casting consultant, was rewarded with the credit "Voices, Jerry Hausner" in *Four Wheels No Brakes* (1955). Radio veteran Jack Mather had done many cartoons for Lantz and Paramount but until now, no credit. He finally received one as "Voice, Jack Mather" for his wry storytelling in UPA's *The Man on the Flying Trapeze* (1954). Teenage radio actress Anne Whitfield also got "Voice" credit for *Baby Boogie* (1955).

And yet, once this welcome trend in screen credit got underway from 1951, there remained as many UPA cartoons that failed to list any voice talents, which seems an odd inconsistency for a studio eager to hire so many fresh voices new to animation. There was no voice credit, for instance, on the studio's whimsical adaptation of humourist James Thurber's *The Unicorn in the Garden* (1953), with its subtle doubling of husband and psychiatrist by actor John Brown; he had earlier done the Brooklynese storyteller at MGM for Tex Avery's pun-fest *Symphony in Slang* (1951). It should be noted that in Brown's case he may have declined credit, because the "progressive" actor was at the time a HUAC victim and his once-prolific radio work was on the slide. The atmosphere of blacklist was so thick at that time in Hollywood that it could well be that the studio, with its many left of centre animators and writers, dared not credit one who had been "named."

Miriam Wolfe did a fine female character in *Stage Door Magoo* (1955) but was unbilled. Comedian Stan Freberg played the talking horse in *Giddyap* (1950) for director Art Babbitt but was not credited. Earlier, Freberg contributed all the voices in *Big Tim*, a fine industrial short made by UPA in 1948 demonstrating railroad safety. Walter Tetley was unnamed in *Georgie and the Dragon* (1951), for which he revived his old "child with the Scottish burr" heard in early Fred Allen radio shows, while actor Peter Leeds, one of Freberg's reliable stock company, missed out on screen credit for the Magoo cartoon *Safety Spin* (1953). Other deserving actors who lacked credit were the veteran deep voiced tough guy Billy Bletcher who played the canine's nemesis in the Magoo cartoon *The Dog Snatcher* (1952), Colleen Collins who voiced the snarky wife in *The Unicorn in the Garden* (1953), Isabel Randolph who recreated her famous radio role of Mrs. Uppington for the snooty society woman from *Hotsy Footsy* (1952), and session singer Gloria Wood who trilled the title role in *The Miner's Daughter* (1950). [16]

Those quibbles aside, the small UPA studio was indeed the first in cartoon history to finally give a range of important voice talents that much needed screen recognition in animated shorts. UPA finally reverted to crediting just Backus when the studio finally dropped all but the Magoo series in 1956. The final one-shot cartoon that year was *The Jaywalker*, for which director Bobe Cannon hired local Los Angeles TV weatherman Eugene Bollay as the sole voice. It was still another meek and mild character for Cannon, who much preferred the non-threatening to the raucous.

With some one-time voices, even this most progressive and for-ward-thinking of all the cartoon outfits wasn't beyond the oldest casting trick in animation, employing its own in-house talent. In the case of UPA, that talent was of high quality, with a writer like Bill Scott and a comic musician like Earl Bennett on staff. Both were skilled actor-comedians.

Since 1942, Scott had been acquainted with Hubley, Hurtz and many others at the First Motion Picture Unit. When he came to UPA he had a reputation as a solid writer and a witty gag cartoon-ist. In his late teens while in Denver, Scott drifted into local radio acting for which he possessed a natural gift playing multiple char-acters. Of radio drama Scott averred, "Great training. Lousy pay." He can be heard in small roles in early UPA cartoons like *Georgie and the Dragon* as well as two large parts in *Pete Hothead* (1952). Scott's best voice roles at UPA were in some of the industrial films he wrote, like the cancer awareness special *Man Alive!* and a film for the oil industry called *Man on the Land*. Typical of his modest nature, Scott simply said he did "a couple of fill-ins for UPA." [17] His major acting career would come a few years later when, as co-pro-ducer, he became the immortal TV voices of Bullwinkle, Peabody, Dudley Do-Right and a host of others for the legendary Jay Ward.

Earl Bennett had been with the famous Spike Jones comedy music ensemble for several years. When musician Joe Siracusa took over the UPA editorial department in 1955, he asked his former Jones band colleagues, from Bennett to Roger Donley to Skip Craig, to join him. Each of them found they possessed a natural facility at the film and sound editing process; Skip Craig said, "It was their innate musical ears; they knew that animation and music both relied on beats." Bennett was once nationally known as the fictional stage character "Sir Frederick Gas" who performed comic songs and did impressions. He contributed an excellent Gabby Hayes old-geezer voice in *Magoo Beats the Heat* (1956), and that character proved popular enough to be revived a year later for *Rock Hound Magoo*. [18]

The Mister Magoo cartoons had proven successful and exploitable. While they may have become increasingly formulaic, at least old pros Backus and Hausner continued to provide consistently fine voice acting. For the Oscar-winner *When Magoo Flew* (1955), the female roles were played by Henny Backus, real-life wife of Quincy Magoo's voice. Following *Magoo Goes West*, Jerry Hausner travelled overseas in 1956 and spent time in Europe. Starting with *Magoo's Puddle Jumper* (1956) Hausner's Waldo character was inherited by the gifted Daws Butler, well regarded for his four years with television's witty *Time for Beany* puppet show. He co-starred on that series with comic Stan Freberg and was heard by millions of fans on several of Freberg's fine comedy records for Capitol. By the mid-fifties Butler was already on regular call at cartoon studios like Lantz, MGM and Warner Bros. and he provided several voices at UPA for the next four years, during which time he became the preeminent actor in the emerging television cartoon industry. [19]

Several women enjoyed distinctive voice roles in the later Magoo cartoons. Quincy's dotty old mother was played by ventriloquist Nancy Wible in *Meet Mother Magoo* (1956), although Bea Benaderet played her in some later made-for-TV entries. Other females prominent in the later years included Colleen Collins in *Magoo's Young Manhood* (1958), Nancy Wible again in *Gumshoe Magoo* (1958) and June Foray in *The Explosive Mr. Magoo* (1958).

For the 1956-57 theatrical season the Mister Magoo entries were the only UPA cartoons in sight, but the final release season saw four odd films starring "Ham and Hattie." Lew Keller, an animation layout artist who later landed at Jay Ward's studio, directed the first three, while animator Gil Turner handled the final one. They were really two-fers, each one containing a novelty song nasally warbled by composer Mel Leven, along with a short special subject (*Jamaica, Saganaki, Dino's Serenade*) for the second half. Fading radio star Hal "Gildersleeve" Peary returned to musically narrate two. The final set of five Magoo cartoons were released in 1959, each featuring voice-work by Jim Backus and Daws Butler, and the theatrical release deal with Columbia came to an end.

Some late prestige was claimed by the UPA studio with its two feature length cartoon movies. The first was, naturally, a Magoo feature film that was afforded a good if not over-generous budget. The movie, with its light hearted take on a fairy tale favorite, was entitled *1001 Arabian Nights* (1959). The story had been in development since 1957. While Pete Burness had directed many successful Magoo shorts, he was nervous about the character sustaining a full length feature, and he quit the project after some time developing the story. The ex-Goofy director Jack Kinney had been let go by Disney in 1957 and, although he was soon busy in a studio venture with Hal Adelquist, he hired on as director of the UPA feature after Bosustow contacted him. Technically the film was co-directed by Abe Levitow who was the animation supervisor, and an artist Kinney admired. Bill Scott had passed on the direction gig, but he was happy to relieve Kinney of some pressure by taking charge of the picture's dialogue recordings, which commenced in March 1958. *

20

* This was only one month after Scott had done his first recording of one Bullwinkle J. Moose's voice for Jay Ward's pilot *Rocky the Flying Squirrel*. In the year Scott waited for that TV show to get the greenlight and a new title, *Rocky and His Friends*, he worked on the Magoo feature and continued writing for industrial cartoons and commercials.

The Magoo feature opened to so-so reviews and did just middling business. It proved disappointing for those hoping for a feature-length movie highlighting the early UPA dazzle with eye-popping stylish graphics. While some layouts and backgrounds were lavishly impressive, the animation in parts resembled cheap television fodder. For a film with nine story contributors it was undeniably bland in spots and felt somewhat padded. It was quite a talk-fest, too, and for that reason it boasted a large vocal cast. TV's *Dobie Gillis* star Dwayne Hickman was cast as Aladdin and starlet Kathryn Grant, who had just married Bing Crosby, spoke for the Princess Yasminda. They were stock standard cartoon feature romantic leads. Sadly they were, as is virtually always the case in full-length cartoons, one dimensional and colorless. This was a pity since Hickman exhibited genuine understated comic flair in his quirky TV show.

Jim Backus maintained his usual high level of comic delivery as Magoo in a larger-than-usual role for the character: here he becomes Abdul Azziz Magoo, Aladdin's uncle. However, the feature format definitively proved that the old codger was more suited to short cartoons. Luckily the supporting actors on the film's track were some of the finest voices then employed in animation.

Hans Conried essayed the villainously lecherous Wicked Wazir in his patented, floridly enjoyable style. Conried's fellow radio veteran Alan Reed was cast as the pompous Sultan who was father to Princess Yasminda. Reed was just a few months away from his greatest cartoon role as Hanna-Barbera's booming Fred Flintstone. The mellifluous tones of Herschel Bernardi, Broadway thespian and the ubiquitous voice of animated commercial character Charlie the Tuna, were employed for the vibrant Jinni of the Lamp. Daws Butler, by now the top voice artist in the new medium of TV cartoons, doubled as Omar the Rugmaker and the Royal Accountant. Even Bill Scott had a couple of small parts using voices he would later call on for Jay Ward's Fractured Fairy Tales. The fine vocal trio The Clark Sisters were hired as "The Three Maids from Damascus," but although they recorded a song bearing that title it was cut from the final film. They receive screen credit, but in fact they were reduced to just some giggling as eligible brides on offer to Aladdin.

Mister Magoo would enjoy a TV afterlife following *Terror Faces Magoo*, the last theatrical short released by Columbia in the summer of 1959. A long series of cheaply made-for-TV Magoo cartoons was overseen by long-time promoter Henry Saperstein who had taken over from Stephen Bosustow as UPA's president in 1960. Those 180 cartoons were followed by *The Famous Adventures of Mr. Magoo*, a series of 26 half-hour television specials which were based around famous literary characters like William Tell, Don Quixote and Robin Hood. These were at least a step up visually.

The final theatrical feature cartoon from UPA was released by Warner Bros. in 1962. *Gay Purr-ee* was a story written over the previous year by Mr. & Mrs. Chuck Jones. Sadly, it tanked at the box office, possibly a little pretentious for a mass audience. The story is predictable and slight, but the film looks attractive in spots and has its moments.

Jones, while moonlighting from Warners, and his long-time colleague Abe Levitow, who directed the feature, were in charge of recording the voices. [21] It could be argued that *Gay Purr-ee* was the first true example of a "celebrity-voiced" feature cartoon, coming five years before Disney's *The Jungle Book*, the film usually regarded as the feature that truly kickstarted the trend to wholesale casting of big-name voices. The starring talents here, playing mostly feline characters in a French setting, were indeed top drawer performers, famous in the fields of musical theatre and nightclub comedy.

Legendary vocalist Judy Garland spoke and sang the leading role of Mewsette, an innocent if rather flighty young farm kitten seeking the bright lights of 1890s Paris. The ringing baritone of Robert Goulet, fresh from his triumph as Sir Lancelot in the Broadway run of *Camelot*, was heard as Mewsette's jaunty admirer Jaune Tom. The sophisticated English revue comedienne Hermione Gingold, familiar from her similar role in *Gigi*, voiced the haughty society grande dame Madame Rubens-Chatte. Stand-up comics Red Buttons and Morey Amsterdam were very funny club and TV performers, although cartoon acting might not have been their strongest suit. Jaune Tom's loyal sidekick Robespierre, as voiced by Buttons in a stridently forced falsetto, can be rather tiring.

As always, however, the best cartoon voices in *Gay Purr-ee* were handled by reliable animation character specialists, with Paul Frees playing the suave villain and Mel Blanc filling in colorful small parts like the bulldog. Frees has a large role for once, and his smooth, sonorous voice was perfect casting for the slyly malevolent Meow-rice. The villainous cat's lecherously oily French accent remains memorable, especially suited to his long narration describing the history of the impressionist art movement. Frees could also sing well and here he gets a couple of solo numbers, "The Money Cat Can" and "The Horse Won't Talk." Chuck Jones and Frees didn't hit it off, with Jones sniffing that "Paul liked to direct the directors." (Both men had formidable egos so perhaps the personality clash was inevitable.) [22]

The *Gay Purr-ee* feature aside, UPA's final years were spent in television. An enjoyable and evergreen seasonal favorite, *Mister Magoo's Christmas Carol*, was successfully rerun for decades. The Magoo character had done wonders for both Jim Backus and the studio, appearing in a final 1970 television cartoon, *Uncle Sam Magoo*, after which UPA folded for good. The studio had lasted just twelve years as a theatrical house, but the UPA name was retained for several more years of TV product, including the long run of *Dick Tracy* cartoons.

Chapter 5:

WALTER LANTZ-UNIVERSAL
Cartoon Voices, 1930-72

*Walter Lantz's studio, housed for many years at Universal
Pictures, was always regarded as an underdog of the cartoon industry. But from its animation desks emerged a large
body of often excellent cartoons over its forty-three years. The
Universal cartoons had their own unique identity, ensuring
Lantz's place alongside Max Fleischer, Paul Terry and even
Walt Disney as a leading producer of sound cartoons. Often
parsimonious, a born self-promoter but always well-liked,
Lantz was a congenial man who weathered several corporate
ups and downs at Universal and eventually produced some of
the most strikingly memorable cartoons of the forties. He will
forever be associated with characters like Woody Woodpecker
and Chilly Willy. While never at the top of the tree near Disney, Lantz still managed to remain a well-respected star player
in the theatrical cartoon era. Some towering artistic talents
emerged from his shop, like Tex Avery, Preston Blair, Ed Benedict and the fine director Shamus Culhane.*

The Walter Lantz cartoons began during the crossover from silent
film to sound. In 1928 Universal Pictures decided to open its own
animation studio due to contractual issues over the cartoon property Oswald the Lucky Rabbit, a character which Universal owned.
Studio founder Carl Laemmle was uncomfortable about having to
deal with independent producer-middleman Charles Mintz, who

had been distributing the popular silent Oswald Rabbit films made at first by Walt Disney.

When Mintz and Disney famously fell out in early 1928, the Oswald cartoons continued production at the new Winkler Pictures studio on Western Avenue in Hollywood. The outfit was run by Mintz's brother-in-law George Winkler, with several former Disney animators on staff. Soon after it was up and running, several New York artists, including Walter Lantz, joined the enterprise. Lantz was a proven talent with years of silent film experience in many areas, notably comedy, story gags, animation and as a screen comic. After he moved from New York to the West Coast in 1927 he contributed gags for both the Hal Roach and Mack Sennett comedy factories; he supervised some animated gags in a few Sennett two-reelers.

At contract renewal time, Mintz was at a crossroads: Universal announced it would establish its own cartoon studio on the Universal City lot at Lankershim Boulevard, quite specifically to eliminate the middleman and begin producing "Universal Cartoons." The start-up began in late 1928 with the purchase of equipment and construction of the cartoon production wing. It was the first film studio to have a cartoon facility on its own lot.

Lantz was personally appointed by Universal studio founder Laemmle to head the cartoon enterprise, and he was quickly joined by prolific New York animation savant Bill Nolan as a nominal co-producer. Lantz began building up a staff of young artists, including Ray Abrams, Vern Harding and Manuel Moreno.

All this occurred just as Disney revolutionized the animated cartoon with the addition of synchronized sound via his immensely successful *Steamboat Willie* (1928). Seemingly overnight Lantz and every other would-be animation executive suddenly realized it was imperative to make the new medium of sound cartoons the top priority. At Universal, as his cartoon studio took shape, Lantz began by adding sound to six of the silent Winkler-produced Oswald cartoons awaiting release.

It was a quick learning curve: Lantz and Nolan would watch a completed cartoon as it was projected and stand at a bench which housed various noisemaking items like rattles, kazoos and bells. They also added vocal sounds and whatever else was required to complete the primitive early tracks. Several years later, in the 1935 Lowell Thomas newsreel *Cartoonland Mysteries* which demonstrated how cartoons were made, Lantz can be seen very much in charge of the filmed recording session, still helping to make sound effects and contributing vocal noises himself, while cueing an unidentified actress for her Oswald dialogue lines.

By February 1929, it was officially announced that Lantz would "take charge" of Universal's new cartoon division to commence in mid-March. The first Lantz-produced Oswald cartoons appeared that fall, starting with *Ozzie of the Circus*. Lantz's first decade with Universal was dominated by the famous Oswald, with just a few second-string characters that came and went. The staff of talented artists continued to grow, and they quickly adapted to the challenges of the new medium of sound. In the first two years, dialogue in the Lantz cartoons, as elsewhere, was minimal.

Young animator Manuel Moreno, one of the earliest hires, explained, "Most of the time, synchronization was not that critical. We didn't use much dialogue at that time. We kept away from it. Singing was easy because you had definite measured beats to guide the animators." [1] An early extra-curricular assignment for the Lantz studio was a short cartoon sequence in 2-Color Technicolor, for inclusion in Universal's prestigious color feature musical *The King of Jazz* (1930), starring the nation's top bandleader Paul Whiteman.

Bill Nolan supervised this job, assisted by Moreno. [2] The singing voice for the caricatured Whiteman was supplied by relatively unknown superstar-in-waiting Bing Crosby, the single most famous voice Lantz would ever use. Crosby, Al Rinker and Harry Barris were known as the Three Rhythm Boys, the vocal group who were a fixture in Whiteman's stage show package. Crosby even added a topical Al Jolson "Mammy!!" call, spoken by a menacing lion, and he was accompanied by his fellow Rhythm Boys, Rinker and Barris, on the vocal chorus. The recording session proved easy because veteran musical whiz Whiteman instantly understood how animation would be done to musical beats; he astonished Lantz by conducting the orchestra in one perfect three minute take.

The regular Lantz-Nolan cartoons soon proved oddly eccentric and often deeply strange, yet many of the gags worked. Nolan was one of the fastest straight ahead animators in the business and Lantz soon had a bright young team, all of whom enthusiastically pitched in on gags. The Oswald Rabbit cartoons, while never in the league of Disney's Mickeys, proved popular. The first soundtracks were crude, with Lantz and various staff post-synching the films with the same kitchen cupboard full of noisy effects and props they had used for the six silent Oswalds.*

* This book's "voice-filmography" describes Lantz's output in even more detail than the other studios because of their eccentric soundtracks; I attempt to enumerate how this studio's use of sound and cartoon voices developed over time.

Cartoon historian Bob Coar noted that Nolan provided the earliest voice for Oswald. The transition to sound was relatively smooth, and with their strong New York sensibility the early Oswald Rabbit shorts were, by 1930, the Coast equivalent of the surreal Max Fleischer cartoons. Aside from a brazen miniature Mickey Mouse lookalike cheekily placed in many early Oswalds, Lantz's cartoons soon found their own identity and felt different to those of the other West Coast studios. Some entries seemed positively bizarre with an anything goes quality to the stories and gags.

The Oswalds remained essentially odd cartoons, wildly variable as a body of work, for the first five years of the Lantz studio. Nolan's gags could be outrageous and even abstract. Funny violence was the norm, with Oswald often being turned inside out as in *Henpecked* (1930), or yanking off his opponent's prosthetic leg and beating him with it in *Alaska* (1930). In many ways Lantz, although never a public figure on Disney's scale, exerted an exceedingly strong producer's influence. He was a gagman in the silent era and to the end of his life he remained proudly a gagman. As he put it, "I always loved physical comedy, that was what I went for. Gags were my prime concern." [3] There was much of the silent comedy sensibility present in these cartoons.

After a few Oswald shorts scored by musicians Bert Fiske and David Broekman, Lantz ended up with a permanent musical director in James Dietrich, who had done fine arrangements for both "King of Jazz" Paul Whiteman and bandleader Jimmy Dorsey. The seasoned pianist-arranger would provide an endless variety of jazzy tracks in a range of styles for the next seven years, notching up scores of cartoons to his name.

Describing the early days of sound, Moreno noted, "The recording was always done by Lantz and the music director [Jimmy Dietrich] as supervisors. And the sound effects were no problem. Chief story man Vic McLeod would often record the sound effects, or Pinto Colvig [would].

"[Typically] Lantz rented the sound stage for four hours, on account of the musicians' minimum charge. Even though it was their own stage, Universal would charge overhead fees for the use of their facilities so they could determine realistic costs. I think Lantz always felt this was unfair for low-budgeted cartoons. During all the time I was at Universal, Lantz did all the cutting of sound, synchronizing the three tracks with the picture. And he would be at all the final mixing sessions with the musical director." [4]

This was during the rapidly evolving and experimental first half of the thirties when, as we have seen at Schlesinger, MGM and Mintz, every studio relied on its own staff members for comic one-liners and vocal squawks. A unique early employee was the former clown and vaudeville performer Pinto Colvig. Lantz knew him from their earliest days in Hollywood when Colvig got him some work animating special gags for Mack Sennett comedy shorts. In 1928 before Lantz was ensconced at Universal he and Colvig had unsuccessfully tried to pitch *Blue Notes,* a cartoon starring Bolivar the Talking Ostrich. [5]

Quite early in Lantz's cartoons, Colvig's unmistakeable voice - later world famous as Disney's Goofy - was first heard in the Oswald entry *Hell's Heels* in mid-1930. He was regularly credited on-screen as an animation staffer beginning two cartoons later with *Not So Quiet.* Colvig, whose chief talents were in music, sound and story gags rather than actual animation, worked on some thirty Lantz cartoons before his final credit for *Wonderland,* released in 1931.

Moreno recalled, "[In a session] Colvig didn't need anybody there, he knew just what to do with voices or sounds. Special sounds they couldn't get from Universal's sound library were recorded at the time they recorded dialogue - the music and everything all at once. After the music you come in with the effects and spoken lines." [6] Colvig spent almost one year with Lantz and Nolan, before defecting to the more prestigious Disney plant in the fall of 1930. There he became a gag man, lyricist and pioneer voice artist responsible for enduringly popular character voices like the singing Grasshopper, Pluto the pup, Grumpy and much more.

In 1931 as the Great Depression cut ever deeper, Lantz instituted cutbacks which included making slightly shorter films and the creation of two distinct units. One was headed by Nolan which continued making the Oswald cartoons. Lantz's own unit began working on a new character called Pooch the Pup.

Meanwhile, Fred "Tex" Avery joined Lantz's Universal crew in the spring of 1929. He slowly worked up from washing cels to a supervising animator position by 1934. His name was first seen on-screen in the animation credits for a mid-1930 Oswald cartoon *The Singing Sap.* From the start, Avery was noticed for his endless gag contributions. His innate gift for precision timed comedy was immediately apparent, soon marking him as a standout in the industry. At Universal Avery was recognized by top guns Lantz and Nolan who regarded him as a funny and unique talent with a big future ahead.

While cartoon fans are aware of his several voice contributions for Warner Bros. and MGM cartoons, it is much less known that Avery had been supplying odd voices for years at Lantz. During a spring 1933 vacation in his hometown he was interviewed for a comprehensive article in *The Dallas Morning News*, in which he revealed he was already assisting on the recording sessions as well as supplying many gags and voices:

"We had a heck of a time trying to get the sounds of a falling tree in one of the Pooch shorts [most likely The *Lumber Champ* (1933)]. We found that a bamboo pole slowly split would give the sound of the squeak that precedes a fall and then one of the boys stood on a chair and dropped another chair to give the crash as the tree hit the ground. I do all the talking for Oswald in a little high squeaky voice and it ruins my throat for days. Another boy in the office who can throw his voice even higher talks for Kitty, Oswald's girlfriend." [7]

Avery can be heard as kings, like *The Merry Old Soul* (1933), villains and countless other bit part voices in many Universal cartoons. It is undoubtedly him in *The Zoo* (1933) doing a suddenly moth-de-nuded bear in underwear who speaks straight to camera for a patented Avery line, "Well, imagine that!" In the 1934 *Ye Happy Pilgrims* a funny scream is unmistakably Avery's.

Other staff members also joined in on the recordings. Animator Jack Carr did characters too and possessed a flexible voice. Gagman Cal Howard very likely joined in. Much of this was relatively easy work, as most of the dialogue in the early years was so-so puns or merely functional. The sophisticated wordplay of the forties cartoons was still a long way off.

Starting in 1930 when some limited dialogue was introduced, Oswald's singing and speaking voices literally varied from film to film. Indeed the poor rabbit was voiced in one early entry by both a man and a woman, and as both adult and childlike. And in a few cartoons his voice was that of a real child, performed by a young Mickey Rooney who was then starring in Larry Darmour's *Mickey McGuire* live action comedy shorts. [8] The ten-year-old Rooney's voice is apparent in some 1931 cartoons like *The Farmer* and *Shipwreck*.

It was the same thing with Oswald's girl Kitty, who varied vocally from a falsetto male to a squeaky-voiced actress like Carol Tevis or Helen Lynd. By the time of *Elmer the Great Dane* in 1935, Oswald was speaking in a voice quite similar to his competitor Mickey Mouse. That Mickey-type voice is heard again in Oswald's one bit of dialogue in *Towne Hall Follies*, (1935), a cartoon effectively directed by Avery just before he was fired by Universal management, who had perceived his ambition to head his own unit as a form of disloyalty to Lantz.

By 1933, Lantz began using a few professional voices in several cartoons. Whistling specialists like Marion Darlington and Purves Pullen, heard in *Pin Feathers*, were now on call. Baby-voiced ventriloquist and scat singer Shirley Reed was one of the several female voices used for Oswald, when he wasn't being voiced by various in-house men! [9]

From 1932 radio performers were called to Universal City for occasional cartoons. When Lantz needed imitations to match movieland caricatures, he called on voice artists like Noreen Gamill who did a Mae West in *The Merry Old Soul*. KFWB radio torch singer Jeane Cowan sang "Minnie the Moocher" for Pooch's girlfriend in *She Done Him Right* (1933). Stammering comic Joe Twerp was called in for a fight commentator in the studio's Kong parody *King Klunk* (1933).

In 1934, the baby-voice of Berneice Hansell was poached from Leon Schlesinger to appear in *The Candy House, Wolf! Wolf!* and *The Wax Works*. Billy Bletcher and a vocally flexible voice lady named Dorothy Lloyd, adept at a range of bird and animal sounds, were also hired. It would still be a few years before dialogue gags began to dominate Hollywood cartoons, so Lantz's shorts would continue relying on specialty singers and staff voices until the 1937-38 season.

For two country & western themed Oswald cartoons, genuine cowboy vocal groups were hired. *The Hill Billy* (1935) employed station KMPC radio stars The Crockett Family, who did such a nice job they were called back the following year for *The Barnyard Five*. For the western parody *Bronco Buster* (1935) Universal booked the popular Sons of the Pioneers combo, headed by Bob Nolan and featuring specialty yodeller Leonard Slye, who later changed his screen name to Roy Rogers. Fine singers with light opera backgrounds were heard in many Hollywood cartoons from 1933-38. Music director Jimmy Dietrich employed flexible character baritones like Paul Keast and George Gramlich. An unconfirmed Popeye soundalike did a funny frog tough guy, singing "The Bulldog (on the Bank)" in *Amateur Broadcast* (1935).

For the morale-boosting *Confidence*, made in the heart of the Great Depression in late 1932, the singing voice of President Franklin D. Roosevelt was done by Gilbert & Sullivan baritone Allan Watson, who was also heard in cartoons for MGM, Mintz and Disney's *Silly Symphonies*. *Confidence* was released in 1933. It was one of the last Bill Nolan efforts. He and Lantz began differing over Nolan's rubbery style of animation which began to look a little outmoded as the younger artists improved. Following a contractual rift over the matter of payment, Nolan was gone by late 1934. [10]

The number of musical shorts increased at all the cartoon factories in order to compete with "the Disney style." Some of the strangeness and outrageous gags in Lantz's cartoons were replaced with a tamer approach as the industry wide Production Code was strictly enforced from the 1934-35 season. A degree of cuteness began creeping in to Lantz's formerly wild comedy. The advent of the "Code" was one reason for a general softening of comic elements in cartoons across the board from Fleischer to Columbia.

Lantz enjoyed a brief flirtation with the 2-Color system in 1934-35 for a short series of five musical entries. These were called Cartune Classics, and they were frankly wannabe Silly Symphonies.*Artistically these cartoons suffered by comparison with Disney's higher budgeted shorts, but they were saved by their musical elements. Clever song lyrics co-written by Lantz and Victor McLeod were matched with some of Dietrich's most memorable melodies. The fine girl's trio The Rhythmettes had been singing in a few Oswalds like *Do a Good Deed* (1935) and their attractive close-harmony was the perfect fit for that year's fairy tales, like *Springtime Serenade* and *Three Lazy Mice.*

* Lantz remained in 2-strip color for just a year; financially strapped, he reverted to black and white cartoons until late 1939, when he finally switched full-time to glorious Technicolor.

Candyland (1935) boasted a particularly classy libretto and used the talents of session singers like baritone Paul Keast, perfectly suited to this genre. For *Jolly Little Elves* (1934), child-voiced Berneice Hansell played the elf who sang "Oh, How I Love to Dunk Donuts," one of the catchiest ditties to come from Lantz's studio. It's not that the song is an all-time classic, but it is one of those tunes that, once locked into your head, is never unheard.

It was in late 1935, following a power play which saw long-time Universal founder Carl Laemmle ousted, that Lantz transitioned from being a Universal employee to forming Walter Lantz Productions, which contracted to deliver cartoons to Universal while staying in the old animation studio on the lot. The new business model saw a dedicated push to begin improving the animation and other aspects of each new short. There was also an effort to update Oswald's appearance via a new Manuel Moreno design, into an all-white rabbit. [11] But with the Code now firmly entrenched the films only became blander, and cartoons like *The Softball Game* (1935) felt sluggish and unfunny compared to the zany films of just a few years before.

Several new characters emerged between 1935 and 1937 season, as part of an effort to find a new Universal cartoon star. These included Elmer the Great Dane who was Oswald's forgettable pet, a family of pretty ordinary ducks, and a frankly unmemorable series called The Three Monkeys starring Meany, Miny and Mo. None of these underwhelming characters really did much for Lantz, but the cartoons were slowly improving artistically. The main trouble was that the Oswald Rabbit character was becoming overexposed after eight years and some two hundred cartoons.

On the soundtracks, a raft of new musicians were given composing assignments following the departure of Jimmy Dietrich in late 1937. He had notched up seven years of bouncy cartoon scores to his credit, ending with *Football Fever* (1937). Lantz used George Lessner, Nathaniel Shilkret and even Frank Churchill, who had written so many fine scores for Disney earlier in the decade. In late 1938 MGM's Scott Bradley composed one cartoon for Lantz (*Baby Kittens*) before returning to the Culver City lot. Frank Marsales had been the musical director for Harman-Ising from 1930-33, scoring and arranging all the early Warner Bros. cartoons. He became Lantz's steady composer for a couple of years, returning to cartoons in 1939 after six years of radio and running his own recording business.

By 1938, outside voice experts began being heard far more often in Lantz's films. Dave Weber was one of the best Hollywood professional voices in that period, and his distinctive tones were heard as tough guys in Baby Face Mouse entries from 1938 like *Sailor Mouse* and *Disobedient Mouse*. He was also an accomplished voice mimic and did a range of good impressions of movie and radio stars for Lantz's *Hollywood Bowl*. At the end of 1938 Weber changed his professional name to Danny Webb, continuing to voice many cartoons for Universal. He even created and spoke for Lantz's short-lived Snuffy Skunk character, based on a radio voice he had done two years earlier. [12]

A talented animation director named Alex Lovy came aboard in 1938. In order to compete with the increasingly popular Warner Bros. cartoon zaniness Lovy began using standout radio stooge voices. They included the whiny comic Phil Kramer, who narrated *Slap Happy Valley* (1939), as well as comedic musician Candy Candido who did his trick high squeak-to-low bullfrog voice for a one-off character, *Charlie Cuckoo* (1939). The busy movie and radio commentator Knox Manning spoke for a few entries like *Crackpot Cruise* (1939). Manning, in demand for newsreels and trailers, managed to wangle on-screen voice credit, a true rarity for this era.

Lantz was also the first cartoon maker to use the high-profile comedy talent Bill Thompson from radio's top-rated *Fibber McGee and Molly* soon after that program transplanted from Chicago to Hollywood in February 1939. Thompson, an expert creator of standout character voices, performed his famous Old Timer ("That ain't the way I heer-ed it, Johnny!!! The way I heer-ed it, one feller says t'other feller...") for Lantz's *Arabs With Dirty Fezzes* (1939). In the forties Thompson became famous as the voice behind MGM's mush-mouthed cartoon canine Droopy, for old Lantz graduate Tex Avery.

Aside from these radio notables, the bulk of Lantz's character voices now came from the core of well-established cartoon dubbing specialists who worked regularly for Schlesinger, MGM and Mintz: Dave Weber, Sara Berner, Billy Bletcher and relative newcomer Mel Blanc. It was these prized people who had a natural flair for the singularly broad, caricatured style of zany cartoon acting that many otherwise fine radio performers could never master.

Lantz first used Mel Blanc in early 1937 in his Three Monkeys cartoon *The Stevedores,* upon the recommendation of Warner sound man Treg Brown, following Blanc's successful Schlesinger audition. [13] Blanc was used again by Lantz in 1938 and more regularly the following year, doing characters like the goody-goody hero Dauntless Dan in a series of boo-hiss melodrama spoofs featuring the old-time heroine Nellie. Blanc was soon on call for dialects and tough guy parts in the Universal cartoons.

In his first noteworthy work for Lantz, Blanc spoke the voice of the mercifully short-lived Li'l Eightball, a 1939 series made by ex-Disney director Burt Gillett. Although the animation in these cartoons was excellent, the mischievous Black child lead was a regrettably cringe-worthy stereotype even by thirties standards and, it must be said, one of the most annoying voices Blanc ever essayed.

With his second season releasing through "the New" Universal, Lantz started to compete more seriously with the other animation houses in Hollywood. His cartoons, by now featuring better and fuller animation, began resembling Warner Bros.' fast and furious spot gag shows being made by former Lantz-studio gagman and animator Tex Avery. They also went all-Technicolor starting from the 1939-40 season. Lantz's 1940 hiring of ex-Schlesinger gag man Ben "Bugs" Hardaway in the position of story department head only added to the increasingly similar comic tone: some spot gag cartoons blatantly swiped Avery's travelogue parody concept. Hardaway even brought narrator Robert Bruce to Universal for two of these gag entries in 1941 (*Fair Today* and *Salt Water Daffy*), pairing him with Mel Blanc and thus ensuring the Warner stylistic similarity was virtually identical.

The addition of the outstanding musical director Darrell Calker, who took over from Frank Marsales in late 1940, resulted in a subtle change to the sound of the Lantz cartoons. Some of the voices

Lantz hired in the new decade began reflecting that change as well, as Lantz searched for a star player.

Having tried and failed to find a marquee "name" with various sub-Oswald characters - such as Baby Face Mouse and Peterkin - Lantz finally hit upon a popular character in 1939's *Life Begins for Andy Panda*. The cute title character underwent various transformations over his ten-year screen career, from baby through young bachelor.

The earliest cartoons portrayed Andy as a troublemaking toddler with a voice alternating between a cloyingly sweet little kid and a direct imitation of Fanny Brice's famous radio brat "Baby Snooks." Sara Berner voiced these two roles, before being replaced by young puppeteer-actress Margaret Hill, at which point Andy's now cuter voice became identical to the Warner Bros. star mouse Sniffles, for whom Ms Hill also spoke. This actress didn't last long though, retiring in 1941 to start a family.

Andy's accident-prone Papa, who supplied early comic relief in the stumblebum style of Hugh Harman's Father Bear at MGM, was originally spoken by the prolific Dave Weber in *Life Begins for Andy Panda*, for which Weber also did several other radio take-offs like newsreader Walter Winchell and Jack Benny's raspy valet Rochester. In the long-time Lantz tradition of vocal inconsistency, Weber changed the senior Panda's voice in each cartoon, even offering an imitation of the now-forgotten radio comic Tommy Cecil Mack ("Excited? Who's excited!!!???") in *Crazy House* (1940). Mel Blanc also voiced panda pater for a couple of entries. Finally, the role was inherited by young radio mimic Dick Nelson who became a Lantz Cartunes voice regular throughout the forties.

Philadelphia born Dick Nelson is one of those mystery names who remain intriguingly obscure today. Nelson's sole major acting credit was the colorless live-action juvenile lead in Twentieth Century-Fox's 1941 Laurel & Hardy feature *Great Guns*, a part he got on the strength of his radio reputation. [14] On camera Nelson was bland

and seemed uncomfortable, but behind a microphone he could go crazy. The cartoon role for which Nelson is probably best remembered today is "Rocky," the funny Edward G. Robinson lampoon in the 1946 Bugs Bunny short *Racketeer Rabbit*. Although he did other Warner cartoons, most of Nelson's animation voice work was for Universal.

For Lantz, Dick Nelson played a variety of parts. With his natural talent for mimicry, many of his impressions were send-ups of current radio and movie stars. His fine Frank Morgan imitation narrates *Mother Goose on the Loose* (1941), while he provides straight off-screen commentary as well as funny voices, including a James Cagney mutt, for the topical wartime spoof *Canine Commandos* (1943). Nelson also spoke the voice of Seaman Hook in Lantz's 1943 sponsored cartoon for the U.S. Navy, *Take Heed Mr. Tojo*.

Strangely enough, one of Dick Nelson's weaker impressions was Universal's star comic W. C. Fields. Lantz settled on his distinctive tones as the final father Panda voice in cartoons like *Andy Panda's Pop* (1941). Like many of the versatile radio talents of the period, work for Nelson was highly competitive and often sporadic, prompting him to move more than once between the West and East Coasts for much of the forties. In New York he starred in a CBS radio sitcom, *Tales of Willie Piper*, before returning to Hollywood for whatever opportunities he could find. Just one of hundreds in the broadcasting actors' union The American Federation of Radio Artists (AFRA), he was either busy or reduced to playing tiny bit roles in movies like *Follow the Boys* (1944), where he is virtually just an extra as a recruiting sergeant. Nelson developed a gallows humor about his low industry profile: for his entry in an agents' casting guide, he placed a photo and the words "Alternating between radio and the breadline (at AFRA rates)." [15]

Still, Nelson kept working for Lantz into the early fifties, finally receiving prominent screen credit for the Grantray-produced short *Broadway Bow Wows* (1954), directed by Ray Patterson. For that cartoon, Nelson supplied an uncanny imitation of nasal-voiced Ed Gardner's Brooklynese "Archie," from the long-running radio comedy *Duffy's Tavern*. * While never as busy as top-tier character men like Paul Frees or Mel Blanc, Nelson eventually wound up in TV cartoons for Bob Clampett and in UPA's *Dick Tracy* series.

* Nelson had previously used this voice in the Warner Bros. short *Hush My Mouse* (1946), and for George in Tex Avery's first three George & Junior cartoons at MGM. That distinctive "Archie" voice was also deployed by, among others, Daws Butler in the later Super Snooper cartoons on Hanna-Barbera's *Quick Draw McGraw* television show.

***

By 1940 Walter Lantz finally latched onto his strongest cartoon star for the new decade. For an upcoming Andy Panda story, long-suffering Papa Panda would have troubles with his roof, including a big rainstorm. Lantz biographer Joe Adamson noted, "Walter took one look at the storyboard and said, 'That's too expensive.'" He needed an easier-to-animate roofing problem and suggested a pesky bird like a woodpecker (a couple of Lantz's thirties cartoons had featured incidental woodpeckers). Story man Bugs Hardaway's contribution resulted in "Woody Woodpecker," a wild and zany character with obvious elements of the crazy new Schlesinger star Daffy Duck (in 1937 Hardaway had worked on the cartoon that established that character, *Daffy Duck and Egghead*). The cross-eyed, multi-hued annoying woodpecker proved a huge hit with exhibitors and theatregoers alike from his earliest unnamed supporting appearance in the Andy Panda entry, *Knock! Knock!* (1940).

For Woody's voice, Lantz asked actor Mel Blanc for input. He recalled telling Blanc, "They make a very raucous noise. We've got to get a gimmick. We tried different things that weren't quite right. [The music director] Darrell Calker suggested something based on a bugle call." [16] Hardaway had already used a grating voice by Blanc in some earlier Warner characters like the proto-Bugs Bunny of *Hare-um Scare-um* (1938). The rabbit's musical laugh was adjusted and became the loony bird's vocal signature. In interviews Blanc always defined Woody's five note laugh as the same strident cackle he would do while he was a Portland teenager, testing an echo in his high school's corridor.

The bird's crazy speaking voice was slightly sped up but not as much as it would finally sound. In Woody's debut appearance Blanc's own non-sped voice is detectable when the bird first says, "Guess Who?" There would be a period of on-off tinkering with the Woody voice.

By 1941 the anarchic Woody inherited his own series, and instantly became a top theatrical cartoon favorite. The early Woodpecker was designed in garish colours and exhibited an unforgettable kookiness. At last Lantz had a character he could really merchandise, and he was able to convincingly compete with the now aggressively funny Warner Bros. cartoons. Since 1938 Lantz had been weaning his stories away from the overly cute animals which had once threatened to stamp him as being forever rooted in the thirties. Now he went all out.

Blanc recorded the voice for two more Woody cartoons released in 1941 (*Woody Woodpecker, The Screwdriver* and possibly some of *Pantry Panic*). But a replacement voice for the Woodpecker was needed once Blanc signed his exclusive deal with Leon Schlesinger in the spring of 1941. Lantz said, "I started shopping around." [17] One early press item on 5 July reflected Lantz's pressing need for a "new" voice when the *Ames Daily Tribune* noted, "Robert Cummings' stand-in, Ed Regan, is the voice of Willie the Woodpecker [sic] in a new Walter Lantz cartoon." It is unclear if Regan was simply one of several who auditioned for the part. [18]

Bernard Brown, director of Universal's sound department since 1936, provided many voices in the early days of Warner Bros. cartoons as well as scoring and recording their music. As he did for Schlesinger, he took charge of Lantz's recording sessions. It was Brown who recommended musician Darrell Calker to Lantz. In 1973, Brown spoke of working closely with Lantz while developing the woodpecker's voice: "We spent a lot of time getting what we felt was the right speed-up. [For Woody] it really didn't make too much difference who [spoke] the original [unsped dialogue], if they had the lilt in the voice and the [right acting] feel. I could speed it up this far, or that far, until I'd say, 'How do you like this, Walt?'" Brown also claimed he "did the voice for many of the pictures" but most of the Woody voices are known, so perhaps Brown meant he helped with incidental dialogue; possibly he provided the Woodpecker's strange little sadistic laugh heard in some forties cartoons like *The Loan Stranger* (1942). [19]

According to Bob Clampett, Dave Weber spoke for Woody in at least one cartoon, possibly recording some of the lines in *Pantry Panic* (1941) following Mel Blanc's departure (although Woody's last line, "Yeah? So am I" sounds like an unsped teenage boy, so ... the eighteen-year old Kent Rogers perhaps?). [20]

Kent Rogers is certainly confirmed as the third Woody Woodpecker voice. Rogers, a radio contemporary of Dick Nelson (they had co-starred in a 1940 CBS sitcom, *Your Neighbors the Haines*), was another excellent young impressionist best known to 21st century cartoon fans for all the movie star voices he enacted in Tex Avery's famous Warner celebrity cartoon *Hollywood Steps Out* (1941). Rogers worked on several Lantz cartoons, including two as the short-lived Homer Pigeon: *Pigeon Patrol* (1942) and *Swing Your Partner* (1943). In that same timeframe he was Woody's mechanically sped voice for *Ace in the Hole, The Screwball, The Loan Stranger* and *The Dizzy Acrobat*. Demonstrating his flexibility for *The Loan Stranger*, Rogers also voiced the con-man fox as a topical John Barrymore imitation complete with hammy snorts: the tragically booze-addled Barrymore, by now a shell of the legendary Broadway star he once was, had a weekly radio gig on *The Rudy Vallee Show* at the time this cartoon was released.

The Woody Woodpecker shorts aside, Rogers also provided all the voices for *The Hams That Couldn't Be Cured* (1942), including an imitation of the prissy character comedian Franklin Pangborn. But as with many Lantz cartoons in this period Alex Lovy's voice direction seems a little hurried, and Rogers's voices weren't nearly as precise as those he gave for Avery and Clampett at Warner Bros. Lantz's pronounced distaste for going even slightly over budget often meant recording sessions were hastily completed, sometimes to a film's detriment.

Today it can be hard to tell which voices were done by Dick Nelson and which by Kent Rogers. They often gave imitations of the same current celebrities, like Red Skelton who was at the time a national radio favorite and highly cartoony himself: Rogers provided Skelton's "Mean Widdle Kid" radio brat voice in *Andy Panda's Victory Garden* (1942). He also did Skelton's goofier Clem Kadiddlehopper character for the voice of Homer Pigeon.

A feature article on motion picture voice "doubles" in the *L.A. Times* dated June 14, 1941, mentions both these young mimics: "There's a fellow named Dick Nelson who can imitate Jimmy Stewart and Cary Grant to a fare-thee-well, while Kent Rogers is a sure thing for the job if the voice of any of twenty different stars is needed." [21] Unfortunately, Rogers only appeared in a handful of Lantz cartoons before he was drafted. He was able to do an occasional furlough job, but essentially Nelson and others picked up the slack.

Edwin Schallert's movie column in the *Los Angeles Times* mentioned Lantz's quandary: "The war is cutting in on the voices of cartoon characters it seems. Walter Lantz has had to get a new impersonator of Andy Panda, and has signed Walter Tetley, the Leroy of the *Great Gildersleeve* air show. Ben Hardaway, story editor for Lantz, has had to replace Kent Rogers as Woody Woodpecker, because Rogers has gone into the service." [22]

That item appeared in February of 1944. Sadly, Kent Rogers died just five months later during aircraft training in Pensacola, Florida. Rogers's final cartoon job was a Beaky Buzzard for Warner Bros. Of this talented young impressionist, Bob Clampett recalled thirty five years later, "After he recorded the second Beaky [cartoon] for me [on March 25, 1944], he was in a plane crash and was lost. Otherwise we'd hear a lot more about him." [23] Yet even in the age of Google, Nelson and Rogers remain almost totally elusive today: various research archives were unable to turn up anything of substance on these bright young actors. Are any family members reading this today, grandkids possibly? This author respectfully requests you consider sharing scrapbooks and information on these two neglected voice talents for a revised edition.

In 1943 Dick Nelson filled in as Woody for *Ration Bored* before Lantz realized that the voice was essentially a mechanical effect. "I tried [to record Woody] in the most inexpensive way, so Bugs Hardaway, who was [head] writer on the staff, did Woody Woodpecker. We used Mel's [original] laugh, but Bugs was doing the [dialogue] voice, speeded up." [24] Director Paul J. Smith recalled, "Ben [i.e. Bugs Hardaway] always used to sit in on all the recordings and do little laughs and vocal sounds, things like that." [25]

Ben "Bugs" Hardaway, firmly established as Lantz's story chief, became Woody's voice from late 1943 to the end of the decade. In fact, he ended up doing a fine job in the role. As Lantz admitted, "I wasn't too happy with Bugs," adding that Hardaway was "certainly no actor." [26] But as the studio's chief gag man, Hardaway knew the Woody character better than anyone, and his stilted one-word-at-a-time delivery, double-speeded for playback, manages to suit the crazy bird most effectively.

Hardaway's innate gag mentality and his cynical wise-guy voice blend well in anarchic and high-octane Woody cartoons from 1944 like *Ski for Two* and *The Barber of Seville*. In these entries Woody has two voices: while Hardaway provided the speaking part, the woodpecker's comically operatic singing was dubbed by baritone Lee Sweetland and sped up to excellent comic effect, especially when matched with the funny animation. Sweetland was contracted for the cartoons by Joseph Gershenson (Universal's musical director), who also used him in the feature film *The Climax* (1944), in which he dubbed the voice of actor George Dolenz, father of future TV Monkee Micky. [27] On one dialogue sheet a Lantz pencil notation instructs, "Have Sweetland do Woody's laugh," and this is what we hear at the end of his *Ski for Two* aria. [28]

Those films, and Lantz's studio, reached new heights when a singular talent, director Shamus Culhane, arrived after Lovy joined the navy in 1942. Culhane had notched up long experience on both Coasts with Fleischer, Iwerks and Disney, and recently a short stint for Schlesinger. Unlike workhorse Lovy, Culhane was his own creative person, an auteur who put his own stamp on his work. From 1943-46 Culhane set a high bar for quality in the Universal cartoons, especially noteworthy considering Lantz's budgets. Culhane's own musical taste (running to the classical) fused with Darrell Calker's inventiveness for a run of fine cartoons, including various entries in the Swing Symphonies. [29]

By mid-1943 some in-demand radio actors were being hired by Culhane as fresh voices. Jack Mather, a versatile air artist who later played the title role in the long-running *Cisco Kid* radio show, was tapped to play Woody's new nemesis Wally Walrus who first appeared in *The Beach Nut* (1944). [30] This oafish character was voiced in a pompous vaudeville Swedish dialect. In fact, it would have been a Danish voice had the original talent considered for the role been used. A *Daily Variety* PR item noted that the brilliant comedy pianist Victor Borge "has been signed to play the voice of a character expected to outstrip Donald Duck, Mickey Mouse, etc., in the public's affections. Victor's Scandinavian accent will be used to portray Wallie Walrus." [31] When that casting choice didn't eventuate Mather inherited the part.

It was pure comic stereotype, but Mather's acting ability added depth to Wally's lines: his love-struck mooning over a cross-dressing Woody in *Chew-Chew Baby* (1945) is almost pathetic. As if to point up Lantz's characteristic tendency to inconsistency, Mather next played Wally in a straight, non-accented voice in *Bathing Buddies* (1946), before reverting to the Swedish patter in follow-up appearances. Mather supplied several voices for Paramount's *Speaking of Animals* novelty shorts which led to his first Lantz assignment.

Phil Kramer and Sara Berner enacted two crows in the Andy Panda cartoon *The Painter and the Pointer* (1944), the first Andy cartoon to feature the accomplished radio brat Walter Tetley in the title role. Tetley was a splendid radio actor, and his line readings instantly made Andy seem far more sympathetic, as a likable, mild teenage voice. Tetley also used his perpetually child-like voice as *Reddy Kilowatt*, star of his own Lantz industrial cartoon in 1946.

Arguably the finest Universal cartoons of the forties were the impressionistic Swing Symphony musical series. Each cartoon was unique and visually stylized to match a musical genre, ranging from jazz to boogie-woogie to pop. They were loud, brassy and perfectly in tune with the escapist abandon of World War II. These films, which replaced the CarTunes series, were first masterminded in late 1941 by musical director Darrell Calker. Calker had the industry connections and wherewithal to enable him to call on major musical talents from the fields of jazz rooms, nightclubs, records and radio. The resultant cartoons proved to be the greatest marriage of music and art since the best of Disney's Silly Symphonies ten years earlier.

For the memorably scored Swing Symphony *The Pied Piper of Basin Street* (1945), Calker was able to get top jazz trombonist Jack Teagarden. Comedienne Ge Ge Pearson, who played a wide range of crazy roles on radio's *Red Skelton Show*, did the female voices.

Radio stooge Harry Lang, mainly heard in Screen Gems cartoons, did the blubbery Lou Costello-esque Mayor. Earlier Lang took advantage of his biggest cartoon showcase: he played every voice in the excellent Swing Symphony *The Greatest Man in Siam* (1944), which cashed in on the Middle Eastern novelty song recently popularized by Spike Jones & the City Slickers. Lang did a fine job in a range of eccentric comic dialects. Aside from Lang,* the cartoon was noted for its striking design and relentless pacing, another winner for director Shamus Culhane.

* To show the six degrees of separation in the reciprocal worlds of Hollywood radio and cartoon acting, Harry Lang was heard weekly for seven years on radio's long-running *Cisco Kid* western playing the comic Mexican sidekick Pancho, while Cisco was Jack Mather, aka Wally Walrus.

A similar Swing Symphony to the *Siam* entry was *Abou Ben Boogie* (1944) which revisited the evocative Cairo setting, with Pat Matthews contributing wonderful animation of a sexy female. Her slinky singing voice came courtesy of veteran diva Patricia Kay, with Dick Nelson voicing the support roles. Again the cartoon was strikingly designed with its rococo heavy take on ornate Middle-Eastern architecture. [32]

One of the best of the Swing Symphonies, set in a literal ghost town, was *The Boogie Woogie Man Will Get You* (1943), the first of director Culhane's musically energetic Lantz assignments. Its catchy theme song was composed by Alberta Holiner. For this entry Calker hired the Lou Mel Morgan trio, a popular boogie-woogie musical aggregation. They were contracted for three cartoons but only ended up in this one, for which they receive on-screen credit. Dick Nelson, in the best vocal showcase of all his Universal gigs, contributed the voices of the rhyming ghosts for this atmospheric cartoon. [33]

The eccentrically distinctive thespian Hans Conried had already played a most unctuous taxidermist in *Woody Dines Out* (1945) in a voice that sounded like a precursor to the later character star Victor Buono. In a follow-up Lantz gig, Conried narrated the unusual Swing Symphony *Sliphorn King of Polaroo* (1945), for which he received screen credit. In the forties that was virtually unheard of for any character voice artist beyond Mel Blanc at Warners. This was the first Swing directed by Disney-trained animator Dick Lundy, who arrived at Lantz's studio to assist on various government contract shorts during the war years, and to relieve the overburdened Culhane. Like the earlier *Pied Piper* cartoon, *Sliphorn King* featured the trombone artistry and, this time, the distinctive voice of revered jazz man Jack Teagarden in another of Calker's inspired musical selections.

Unique to the Universal cartoons, Lantz and Calker managed to enlist some of the crazy specialty musicians from Spike Jones's wildly popular City Slickers novelty band. Slickers co-founder Del Porter, who maintained his own song writing business in Hollywood, wrote the lyrics and sang for *Boogie Woogie Sioux* (1942). Porter's bandmate, the violinist and singer Carl Grayson, supplied his distinctive "throat glugging" comic vocal effect (re-used on the soundtrack of *Swing Your Partner*), while actor Dick Nelson handled the spoken dialogue.

Porter next added extra lyrics to his own hillbilly novelty song "Pass the Biscuits, Mirandy!," also recently recorded by Spike Jones, for a 1943 Swing Symphony. Lantz and Calker produced a bucolic cartoon based around that cornball number, and Porter sang the song alongside famed voice man and fellow Oregonian Pinto Colvig at his "Goofy hick" best. Edna Harris, a trick voice comedienne then known as "radio's Aircraft Annie," sang and yodelled the female role. [34]

Finally, Porter returned to sing the catchy "Up Jumped the Devil in the White Nightgown" for Lundy's memorable Andy Panda cartoon *Apple Andy* (1946). The trombonist King Jackson, an early Spike Jones sideman, supplied his own distinctive Teagarden-like country drawl for *Cow Cow Boogie* (1943). Following the Swing Symphonies Lantz made several Musical Miniatures, cartoons inspired by classical music. These were mostly voice-less and relied on tightly synchronized visual gags, featuring some excellent animation by Disney legend Freddie Moore.

For his non-musical shorts of the mid-forties Lantz hired more voices from movies and radio, reflecting Culhane's penchant for trying different actors. The familiar, gaunt character player Will Wright spoke for the highly distinctive wolf who co-starred with Woody in 1946 entries like *Fair Weather Fiends* ("My old palsy-walsy"). Wright also used his sandpaper voice, mechanically sped, for the cackling little devil in *Apple Andy*. [35] For the Navy commissioned medical film *The Enemy Bacteria* Lantz got Mel Blanc back to his studio for the voices of the plug-ugly germs; Blanc was now exclusive to Warner Bros. cartoons but was allowed to voice "non-theatricals" for any producer. For this cartoon Lantz also used the accomplished stage actor Thomas Gomez, a recent Universal contractee, as narrator.

Buck Beaver was a "tryout" character appearing in just two cartoons, *Woody the Giant Killer* (1947) and *Scrappy Birthday* (1949), the last of the Andy Pandas. A flim flam con artist-type, the fast-talking beaver was played in the former by Harry Lang and in the latter by Eddie Marr, reprising his famous radio pitch-man spiel, "Tell ya what I'm gonna do!" A young voice actor, Walker Edmiston, filled in as Wally Walrus when Jack Mather was unavailable, and a few so-so characters were done by radio actor Bill Shaw, who provided falsetto voices in cartoons like *Mousie Come Home* (1946).

Gravel-voiced movie character star Lionel Stander played a cat villain in the funny, Oscar-nominated *Fish Fry* (1944); Stander's ex-wife Alice was working at the Lantz studio. The left-leaning activist actor was an early victim of the HUAC investigations into

Communism and by the late forties Stander was already in need of work. He was rehired by Lantz, returning to play Buzz Buzzard in *Wild and Woody* (1948), alongside cartoon veteran Pinto Colvig who was also back with Lantz to play the grizzled old sheriff. [36]

Meanwhile, various female voices were now being handled by Lantz's actress wife, Grace Stafford. She told Lantz biographer Joe Adamson, "I'd been doing the voices of crazy characters and all the women, but I wanted to do Woody. I asked Walter about it, and he said, 'Woody's a boy, you can't do Woody.' So I skipped it." But when Lantz was auditioning actors for a post-Bugs Hardaway Woody voice she went ahead and recorded a tape and, as she recalled, "When they played back [the tapes] they all went for [auditionee] Number Seven. Well, I was Number Seven." [37] Gracie finally took over the role of Woody starting with the character's special appearance in George Pal's sci-fi feature *Destination Moon* (1950).

United Artists and Lantz's Return to Universal

Following World War II the theatrical cartoon landscape became much tougher financially. The government won a long-running antitrust suit, finally ending the old studio practice of block booking, which had compelled theatres to take all of a studio's product. Post war costs for animation production hit an all-time high. Lantz and the new management at Universal-International experienced a falling out when the studio sought ownership of Lantz's characters. In early 1947 he signed with United Artists to distribute his next twelve cartoons for the 1948-49 theatrical season. But within months the UA deal was proving problematic and Lantz laid off his staff. Universal was successfully reissuing Lantz's older cartoons. Lantz closed down for a year in late 1948 and on the advice of his banker, decided to travel to Europe with Gracie.

Upon his return Lantz patched up his differences with long-time associate Universal. Having repaid some loans, he signed a new contract in 1950 to specifically make just Woody Woodpecker cartoons. He re-opened his studio in time for the calendar year of 1951. His budget would be tighter from this point and Lantz watched every dime like a hawk. He had to start over, directing cartoons himself, with just a loyal skeleton staff and no writers. Luckily he was able to take older boards and stories which had been awaiting the green light back in 1948, including cowboy parodies and other material (*Puny Express* and *Sleep Happy*). Drawing on his years of experience Lantz managed to put together ten cheap Woody cartoons, after which one of his top animators Don Patterson became a director.

To save on costs, the first ten films were virtually voice-less. Any minimal dialogue was handled by Mrs. Lantz, aka "Gracie," now Woody's voice for all time. Musician Clarence Wheeler - recommended to Lantz by his friend, the Puppetoon master George Pal - would supply music that, because of the lower budget, could never again equal the bold and brassy work of maestro Darrell Calker, whose unique musical contributions from Swing Symphonies to Musical Miniatures had so stamped the Lantz studio over the preceding decade.

Woody himself had been redesigned in the mid-forties to make him less grotesque looking. Now he was further altered to an easier-to-draw, smaller sized bird to save on costs. But despite the low budget, fate still seemed to smile on Lantz. His recent pantomime Woody cartoons proved as popular as ever, and that feather in his cap meant he could renegotiate terms after thirteen films. Don Patterson proved to be one of Lantz's most successful directors of the early fifties. He was another strong animation talent whose Woody cartoons were funny and as always, totally illogical. The ex-Disney story man Homer Brightman, a victim of Disney's own studio cutbacks, could now afford to be hired. Once Woody's streamlined appearance was okayed, Patterson produced memorable cartoons in the 1952-54 period, including *Belle Boys*, *Alley to Bali* and *The Great Who-Dood-It*.

In 1954, Lantz was able to secure short tours of duty by two of the most ingenious men in the business. Tex Avery did his final four theatrical cartoons for old boss Lantz, turning the cute new penguin star Chilly Willy on his head, in the usual Avery manner of subverting all the rules, for *I'm Cold* (1954). He also produced a typically offbeat cartoon, *Crazy Mixed-Up Pup* (1955). Avery's old colleague, Warner Bros. story man Mike Maltese was regarded as the funniest of that studio's team of scribes. He took advantage of a half-year closure at Warner Cartoons to work for Lantz. Maltese produced a string of Woody and Chilly Willy stories along with several one shot cartoons in 1955 like *Flea for Two* and *Bunco Busters*.

As for his famous woodpecker, Lantz was now happy both creatively and financially that he had approved Gracie in the vocal role. In one interview he said, "She had been in the theatre all her life, and she could project without a mike. She's such a good reader… you look at the early cartoons, the ones Mel [Blanc] did, and the diction is not as clear as it is in the later ones. We don't speed up the voice as much as we used to, because I'd rather have good diction and understand every word." [38]

Unfortunately just as Lantz began using Gracie's voice for his leading character, his cartoons had begun their slow downhill march to the merely formulaic. Certainly by the sixties the quality level of the studio's output was clearly not what it had been twenty years before. And because Woody never progressed beyond being a purveyor of endless physical gags, the dialogue Gracie read sounded just as mechanical as Hardaway's earlier delivery. In any event, following the success of his voiceless Woody cartoons, the budget was at least increased, and Lantz was once again able to hire outside voice actors.

While character voices would become prominent again in Lantz's cartoons, as always cost remained the main factor with Universal. In the mid-fifties budgets for theatrical cartoons faced further industry-wide pruning. Lantz, notorious for being cautiously mindful of the bottom line, decided to consolidate in 1954 and rely on a small core group of voices. The range of casual hired talent, a wide open net in the forties, was reduced to a handful of three or four. It was fortunate that, for his final twenty years of cartoon production, Lantz was able to attract excellent voice artists who somehow made the increasingly bland material sound far more interesting than it actually was.

Actor Dallas McKennon, a former Oregon stock company character man, became the first chief utility voice for Lantz in this phase of the studio. McKennon described himself as a "trick voice" specialist [39], and that he was, speaking for many Lantz cartoons over the remaining years.

McKennon came recommended by veteran voice artist Bill Thompson, the famous Wallace Wimple from radio's *Fibber McGee* show. Thompson had liked a couple of character bit roles McKennon played on that program and urged him to contact cartoon makers. At the time, McKennon was still establishing his acting career in Los Angeles. He was working a day job as an assistant in the sound room at Universal. It was there that Bill Thompson bumped into Lantz. McKennon, standing near a loudspeaker, overheard his own name being mentioned favorably. After auditioning in 1952, he became one of the most regular on-call voices for the rest of Lantz's theatrical career. [40]

McKennon worked with other one-off artists in his first couple of years with Lantz, actors like John T. Smith in *Wrestling Wrecks* (1953) and Nestor Paiva in *Alley to Bali* (1954). McKennon said, "Walter was my stepping-stone out of which I became acquainted with an animator at Disney. A call from Walter Lantz would always be Number One on my list." [41]

Like an acting coach, McKennon referred to his voice as an "instrument," placing characters from three parts of his body. He enjoyed demonstrating how deep voices emanated from his diaphragm, mid-range characters came from his throat and all the high-pitched voices were projected from his nose. He learned to shape his mouth to alter tonalities and could remember precisely what he did on each character voice, even if he was re-booked months later for a few pick-up lines. [42] McKennon enjoyed a long voice-over career because he was a self-starting, instinctive actor.

At first, McKennon was hired to take over the Buzz Buzzard role from Lionel Stander. "Walter needed that voice, and the guy who had been doing it before had moved away." * [43] McKennon's first cartoon was 1952's *The Great Who-Dood-It*, coincidentally the first of many story credits on Lantz cartoons for ex-Disney scribe Homer Brightman.

> *Putting the euphemism to one side, the politically active Stander had been blacklisted by the House Un-American Activities Committee. Virtually all his work for the next decade dried up and in the fifties he moved to Europe.

The scores of roles played by McKennon included Woody's endless adversaries, as well as later characters like Inspector Willoughby, Dapper Denver Dooley, Professor Grossenfibber, and Champ to Paul Frees's Doc. He even became a new voice of Wally Walrus, that character now being virtually interchangeable cartoon by cartoon, from Swedish to Irish constable to British.

McKennon recalled that Walter and Gracie were always present at the recording sessions, along with director Paul Smith and top animator LaVerne Harding. Many times McKennon would be all the voices in a cartoon, such as the breathlessly fast and funny *Legend of Rock-a-Bye Point* (1955) for Tex Avery during that famous director's brief stop at the Lantz studio. That cartoon remained McKennon's personal favorite, "because it was designed for me to do all the voices." [44] He also noted with pride that Lantz created the cartoon *Woodpecker from Mars* (1956) just for him. It was soon after Lantz had seen McKennon hosting a CBS TV kiddie show, playing the space man called "Captain Jet."

Besides recalling his Buzz Buzzard role with affection, McKennon added he was cast "often as a corny hillbilly character or a queasy professor-type. And any kid or animal sound effects, squeaky doors, etcetera." [45] Lantz next introduced McKennon to George Pal, for whom he would work in the feature *The 7 Faces of Dr. Lao* (1964). Eventually he toiled for Art Clokey, becoming the long-running voice for television's famous Claymation character Gumby.

Eternally grateful to Lantz for giving him his animation break, McKennon passed the torch by recommending his Oregon pal Bob Johnson to the cartoon maker. Johnson was a trained baritone singer and actor with an uncommonly strong voice who was hired by Lantz for the cartoon *Calling All Cuckoos* (1956) just two days after his arrival in Hollywood. [46] Johnson also played the ranger in *Niagara Fools* (1956) and was heard interpreting Rossini's "Largo al Factotum" in Alex Lovy's *Plumber of Seville* (1957), for which he was billed on screen as "Vocalist."

Vintage TV buffs will certainly know the obscure Robert Johnson, whose day job as an accountant at Daystar Productions was augmented by voicing various monsters for *The Outer Limits*. They will also surely recall Johnson's seven seasons as the stentorian voice-on-tape at the start of every instalment of *Mission:Impossible* ("This tape will self-destruct in five seconds..."). Johnson returned once to the Lantz studio a decade later to sing for Maxie the polar bear in *Chiller Dillers* (1968).

McKennon was soon sharing cartoon assignments with the top-drawer trio of Daws Butler, June Foray and Paul Frees, who began working for Lantz just before their stellar careers in TV cartoons began taking off. From 1955 McKennon and Daws Butler virtually tied for the number of bookings each got from Lantz, where they worked alongside his wife Gracie in scores of shorts.

Daws Butler and Paul Frees, described elsewhere in this book, were Hollywood's top character voice go-to's in the late fifties, so busy with television and commercial voice-overs that they could have managed very well without any Lantz jobs. But the producer earned their unwavering loyalty. June Foray, who also worked on Lantz cartoons, never forgot that he was the first cartoon producer to regularly give screen credit to all his voice artists. [47] There had been a handful of occasions when an actor other than Mel Blanc was given voice billing in the opening titles, such as Sara Berner's credit on the 1953 *Chilly Willy*. In fact UPA was the first studio to actually give screen credit to cartoon voices on selected shorts in the early fifties. But from the start of 1956 all the way to his final theatrical entry in 1972, Walter Lantz's voice actors were always assured of on-screen "Voices" billing.

Indeed it was only after several years that a Screen Actors Guild union ruling took effect and animation actors finally received screen credit as a matter of course, whether at MGM, DePatie-Freleng or Warner Bros., from 1962 onwards. Back East, Famous Studios and Terrytoons still lagged behind on the issue of voice credit in the fifties.

Daws Butler was able to perform some of his most amusing voices for Lantz, particularly the low-key guard dog Smedley in various *Chilly Willy* entries. Tex Avery first used Butler's amusing North Carolina dialect voice at MGM in *The Three Little Pups* (1953); while he was briefly back as a director with Lantz, Avery asked Butler to do the same taciturn guard dog in *I'm Cold* (1954). The voice was similar to what would become his enduringly famous Huckleberry Hound voice for TV. Windy the bear was another Butler character, which he voiced as a gruff Jackie Gleason-like blowhard. By the late fifties, Gabby Gator was one more dopey voice Butler added for Lantz, while many other one-off characters he played in these cartoons would be used again in his fabled television career for the Hanna-Barbera and Jay Ward dynasties.

Butler knew that his guaranteed five or six Lantz-Universal cartoons each year were always relatively low paying jobs. But the invaluable screen credit meant a lot: he didn't get credit on any of his MGM, UPA or Warner cartoons. And Lantz's loyalty meant a lot too. In his eighteen years with Lantz he never bugged his agent, Miles Auer, to up the fee. [48] Butler recalled, "Walter would always ask his actors to come to his studio on Seward Street and rehearse the storyboard. Then he would call a limo, and Gracie, he and I would travel in style up to the studio on Sunset [Boulevard], do the job in a couple of takes and I'd be driven back in the limo to pick my own car up at Walter's place. It never varied and they were always fun, just marvellously enjoyable sessions." [49]

Lantz appeared in the 1987 documentary *Daws Butler: Voice Magician* and had this to say about his prized voice artist: "Well, [Daws is] one of the loveliest persons I've ever met, and he's so co-operative. In fact he'd always give you more than what you asked him to do. He's just so darned creative, he really makes the character what it is, and I just can't say enough about him. My wife Gracie insisted, 'Be sure and give Daws my love, too.'" [50]

Starting in 1958, the in-demand dialect expert Paul Frees was hired on two Walter Lantz series. In the Hickory, Dickory & Doc cartoons he played the suave conman Doc in an amusingly pompous voice based around a seedy, down-on-his-luck (but ever-dignified) theatrical. For his second series Frees portrayed the harried father Charlie Beary in the long-running Beary Family's Album animated sitcom, which has the dubious distinction of being Lantz's least loved cartoon series. Frees used a Wallace Beery-type voice, similar to the one he had used for Barney Bear at MGM.

Frees was also one of the several Wally Walrus voices over the years, and he portrayed a slew of other fine characters in Cartune one-shots like *Ballyhooey* (1960). From the mid-fifties Paul Frees was prominent and ceaselessly busy on television, especially for Disney and in the Jay Ward cartoons, often voicing much better material than he was given at Lantz's. His movie dubbing and trailer work made him one of the wealthiest of voice artists. Yet he thoroughly enjoyed working with Gracie on the Beary Family shorts, recalling "they were always wonderful, fun get-togethers."[51] (Little wonder: a surviving session audiotape for one of the Beary Family cartoons has Frees, the eternal industry ham, reducing Mrs. Lantz to helpless laughter, just as he did his Jay Ward co-stars at each and every recording date.)

McKennon, Butler and Frees aside, the only other voices of note in Lantz's last fifteen years of theatricals were comedians Benny Rubin and Jerry Mann who did just one cartoon apiece in 1963, *Science Friction* and *Shutter Bug* respectively. That same year Chicago radio veteran Johnny Coons, along with Paul Frees, voiced a TV pilot for Walter called *The Secret Weapon*, featuring the character Space Mouse. Sadly, June Foray became a rarer performer as Lantz's budgets shrank ever tighter, with Gracie handling virtually all the female parts. For a non-full time voice specialist Gracie managed to come up with a flock of amusing one-time characters, but her range was frankly limited when compared with the top female voice creators like Foray and Sara Berner.

Due to the enormous popularity of his older cartoons on ABC-TV's high-rating *Woody Woodpecker Show*, Lantz's theatrical cartoons continued being made on a regular basis, outlasting every animation house in Hollywood except for De Patie-Freleng. By the mid-sixties cinema cartoons were still being enjoyed, or occasionally tolerated, but their days were plainly numbered. Lantz was as aware as anyone that the glory days of the forties were long past. It was apparent that several TV cartoons now seemed livelier than their theatrical cousins, which collectively had dwindled into a tired and often lacklustre breed.

However there were still bright moments in various Lantz cartoons of the sixties because some of the people who worked for him were top drawer talents. Alex Lovy returned in 1955 when Tex Avery vacated after directing four cartoons. Lovy began with a strong Chilly Willy, *Hot and Cold Penguin* (1955), a cartoon that felt as though it had been started by Avery. Lovy continued making the Chilly Willy's, an occasional Woody Woodpecker, and some interesting one shots like *The Bongo Punch* (1957) which auditioned a character named Pepito Chickeeto, the one occasion for which voice actor Hal Smith did a Lantz cartoon. Lovy also directed the early Hickory, Dickory & Doc cartoons like *Space Mouse* (1959). He completed a five year post as a Lantz director. When he left for Hanna-Barbera, his position was filled by the ace ex-Disney man Jack Hannah who directed many fine Donald Duck and Humphrey Bear cartoons in the mid-fifties.

Hannah made one freelance cartoon for Lantz in 1959, *Bee Bopped*, featuring the bear characters Windy and Breezy. Like Homer Brightman before him, Hannah was a victim of Disney's short cartoon cutbacks in the mid-fifties. Universal studio veteran Clyde Geronimi put in a word for Hannah who soon landed the directing spot at Lantz's Seward Street studio. He began by helming some of the one shot Cartunes, then alternated with Paul Smith on various Woody, Chilly and Doc-Champ cartoons. Hannah and Lantz shared a keen interest as hobbyist painters and would socialize on weekends.

Some of the cartoons in this period were a little Disney-esque, not surprising when considering Hannah's strong influence and the addition of ex-Disney story men Al Bertino and Dick Kinney. The gag element was even more to the fore in mid-sixties Lantz cartoons made by veteran animator-writer-director Sid Marcus who had always possessed a comic bent. Marcus joined in late 1964, and worked with his long-time Screen Gems animator colleague Arthur Davis, making a few funny entries like *Teepee for Two* (1963) and *Half-Baked Alaska* (1965). Marcus and his seasoned story-gag man Cal Howard, who had last worked together in the dying days of the old Screen Gems studio, were the final new hires. Howard's relationship with Lantz stretched back to the early thirties.

To the end, Lantz was one of the most loyal of animation bosses. Aware that theatrical cartoon costs were plunging even further, he groused ever louder to the trade papers. As ever Lantz sided with his creative people, whether long-time animators or his ink-&-paint crew. What he constantly fretted over was that he could never get any increase from exhibitors, season after season. Cost-cutting around his studio became the norm as storyboards and layouts were examined for any money-saving areas, as was often glaringly obvious in the later films.

With better offers in the television cartoon field, Lantz lost three of his talented directors in his last decade, as he watched Alex Lovy, Jack Hannah and Sid Marcus gradually depart; Marcus ended up at DePatie-Freleng working on some of the early seventies shorts like *The Blue Racer* series. This left just Paul J. Smith to handle the final eighty cartoons! Little wonder that most of Lantz's pictures in the last six years of his Universal release looked pretty dismal, akin to the cheesiest of TV animation, and in the last films often below that level.

The overworked Smith, while a fully competent animation veteran, was not simply hampered by the continuing budget cuts. His eyesight had gradually failed to the point of legal blindness, and his daughter had been trained by him to fill out his exposure sheets. [52] And to be honest, Smith, although a total professional, lacked the deeper comic gift of men like a Tex Avery or even a Sid Marcus: his many cartoons often appeared to be made on a treadmill, the gags produced on Valium-induced autopilot.

At best, the last decade of Lantz studio shorts were pleasant time fillers. The Woodpecker's own competing TV show, which reran the studio's golden age classics, proved that Lantz's glory days were now far behind him. But at least there was consistency of employment for loyal staff members, from background artists to long-time sound editors. In this period, it was Lantz's talented company of voice artists who performed the old actor's magic of "plussing up" what were, increasingly, uninspired stories, hackneyed dialogue and cookie-cutter comedy situations.

If Lantz's many one-off characters like hunter Colonel Potshot or Western villain Dirty McNasty were strictly one dimensional ciphers, their voices at least were amusing to the end. And each year from 1961 to the end of production in 1971, actors Dal McKennon, Daws Butler and Paul Frees unfailingly found Lantz cartoon bookings in their busy schedules, with each artist continuing to enjoy a fond relationship with the veteran producer. It is unfortunate that his late-era films were so lamentable, the equivalent of how far the Warner cartoons had fallen.

Still, Lantz's long career as a successful producer lasted over forty years and he is considered one of the animation industry's bona fide legends. Certainly some of his forties output was often as good as short cartoons could get, and his reputation remains secure today. It is obvious he loved doing what he did from his silent film days to the last. Year after year his cartoons were gagfests, pure and simple, with zero artistic pretensions beyond that goal. Walter Lantz remained supremely happy knowing that his films had made millions of people laugh. And that's surely a noble achievement in the entertainment game.

Chapter 6:

WALT DISNEY Cartoon Voices, 1928-70

On the West Coast Walt Disney was the acknowledged industry leader, almost from the advent of sound. Disney's studio was where the art of the short cartoon was developed. From story to animation drawings to specialised areas like character layouts, effects animation and backgrounds, in every detail the Disney studio excelled. And it was all dominated by Walt himself, and that made the difference. No other cartoon plant had an overall genius in charge of every nut and bolt. The smaller animation players all knew it and were glad to be in the same game, to enjoy the benefit of each Disney advance. When viewed chronologically, Disney's output can clearly be seen improving, film by film. By 1933 the best artists wanted to gravitate to Disney. Not only was it the one studio where the art of animation -"the illusion of life"- was lovingly perfected along with characterization and caricature, but the main emphasis with the new sound cartoons was the uncanny synchronizing of action with music. Most of the early Mickeys and Silly Symphonies had virtually no dialogue, but there were musical and dance sequences aplenty, all calculated to delight movie audiences with unexpected comic effects. It was obvious the whole of team Disney was experimenting, undertaking training programs, stretching each artist's abilities, and developing and refining their cartooning skills with each project. The great creative experiment that was "Walt Disney ani-

*mation" spanned a full nine years between 1928's Steamboat
Willie and Disney's triumphant feature film* Snow White and
The Seven Dwarfs.

Part 1: Beginnings and Voices in
Walt Disney short cartoons

Unlike this book's other chapters, it would be pointless to attempt
a potted chronology of Disney history to accompany this study of
the many voice talents who worked for the studio. Disney history
is a gigantic topic and material on its many areas exists in abun-
dance. Specific films and animators, as well as biographies of Walt
and innumerable other topics have been scrupulously covered by
the most accomplished animation historians including Leonard
Maltin, Michael Barrier, J. B. Kaufman and John Canemaker. Revisiting various well known high points in the studio's development
would simply be redundant in this book. And so this chapter will
deal solely with the many unique voice talents who worked for Walt
Disney Productions.

Almost all Disney's early recording department logs have sadly
been lost to the ages. The late David R. Smith, creator and long-
time head of Walt Disney Archives, its famous repository of studio
records, admitted to *Funnyworld* magazine that, "Our files on voices
are not well-arranged, and on some films we have to dig from several different sources." [1] It is only from mid-1935, seven years after
sound cartoons began, that any paperwork of value on the voices
begins to survive. And solid information remains patchy for a few
more years.

In the thirties the Disney Studio could deservedly boast about
having the most famous characters in the world of animation. However the area of voice artistry was actually not a top priority in Disney's first five years of making sound cartoons. Far more important
was the imaginative synchronizing of music with the animation.

That said, however, voices were certainly there from the start of sound.

As we saw in Chapter One, the Disney cartoon voice saga begins in late 1928 with the New York recording session for the legendary *Steamboat Willie*, the first cartoon to use and blend sound effects, music and even primitive voices creatively and entertainingly. And it is entirely appropriate that the very first cartoon character voice of any consequence, a mocking ship's parrot, was spoken by the greatest name in animation history, Walt Disney. [2] A tad unintelligibly, the bird squawks, "Hope ya don't feel hurt, big boy!"

Note that Disney's famous mouse doesn't actually speak in *Willie* - his happy whistling was supplied by the orchestra's piccolo player - but Disney does provide vocal noises for Mickey and villain Pete, as well as doing Minnie's famous greeting, "Yoo hoo!" And it is this cartoon, as primitive as it might look and sound ninety five years later, that hinted at what could be done with the use of character voices in animation. It took a while at the Disney studio, however.

The earliest actual vocal artists, beyond occasional squeaks and grunts provided by staff members, were specialists in the art of what was then called "barnyard mimicry," a vaudeville and tent show novelty performance genre. Its practitioners were anxiously on the lookout for any new avenues for work: by the mid-twenties, many of their opportunities for live entertainment (such as vaudeville or the more family-oriented Chautauqua circuit) were already dying out. The old stage venues had seen business drop off dramatically, fallen victims to the advent of 20th century show biz technologies exemplified by the newfangled "talkies" and the ubiquitous radio set in every home.

Indeed, both radio and sound cartoon opportunities came along just in time for these artists. Unique and eccentric talents like Count Gaetano Cutelli, A. Purves Pullen and Melvin J. Gibby made themselves and their career résumés known to the Disney brothers. As we will see, animation with sound meant they would be called upon to crow like roosters, whinny like horses and croak like a genuine frog. These oddly gifted artists, most of whom had practiced animal sounds since childhood with a perfectionist's zeal, thrived in the field of thirties cartoons, also toiling at MGM, Schlesinger, Mintz-Columbia and any other animation makers who were attempting to copy the Disney model. While their vocal sound effects could be startlingly authentic, it was their native performing skills that mattered: being musically talented meant they could augment their already striking abilities at vocal noises by making them sync in rhythm to jazzy music. These show business "one-offs" were marked as valued players in the pre-dialogue era of sound animation.

Aside from the barnyard imitators, there were the finely honed talents of whistling and chirping specialists. Esther Campbell, Ruby Ray and Marion Darlington, whose abilities at mimicking and trilling a wide variety of birdlife, were astounding performers. Their talents were so realistic it was almost as if the animated canaries, robins, quails, crows and chickens on screen were being accompanied by field recordings of actual avian life. These dedicated artists might have appeared a little strange to outsiders, but the directors of cartoons like *The Bird Store, The Wayward Canary* (both from 1932) and *Birds in the Spring* (1933) benefited tremendously from their contributions.

Along with the bird whistlers were various in-house voices by both animation and sound staff including some with musical ability, and others with a flair for comic exaggeration like the audio specialist Hal Rees who was put in charge of the Disney sound effects department.

As for Mickey Mouse himself, confusion about his earliest voice remains a mystery almost a century later. Disney's first staff musician, the gifted and capable Carl Stalling, owned up to doing some of Mickey's earliest noises before Disney himself famously became the definitive voice of his starring rodent. Stalling also claimed other studio staff were called on to speak into a microphone. [3]

This meant that for some ten cartoons in 1929, Mickey's limited early dialogue was shared. A couple of early attempts sound distinctly non-Mickey, and one falsetto voice is plainly not Disney's. Indeed, although it's unconfirmed, several Disney scholars have posited that Stalling was likely the slightly feminine singing voice when the mouse warbles the memorable "Minnie's Yoo Hoo" show-stopper in *Mickey's Follies* (1929).

As for actual voice acting it sounds much like Disney doing at least some of the mouse's dialogue in *Mickey's Choo Choo* (1929), the first Mickey cartoon to feature a small spoken exchange between Mickey and Minnie. Yet Carl Stalling claimed to have done that speech too. Stalling even owned up to singing for an off-key bass walrus in *Wild Waves* (1929), his final Disney cartoon before he departed in early 1930, eventually working at the animation studio of Walt's former colleague Ub Iwerks. [4]

Was Mickey himself ever voiced by a woman? A note appeared in a late 1930 issue of *Variety* stating that Helen Lynd had been a fill-in Mickey voice. [5] Ms Lynd was one of several high-voiced female artists heard in thirties films and animation using their distinctively squeaky "little" voices that were perfectly pitched for portraying exaggerated children and comically cute animals. So where do we place her? Her name doesn't appear in the Disney Archives character voice files.

It's all moot, however. The definitive voice of Mickey Mouse was, as everyone knows, Walt Disney himself. By sometime in 1930 his familiar falsetto voice can be heard regularly, even if the rodent's dialog was still minimal at this point. Disney knew, precisely, the character he was after for his star attraction and he could project just the right emotion when the little mouse was still a feisty, somewhat mischievous character. And always with that appealingly authentic Midwestern twang that Disney carried in his own voice.

Disney himself admitted in one interview, "I've always [sic] done The Mouse's talking. He's a shy little feller so I've always provided the voice. I use a falsetto. His voice changed after I had my tonsils out. It became a little deeper. I kind of like it better. [But] I'm sorry I started the voice. It takes a lot of time and I feel silly doing The Mouse in front of the sound crew." [6]

Minnie Mouse was another voice that took a few cartoons to get right. In 1971 director Wilfred Jackson told Archives founder Dave Smith, "At first we didn't pre-score the voices; everything was recorded at the same time onto one track. We could only use short, little phrases, so they could be said to rhythm. [Assistant animator] Merle Gilson's wife [Marjorie], who worked in Ink and Paint, sometimes did Minnie until Marcellite started." [7] Disney finally settled on Marcellite Garner for Minnie's voice in *The Cactus Kid* (1930). Ms Garner was another of the studio's regular Ink and Paint artists, although she occasionally worked at other studios in this capacity, like Harman-Ising.

Almost half a century later Marcellite Garner recalled doing her earliest voice work for director Burt Gillett, who needed a voice with a tinge of Spanish for *The Cactus Kid*. "Most of my direction came from Walt, as he was Mickey's voice. He would go through a whole situation and act out all of the characters and explain the mood 'til I really felt the part. No one else could 'become' all the characters as Walt did." [8]

Ms Garner remembered the early Melrose Ave. sound studio Tec-Art which Disney used before the recording stage was built at his Hyperion Avenue studio. She recorded some early soundtracks "in one" with the orchestra and sound effects people: "The dialogue was written on a music score, with the words falling at certain points or bars of music and we worked it into a sort of rhythm with the director giving us the signal when to come in, just as he would some instrument. I was Minnie's voice from early 1930 to sometime in 1941 when I left the [Los Angeles] area. Other sounds I did were just miscellaneous animal sounds…barking, meowing, etcetera." [9]

In a letter to her long-time industry friend Bob Clampett, whom she met while working at Harman-Ising, she wrote, "So often Minnie just screamed or la-la'd or just said a phrase or two. In one recording [for *Blue Rhythm* (1931)] Minnie sang 'St. Louis Woman' in a raspy voice, low down and dirty, of all things. What a day! By the time we finished that I couldn't even talk. In *The Gorilla Mystery* (1930), Minnie sang 'All Alone by the Telephone' and then screamed her way through the rest, and I do mean scream. I used to give it my all." [10]

Marcellite Garner had just the right modest and giggly vocal quality for the plucky, piano-playing girlfriend role. The early thirties was a period that is essentially alien to most of today's far more jaded and harsh society, almost a century on. A huge portion of the moviegoing population back then was still rural, and the small town values of virtue, reticence and a general air of a much more innocent time are reflected in the early Disney films.

But as primitive as those early cartoons might appear now, Mickey and Minnie still come across as essentially authentic, with their nervous shuffles, slightly embarrassed giggles and awkward pauses. They are certainly a far cry from the streetwise urban world of the Fleischer Studio characters from that period, let alone the wiseass Hollywood cartoon stars to come. Disney had the common touch sewed up: from the early thirties audiences in the farm belt and vast areas of middle America related emotionally to the likable naiveite of Mickey and his gang, making him easily the most popular cartoon character in the first part of the decade.

Mickey and Minnie were well established in 1931, and the Disney brothers no longer took a sound truck to the Tec-Art Studio. Disney's own building now boasted its own recording facility, headed by chief audio engineer William Garity.

The sound room was colorfully described in a 1932 *McCalls* article. It was just one of many thirties pieces about Disney and the "how-to" making of cartoons, a topic of unending fascination for moviegoers who read movie magazines and even general interest publications.

After detailing the story and animation departments at Disney's Hyperion Avenue studio, author Henry Pringle reported, "The second division of the work is under way; the recording of the music and sound effects. The sound-proof room is the maddest of all the weird subdivisions of the Disney Studio. It is a large hall, rather similar in appearance to the average broadcasting studio. A small orchestra is seated in the left-hand corner, as you enter. At the opposite end is a glass-enclosed control room from which the orchestra is conducted. Stretching almost the length of the room at the right is a long table with a conglomeration of instruments and four or five men standing in front of it. A microphone is in front for each of them, and several [more mikes] are near the orchestra. These are the sound experts and they can simulate any noise imaginable. On the day I was there they were recording for a film called *Mickey's Revue* [1932], the idea of which is a musical show staged by Mickey, with his barnyard family as the cast. One young man barked repeatedly into a microphone and did it with incredible artistry. Another imitated a cow. Another was a pig. They made thunder by rattling tin sheets. Tap dancing was done by a shirt-sleeved youth who slapped on a cushion with the palms of his hands."

One of the earliest "outside" professional voices was a distinguished stage actor from Oakland, California named Lee Millar who happened to possess a secondary skill for realistic animal effects, which kept him busy on various radio drama calls. He was the first to do the canine sounds that would soon define Pluto the pup, after he was hired for the embryonic bloodhound noises in *The Chain Gang* (1930). Millar, long married to actress Verna Felton, herself a Disney character voice to come, was gainfully employed in many thirties Disney cartoons until his untimely sudden death on Christmas Eve of 1941.

But the first truly outstanding funny cartoon voice at Disney's belonged to a former circus clown, newspaper cartoonist, silent film comedy gagster and musician named Vance "Pinto" Colvig. Always ambitious, he joined the Disney outfit late in the fall of 1930, after almost a year at Walter Lantz's cartoon shop at Universal City. Colvig had performed a raft of sound effects, music and a few cartoony voices there (he was one of the many voices for Oswald the Lucky Rabbit). But it was at the Disney plant where his vocal talents developed into much sharper focus. Although Colvig's main role at Disney was ostensibly in the scenario and gag department, contributing funny material, the sound stage would end up being his main venue.

Beyond Colvig's ability at funny voices, he showed boundless creative ingenuity at adding sound effects, both vocally and mechanically, to a cartoon's track. These included airplane effects achieved on a slide trombone, cow moos via his ever-present yellow clarinet, motorboat noises made on a derby hat, an old car engine via his throat, and the sounds of creatures like a fly, a beetle, a bird, dogs, in fact you name it. [11] Indeed he had already done much in this field for both Lantz and Harman-Ising. But it was as a Disney character voice that Colvig would become one of the Disney Legends.

For the Mickey Mouse entry *Barnyard Olympics* (1932) Colvig came up with the dull-witted laughter of an annoying old audience member. That unique guffaw had an infectiously funny quality that greatly amused cinema audiences. It was a voice Disney was quick to use again, and a month later the chortling character was given the name of Dippy Dawg for *Mickey's Revue*. By year's end the voice had developed further and he was renamed Goofy. Slowly that "cornfed hick," as Colvig described both himself and the cartoon character, became one of the all-time popular members of Mickey's gang. [12]

In interviews Colvig often referred to him as "Goofy the half-wit." For one story he recalled, "It's funny where I got the idea for Goofy's voice. Every American small town has a Goofy, a village character. Disney was rapidly developing [Goofy], and he seemed to me more and more like one of those big bucolic youths of the village who have no particular aim in life...I knew one such lad in Oregon. He was a flagman at the railroad crossing. His voice was perfect and I studied it until I had every shade and nuance down." [13]

Colvig also contributed occasional barks and yipe-ing noises for Pluto when Lee Millar was unavailable. Story man Homer Brightman recalled that for the Mickey cartoon *Alpine Climbers* (1936), Disney suggested the end gag where both Pluto and the hefty St. Bernard get drunk and dog-sing together. He paraphrased Disney at a gag meeting: "At the end both dogs lean together for a long chord. Get [Pinto] to do the dog voices. The St. Bernard should have a deep bass voice and Pluto a high one. After he does both voices, we'll dub them together." [14]

Colvig's eccentric talents were always good for a human interest story and he was frequently interviewed in the thirties for radio and movie columns describing his eclectic range of duties. In one of these he even discussed his boss: "[Walt] Disney is the voice of Mickey, and he is pleasing to work with. [In some ways he is] just a big boy, who will never grow up. He's a young fellow, about thirty two or thirty three, who takes humor very seriously." [15]

Unlike some of the earliest Disney studio voices, Colvig had been a stage performer. He possessed genuine acting and singing ability and his talents were given a fine showcase in the Silly Symphony *The Grasshopper and the Ants* (1934). The grasshopper's voice was close to his own straight voice in a moralistic tale calling for restrained performance while remaining charmingly cartoony, as he sang the catchy song "The World Owes Me a Living." Colvig, who contributed to the song's original lyrics, said his voice was recorded in four different ways before the final take was selected. "We had to be particular about [that] voice. It would spoil the grasshopper's personality if we used the wrong one. We decided the grasshopper was just a country boy who had been misinformed."

Typically, he couldn't resist adding, "It wasn't the words I wrote for [the cartoon] that I was particularly proud of, it was the high, wide and fancy spittin!'" [16] *

*Many early thirties cartoons have characters spitting tobacco juice; in the 21st century, when cigarette smoking has declined markedly, the sight must appear totally alien to millions of younger viewers who have never heard of tobacco chewing. But decades ago it was relatively common for some folk to chew or suck on cured, flavored tobacco, the excess juice from which was spat. (Perhaps a hundred years from now someone might need to explain if a 21st century cartoon character is seen vaping!)

Colvig's other famous early role, before his great Goofy voice attained full stardom, was the industrious bricklaying Practical Pig in Disney's most successful short cartoon *Three Little Pigs* (1933). Colvig recalled, "We were going to have an off-screen voice telling us about each of the little pigs, then it seemed better to have each pig [sing] about himself." Colvig also contributed to the instantly popular feel-good Depression song "Who's Afraid of the Big Bad Wolf?," explaining, "At first, the idea was to have the three little pigs dancing around singing 'Who's afraid of the woo-oo-oolf?' For no reason at all I said, 'Big bad wolf.' It sounded silly. But [musician] Frank Churchill said, 'That's it!' And in about five minutes he worked out the tune with one finger on the piano." [17]

Colvig's co-stars were the two carefree pigs voiced by girl singers Dorothy Compton and Mary Moder who were members of a busy radio trio called The Rhythmettes. Ms Compton recalled, "[Mary] and I started singing as a duo. We were on early [Los Angeles] radio programs like *Dot and Mary* for a long while. Our voices just blended beautifully. And Mary Moder, she didn't have any training whatsoever. I was [studying at first to be] a concert pianist." [18]

The young women soon decided a close harmony trio would make more money than a twosome. In fact their trio, named The Rhythmettes, had already done several cartoons starting in 1931 with Harman-Ising's Merrie Melodies.

For Disney's *Pigs* classic, they were a duo once more, singing as they always had. Dorothy Compton: "I had the harmony. [Mary] had the melody." Disney worked with them, as he did with all outside talent. "He'd first of all tell us what the story was, and what we were supposed to sound like, and when we were frightened and when we were not, and to put it into our voices. So we kind of just did it naturally, we would get childish voices like, 'I build my house of twigs'…high voices. I know we didn't spend much time [on the recording], because we only got ten dollars for it, according to Mary." [19]

Dorothy Compton did *Three Little Pigs* and its 1934 follow-up *The Big Bad Wolf*, before she left The Rhythmettes to sing with Ted Fio Rito's orchestra in a vocal trio called The Debutantes. She recalled that Disney "always had a musician, an arranger, so we'd follow the notes and the lyrics. Frank Churchill was the pianist. [And Pinto Colvig] I remember so well. He did a lot more things [around the studio]. He was working for Disney's a great deal." [20]

It was for the milestone *Pigs* cartoon that Colvig, who had been appointed a voice casting consultant for Disney, invited his actor pal from silent comedy days, William Bletcher, to audition his very deep voice for the memorably villainous wolf role. Long before Mel Blanc was regarded as the top voice man in Golden Age animation there was the remarkable Billy Bletcher (1894-1979).

Bletcher was the earliest freelance artist to specialize in "character" voices, unlike his contemporaries Clarence "Donald Duck" Nash and Walt "Mickey Mouse" Disney, who basically did just one starring voice each. Today Bletcher remains one of animation's vocal heavyweights, notching up a gallery of superbly menacing performances in scores of classic-era cartoons. His voice was an incredibly elastic bass instrument which he had been using since his days as a young comedy singer.

Bletcher, born in Lancaster, Pennsylvania, stood just over five feet tall, making his incongruously belligerent basso even more striking. Bletcher's father appeared in comic opera, and young Billy began as a spotlight singer for slide shows, interrupted by a brief fling in music publishing, before he worked as a character-singing waiter in a restaurant at New York's Sheepshead Bay. "It came easy to me because when I was a kid I used to sing all the old dialect songs like 'I'm Not Homesick for Germany.' You picked up a sheet of music that called for a dialect, and you did it that way." [21]

A movie comedy troupe from the Vitagraph company saw him performing at the diner and invited him to their studio, where he scored a role in a Mabel Normand short followed by some parts in feature pictures. Bletcher, keen to explore the production end of movies, became an assistant director, learning aspects of the film business thoroughly.

With his wife Arline, Bletcher next transferred to the Vim Comedy Company in Jacksonville, Florida, where a youthful, chubby actor named Oliver Hardy was being nurtured. He finally headed west to the booming Southern California picture industry. Once settled in Hollywood he played a Keystone Kop for Mack Sennett, while working steadily as both an actor and behind the camera for film outfits like Christie Comedies and Universal. Bletcher's years in short comedies, dating from 1914, honed his natural comic sense of timing to pinpoint sharpness.

With the advent of the "talkies," Bletcher appeared in Hal Roach comedies, where his rich, deep voice suddenly became his fortune. In 1930 he began dubbing character voices for live-action animals in MGM's *Dogville* novelty shorts. He said, "Once sound films came into being, I went almost completely out of [on-camera acting] and into the voice business. That part of my career was something of an accident. I never had any voice training. It's just one of those natural things, I suppose." He was soon specializing in voice dubbing work for major directors like Cecil B. DeMille: "I think I worked on the sound stage with him on every big picture that he made. Re-dubbing noisy crowd scenes." [22]

It was in late 1932 that Bletcher met Disney. As he recalled, "[Pinto Colvig] was a gag writer for Mack Sennett when I first came out to California." Disney had expressed his need for a truly distinctive villainous voice for the Big Bad Wolf in his upcoming *Three Little Pigs* (1933). "Pinto invited me to come over. [The audition] wasn't much to do except voices saying things like, 'I'll huff and I'll puff and I'll blow your house in!!'" [23]

For the menacing wolf Bletcher provided a memorably malevolent performance, cementing a solid relationship with Disney and starting his long cartoon career as the first vocal performer to be recognized by the public. Bletcher said, "I sort of made a hit with Walt, and stayed with him for [over twenty years], without ever being on steady salary, but always sure of three or four calls per week. I was the Big Bad Wolf and another character, Pegleg Pete, a tough sort of a guy who snarled all the time. It was a lovely engagement." [24]

Bletcher's vocal range was impressive: along with his thunderous bass, he could also affect a falsetto whining tone. "I gained a fairly substantial reputation for doing odd voices and dialects." He handled comical singing and specialized in burlesque accents: "In vaudeville, almost everybody *except* basso profundo used dialect!" He did French, such as the hulking Pierre in Disney's *Timber* (1941), what was commonly known in vaudeville as "Dutch" dialect for his lead role in MGM's Captain and the Kids series, and stock Irish for burly cops in Disney's *The Autograph Hound* (1939) and Donald Duck's moody fever-dream *Duck Pimples* (1945). [25]

From the mid-thirties Bletcher was also a fixture in Warner Bros. cartoons including the title role in *The Lone Stranger and Porky* (1939), as well as working for Iwerks, Lantz, Mintz-Screen

Gems, and dubbing the offstage voice of *The Lone Ranger* in two Republic live action chapter serials in 1938-39. Later he added dubbing work for George Pal's Puppetoons.

Bletcher immediately sensed that Disney was a standout director. "Walt was a great man for story. They'd sit around for weeks and weeks arguing some story point. His ability to visualize when he was listening back to recordings was marvellous; he'd say, 'That just doesn't ring true to me.'"[26] In the mid-thirties for dialogue heavy cartoons a director would sometimes photograph a voice talent as they were recording. When Bletcher voiced the voracious King Midas in *The Golden Touch*, a cartoon directed by Disney himself, he recalled "They put white on my lips, for the animator to animate from, and photographed me that way." [27]

Bletcher remembered, "At that time [mid-to-late thirties], there were only four or five voice pros [like me] including Mel Blanc and Pinto Colvig and Clarence Nash. We didn't make a lot of money, but we had regular work. In the old days we got no screen credits. Also, the voice people were never under contract. Graphic artists made the real money. We received seventy dollars for one session, and a session could last all day, although we tried to get out as quickly as possible." [28]

One of Bletcher's claims to film immortality was re-dubbing the voice of the dwarf actor who played the Mayor of Munchkin City in *The Wizard of Oz* (1938). This author's favorite, however, is Bletcher's hilarious on-camera performance in the 1953 George Pal production *Houdini*, starring a young Tony Curtis. In the film he plays "Larrazini, the Little Man with the Big Voice," a down and out opera basso working a strictly tank-town vaudeville circuit. He is seen on a dodgy makeshift stage in a show for a bunch of rough and raucous miners, and as he sings the unbelievably deep notes of Preston Sturges's song "Boom Boom, Tolled the Bell in the Bay," he is ignominiously pelted with rotten tomatoes by the unruly hecklers. Bletcher is not only vocally funny, but he draws on his years in silent comedy to be visually hilarious as he calmly ducks and weaves, as if practiced in the art of dodging audience missiles over a thousand awful one-night stands. He affects a comically offended look, bringing a magnificent seedy elegance to his role. It is an unforgettable bit part, one of scores of minuscule live action roles Bletcher essayed from the thirties onward.

Billy Bletcher died in January 1979, soon after filming a role in TV's *Charlie's Angels*. It was the end of a sixty five-year career as one of the most unique specialty talents in Hollywood. He is, naturally, one of this book's heroes.

In 1932 as the music in the cartoons became richer and more melodic the use of professional singers increased. The groups included male quartets like The Uptowners and the Three Rhythm Kings along with various female trios. Trained vocalists from the field of comic operetta found a place in Hollywood choral work for endless features and shorts. Allan Watson was a full voiced baritone who was a leading Gilbert and Sullivan interpreter. He sang for the Silly Symphonies, giving life to jolly kings and characters like Noah, Santa Claus and Neptune. For the deepest of deep notes, basso profundo Delos Jewkes was called in, while the ringing tenor voice of young Kenny Baker, some time before he gained fame as the addled vocalist on Jack Benny's comedy program, was a singing narrator in Silly entries like *The Goddess of Spring* (1934). [29] The cartoon industry provided considerable employment for Hollywood's vocal fraternity during the thirties, and much of their classiest work was for Disney.

Colvig remained a voice caster at Disney's until he departed in the fall of 1937. While at the studio, he gave opportunities to a range of outré talents. He was in on the auditions for bird whistlers like Esther Campbell and Marion Darlington, and the singular Miss Florence Gill, an elderly British-born operatic soprano who had an ability to mimic hens and chickens and comically time their cackling to music. [30] She became known on radio by her cartoon moniker "The Barnyard Nightingale" and was called to Disney's mainly to cackle for the grandiose character of Dame Clara Cluck. She and another lady named Dorothy Lloyd handled virtually all the hens and baby chick sounds in West Coast cartoon-dom.

Others odd voices included a range of indefinable character people now relegated to almost total obscurity. Purves Pullen was one barnyard mimic who had a specialty of whistling. He reproduced over a hundred rare bird species and had a melodious ability at different types of chirps and tooth-and-lip puckers. Pullen had a featured stage act with bandleader Ben Bernie where he was billed as "Whistling Pullen." After doing realistic animal dubbing like Tarzan's cheetah and for other jungle features, he joined the Disney bird whistle fraternity. Pullen's own straight whistling can be heard at the start of *Who Killed Cock Robin?* (1935) and in the forties he toured for several seasons with Spike Jones's comic band, recording novelty sides like "Old MacDonald Had a Farm" and "Mother Goose Medley" featuring many of his cartoon sounds.

Another talented barnyard mimic was Melvin J. Gibby who was working for Charm Cosmetics when he auditioned for Colvig at the studio. His hobby was being "an imitator of almost any kind of animal you can mention" [31] and he was good enough to impress the Disney people instantly. Gibby ended up in thirties cartoons at various studios as realistically guttural horses, dogs and donkey brays. For his 1939 memoir *It's a Crazy Business*, Colvig wrote, "No doubt you've since heard [Gibby] dozens of times in many animated cartoons, motion pictures and on the radio."

In that autobiographical work Colvig helpfully recalled some even rarer voices that would otherwise have slipped under the radar. He noted that the jolly laughing used for Santa Claus in *Santa's Workshop* (1932) belonged to a tall Hollywood undertaker named Bill Geiger. And, discovered in-house, Disney's legal counsel Gunther Lessing could apparently produce excellent rooster and goat sounds!

But by far the most long lasting of all the many auditionees was Clarence Nash (1904-85) who became world famous as Donald Duck. Nash was described by Colvig as "a serious young man dressed in a milkman's unform" [32] who was a promotional actor working for the Adohr Milk Company. Nash performed various bird calls, horse-whinnying and trick voices like baby cries. People amused by his talents began to suggest he seek professional opportunities in the movies and broadcasting. By late 1931 Nash appeared on a local Los Angeles radio comedy called *The Merry Makers*. Soon after, he dropped in to Disney's Hyperion Avenue studio (after spotting the large Mickey Mouse billboard on the roof). He left a circular describing his range of bird sounds, and a few days later got a phone call from animation director Wilfred Jackson.

Nash dropped into the studio. He recalled that Jackson "liked my bird sounds. He said, 'We can use them. What else can you do?' So I did my whole act, all the farm animal sounds and my specialty, 'Mary Had a Little Lamb' as recited by a baby goat. Right in the middle, [Jackson] reached over and secretly switched on the intercom. The sound went into Disney's office. Walt came down. After I finished my recitation I said, 'Now we will hear some chickens, baby turkeys, baby ducks...now mama and papa duck.' Walt looked at [Jackson] and said, 'That's the duck we've been looking for.'"[33]

As it transpired, Disney had heard Nash on the *Merry Makers* show that week and was interested in hiring him. "Walt really wasn't ready yet to make a cartoon with a duck [that was months away] but the same day of my audition he did have me record some bird sounds for a 'Silly Symphony' cartoon, *The Bird Store* [1932]." [34] As Nash was leaving, he met Ted Osborne who was his radio producer on *Merry Makers*. "He said, 'Hey, Walt heard you that night, he was going to look you up.' So it was just one of those things [like fate]. We had to meet." [35]

Over the next two years Disney continued to call Nash in for various sounds like birds, horse whinnying and more. Nash also began getting live entertainment bookings for parties around the

Los Angeles area along with Florence "Clara Cluck" Gill. Soon he was appearing on occasional radio shows with Disney; he winkingly recalled, "When we did radio work, [Walt] had a little false courage in his hip pocket." [36] Nash claimed he also filled in as Mickey Mouse's voice for some nine cartoons [possibly in 1931-32 when Disney took a break after suffering exhaustion from overwork]. At one radio rehearsal, Disney confided to Nash he was "about ready to make [that] picture with a duck."

Coincidentally, Nash had a call the next day from story man Otto Englander who had heard the latest radio show featuring his funny duck voice. Englander had already contacted Nash once before for a possible Harman-Ising voice job which finally didn't happen. Now Englander was at Ub Iwerks's studio, working on the ComiColor cartoons, "and he said, 'We're going to make a picture with a duck in it.'" Feeling a tad conflicted, Nash called Disney to let him know of the job offer. Disney graciously but cannily said, "'Sure, go ahead [and do quacks], but don't do any dialogue.'" [37]

After calling in to the Iwerks outfit to see the storyboard, Nash returned to his Adohr Milk Company office and tried calling Disney, who couldn't be reached. So Nash left the title of Iwerks's cartoon story, *The Little Red Hen* (1934), with the Adohr secretary. Disney finally got back to her and said, "'Tell [Nash] not to do a damned thing for them.'" [38] It appears Disney had been intending to make a Red Hen Silly Symphony story himself. The cartoon eventually became *The Wise Little Hen* (1934).

Soon afterwards Nash was asked to attend a Disney story session where he ran into Colvig who said, "'Walt told me about you [phoning him regarding] Iwerks. [Walt] said, 'I like the loyalty in that guy, I'm going to put him on the payroll.' Sure enough, before the meeting ended, Disney asked Nash, "'Come up to the office, I want to talk to you.' He wanted to put me on, on a retainer." [39] Nash now had a steady job with Walt Disney Productions starting December 2, 1933.

By this point Nash had begun developing the voice for the explosive character who would quickly become one of the most famous in cartoon history. Work was progressing on the Silly Symphony *The Wise Little Hen*, for which Florence Gill was engaged for the title character's voice. But there were two other farm animals in that story that needed distinctive voices just at the point when dialogue was becoming more prominent in the Disney cartoons. One character was Peter Pig and the other a sailor-suited duck named "Donald" (after Disney had named a Nash-voiced duck by that moniker on their most recent radio appearance).

Nash was given the nod to do both voices. For the pig he talked in a snorting inhalation, while the duck now sounded fuller and more quackingly distinctive than the original goat template from two years prior. While the hog's career fizzled out and he returned to obscurity in the great animation pigpen, audience reaction to the explosive little duck was highly favorable. Disney immediately placed him in the next Mickey Mouse, *Orphans' Benefit* (1934), where his blustery, tantrum-prone character burst fully forth. Within just two years it seemed like the hot tempered duck might take over in popularity from Mickey as the studio's top star.

Nash was another voice artist who felt that Disney was a creative force. "Before Walt came up with the idea, I had never even thought of being angry or laughing in a duck's voice. But the more I learned to use it, the more it developed. Walt believed it was important for Donald to have a strong personality."

Donald's shorts as a starring character ran over twenty years, starting in 1936 when he got his own series. Over the years the directors kept their ears open for standby duck voices, because Nash was occasionally hard to understand; dialogue was sometimes modified so the quack-talk would be clearer. Nash himself admitted, "My first problem was the choice of vocabulary that would insure Donald could be understood. The most important thing about Donald was his voice. That was his asset. The writers always kept the Duck dialogue down to a minimum because they discovered it worked best when his sentences were kept short."

By the late forties Donald's main director was Jack Hannah. Hannah told historian Jim Korkis that he eventually found the Duck's dialogue recordings difficult, "knowing that the audience had a hard time understanding [the duck's] words." Hannah said that recording sessions for Donald's shorts occurred approximately every six weeks, and he admitted to tiring of hearing the Duck's voice so many times: "I not only heard the voice when I was recording it [but also] time after time when I was [reading the soundtrack and] studying it to layout the animation to it. I got to the point where I really resented having to go over and record [Nash's] voice."

Indeed, Hànnah reached a kind of burnout, revealing that he found the voice "irritating...every once in a while I got a couple of Goofy's to do and a Mickey, and, oh, it was a pleasure just to change." He recalled Nash being proud of his famous duck voice, but as the series' director Hannah finally resented the endless sameness noting, "The duck was either nice or he was mad, and he was never [anything] in between." Working with the soundtrack backward and forwards on the Moviola drove him to near distraction: "Speed it up, slow it down, and in slow motion...I heard the same duck lines for six solid weeks, before I got to a new one, when those [new] lines sounded the same for another six weeks!" [40]

Nash, despite unknowingly driving his director quack-crazy, was the last of the six important recurring voice actors in the Disney short cartoons. Mickey, Minnie, Goofy, Pluto, Pete and now Donald Duck formed the main stock company of Disney cartoon stars, and most other voice talent hires would be one shots from radio who would speak for various non-regular supporting characters.

By 1933, the Disney cartoons were generally regarded as technically the best in the business, particularly by his rivals. Supervisors and animators at other cartoon studios envied Disney's story department. They had heard the talk of Disney's unique methods, such as not settling for story approval until he had refined the details of gags growing naturally out of character, and the considerable time the studio spent analysing and re-analysing varied aspects of each single cartoon. None of the other animation shops, tied as they were to majors like Warner Bros., Columbia and Universal who all notoriously counted every penny, were allowed anything like the Disney studio's creative luxuries.

A look at various Disney cutting records graciously shared by historian J. B. Kaufman, discloses that a single short cartoon like *Who Killed Cock Robin?* enjoyed seventeen separate recording sessions between December 1934 and the final orchestra scoring in mid-April 1935. And that was not unusual: in the same timeframe *The Cookie Carnival* (1935) took eleven recording dates, the first of which was a quartet of male singers rehearsing with piano accompaniment, followed three weeks later by two members of The Blackbirds vocal group to record the "Devil's Feud Cake" number. A week later was the first dialogue recording with Pinto Colvig and Shirley Reed, a follow-up session two days later with Colvig, Ms Reed and the Homer Hall quartet singers, and in the early weeks of 1935, separate sessions for Ms Reed and Jack Dale, a specialty whistler. Then an organ track by Leigh Harline was recorded, and a fortnight later the full nineteen piece orchestra completed the scoring session, followed a day after by a musical effects session, and finally a recording date with two male quartets singing "Hail the Cookie Queen" with full orchestra. Schlesinger's directors, by contrast, were lucky to get more than one dialogue pre-record session, maybe some dialogue pickups and then they waited months for the final orchestra scoring session.

In mid-1937, as the long and challenging production of Disney's first animated feature *Snow White and the Seven Dwarfs* (1938) was nearing completion, Pinto Colvig was let go. Always an ambitious and slightly undisciplined talent, the eccentrically gifted Colvig went a step too far big-noting himself and whining about trivial things. He managed to irritate Disney to the point of getting himself fired. [41] It was a pity of course, and the loss of the great Goofy voice was noticeable.

Once the backlog of cartoons featuring Colvig's pre-recorded dialogue tracks had been completed and released, replacement voices were sought. Colvig's character voices like Goofy and the Practical Pig were tried by lesser talents - George Johnson, Tommy Wiggins - who were adequate for the limited Goofy dialogue in 1940 releases like *Tugboat Mickey* and *Baggage Buster*. But it was soon apparent that the genuine Goof spirit simply wasn't there. Another who claimed doing a Goofy role for Disney was Jack Bailey, later famous as a fifties TV personality (he was popular as the quick-witted host of *Queen for a Day*). It is possibly Bailey's voice as Goofy in *Goofy and Wilbur* (1939). In the end none of these Goofy wannabes were able to enter Colvig's uniquely creative head, or fully capture his voice quality.

One way the studio got around his glaring vocal absence was by re-using brief recordings of Colvig's old yells, guffaws and quirkily odd noises. Another was the fine series of Goofy "How To" cartoons made by director Jack Kinney from 1941. These relied on an off-screen narrator: Goofy became essentially a pantomime character demonstrating many beautifully animated disasters and pratfalls. [42] But the likable Goofy voice was still missed and it was a relief when Colvig was able to finally shake hands and make up with Disney as a freelance voice for hire sometime in 1942. From then onwards he was back as the genuine Goof, voicing Disney cartoons and children's records all the way to his passing in 1967.

Rounding out the supplementary Disney voices was the singular James Macdonald, a studio mainstay from 1934 to the early eighties. "I'm primarily in charge of sound effects. I've also done many, many of the voices. [Since 1946] I've been Mickey's voice, plus the bears, the gorillas...." said Macdonald, who supplied grunts, groans, roars and countless other comic noises in scores of Disney cartoons. His bottomless pit of subliminal vocal effects added much to the characteristic sound of those Disney shorts. [43]

In 1934 Jim Macdonald was a drummer in a band that was called in to supply music for a Mickey cartoon. He stayed on at the studio as one of two people hired to start-up the new Sound Effects department. From the outset Macdonald proved ingenious in manufacturing hundreds of individual noises from scratch or via home-built contraptions. He also filled in vocally when other voices couldn't make it, doing endless minor recordings like extra barks for Pluto, pickups for the sped voices of chipmunks, whistling, coughing, yodelling, things like extra sneezes for Sneezy the Dwarf, the gibberish voices of mice Jaq and Gus in *Cinderella* (1950), Humphrey the bear and literally dozens of others. He was happy to go unnoticed for this vast menagerie because the work was purely functional, augmenting and fine tuning the soundtracks.

Macdonald was always aware that Disney himself loved sound effects and he went the extra mile. "Back in the early days, Walt used to love to come [to recording sessions]. I remember he used to bring guests around." [44]

It was in 1946 during production of *Mickey and the Beanstalk* that Disney entrusted Macdonald to take over the famous voice of Mickey Mouse. Macdonald recalled Disney - an inveterate cigarette smoker - was getting a little hoarse to record some lines for "Mickey and the Beanstalk," claiming he was too busy. He recalled Disney saying he couldn't do Mickey any more: "One day he said, 'Call Jim up here.' He said, 'Have you ever tried to do Mickey?' I said, 'No, Walt [meaning Mickey has always been *your* voice].' He said, 'Do it. Just say something.' So [falsetto, I said], 'Hello Walt, how are you' [with that little giggle]. He said, 'Fine, that's it.'" He [then] told the directors 'Have Jim do it, in the future.'" [45]

Macdonald revealed he was given some sage advice regarding that most famous of cartoon voices, essentially vocal tips on speaking for Mickey from Disney himself. "[Walt] said, 'Don't let them give you long speeches. [In falsetto you only] have a couple of inches of area for inflection.' You're already [speaking high] up there. And if you get too low, you start to yodel, and yodel out of [the character]. So it was always best to have short speeches." [46]

The Disney studio's cartoon shorts relied heavily on all these striking voice artists for thirty years. It was a singular stock company of eccentric and oddball talents like no other. Meanwhile Disney's casting department headed by actor Stuart Buchanan hired almost every actor in town when it came to providing all the secondary character roles.

Some unique voices were essentially one-offs from film and radio. Actors hired included child performers like Tommy Bupp, the cheeky on-screen son of W. C. Fields in the classic comedy *It's a Gift* (1934) who played the little sailor in Disney's *Broken Toys* (1935). African American jazz club comic Billy Mitchell did the raucous voice of the Genie in *Pluto's Dream House* (1940). Disney regular Billy Bletcher originally auditioned for that part but in this instance Mitchell got the gig.

Two Disney regulars possessed unique vocal gimmicks. Actor Don Brodie had a gruff voiced wise-guy sound that was perfect for cartoons. Brodie told historian David Johnson, "I did a lot of voices for [Walt] on the Mickey Mouse and Duck pictures: not the principal characters, but all the other characters that worked with the Duck." [47] Brodie was heard as "internal" voices, like Pluto's conscience in *Mickey's Pal Pluto* (1933) and *Mickey's Kangaroo* (1935), or as a wickedly prodding voice like the little devil in *Mickey's Elephant* (1936) or *Donald's Better Self* (1938). He was a great utility voice in parts like the attendant cat who pushes the nervous cat in the wheelchair for *Pluto's Judgment Day* (1935). The Cincinnati native was a veteran actor and theatrical director who ran a Hollywood school for young acting hopefuls. Brodie was seen onscreen in scores of bits playing endless reporters, and he spent some time working for the animators' reference during production of *Snow White,* where his stage training had him enacting some of the Wicked Witch's gran-diose movements. Brodie was the gravelly-voiced one of the four *Lonesome Ghosts* (1935), and he pops up in the forties as a General in *The Vanishing Private* (1942).

The other notably eccentric Disney voice artist of the thir-ties was an obscure talent named Billy Sheets. Possibly a musical comic from the stage, Sheets did an excellent froggy gruff voice that matched Popeye's odd sound, for roles like the spider in *Gulliver Mickey* (1934). As the mocking chief Bat in the "Silly Symphony" *The Flying Mouse* (1934) he memorably sang "You're Nothin' But a Nothin'" to the beleaguered little hero. Sheets also used that raspy voice for the Judge in *Pluto's Judgment Day* (1935) and other shorts, and was heard as the second of the Pleasure Island barkers in *Pinoc-chio* (1940), spruiking "The Rough House, it's the roughest, tough-est joint you've ever seen!!"

Sheets is yet another of those elusive performers who have man-aged to remain totally mysterious for almost a century through a complete lack of any information to date. Nothing biographical was found at Disney Archives, where Dave Smith and Robert Tieman admitted to having nothing on file and in fact neither archivist had even heard of Sheets. Was he a trick singer, an actor, a comedian, a staff member? Nobody seems to recall, but whatever, he sure had a great voice for cartoons! Sheets appeared on several thirties radio shows with Disney and the other regular voices, and whenever he revived his *Flying Mouse* bat song, the audibly amazed studio audi-ences would burst into delighted applause.

Aside from trick voice types, busy radio announcers might be called on for special narration, like Gayne Whitman's for *Little Hiawatha* (1937). This was the Disney short that Tex Avery claimed swiped his pioneering use of an offstage commentator voice: Avery was often quoted lamenting, "It was the one thing Disney stole from me!" [48] The slightly pompous sounding Fred Shields was used when Disney wanted a purely straight and authoritative voice, like the announcer of *Victory Vehicles* (1943), while a more flexible artist like Frank Graham, who had a pronounced comic flair, was used for the wry, ironic narration in Jack Kinney's marvellous Goofy cartoon *African Diary* (1945). A more specialized voice was authentic sports announcer Frank Bull whom Kinney hired for themed Goofy entries like *Double Dribble* (1946) and *Football (Now and Then)* (1953).

Radio was also the source for various comic stooges like Cliff Arquette, famous years later as "Charley Weaver" on TV's *The Hollywood Squares*. For Disney he was the jovial radio voice of Uncle Smiley in the Donald cartoon *Self Control* (1938). A Silly Symphony needing specialized mimicry benefitted from the excellent Martha Wentworth, who played hags, gentle mothers and many other voices. For *Who Killed Cock Robin?* (1935) she was called in to recreate her sublime Mae West impression for buxom Jenny Wren. Wentworth had gained some fame with that voice having done it twice on the local Los Angeles radio police drama *Calling All Cars* for a 1933 episode, "The Mae West Jewel Robbery," which was remade by popular demand in 1934 as production on *Cock Robin* was underway.

"Live on stage" comedians were also occasional Disney voices, like the zany Doodles Weaver who is mostly remembered today for his Spike Jones recording of "The William Tell Overture" as a monotone race caller ("And there goes the winnerrrrrrrrr....Feetlebaum!"). His uniquely whimsical tones narrated cartoons like *Duck Pimples* and *Hockey Homicide*, both 1945 releases. Movie character actors were often called to Disney, such as the resonant dialect expert Nestor Paiva who for several years had been enacting the hammily villainous Squire Cribbs in the long-running Los Angeles Theatre Mart production of *The Drunkard*. When director Dick Lundy caught that show he hired Paiva to voice the cunning con artist Ben Buzzard for his upcoming Donald cartoon *The Flying Jalopy* (1943). Earlier Paiva was another of the actors, along with Don Brodie, who spent time on Disney's soundstage dressed up as the Wicked Witch for the team of animators to study exaggerated, villainous theatrical movements for *Snow White*.

When it came to celebrity imitations, the Disney studio wasn't as prominent in that line as Schlesinger or Mintz, but they did a few. In 1933 a young comedian who did impressions in a Hollywood night-club engagement was called in to Disney's to voice various movie stars to be caricatured in *Mickey's Gala Premier*. His name was Jerry Lester, and years later he would end up on television as the first host of *Broadway Open House*, the 1950 NBC talk program that was the template for all succeeding versions of *The Tonight Show*. In terms of draftsmanship the finest looking movie star caricatures of any animated cartoon were those in one of the last Silly Symphonies, *Mother Goose Goes Hollywood* (1938). As was typical of Disney by the late thirties, this short had been in development a long time.

Various nightclub and theatre impressionists were auditioned and the chosen ones are heard bringing a raft of then-famous stars to delightful vocal life in the film. It is not certain who did the final versions of several, but it is known that Sara Berner did the fine Katharine Hepburn and Greta Garbo voices,* and Dave Weber recreated the radio voices of Joe Penner and Charlie McCarthy. Nightclub mimic Al Bernie remembered getting a call to audition for Disney following his successful guest appearance on George Jessel's radio show *Thirty Minutes in Hollywood* in early 1938. On that program Bernie, announced as "Mister Everybody," did the same Charles Laughton impression that appears in the cartoon, imitating the actor's famous Captain Bligh role from the 1935 MGM drama *Mutiny on the Bounty*.

* Disney's characteristic attention to every detail extended to hiring actual stand-ins for top movie stars. An example was Greta Garbo's regular stand-in, Elizabeth Talbot-Martin, who modelled for the animators working on the Garbo caricature.

Bernie recalled, "The director [Wilfred Jackson] was a very nice man, he was great. He let me take as long as I wanted, as many takes to get the voices just right...they used my Charles Laughton, then they asked me to try a few more. In the cartoon it's me doing the W. C. Fields, and Laurel & Hardy with the pies. All the [impersonators] who worked on that cartoon, and I knew some of them, said how nice it was to work for the Disney boys because they made you feel like real pros. They had reference samples of all the real celebrities on these huge records and they'd play it to me in the ear-piece just before a take so I could get the pitch of the voice just right. But they also allowed for some exaggeration because they were going to be caricaturing them in the drawings for the cartoon."[49]

Vocal trios, though not as prominent after the thirties, remained busy in Walt Disney cartoons. A girls trio called The Coquettes did atmospheric warbling for *Little Hiawatha* (1937), while the versatile King's Men quartet augmented cartoons like *Donald Gets Drafted* (1942) and *The Brave Engineer* (1950). Cowboy actor-singer Cactus Mack Peters lent his authentic Western twang to *The Legend of Coyote Rock* (1945), and in the fifties the Mello Men quartet were frequently heard. As late as 1961, the famous Sons of the Pioneers country-western group was contracted to sing for *The Saga of Windwagon Smith*.

Occasionally a musical sub-specialist skilled in the art of yodelling would be hired and the recording was afforded a special place in the sound library, to be re-used for years after. Hannes Schroll was the familiar yodeller in *The Art of Skiing* (1941) and his track was famously re-used for Goofy on several more cartoons whenever he fell from a great height or was in any sort of imminent danger ("WAAAHHH HOOO HOOOEYHOOEY"). The vocal effect was sometimes married to one that Colvig himself had done, used for gags requiring various awkward sounding yells of fright.

The first of the famous Goofy "How to" cartoons was *How to Ride a Horse*, included within the 1941 feature *The Reluctant*

Dragon. It needed an offscreen commentator with a unique attitude. John McLeish was a Disney staff member who, unusually,
became an outstandingly distinctive voice artist. We already met
McLeish in the Warner Bros. and Screen Gems studio chapters, but
it was at Disney Productions where he first worked. Jack Kinney,
the director of the Goofy horse picture, noted in his book *Walt Disney and Assorted Other Characters* that McLeish, a Canadian born
American, "was swept up in Disney's worldwide talent hunt" in the
late thirties. [50] McLeish was by general consensus one of the most
singularly gifted artists ever to toil for Disney. A superlative drafts-
man with exceptional color skills, he was also a story man whose
biggest strength was his fine storyboard work.

Along with his artistic skills, McLeish also enjoyed a lifelong
and consuming devotion to the legitimate theatre. At an early age
he'd become obsessed by the most famous actor of his generation,
the legendary John Barrymore. McLeish was able to cultivate one
of the most unique speaking voices in animation, with all the resonance and sepulchral timbre of his stage hero. When Kinney was
casting for an off stage narrator for his Goofy short, he said "I put a
lot of Hollywood voice boxes over the jumps: radio, stage and film
speechifiers..." [51] But it was the in-house McLeish who instantly
understood Kinney's direction when he tested: the narration had
to point up the cartoon's silliness by remaining heavy, pontifical,
supercilious. McLeish's was such a fine reading of a cartoon script
- different yet as good as any voice professional - that his fruity,
hammy tones were soon poached by Warner Bros. and heard to
great effect narrating Chuck Jones's *The Dover Boys* (1942). *

*At the Schlesinger studio Jones and Norman McCabe both
wanted to use McLeish, having first heard his voice in the
Pluto cartoon *Lend a Paw* (1941). McLeish had started
speaking for Disney cartoons even earlier with minor voice
work in 1939's *Tugboat Mickey.*

For the Disney studio John Fraser McLeish's dulcet tones enhanced classic Goofy cartoons like *The Art of Skiing*, *The Art of Self Defence* (both from 1941), *Symphony Hour*, *Donald Gets Drafted*, *The Olympic Champ*, *How to Swim*, *How to Fish* (all from 1942) and *Motor Mania* (1950).

Background artist Paul Julian described the brilliant McLeish as insecure and troubled his whole life. "He was highly intelligent, yet intensely neurotic…he had a contempt for his own drawing ability," and he was psychologically affected since childhood by a deeply split "almost warring family," half of them based in Quebec, the others in the southern part of America. The gifted fine artist was "sort of a lovely guy, but totally warped."

UPA historian Adam Abraham noted in his fine book *When Magoo Flew* that after McLeish became an American citizen in 1945 he changed his last name to Ployardt (which was his father's mother's maiden name). His one screen credit for voice work was for the 1949 Disney feature *The Adventures of Ichabod and Mr. Toad*, which has him listed with the name John Ployardt.

Designer Zachary Schwartz declared McLeish was "Just too original and too remarkable to ever really have a possibility of expressing himself within the limitations of [the Disney] studio. [Later] at Screen Gems, he [proved] a fantastic caricaturist, a remarkable artist, and he and John Hubley were very close friends. As a matter of fact, I think that John McLeish was a very strong influence on Hubley." McLeish's later life got progressively worse as his addiction to alcohol took hold; the one-off artist and voice talent died in a tragic auto accident in October 1968. [52]

By the fifties radio artist Bill Thompson, famous in cartoons as MGM's Droopy, started doing much work for Disney, including voices like The White Rabbit from *Alice in Wonderland* (1951), nervously muttering "I'm late, I'm late, for a very important date," and Mr. Smee in *Peter Pan* (1953), along with his fussbudget voice for the Park Ranger in the Humphrey Bear shorts. Other gifted radio comedy voices like Alan Reed, Jim Backus and Stan Freberg were hired for occasional roles. The splendid British character actor Alan Mowbray's cultured tones were called on to enhance the Jack Kinney special *Social Lion* (1954), while stentorian narrator William Woodson, usually heard as a commentator for tough film noir pictures like the 1950 cop drama *Where the Sidewalk Ends*, gave a memorable reading of the witty rhyming script for *Pigs is Pigs* (1954).

A number of the fifties shorts, while still boasting the usual high quality Disney animation, were burdened by somewhat duller soundtracks at this point. Many had "voices" that were often simply sped up staff members: Chip 'n' Dale's chipmunk dialogue was really just nonsense syllables triple sped to the point of gibberish, and their lines were delivered over the years by ink and paint employee Dessie Flynn and soundman Jim Macdonald, or occasionally another inker named Norma Swank. There were a few too many cartoons featuring Donald Duck and his three nephews where a little too much of Clarence Nash could became grating. And by this point there were a few too many Pluto cartoons with just vocal noises and snorts but no amusing dialogue from any speaking characters. When an occasional picture, like two 1952 Goofy cartoons *How to Be a Detective* and *Two Gun Goofy*, used the character voices of Pinto Colvig and Billy Bletcher, it was like a breath of fresh air to finally hear great cartoon acting again.

Acknowledging the ever present need for such standout cartoon voices, story man Don Christensen observed, "Sometimes we [of the story staff] got a chance to hear recordings that were made in testing various voices. [We were often] so disappointed hearing the way many actors would do it, with the exceptions of the ones that had become the standbys for the studios."[53] He was referring of course to the evergreen animation acting reliables, recognized voice experts like Bletcher, Colvig or Bill Thompson. Paul Frees once described the top tier of voice people as "insurance policies.

[Directors] know they can always rely on us. If they want B flat we give them exactly that." [54]

Christensen added, "The guys who can do [cartoon acting], they can do it so well, and you don't realize how much they're doing it so well until you hear other actors...good actors in live-action pictures. I couldn't understand how they missed what seemed like the obvious inflection, or way to deliver a particular line." [55]

Christensen was speaking in the seventies. One wonders what he would have made of the wholly changed new millennium where many multi-voice cartoon specialists have been displaced by the now automatic hiring of endless superstars, from Brad Pitt to Bruce Willis to Jennifer Lopez, as part of a modern movie's mega-selling points. That trend will be discussed further at the end of this chapter.

In the almost forty years of sound cartoons before Walt Disney's death in 1966, his studio cast the widest net by far when it came to an endless variety of voice talents. To list all the non-regulars here would be pointlessly redundant, akin to printing out a lengthy shopping list. Interested "voice geeks" can discover the full range of Disney cartoon acting talent listed in this book's filmography.

Overall it could be argued that the dialogue for a large number of Disney cartoons was often unremarkable, with few quotable lines that stay in the memory. This is one reason the majority of Disney's shorts have a totally different dynamic to the funny, broad and increasingly wiseacre comedy that became the Warner cartoon's house style. With Disney, it was marvellous character-based animation, caricature and expertly rendered visual gags that were paramount, the so-called "illusion of life." Actual comedy lines quoted from Disney cartoons are rare indeed compared to Blanc's endless Looney Tunes catchphrases. Disney definitely did not want a Mel Blanc style of actor dominating the soundtracks of his films. His star players like Donald and Goofy already had some of the most unique voices in animation, and a lifelong experimenter like

Disney had neither the desire nor the need for a one-man stock company.

As story man Chuck Couch recalled of *Donald's Cousin Gus* (1939), "Walt had this idea for a goose cousin for Donald. We'd worked for months trying to get a story [and nothing pleased Walt]. I remember we recorded Mel Blanc; we were trying to get a voice for Gus Goose. When Walt found out we'd tested Mel, he about had a haemorrhage. Warner Bros. and everybody else used Mel Blanc [but not the Disney Studio!]. [Mel] did a very funny goose with a kind of Nordic accent ... I think it was partly because story man Carl Barks was a Swede." [56]

Part Two: Voices in Disney Features: New Levels of Animation Acting

As everyone knows, Walt Disney pioneered the animated feature film, and when *Snow White and the Seven Dwarfs* was in its early stages of development, the voices for the "little men" were being discussed and discarded as early as 1934. By the next year as the cartoon feature commenced its long and tortuous production, several voices were decided upon after much discussion and analysis. Carefully chosen were the various actors for the dwarfs, the critically important "cartoony" element of the film. The romantic leads and the villains were a different matter altogether: for the first time in cartoon animation, an entirely new discipline in the craft of vocal acting was going to be required. Realism, sincerity and the difficult actor's art of underplaying in an essentially caricatured medium marked the new approach. Snow White, the Huntsman and the evil Queen were virtually "straight" voices, with only the Queen's transformation into the Wicked Witch allowing her voice to veer into the melodramatic and larger than life.

The dual roles of the evil Queen and wicked Witch were brilliantly portrayed in a multi-layered characterization of a deeply insecure and dangerous woman by the veteran stage actress Lucille La Verne. She was a distinguished artist who had been emoting in a lengthy career that began in the 19th century, and she brought her lifetime of theatrical experience to this role.

Aside from her long years of stage work Ms La Verne had been seen in recent prestige films like MGM's *A Tale of Two Cities* (1935) in which she played another great hag role ("The Vengeance"), and when she began the dialogue recordings for Disney, she was being heard on NBC radio every Sunday afternoon for a full year (December 1935 to December 1936) in the leading role of a dramatic series called *The Widow's Sons*. When recording her dialogue from mid-1937 she often left her sequence director Bill Cottrell - and Disney - gaping as she grasped the emotional weight and meaning of each scene in virtually single takes.

Her excellent interpretation of the vindictively jealous and unbalanced Queen was a perfect example of the less is more approach, and her subtle reading of the coldly menacing monarch remains superb. When she morphed into the villainous witch it was with a realistic step into insanity and not the usual cliched cackling crone of typical comedy cartoons. Bill Cottrell confirmed that several radio actresses auditioned and indeed fell into that expected comic witch delivery. But "Lucille LaVerne was a stage actress. She came in and glanced at the storyboard, took the script and read it, and you could have recorded and used the dialogue as she read it, she was so great. I thought she was marvellous." Cottrell added that she made the transition vocally from Queen to ancient hag by doing exactly what Walter Brennan did to play older parts...she removed her set of false teeth.

Likewise, the Queen's Magic Mirror slave required a special voice, chilly and virtually emotionless. It had to be serious and dispassionate but not merely a "straight" announcer-style voice. Boomingly resonant screen actors like John Carradine and Irving Pichel were considered. Character player Moroni Olsen finally got the nod.

Encased in a layer of ethereal echo, the distinguished Olsen, tall, ramrod straight and thoroughly theatre trained, deployed his quietly resonant vocal instrument to excellent effect, with just a sly hint of malicious enjoyment of his Queen's turmoil. The first audience who saw this film at the Hollywood premiere just before Christmas of 1937 had, until that evening, only known funny cartoons with trick voices like Donald Duck, Popeye or Porky Pig, and it must have seemed astonishing to hear animated figures speaking with voices enacted in the manner of the finest dramatic radio programs.

Of course the Seven Dwarfs were the brilliant and much needed light relief, contrasting most effectively with the darker elements within the show. From the earliest days of work on the movie, the intention was to have strong comedic personalities for the dwarfs. Choosing their voices began in 1934, four years before the film was released, and early choices included radio personalities like Eddie Holden as well as screen actors like trembly-voiced Sterling Holloway.

Their dialogue was finally provided by several movie and radio old timers from the ranks of character actors. These included unique stage bred comedy specialists like Billy Gilbert, cast in the role of Sneezy. Gilbert was able to use his special party trick "chronic sneeze" bit, already seen in a few comedies like the 1934 Roach short *Maid in Hollywood*. Gilbert's sneeze routine, at its funniest when Sneezy was trying in vain to suppress the inevitable, was used judiciously so it didn't seem like an intrusive and tacked-on gimmick.

By early 1936 when dialogue recording sessions commenced, comedian Roy Atwell was the final choice to play the Dwarfs' leader Doc. Atwell, a veteran Broadway actor and playwright, was the most prominent of those thirties stage and radio comedians who developed odd verbal characters who specialized in stammering and spoonerisms, mixing up their words in escalating nervous tics of befuddled confusion. One Hollywood talent who was considered for a Dwarf voice as early as 1934 was Joe Twerp, who wrote and performed comic routines on local Los Angeles radio shows. He too did a funny word-mix-up routine and would finally get to use it in a few Schlesinger cartoons like *I Only Have Eyes for You* (1937).

Another seasoned stage artist who went back to the 1880s treading the boards as a comic specialty in leading vaudeville houses was Otis Harlan, who played the Dwarf named Happy. He gave a fine performance as the roly poly with boundless sunny optimism. Many of Harlan's own personal mannerisms were keenly observed by Fred Moore and other dwarf animators, and his distinct walk and hand gestures end up in Happy's onscreen movements. The shy dwarf Bashful was voiced by the corpulent character actor Scotty Mattraw, with a winning, red-faced, self-conscious "Oh goorrrsh!!" manner, slowly revealing that he was as besotted with Snow White as was the mute Dopey.

Studio staffer Pinto Colvig, already a proven and expert voice talent at the Disney plant, was given two of the dwarf's voices and he carried them off in fine style. Colvig played Sleepy, a role he inherited after the whiny-voiced radio actor John Gibson had been auditioned. Colvig's Sleepy voice had a slight resemblance to his Goofy tones. With his ability at doubling, Colvig was then cast in the vitally important role of Grumpy. His acting of the deceptively crotchety Grumpy was superb, showing a far deeper ability beyond his amusing cartoon voices like Goofy and the lazy Grasshopper. Vocally Grumpy was a more refined and credible version of the gruff little gnome assistant Colvig had voiced for a 1932 Silly Symphony, *Santa's Workshop*. Indeed the Grumpy character, with his surface belligerence hiding a caring nature, ended up the most fully dimensional and believably human of the seven. Colvig's excellent line readings were enhanced by the wonderful animation of his character by such gifted artists as Bill Tytla and Frank Thomas.

One of the thirties Disney voice regulars badly wanted to be in the much-anticipated movie. Billy Bletcher recorded the Big

Bad Wolf in late 1932 and he knew he was "in pretty solid with Walt." A while after the casting had commenced for the Dwarfs he approached Disney at a session. "I wanted to contribute one or two of the voices in *Snow White*. Walt's answer to me was, 'Billy, your voice is heard so much in all of these singles that I make, I don't think I'd want to use you as one of the Seven Dwarfs.'" [57] Disney's reaction was most likely from a gut feeling that Bletcher's obvious and proven ability at scene stealing could possibly be jarring to the delicate tone of various Dwarf scenes. Whatever, it was a bee in Bletcher's bonnet for the rest of his life (although he was most likely unaware that for about a year starting in the winter of 1934 he was in fact being touted as a likely contender for the role of Doc).

In his comprehensive book-length study *The Fairest One of All*, Disney historian J. B. Kaufman notes that the "casting of the dwarf's voices was extremely flexible," and that the soundtrack, over the long production process, consisted of "hundreds of bit and pieces." [58] Typical of the Disney approach, these miscellaneous voice effects, such as gulps, gasps and minor dialogue changes, were added as the story was refined, and it was staffers like voice men Colvig, Clarence Nash and sound wizards Hal Rees and Jim Macdonald who recorded these various dwarf pickups and vocal noises.

As was traditional for musical numbers, the dwarfs' singing voices were always different to the actors who spoke their dialogue. Busy session singer and chorus master Freeman High, who had contributed to various Silly Symphonies, contracted the ensemble of vocalists who sang the eternally catchy dwarf numbers like "Heigh Ho, Heigh Ho."

As for the pivotal title character, teenage soprano Adriana Caselotti, the daughter of a prominent Los Angeles based singing coach, was cast as the voice of the childlike and sweet Snow White. She was an early auditionee, and was almost announced for the role immediately. After the studio decided to play it safe by trying various other lyric sopranos, Adriana signed on as Snow White in late

1935. It's understandable why she was almost chosen straight away. As cartoon expert Mark Kausler noted, "Her singing and speaking voices have an innocence along with a bit of Betty Boop sauciness. She was able to create such great sympathy for Snow White."[59]

While Adriana Caselotti delivered most of the young heroine's dialogue, over the long three years of recording sessions the seasoned radio actress Thelma Hubbard, who played the Snow White lead role in the *Lux Radio Theatre* adaptation for Christmas of 1938, recorded some miscellaneous parts of Snow White's vocalisings, including the girl's terrified screams in the early forest sequence as she flees from the Huntsman.[60]

The role of the Prince who loved Snow White at first sight was played by tenor vocalist Harry Stockwell, who came aboard in 1936. The Prince was the first example of what some have labelled the stock bland cartoon hero, traditionally a model of goodness and virtue, but ultimately and inevitably a little dull. It was the template for eighty years of feature cartoon heroically upright Princes to come. There was nothing essentially wrong with having storybook heroes and heroines, but they are invariably happy ending plot devices-cum-romantic leads, their voices always necessarily straight, idealistic and, some will argue, vanilla plain. It was obvious from *Snow White*, and each fairy tale cartoon that came after, that the characters of actual interest in any feature length story were either dastardly villains who finally get their comeuppance, or the various comic relief types. Those are still the feature cartoon voices that movie audiences fondly recall.

Snow White opened in early 1938. It was indeed a gigantic success, and remains arguably the Disney studio's crowning achievement over its long history. The film remained the all-time favorite of certain studio veterans like Frank Thomas and Ward Kimball. It was said to be Disney's abiding favorite too. With hindsight, what animation scholars still find most unbelievable are the tremendous advances and improvements in the art of the film cartoon in the mere nine years from *Steamboat Willie* to *Snow White*, an arc of stunning progress led by the visionary "Walt." Disney was confirmed as a singular genius by his own animators and story staff, a description agreed upon by everyone else in the industry from Walter Lantz to Chuck Jones who knew that Disney was the one person truly responsible for "leading the way" and benefitting the entire animation industry.

Disney's next feature *Pinocchio* (1940) was a film of such visual richness it requires multiple viewings to even notice, let alone appreciate, all of its gorgeous details. It repeated the successful formula of *Snow White* when it came to casting unique voices. And once again it was the uniquely talented character performers who stood out on the soundtrack, creative performers like Walter Catlett, Charles Judels and Cliff Edwards, known to audiences of the day from live action movies and theatre appearances.

Walter Catlett, who voiced Honest John (aka J. Worthington Foulfellow) the opportunistic Fox, was a distinctly familiar actor to filmgoers by the year 1940. He had made an indelible impression on audiences throughout the thirties with marvellously etched eccentric characters in movies like *Bringing Up Baby* (1938) and *A Tale of Two Cities* (1935). His garrulously tipsy poet in *Mr. Deeds Goes to Town* (1936) was a great comic turn, the sort of strikingly original performance that often has 21st century viewers asking, "Why do many of today's actors seem so bland?" Catlett's unique voice with its way of tumbling a torrent of words together quickly was perfect casting for Honest John, a slightly seedy theatrical type who was essentially a pure con artist with the gift of endless gab, a streetwise character who saw suckers coming a mile off. Catlett's crowning vocal moment was John's rousing rendition of the clever novelty number "Hi-Diddle-Dee Dee," as he overwhelms Pinocchio with his description of an actor's cushy life.

Joining the cast of standout voices was the stocky actor Charles Judels, expert at any number of national dialects. He was awarded the roles of the two important villains in *Pinocchio*, Stromboli and the Coachman. Judels gave the explosively brash puppet master Stromboli a broad Italian speech pattern, creating a vocally bullying and bombastic puppeteer with a fearsome temper, a perfect match to his dark visual appearance as a constantly intimidating force of nature. Judels was also filmed as a reference model for Stromboli. His other voice for the coldly unscrupulous Coachman was a gruff Cockney accent, dripping with malevolence, hinting at a streak of sadism. This was top notch vocal emoting, and Judels brought off the clever character actor's trick of sounding so different in these two strong parts that, to the audience, it seemed entirely plausible to believe the roles were actually voiced by two actors.

Pinocchio's "father" Geppetto was a gentle but essentially non-comic character, and, as Michael Barrier noted in *Hollywood Cartoons*, "Art Babbitt's animation of Geppetto made that character a virtual duplicate of Christian Rub, the Austrian actor who provided the voice and appeared in live action [reference footage]." [61] Rub, a small part actor seen in many films of the thirties, gives a sincere performance of a humble, elderly man who, although a popular toy-maker, is essentially lonely. He craves some company, and regrets never having had a son. While essentially decent, his voice never sounds cloyingly sweet. His gentle Germanic tonality carries with it an old-world quality that jells with the beautifully rendered European settings of the story. The actor had to do multiple recording sessions: Disney wanted Rub's prominent dialect but he had quite a bit of talking in the movie, and it was often delivered in a way that was hard to understand. Disney's concern was that each of Geppetto's speeches had to be perfectly clear to the audience. Rub wasn't even the first choice for Geppetto: earlier the veteran small part actor Spencer Charters, who specialized in playing old codgers but with a distinctly American twang, was on the cards.

Similarly, Pinocchio's Pleasure Island companion Lampwick was at first envisioned as a role for Mickey Rooney, the versatile young

MGM star. But Disney's inner ear heard differently, and he asked for Frankie Darro. [62] The juvenile "tough kid" actor Darro, familiar from scores of thirties movies like *Thoroughbreds Don't Cry* (1937) and *Wild Boys of the Road* (1933) was indeed a fine choice for the wayward youth in *Pinocchio*. His voice carried chip-on-the-shoulder attitude, and the cracking sound of a recently "broken" teenage voice, although he was over twenty when he recorded his Lampwick lines. Darro's performance was excellent, especially in the chillingly effective transformation sequence where he changes attitude from swaggeringly cocky to fully terrified as he suddenly morphs from human boy into an uncontrollably braying donkey.

Undoubtedly the dominant character voice in the film was Jiminy Cricket, as portrayed by entertainer Cliff Edwards, who had abundant comedic and musical gifts. Edwards had been famous for the preceding twenty years in stage shows like the *Ziegfeld Follies*, and on records as a pioneering vocalist who had reached a pre-Bing Crosby level of popular fame throughout the twenties. Edwards could sing in his own patented hot scatting style or croon sweetly with a natural tenor that could slide into a strong falsetto. His trademark was his instrumental self-accompaniment and he earned the famous showbiz nickname of "Ukulele Ike." Jiminy Cricket is essentially the film's storyteller and Edwards's charming rendition of the scene setting opening song "When You Wish Upon a Star" is now inextricably linked to the *Disneyland* TV show in the collective memory. His folksy, soft speaking voice, with its low tenor and warm conversational quality, was the epitome of a Disney character. It had a little of that mid-Western Mickey Mouse modesty, a little in fact of Walt himself in its tone. Edwards was a naturally creative comic performer and he was allowed to go "off-script" in the recording sessions. His ad libs delighted Disney's crew and were incorporated into the film. Visually the character of Jiminy had the good fortune to be animated under the supervision of one of Disney's strongest young talents, Ward Kimball.

The straighter voices of Pinocchio and the Blue Fairy delivered their lines over several recording sessions with the assistance of a specially hired dialogue coach. Child actor Dickie Jones, a movie professional for most of his eleven years, was the final choice for the title role, although during the audition period the character of Pinocchio was still intended to match the more mischievous puppet from Carlo Collodi's original book. The comically talented radio "brat" Walter Tetley auditioned and was seriously considered for a time. Over the months of pre-production, however, Disney finally decided to go with the more naive, cuter approach of young Jones's voice. Disney had noted his acting as a newsboy in a recent Warner Bros. drama *The Kid Comes Back* (1938). For the last of the film's major parts, screen actress Evelyn Venable evinced a perfect fairy tale quality in her pleasant stage trained voice for the Blue Fairy. The prominent radio actress Lurene Tuttle had auditioned for that role, but Disney finally signed off on Miss Venable, who managed to make this softly spoken make believe spirit, by turns magical and protective, even motherly, seem entirely credible.

Of course, readers of this book are no doubt aware that Mel Blanc was reduced to just a single hiccup or two in the movie.[63] Blanc, who was doing voices all over town in 1938, had been a weekly regular on that year's *Mickey Mouse* NBC radio show for Pepsodent, on which he played a zany recurring character who broke into uncontrollable hiccups. He recorded an early track with dialogue for Gideon the Cat, for a sequence at an Inn where the feline gets progressively more drunk. The dialogue relied on that hiccupping radio voice, but Disney's decision to eliminate this material and have Gideon be essentially a mute character was well judged. Blanc's nonsensical hiccups would have been distracting and extraneous to the story. And it could have appeared like gimmicky schtick simply to get an obvious and unnecessary laugh. Mel Blanc was eventually called back a year later in the post production phase for a pickup session to record just a few short hiccups; they also had him do some miscellaneous donkey braying used for the Pleasure Island sequence.

Pinocchio was followed by the triumphant *Fantasia* (1940), a stunning Disney achievement in the new stereophonic process Fantasound. The film showcases an often astonishing eight-part blend of classical music accompanied by a wide range of superlative animation. Mickey Mouse appears in the most famous segment, "The Sorcerer's Apprentice," but he doesn't speak, and we only hear a few brief words afterwards as the famous rodent shakes the hand of orchestra conductor Leopold Stokowski. Although *Fantasia* is considered a studio milestone and much meticulous Disney research has covered the film in detail, for the purposes of this book there is only one other off-screen voice heard in the two hours of running time: soprano Julietta Novis sings Schubert's "Ave Maria" which accompanies the "Night on Bald Mountain" sequence. (In fact music critic Deems Taylor, the film's live action master of ceremonies, is technically the only other speaking voice heard.)

With *The Reluctant Dragon* (1941) Walt Disney produced his first combination feature, essentially a live action tour of the Disney Studio by the famed Algonquin Round Table humorist Robert Benchley. The movie included glimpses of Disney's recording stage orchestra during a music scoring session, along with the Disney sound crew including young effects wizard Jim Macdonald. It also allowed the theatre audience to finally see Clarence Nash and Florence Gill on camera, performing at the microphone as their famous Donald Duck and Clara Cluck cartoon characters. The animated portions included the opening instalment of the fine Goofy "How to" cartoon, *How to Ride a Horse*, featuring the first example of John McLeish's amusingly pontificating commentator voice.

The title cartoon continued the tradition of hiring movie character talents for voices, with prissy comic actor Barnett Parker as the outrageously effusive Dragon, and fellow British player Claud

Allister offering a drily amusing parody of the already stereotyped English "silly ass" from innumerable stage farces, as the vague Sir Giles. The contrast between the dragon's high camp declaimings and Giles's dry underplaying is amusingly achieved. The most interesting of the cartoon segments was *Baby Weems*, essentially a storyboard come to life with the vitality of superb character layout drawings by John P. Miller, as narrated by the smooth radio actor Gerald Mohr. Announcer Art Gilmore contributed the fine imitation of President Franklin D. Roosevelt.

Dumbo (1941) was the next Disney feature, one of the studio's shortest and most enduringly beloved animated films. The leading voice artist was the familiar movie character player Edward Brophy, who portrayed ineffectual comic gangsters, incompetent police officials and a raft of Runyonesque types in the thirties and forties. His voice was the essence of Brooklynese wiseguy. Brophy was fine casting for Timothy J. Mouse, a surface tough guy with the proverbial soft heart who befriends the baby elephant. Among the other memorable voices were the windbag matriarch elephant played by the funny Verna Felton and her cattily gossiping companion enacted by radio stalwart Noreen Gamill.

Dumbo also marked the Disney debut of timid-voiced Sterling Holloway as the Stork. Disney had noticed his unique voice years earlier, and in the initial stage of *Snow White*'s development, circa 1933-34, Holloway was temporarily considered for the vocal role of Sleepy in that film. But even before work on *Dumbo* commenced, Holloway's high and nervously husky tones had already been recorded for the adult version of the skunk named Flower in *Bambi* (1942). That feature, however, experienced several years of stop-start development and production, and so *Dumbo* was the first Disney role for which the public heard Holloway's unmistakable voice. In fact Holloway's singular tones became something of a regular Disney sound over the next thirty years, and he was heard in several of the special shorts like two 1952 releases, *Suzie, the Little*

Blue Coupe and *The Little House,* before finally ending up as the voice of Winnie the Pooh in the mid-sixties.

The circus Ringmaster was given voice by the explosively Germanic Herman Bing, still another effective small part actor seen in many movies of the thirties. It's always important to keep in mind that the original audiences for these features would have recognized each character actor's voice the minute their animated selves began to talk. Following his endearingly likable Jiminy Cricket role in *Pinocchio,* the talented musician-performer Cliff Edwards was hired again, this time for the memorable sequence featuring the four black crows and the feather, animated by Ward Kimball. He supplied the dialect singing voice of the lead crow who comically warbles "When I See an Elephant Fly," with fine backup by several members from Hall Johnson's famous choral group. Other singers from the long-established Johnson ensemble sang in the circus laborers' "Roustabout" number earlier in the picture, arranged by the choral group's long-time vocal coach, actor Jester Hairston. *Dumbo,* lower budgeted than the preceding animated features, proved an immense success and remains a revered Disney favorite.

In the next feature *Bambi* (1942) the tone was far different to *Dumbo's.* This was the most realistic Disney cartoon to date, reflecting the years of intensive art training undertaken by the studio's top animators. The film's production stretched over five exacting years, including a temporary break while Disney and the story team reconsidered several points. The story itself was adapted from the famous Felix Salten book, the theme of which was the cycle of life, as experienced by a community of forest creatures. Because voices would be such an important element the casting was handled with great care. Much of *Bambi's* dialogue was underplayed. often serious to match the tone of the story, and it was mostly a team of anonymous radio artists who supplied the realistic voice work for the various animals.

The main characters would be the four youngsters: Bambi, Thumper the rabbit, Faline the female deer, and the skunk named Flower. Their voices would span the timeframe from birth through the coming of age, which meant that several performers voiced each character, although the bulk of the film's running time was concerned with the period of childhood. Uniquely, there were no instances of adult females portraying children, as had been common casting in animation voice work. For this production Disney insisted on real children's voices for verisimilitude.

Announcer Fred Shields was hired as the voice of the elder deer. Disney's opinion of Shields, a seasoned radio voice, varied over the years. He once said, "In Shields you haven't got a clever guy." What Disney meant was that Shields wasn't naturally comedic like certain cartoon actors, and could veer towards dull and flat in his delivery unless coached. However for *Bambi* he proved a fine choice as the elder, known as the Great Prince of the Forest, and Shields's solemn and portentous reading of lines like "Your mother can't be with you anymore" were performed with subtle skill. Paula Winslowe, one of West Coast radio's most in demand actresses, was cast as Bambi's mother, comforting and soft spoken with a hint of constantly cautious concern in her delivery. Her emotional reading of "Man…was in the forest" was perfectly judged.

Balancing the solemnity was the always present light relief of characters who provided gentle comedy. The most cartoony yet still dramatically effective adult character voice was spoken by Will Wright, a familiar, gaunt looking actor who often played old codgers, sheriffs, newspaper editors and judges in live action movies. Wright had a resonant vocal edge that brought him much radio work, and for *Bambi* he was awarded the role of the wise, kindly Friend Owl.

Among the various child actors who recorded for the film, the one with the most winning and natural personality in his voice was the younger version of Thumper as played by Peter Behn. Bambi's own childhood voice was provided by Donnie Dunagan who had recently enacted the role of the youthful child living amid the strange goings on in Universal's 1939 horror classic *Son of Franken-stein*. And Cammie King, the very young girl who voiced Faline, had famously played the doomed child Bonnie, daughter of Scarlett and Rhett, in *Gone with the Wind*. Dialogue coaches attended the children's recording sessions and worked diligently and sensitively to get precise line readings from the youngest members of the cast.

What is less known about the original *Bambi* soundtrack was disclosed in a pioneering 1942 book *The Art of Walt Disney* by Robert D. Feild. As animator Mark Kausler noted, *Bambi* originally had many more voices; the leaves which fall from a tree to the ground at first spoke to each other. Raindrops sang the song "I Like Falling" and even the wind was given voice. The hunters had lines of dialogue. The grouse who says, 'I can't stand it any longer' is one of the few remaining vestiges of the original *Bambi* sound concept. The final track was pared down until there was a real economy of dialogue. As Feild wrote, "Each word of the dialogue had to be phrased with the greatest artistic delicacy" and he noted that this material was finally "omitted because of the length of the film." [64] Even small roles like a squirrel and a chipmunk in the film had much more dialogue at one stage.

Bambi was happily a triumph for Disney Productions and remains one of the studio's major accomplishments. In so many areas - the animation, both marvellously realistic yet winningly caricatured, the special effects, the forest design, Frank Churchill's fine music - the Disney plant's level of accomplishments in this film can still seem unsurpassed over eighty years later. Inarguably, the five years covering *Snow White* through *Pinocchio* to the often stunning work produced in *Bambi* represent the pinnacle of Disney feature cartoon production.

The war years kept the Disney studio busy with much Government-commissioned work on war-related training films, and full-length cartoon features with their attendant lengthy production periods were necessarily put on hold. Disney's next group of features did not contain movie-length stories. Rather, they were mixed bags containing various shorts and sequences. *Saludos Amigos* (1943) was an animated propaganda travelogue with music, made for the Pan America Union. It featured Donald Duck in his first feature film teamed with a new character, a South of the Border parrot named Joe Carioca from Brazil. He was voiced by the Argentinian entertainer Jose Oliveira, who projected a fine personality. The film, short enough to be labelled a featurette, was a mix of shorts linked with narration supplied by radio announcer Fred Shields, who became the first voice artist to get screen credit on a Disney production. Two of the sequences featured established star characters, with Donald appearing in *Lake Titicaca*, and Goofy starred in the funny *El Gaucho Goofy*. The lavish musical number *Aquarela do Brasil* paired Donald with the dapper Joe Carioca, and was a colorful feast for the eyes. The film was nominated for two Oscars with the title number winning for Best Song. Some segments originally planned for this feature were released as separate shorts, such as *The Pelican and the Snipe* and *Pluto and the Armadillo*.

Victory Through Air Power (1943) was another unique Disney film, definitively proving the singular ability of specialized animation to educate and instruct. A topical and didactic film released halfway through America's involvement in World War Two, there was fine narration by Art Baker who blended a straight informational tone with dramatic touches, both calm and urgent, in his reading. Baker was a radio announcer who became a principal offscreen commentator for many of Disney's government sponsored training and instructional shorts.

The next portmanteau style feature was *The Three Caballeros*, released in early 1945 as the second of the two South American compilation films. This time several character voice talents actually received screen credit, a first for the Disney studio, with Clarence

Nash, Sterling Holloway, Frank Graham and others finally being noted for their important contributions to an animated film.

The versatile Frank Graham, who had been doing multiple cartoon jobs for Schlesinger, MGM and Screen Gems, not to mention Disney shorts like *Chicken Little* (1943), was the opening narrator who interacts with Donald Duck. Next, Sterling Holloway, in his third Disney feature, narrated *The Cold Blooded Penguin* sequence, while Fred Shields, who we heard as the Great Prince of the Forest in *Bambi*, was unrecognizable here, narrating *The Flying Gauchito* in a light-hearted Latino dialect. Jose Oliveira's character Joe Carioca returned from *Saludos Amigos* to team once more with Donald Duck and a new player, the confident and extrovert rooster Panchito Pistolas who was voiced by Mexican-American tenor Joaquin Garay. A bandleader of renown, Garay had been signed in late 1943 after Disney talent scouts heard him singing in a San Francisco nightclub where he and his musicians had a regular engagement.

The film featured several fine vocalists from South of the border accompanying the live action segments, as well as two solos: "Baia" was warbled by Brazilian singer-conductor Nestor Amaral, while the powerful operatic baritone Carlos Ramirez, a Colombian native, sang "Mexico." Ramirez, contracted to MGM for musicals of the forties, was loaned out to Disney, originally to voice one of the titular caballeros. Cartoon fans will recall Ramirez's later cartoon connection, where one of his vocal tracks was "lifted" and matched to the melodically hapless bulldog Poochini in Tex Avery's MGM cartoon spoof *Magical Maestro* (1952).

Disney's next feature, *Make Mine Music* (1946), was the first of the so-called "package films," grouping several musical shorts of varying styles. A natural progression from *Fantasia*, which had grouped a set of short films featuring animation set to famous examples of classical music, this new feature was a similar gathering of cartoon shorts featuring various genre offshoots of so-called popular music. They ranged from country and western to ballads to swing and even the grandly operatic, and featured major musical names on the accompanying vocals or narration.

Sterling Holloway, who was now being heard in Disney's short cartoons as well, was back once more to narrate *Peter and the Wolf* which, along with its instrumental effects, featured Pinto Colvig supplying various animal sounds. Nelson Eddy, the famed baritone of thirties MGM operettas like *Rose-Marie* (1936) and *Naughty Marietta* (1935) gave a tremendous performance as all the voices in *The Whale Who Wanted to Sing at the Met.* His acting was assisted by a technical process allowing him to sing in four ranges, from tenor to bass. Eddy, along with radio diva Dinah Shore, crooner Andy Russell and the top tier vocal ensemble The Pied Pipers were all names of marquee value at the time, each heard regularly in the mid-forties on musical-variety radio programs. They all enjoyed effective showcases via this feature.

The only cartoon-style voices in the movie were in the two segments that most felt like actual comedy cartoons. *Casey at the Bat* was narrated by the unique musician and radio stooge Jerry Colonna. A standout trumpeter long associated with Bob Hope's radio show, Colonna was a one-off. His husky tenor voice, capable of incredibly long notes that started out almost inaudibly and finally became ear-piercingly shrill, was used to great comic effect as narrator of the baseball saga. The prolific vocal quartet The King's Men, who performed intricate novelty comic songs each week for ten years on the *Fibber McGee and Molly* radio program, sang the hillbilly feud *The Martins and The Coys* with their most flexible voices doubling for the various mountain denizens. They were fine accompaniment for Jack Kinney's fast paced and amusingly animated segment.

The King's Men were the vocal group heard in the early Merrie Melodies for Warner Bros. from 1931-33 and were led by the fine bass singer Ken Darby. By this point, while still maintaining his quartet, Darby, whose extensive music training went back to his childhood, was the top choral arranger for movies. In 1944 he

330 • Keith Scott

signed a contract with Disney to provide his talents for upcoming features. He assembled the Ken Darby Singers for the *Blue Bayou* sequence in this film.

Darby knew every specialty singer in Hollywood. He had been praised for his work as recording director in charge of all the character voice sessions for *The Wizard of Oz* at MGM in 1938. Darby was responsible for the brainwave of vocally replacing the live action Munchkin dwarf actors with top cartoon voice talents like Billy Bletcher, Pinto Colvig and bass singer Harry Stanton. Their voices were recorded with the music tracks slowed down. When played back at normal speed they sounded comically "little" for numbers like "As Mayor of the Munchkin City" and "We Welcome You to Munchkin Land." The Munchkin actors then mimed to playback of these tracks during principal photography. Darby also supervised the recording of the talking trees sequence with other cartoon actors.

The next Disney feature was *Song of the South* (1946), a mostly live action movie with three wonderfully produced cartoon sequences supervised by master director Wilfred Jackson. These featured the roguish and charming characters from Joel Chandler Harris's internationally loved folk tales, namely Br'er Rabbit, Br'er Fox and Br'er Bear. The trio of comic characters were distinctly defined personalities with brilliantly caricatured animation movement. The voices were carefully cast using African American radio talents like Johnny Lee and Nicodemus Stewart. But the top acting honours went to James Baskett who portrayed Uncle Remus, the film's leading live action role.

Baskett was described by Disney as one of the finest actors he had ever known. A seasoned stage veteran who had notched up decades of stock company theatrical training, he enacted the Remus role with total sincerity and dignity, transcending those stereotypical elements that were a cause of contention then as well as now: his threadbare costuming, occasional diffidence to the plantation owners, a slight tendency to cliches of what was then called stage-negro dialect.

And yet Baskett's interpretive genius made a three-dimensional man out of what could simply have been a hackneyed "heart of gold old-time worker on the plantation," and it is made clear that the story is set in the post-Civil War reconstruction era of emancipation. Baskett was also a marvellous visual actor who adapted to the logistically difficult filming job of marrying live action with still-to-be animated sequences so seamlessly. His intelligence was apparent in the early song "Zippity Doo Dah" in which he truly appears to interact with Mr. Bluebird and the other animated creatures and manages to look totally at ease with the technical details of eye contact and subtle physical movement. Even more impressively, Baskett was not a physically well man at this stage of his life and was occasionally hospitalized during the film's production.

Added to these attributes was Baskett's instinctive flair for voice acting. It was so good that it seems impossible to hear his rich and underplayed mature age voice and realize that he is also enacting the cartoon role of Br'er Fox. That character's voice is a fast-talking, fussbudget comic villain with a catchy high giggle, and is a variation of the radio role he played on *The Amos & Andy Show*, a motor-mouth shyster lawyer named Gabby Gibson.

Still more amazingly, when Johnny Lee, another regular on *Amos & Andy* as Lawyer Calhoun, and the voice of Br'er Rabbit in the film, was away on a USO tour in France, Baskett stepped in when further recording was suddenly needed for the "Laughing Place" sequence. He matched Lee's voice and did part of the Br'er Rabbit dialogue which remains in the movie. As animator Eric Larson told John Culhane, "You can't tell the difference." The film benefited yet again from Ken Darby's excellent choral arrangements. It is regrettable that, today, the controversial status of *Song of the South* has seen the film shelved indefinitely, preventing latter day appreciation for its many technical accomplishments in combination work, its admirable acting, and the truly excellent character animation.

The tenth Disney cartoon feature was a film which had begun back in 1938, when the monumental success of *Snow White* had Disney pondering a Mickey Mouse feature with music. In that year he approved a "Jack and the Beanstalk" two-reel short concept. Soon after, an expanded version was assigned to Frank Tashlin who had joined the studio's story division after a successful directing stint at Leon Schlesinger's. The eventual "Mickey feature" went through one of the most convoluted production histories at the Disney studio.

It was twice shelved for a number of reasons, including the loss of the war-torn European market. By 1941 some early dialogue had been recorded by Disney speaking as Mickey Mouse, with writer Ford Banes performing Mickey's singing voice. In August *Daily Variety* noted that Disney had signed Lee Sweetland, "a baritone for NBC," to do narration for the proposed picture. [65] But Banes's and Sweetland's work wasn't heard in the final film. Some early animation was begun just as the divisive Disney strike occurred, and by year's end America was plunged into the World War, meaning the film was on hold once again.

When hostilities ceased the show was revived in late 1945 and put back into production, renamed "Slap Happy Valley" then finally *Fun and Fancy Free* (1947). By now it was another of the feature films in the combination format, with live action sequences featuring popular radio comedy ventriloquist Edgar Bergen and his famous dummies "Charlie McCarthy" and "Mortimer Snerd" telling stories to Disney's two contracted child actors from *Song of the South*, Bobby Driscoll and Luana Patten. The film was essentially a two-parter, the first half featuring an animated adaptation of Sinclair Lewis's story *Bongo*, the tale of a unicyclist circus bear. *Bongo* was narrated by top radio singer Dinah Shore, previously in *Make Mine Music* and returning for a second Disney appearance. The long-planned *Mickey and the Beanstalk* story took up the second half, reuniting the old thirties starring-trio of the Mouse, Duck and Goof.

The voices included two return engagements from previous Disney cartoon features, with Cliff Edwards as the ever-popular Jiminy Cricket who hosts the picture, and character comedian Billy Gilbert - alias Sneezy in *Snow White* - providing the oafish voice of Willie, the lumbering giant. Willie's singing harp was warbled by Anita Gordon, then a weekly pop vocalist on Red Skelton's top-rating radio show. With all this quality voice talent on board, it was still the reliable old studio hands Pinto Colvig and Clarence Nash who stole the vocal honors in a brief but funny bit where Goofy and Donald Duck sing parody lyrics to the Neapolitan perennial "Funiculi Funicula."

The *Beanstalk* cartoon was enjoyable if far from top notch Disney, but it was mainly significant in that it marked the first time James Macdonald was asked by Walt Disney himself to take over Mickey's voice, as already related in the "shorts" section of this chapter. Disney was simply too busy in 1946 to complete the task of recording dialogue he had started five years before, and he might have noticed a slight change in his vocal pitch owing to his years of heavy smoking.

Melody Time (1948) was the second of the "package" features. Like the earlier *Make Mine Music* it boasted a potpourri of musical styles accompanying various animated short stories and *Fantasia*-esque mood pieces. As before, most of the featured voices were musical stars of the period who sang or narrated the stories. These talents included the movie's MC, crooner Buddy Clark, and the popular chanteuse Frances Langford from Bob Hope's radio show. Actual cartoon-type voices were not really apparent in this feature, aside from comic vocal effects by Pinto Colvig and Jim Macdonald: in *Little Toot*, told in song by the popular Andrews Sisters trio, Colvig does the sounds for Toot's older Ferryboat father. Although Donald Duck and Jose Carioca are back in *Blame it on the Samba*, featuring another fine girls' trio, The Dinning Sisters, the duck and parrot are, for once, pantomime characters. Colvig provides the eccentric noises for the zany Aracuan bird, who was last seen in *The Three Caballeros.*

The famous folktale *Johnny Appleseed* showcased radio singer Dennis Day who supplies every voice. This was not difficult for the accomplished Mr. Day, the addled Irish tenor from Jack Benny's top-rated radio comedy, because he was a most accomplished impressionist as well. For *Johnny Appleseed* he not only narrates the segment but provides the voices of the title character Johnny, his Guardian and the Square Dance caller. The one genuinely "cartoony" segment was *Pecos Bill*, an excellent Western movie take-off supervised by the satirically inclined Ward Kimball. It used the distinctive voices of star singing cowboy Roy Rogers narrating the saga, and his old vocal group The Sons of the Pioneers, who had done occasional short cartoons for Walter Lantz and Leon Schlesinger, singing and speaking all the sagebrush cowpoke character parts.

Next in Disney's feature line-up was *So Dear to My Heart* (1949), a mainly live-action rural story with songs adapted from the 1943 children's book *Midnight and Jeremiah*. The twelve minute animated sequence featured veteran country and western singer Ken Carson, a one-time member of the Sons of The Pioneers, as the voice of the Wise Old Owl who imparts musical encouragement to the live action child star Bobby Driscoll. The gifted vocal contractor Ken Darby was once again in charge of directing the singers, with chorus master Judson Conlon arranging the vocal numbers. Conlon's group The Rhythmaires, long-time regulars on Bing Crosby's weekly radio show, were heard as the backing vocalists.

The large cast of voices for the *Wind in the Willows* segment of the 1949 release *The Adventures of Ichabod and Mr. Toad* had been recorded back in 1941, when Disney had intended that story to be a feature length animated show. As with several other studio projects, the advent of war in Europe and the consequent diminished overseas market affected the studio coffers. Disney's bankers imposed a wartime budget ceiling which left Disney feeling that the work required on *Wind in the Willows* would inevitably be below par in quality. The result was that this film was also put on hold for several years. Although pencil animation had begun before the summer of 1941, Disney halted the work that fall. Sometime later he decided to pair that story with another "featurette" length segment, and when work resumed in 1947 Disney chose Washington Irving's famous tale of American folklore, *The Legend of Sleepy Hollow*, as the second of the two cartoons in this, his final package feature.

Bing Crosby was still the nation's top vocalist after sixteen hugely successful years, and he was chosen to narrate the *Sleepy Hollow* story featuring the string bean schoolmaster Ichabod Crane. Although there were no other voices beyond Crosby and his radio vocal group the Rhythmaires, for a short time Disney had considered filming a live action sequence featuring the crooner's four young sons, who had been well received in some light hearted skits on Crosby's *Philco Radio Time* show in 1948. But the live action idea was dropped and the Ichabod tale was paired with the famous Kenneth Grahame story *Wind in the Willows* to make up a fully animated cartoon feature.

By 1946, when work resumed on the long-delayed *Wind in the Willows* segment, the very British feel was set to be enhanced by having famed Lancashire music hall legend Gracie Fields both singing in, and narrating, the story. The *Hollywood Reporter* announced she had been signed for this role, but by 1948 leading character star Charles Laughton was also in the running for storyteller. The famous Mr. Toad saga was finally narrated by the distinctively clipped and whimsical tones of Basil Rathbone, one of the screen's finest actors and famous for his long-running movie and radio portrayal of Sherlock Holmes.

The earlier dialogue track from 1941 was married to the newer work, resulting in Disney's best use of a range of funny character voices since his earliest features. The plummy Eric Blore, famous as the butler in classic Fred Astaire-Ginger Rogers musicals like *Top*

Hat (1935), was that rare example of a prominent screen actor who could emote in a caricature based cartoon as handily as animation specialty voices like Mel Blanc or Pinto Colvig. Blore's line readings for Mr. J. Thaddeus Toad, a giddily hyperactive eccentric, produced a great voice. Little wonder Paul Frees closely imitated Blore's distinctly fey tones years later on TV for the Inspector Fenwick role in Jay Ward's Dudley Do-Right cartoons.

Toad's friends were voiced by a collection of Hollywood's British character contingent of the early forties, including Claud Allister as Ratty. Allister had spoken for the diffident Sir Giles in *The Reluctant Dragon*, recorded around the same period in 1940-41. Pat O'Malley contributed a funny Cockney dialect voice for Toad's equally eccentric horse, named Cyril Proudbottom. An appearance by the studio's fine layout artist and voice expert John McLeish, who had been narrating the Goofy "How To" sports cartoons, gave life to the wily Prosecuting Attorney. A further example of an in-house Disney voice was that of talented studio artist Campbell Grant, who provided the Scots-tinged accent for Angus MacBadger. Colin Campbell, another familiar English small part screen actor, supplied the very few lines for Mole, indicating that after the story was whittled down to a manageable length, some dialogue from the 1941 sessions had been relegated to the cutting room floor. A couple of musical numbers were excised for length, including an English "Drinking Song" that sounds tantalizingly humorous. We can only hope that track survives somewhere in the Disney vaults.

Finally in 1950 a Disney feature cartoon emerged that was almost as popular, and profitable, as *Snow White* from a dozen years earlier. *Cinderella*, still another of the many on again-off again studio projects both pre-war and during, had an early storyboard underway by 1943. Other work intervened including Disney's large slate of Government and instructional films. Then a new *Cinderella* treatment was approved in 1947. The following year preliminary animation finally commenced.

It had been several years since a full Disney cartoon feature and much in the Hollywood landscape had changed. The motion picture studios lost the federal antitrust suit (*United States vs. Paramount, et al*) which meant that film studios no longer monopolized the way movies were sold and exhibited. Post-war labor costs had risen markedly, affecting animation as well as live action. The advent of television in households starting from mid-1948 was perceived as a potential long-term threat to the movie industry. For this full length cartoon costs were to be closely monitored, and so all the human characters were performed at first by live actors working to dialogue playbacks, while being filmed as live action reference footage for the animators.

Cinderella herself spoke with the pleasantly soft yet breathily expressive voice of Ilene Woods, a radio singer who won the part when songwriters Mack David, Jerry Livingston and Al Hoffman presented their song "A Dream is a Wish Your Heart Makes" to Disney as a demo record. Their number was sung on the disc by Ms Woods, whom Mack David had remembered from a radio show on which they had worked in New York. Disney was instantly impressed by her voice and felt she was much more the Cinderella in his mind's ear than many of the earlier singers who had auditioned. Ilene Woods recalled, "Walt would come in at the end of each recording session and suggest different ways of doing things." She spoke of an aura about Disney, saying, "You definitely felt you were in the presence of genius." [66]

By far the most memorable voice work in *Cinderella*, however, was by stage and radio veteran Eleanor Audley who was splendid as the icily nasty stepmother, a well written, near-villainous role that echoed hints of the jealously evil Queen from *Snow White*. Two more radio stalwarts supplied some fine voice acting: Verna Felton, last heard as the gossiping old elephant in *Dumbo*, was back as the kindly Fairy Godmother who introduced the catchy song "Bibbidy Bobbidy Boo." New York based actor Luis Van Rooten was a brilliant author, and a multi-lingual master of dialects. A Broadway stage and Manhattan radio staple, he was in Hollywood for several Paramount film roles when he recorded his dialogue for *Cinderella*. Van Rooten doubled as the flustered King and his nervous Grand Duke, the most cartoony pair of all the human characters, if you don't count Cinderella's homely stepsisters.

Beyond all the realistically animated humans it was the large cast of cartoon animals, intensely loyal to the mistreated Cinderella, who were the film's true scene stealers. The chief mice were Gus and Jaq-Jaq, and they were voiced by long-time staff member Jim Macdonald of the Disney sound department. He described the mice voices as "trick" work, "something we'd try because I was on staff." [67]

The voices were sped up, each mouse at a different pitch, one being somewhat lower than the other to achieve a unique chattering sound. Macdonald related how Winston Hibler had written a bunch of unintelligible words for the mice, "'Mouse Latin,' as Hib called it." [68] The mice dialogue was recorded as fast nonsense syllables, but after a rough cut screening "everybody loved the mice, but they said we wish we could understand what they were saying. [So] Hib wrote more dialogue and cleared it up." The final revised tracks created a technical problem with the speed ups in synching the mice voices with their animated mouth movements. Because the dialogue was recorded on film and transferred to discs (the more user-friendly recording tape was still a year away from being adopted), the pitching up at two different speeds was a trial and error learning curve: "We would hold our finger on discs [for the] slow down." [69] But the final result was excellent and the little mice were truly heroic characters. Their travails with the overweight cat Lucifer, who was voice legend June Foray's first Disney assignment, boasted some of the film's most amusing animation.

The next feature cartoon was *Alice in Wonderland* (1951), again a story that had been on the studio's watch list since the late thirties. Some storyboard work had begun in 1943, but by 1945 it was being conceived as a combination live and animated feature. Ginger Rogers, who had recorded a Decca record of *Alice in Wonderland* in 1944, was temporarily in the running to play the lead. However by 1947, following the disappointing returns from the previous combination film *Song of the South*, it was decided to make *Alice in Wonderland* as a full cartoon feature, scheduled for a 1951 release.

As animation historian Michael Barrier observed, when discussing Disney's feature voices in *Funnyworld*, before *Alice in Wonderland* the voices of familiar screen actors like Edward Brophy in *Dumbo* and Eric Blore in *Wind in the Willows* "had only colored the characters they portrayed. [Whereas in] *Alice*, Ed Wynn as the Mad Hatter and Jerry Colonna as the March Hare dominated their characters...the voices were not appropriate for the film." [70] Wynn and Colonna were two highly unique show business performers who had overwhelming personalities, the kind that other comedians would be scared to follow in a live show. That level of overpowering nonsense is a hallmark of the movie. Barrier described the resulting feature as "frantic," pitched at a sometimes zany level that was "disguised as high spirits."

The story by Lewis Carroll was rich in highly eccentric characters perfect for the cartoon medium, and the casting department populated the feature with a range of radio talent adept at broad vocal caricature. Bill Thompson, who provided the famous Droopy voice at MGM, made his Disney debut as the harried and fidgety White Rabbit. Verna Felton was back as the Queen of Hearts, a termagant to end them all, and the henpecked creampuff voice of Francis "Dink" Trout played her woebegone hubby, the King of Hearts. The fine and prolific radio artist Joe Kearns was the talking Doorknob, and it is a pity his voice wasn't used more in animation; Kearns was one of actor Daws Butler's own radio inspirations.

British actresses Kathryn Beaumont and Heather Angel played the straight roles of Alice and her older sister, the only sane voices among the often cacophonous absurdity. Another English artist, the flexible Pat O'Malley who had been such a fine Cockney equine in *Mr. Toad*, was back as two famous character pairs from the story, Tweedle Dee and Tweedle Dum, and the Walrus and the Carpenter.

Also returning was another regular, the eternally timid sounding Sterling Holloway as the memorably eccentric Cheshire Cat, while the studio cast the unique British revue artist Richard Haydn, who enacted the priggish Caterpillar using his fussy "Edwin Carp" radio voice. The film was originally to feature popular young satirist Stan Freberg as the Jabberwocky. Freberg recorded dialogue for the character, but that sequence was finally cut from the film.

It was two years before the next Disney animated feature, *Peter Pan*, was released in 1953. This was still another in the long line of projects that had been lingering since the late thirties. Sir James M. Barrie's famous play about the astral travels of a family of English children following a magical boy who never wanted to grow up was adapted to become one of Disney's most enduringly popular fifties films. Vocally, it was the by now usual feature mix of "straight" voices for the Darling family (Wendy, John and Michael) juxtaposed with comical character voices for the villains and other supporting players.

Of all the voice talents in this film, it was Hans Conried (1917-82) who was forever immortalized playing the comical villain Captain Hook. Conried's previous Disney experience had only been a few parts on the 1938 *Mickey Mouse* Pepsodent-sponsored radio show. In 1951 he was cast as the on-camera "Slave in the Magic Mirror" for Walt's first TV special. Following that performance he auditioned for, and won the Hook role in, *Peter Pan*.

Conried was one of the most original artists in the Los Angeles radio circle, an arch personality with a truly singular voice and a range of striking dialects like no other. A born actor who always relished the opportunity for hamming it up, he was a student of John Barrymore and an ardent Shakespeare buff whose knowledge of the Bard was rivalled only by actor colleague John Carradine;

coincidentally, when Conried was unavailable for the *Lux Radio* adaptation of Disney's *Peter Pan*, Carradine took the part of Captain Hook on the air. Conried was a Hollywood eccentric who was famous along Radio row for his daily pair of socks, one green and one red. Once heard, Conried's juicy exhortations of blustery full throttle villainy ("Blast you, Pan!!!!") could never be forgotten. In typical fashion he completed his recording for the film relatively quickly; he recalled years later that he was reading dialogue which had been written as far back as 1937. But once his lines were in the can he spent almost three years on call playing both Hook and George Darling, the children's father, in live action reference film for the animators that was shot intermittently on the Disney soundstage.

For the Indian Chief role, veteran musician-comic Candy Candido did his trademark guttural voice which he had made famous on radio's *Jimmy Durante Show* in recurring skits where he went from a squeaky falsetto to his deep, froggy voice using the defeated expression, "I'm feelin' mighty looooowwww!" June Foray modelled as live action reference for one of the Mermaids as well as voicing the grouchy old Indian squaw. Fresh from his Disney debut as the Dodo and White Rabbit from *Alice in Wonderland*, Bill Thompson was back in what was undoubtedly his most versatile showcase to date in his lengthy cartoon career. Not only was he cast as Captain Hook's toadying first mate, the nervous Mr. Smee, but he enacted the voices of seven other pirate crew members, all of them sounding totally distinct.

Among the straighter voices in the cast was young Kathryn Beaumont who went from recording the lead role of Alice for *Alice in Wonderland* to playing Wendy in *Peter Pan* almost without a pause for breath. A group of Hollywood radio's best child artists played the "Lost Boys," with Bobby Ellis supplying a rare example of a real kid doing a cartoonish character voice - the large, goofy sounding boy - rather than simply playing a straight child role.

Finally, it should be noted that the title character of this film, the famous "boy who never wished to grow up," was voiced by Disney's long-time contract juvenile artist Bobby Driscoll. Ironically, however, by the time he got around to recording Peter's dialogue, young Mr. Driscoll was now a teenager whose voice had obviously changed! So Peter Pan, in fact, sounded much like a young high school student who'd recently been through puberty and was definitely growing up! It was no wonder that a long held theatrical tradition was to always have the role of Peter Pan portrayed by a female.

Lady and the Tramp followed two years later in 1955, and was the first Disney animated feature in which the lead characters, a boy and girl dog, have voices as straight as the human characters in whose house the female dog resides. Only *Bambi* from a dozen years before had animal characters speaking in straight, believably human voices.

The female roles were played by some fine talents. Radio actress Barbara Luddy, famous for her years as resident leading lady on *The First Nighter Program*, played the main role of Lady in an effectively soft and husky voice. The great song stylist, composer and jazz artist Peggy Lee played Lady's human mistress, nicknamed Darling, while doubling as not only the worldly-wise Pekingese named Peg, but also the destructive twin cats who sing the amusing "Siamese Cat Song" (it was composed for the film by Ms Lee herself). Rounding out the relatively straight voices were Verna Felton, returning with another fine matronly part as Aunt Sarah, and her real-life son Lee Millar Jr. who played Jim Dear, Lady's master.

The title role of canine hero Tramp was voiced by youthful Larry Roberts who was a triple threat talent. An actor, singer and comedian, he was discovered by a Disney story man who saw him in a production staged by the little theatre group The Player's Ring, which Roberts had formed. All these voice actors delivered their roles with total naturalness and great conviction. For a film with such a sustained level of quality animation *Lady and the Tramp* was an unusually talky film. *Alice in Wonderland* had been just as dialogue heavy, although the speaking parts in that film were much more frantically pitched.

But despite the many straight roles, lovers of great "cartoony voices" needn't have feared for *Lady and the Tramp* boasts just as many funny supporting characters. These voices are dominated again by the excellent voice talent Bill Thompson who plays three prominent dogs. These were Jock the Scottie, a British bulldog and the dachshund, with the inventive Thompson adding Joe the Italian restaurant chef, and an Irish policeman. Stage actor Bill Baucom, who did much radio in the early fifties, played the loyal and slow-talking old Southern bloodhound Trusty, while veteran stage comedian George Givot, famous for his "Greek Ambassador" dialect character, was the sympathetic restaurant owner Tony, a loyal friend to Tramp. Tony's singing voice for the love song "Bella Notte" was dubbed by Bill Lee, baritone singer in the Mello Men, the vocal group who sang and howled for the pound hounds.

Assisting Thompson in filling out the sundry other animal and human characters was a raft of Hollywood's leading radio trained specialists including the popular young satirist Stan Freberg as the beaver with the whistling front teeth. Freberg's own whistle effect was enhanced by a device invented by sound whiz James Macdonald. Dallas McKennon, by now established as a leading cartoon actor for Walter Lantz, did several nutty voices including Pedro the chihuahua, a crazy laughing hyena and even some extra whistling teeth effects augmenting Freberg's beaver voice track. The excellent character actor Alan Reed, just a few years away from his career-defining Fred Flintstone cartoon role, played Boris the Russian wolf hound.

Lady and the Tramp proved successful at the box-office, raking in the most for a Disney cartoon feature since *Snow White*, and its distinct charm has remained strong for over sixty years. But despite the plaudits it would be another four years before the studio's next full-length cartoon appeared. This gap reflected the now older Disney's time and preoccupations slowly shifting from animation to his many live action movies, television shows and his new all-consuming Disneyland park, throughout the later fifties.

As the end of the decade approached, Disney Productions finally released the long-awaited feature *Sleeping Beauty* (1959). It was the third in the classic fairy tale tradition, a genre at which Disney's team of gifted animators excelled. The film had commenced story meetings some eight years before in 1951 and it was finally decided to base it on two sources, the original Charles Perrault fairy tale blended with the Russian musical adaptation from two centuries later, featuring music by Peter Tchaikovsky. Finally, some original songs were added to the mix.

Disney dithered quite a lot with the story elements, and production delays kept increasing as he seemed incapable of the once decisive qualities he showed as far back as the early thirties. Artistically, though, Disney had made it clear that he desired achieving something new and striking with the film's design. Two studio artists, veteran layout man John Hench and a recent hire Eyvind Earle, a gifted painter, were able to influence the course of the feature in a dazzling way. A "medieval" approach was based on museum tapestries, while Earle's singular ability at detailed backgrounds stressed an overall vertical look to everything from castle interiors to the surrounding forest. The resultant visual finery eventually came to dominate the efforts of even Disney's top animators. While undeniably beautiful, the very busy backgrounds often seemed like too much of a good thing to the point of overkill.

The movie gave the greatest prominence to a range of talented female voices. Certainly it was a treat to again hear the superb stage actress Eleanor Audley, in a villainous role that exceeded her horrid stepmother from *Cinderella*. The evil Maleficent was in some ways closer to the Wicked Queen from *Snow White*. That said, the Wicked Queen remains the superior villain, being slowly driven mad by a self-loathing psycho-sexual jealousy. In *Sleeping Beauty* Maleficent is less motivated by vengeful hate and often seems evil simply for the sake of being evil. But that aside, the superb Miss Audley, despite suffering a tubercular illness during the film's production, was as marvellous in her malignant line readings as ever.

The regular straight roles of Aurora and Prince Phillip were handled by two gifted and experienced singers. Mary Costa possessed a bell-like clarity that Disney deemed perfect for the heroine, while Bill Shirley's attractive bel canto voice was just how a noble knight in shining armour should sound. They recorded their roles over multiple sessions, as was the Disney production norm. But it must be noted they remained the blandest of all the inescapably bland hero-heroine roles of any Disney feature. (Coincidentally Ms Costa was married to Frank Tashlin, not only a leading comedy filmmaker but also one of this book's heroes, a fine director of classic era cartoons for Schlesinger and Screen Gems as well as spending several years in Disney's story department.)

Character actress Verna Felton, by now considered a Disney regular, returned as the main member of the three magic fairies who are essentially the heroine's guardian angels. Her warm, motherly tone supplied the light touch badly needed in a film far less populated with eccentric or comedic characters than any previous Disney feature. And while the fairies and the older royals are likable, they lack depth and come across as two-dimensional characters.

Taylor Holmes, an accomplished stage and screen veteran whose career was in its sixth decade, recorded the voice of King Stefan. Sadly, Holmes died in the year the film was released. Actor Hans Conried was the live action model for the Stefan character. As he had previously done for *Peter Pan*, Conried was filmed for the animators' reference. In hindsight, it seems a pity that the studio chose Holmes and not Conried to voice Stefan. While the role was regal and distinguished, Holmes sounded too "normal" when contrasted with the bumbling King Hubert, the father of heroic Prince

Phillip. Hubert was played for laughs by familiar voice specialist Bill Thompson, and he was the only real cartoon-style "funny" voice in the show (if we don't count the froggy mumblings of trumpeter-comic Candy Candido who grunted the role of Maleficent's chief goon).

In this author's opinion, had Hans Conried also been cast as King Stefan's voice, he and Bill Thompson would have been a more distinctive duo in their scenes together, as they had been so effectively as Hook and Smee in *Peter Pan*. Serious or comedic, Conried always added a vocal flavoring that was fascinating to audiences, and he was a born animation actor.

Incidentally this was the next-to-last Disney feature to employ the voice of Thompson, one of the all-time great cartoon voices. In 1960 he moved from show business to an executive position with Union Oil and effectively retired from full-time performing.*

*Thompson returned for two final roles in the late sixties: he played Uncle Scrooge in the short *Scrooge McDuck and Money* (1967), while for his final feature film he voiced the inebriated goose Uncle Waldo in *The Aristocats* released in 1970, a year before the versatile voice-man's death.

Another voice artist who would soon be missed in animation was the unforgettable Verna Felton, who excelled at all her roles from battle-axes to good fairies. After *Sleeping Beauty* she remained on call but she was aging and her career was inexorably winding down. She would record just one more cartoon feature, *The Jungle Book*, before she died in 1966 on 14 December 1966, just one day before Walt Disney passed.

Poor *Sleeping Beauty*. Despite the eight long years of meticulous work, and the vast sums of money spent, it was not the huge hit Disney Productions had expected. Without indelibly memorable and funny characters like the Seven Dwarfs or even Cinderella's animal friends to offset the evil Maleficent, the slight story seemed a tad unengaging throughout and it finally couldn't compete with all the visual finery on display. The climactic chase sequence was excitingly paced and staged, and Maleficent's battle with Prince Phillip is an excellent blending of animation with sound design. But the endless magnificence of those detailed backgrounds couldn't help dominating the animation, no matter how stunningly accomplished Disney's character animators had become by this point.

Inevitably, the box office returns on the film proved disappointing. The *Disneyland* TV show and the successful venture into the Anaheim theme park had provided a big boost to studio coffers in the three years preceding the film's 1959 release, but the final cost overruns of *Sleeping Beauty* wiped out much of those profits. Fortunately for Disney, the next animated feature was to cost much less and make a whole lot more.

The decade of the sixties dawned with a film that had one of the largest voice casts of any Disney feature. *One Hundred and One Dalmatians* (1961) adapted from Dodie Smith's British novel, was not only vocally different in tone to the overall sound of *Sleeping Beauty*, but it was also the first feature to boast the new xerographic method of transferring animation drawings to cels. This new technology was first tried in some shorts and on UPA's *Boing Boing* TV show in 1956. It effectively did away with the costly and labor intensive method of hand inking each individual animation drawing that had been the "ink & paint on celluloid" norm for decades.

Dalmatians was a story that felt contemporary and was a departure from the by now familiar fairy tale genre set "once upon a time." Set in and around London, the film had an evocative, wintry English feel. The new Xerox process added to that ambience with the decision to visually match the backgrounds with the character drawings. It imparted a kind of *Punch* Magazine bamboo pen-scratch cartoon visual, definitely a break with the long-time Disney cartoon look.

Many of the adult voices reflected that British aura, such as pro-lific radio artist Ben Wright who played the songwriter Roger Rad-cliffe. He was just one of a group from West Coast radio's so-called Limey actor contingent, with Ramsay Hill, Frederic Worlock and Tudor Owen all doubling up with at least two voices each. The film had many parts, most of which were small but telling canine cameos, and they each needed to sound unique. Disney regular J. Pat O'Malley, a most flexible English artist, supplied four distinct voices, including the uncouth human Cockney villain Jasper and the haughty sounding dog known as The Colonel.

Martha Wentworth voiced the household's Nanny-cook who looked after the Dalmatian's litter of pups. This fine actress gave a magnificent reading to the scene where she realizes her "babies" have been dognapped and she runs into the street desperately screaming for help. It is hard to believe that way back in 1935 this same Miss Wentworth was the funny Mae West-inspired voice of Jenny Wren in Disney's *Who Killed Cock Robin?* Small wonder that Martha Went-worth, thoroughly theatre trained, was the first actress to be given the label "the Woman of a Thousand Voices," many years before the emer-gence of other multi-voiced women like Sara Berner and June Foray. [71]

But far and away the most distinctive character in *Dalmatians* is the horridly overbearing and nasty-to-the-core Cruella de Vil. This reptilian hag was played to the hilt by Betty Lou Gerson whose slightly cigarette-husky voice and Gothically evil manner were unforgettable, perfectly matched with master animator Marc Davis who brought Cruella to florid visual life. Ms Gerson had been play-ing slinky and seductive bad girl roles on radio crime and mystery dramas for twenty years and she was a great casting decision for this ghastly woman. Like Eleanor Audley and Lucille LaVerne before her, Ms Gerson helped create another in the long line of indelible female Disney villains.

The strong British tone was affected to only a slight degree when the small pups spoke in the voices of obviously American children. But overall the cast was exceptionally well chosen and the soundtrack maintained its consistency. This was no doubt due to the film's expert story man Bill Peet, who personally directed all the film's dialogue recording sessions.

No well-known voices dominated this feature as Ed Wynn and Jerry Colonna had so dominated *Alice in Wonderland*, if we don't count Australian-born movie actor Rod Taylor's subtle under-playing of Pongo, the story's chief canine. Disney's next two fea-tures would continue to rely on voice talents with a proven track record in radio drama, a wonderful entertainment medium that had recently been pronounced definitively dead and buried. Hol-lywood radio's still active practitioners of the art of voice emoting would be relying on voice-overs and animation producers more than ever after 1961.

The Sword in the Stone (1963), from T. H. White's Arthurian legend, was the penultimate feature in which Disney himself was creatively involved. It was yet one more of the countless projects first mooted as a cartoon feature in the late thirties. But by this point in the early sixties, Disney was much more occupied with his non-animation projects, especially the hugely successful Disney-land theme park. As Michael Barrier noted, Wolfgang Reitherman was the sole supervising head of *Sword*, and the chief animators were now essentially full directors. [72] While the film's lush settings and Olde-England atmosphere are beautifully achieved, it feels somewhat uninspiring and cold when compared with the top Dis-ney feature cartoons.

Bill Peet provided another of his detailed story treatments, and the actors chosen were mostly seasoned pros from radio, stage and film. Karl Swenson, a long-time veteran of New York's radio row, played Merlin the Magician in a believable interpretation that had the requisite crusty, absent-minded quality of a venerable wizard but was subtly underplayed so as not to be just another dithering "old coot" voice. However the character finally lacked the awe inspiring charisma required of such a learned sorcerer, and his constant chatter did indeed become tiring.

The narration was supplied via the rich English tones of Sebastian Cabot who would become famous later in the decade as Mr. French the housekeeper on TV's long-running sitcom *Family Affair*. Cabot had first appeared in live-action roles for Disney, such as Bissonnette in *Westward Ho the Wagons!* (1956). He doubled in *Sword* as the voice of Sir Ector, the boy's bombastic stepfather. Another distinguished British voice hired for the role of Sir Pelinore was the cultured stage and screen character actor Alan Napier. He too would become a television favorite starting in 1965 when the camp classic *Batman* series first went to air, with Napier prominently cast as Alfred, the unflappable butler to Bruce Wayne.

Voice-wise, the major problem with the movie was the lead character of Wart, the future King Arthur. In fact he ends up with three voices. Rickie Sorenson, a fifties child actor in television and films, had done a small part for Walt Disney in *One Hundred and One Dalmatians* as one of the endangered puppies. He was cast in the role of Wart for *Sword in the Stone* but when recording commenced he was entering puberty. It is obvious listening to his strained line readings that he was experiencing a degree of difficulty with that early teenage period where a boy's voice is changing, and vocal cracks, break-ups and a general self-conscious awkwardness are common.

In several places throughout the film some of Wart's lines were read by director Wolfgang Reitherman's two sons Richard and Robert, and it was possibly assumed audiences would only hear a "young boy" voice and not notice the dissimilar vocal timbres. Alas, the voice differences are in fact apparent and they tend to mar a viewer's enjoyment - the film is certainly talky - and it is compounded by the medieval English setting and ambience. The boy, alone among the rest of the very British cast, sounds like a typical sixties American kid from television sitcom suburbia.

The most "cartoony" voices, in a film that badly needed some comic relief to balance the overall serious tone (somewhat earnestly stressing the benefits of continuous education), were provided by old-time radio artists of proven reputation. Junius Matthews, a diminutive actor with an unusual voice quality had been a regular on the long-running children's radio serial *The Land of the Lost* as well as in many dramatic shows. He supplied a fine characterization for Merlin's comically contentious pet Owl named Archimedes. And returning for one more Disney booking was the excellent actress Martha Wentworth who played the most traditionally caricatured member of the cast, Mad Madam Mim the sorceress. Essentially a cameo role, her magic duel with Merlin was an enjoyable sequence, the funny and action-filled highlight of an otherwise disappointing and occasionally dull feature.

Soon after *Sword in the Stone*, Disney enjoyed a monumental success in 1964 with the live action fantasy film *Mary Poppins*. This eternally popular movie featured some animated combination sequences that are enjoyable, well executed and which rather resembled the effects achieved years before in *Song of the South*. The voices were essentially an ensemble of one liners, so brief as to be inconsequential to this narrative, except to note that the recording sessions for the cartoon animals managed to corral a large contingent of Hollywood's leading sixties specialty voice artists like Daws Butler, Paul Frees, Thurl Ravenscroft, Dal McKennon, and Ginny Tyler. These talents were then buttressed by some of the live cast members also supplying bit voices. Julie Andrews, David Tomlinson, Alan Napier and Sean McClory were among the latter group, and everyone seemed to contribute to the large collection of animated penguin waiters and London Pearlies. For any voice-minutiae buffs this book's filmography enumerates who was who.

And so we come to the final Disney feature of what can be called sound animation's Golden Age, the forty year period which is the purview of this book. *The Jungle Book* (1967) as everyone surely knows by now, was the final animated feature to benefit from at least some creative input by Disney, indisputably the leading figure of the theatrical cartoon medium, who died in December 1966 as the film was over halfway to completion. In truth *The Jungle Book* was actually much less a Disney film and more continuation of the Reitherman style established from *The Sword in the Stone*. Indeed Reitherman's domination continued for the next few features after *Jungle Book*. As noted earlier the reality is that Disney had slowly lost much of his once all-encompassing enthusiasm for great character animation by the mid-fifties.

As this chapter on Golden Age Disney animation voices enters its final stage it is time to discuss the lasting legacy of *The Jungle Book*. The film is now widely regarded as the very first animated feature to kickstart the modern-day trend of hiring what are now called "Celebrity Voices" to portray a range of cartoon characters. This was the single biggest change in cartoon features, which had until this point traditionally relied on the older style of animation voice experts like Bill Thompson or Pinto Colvig to speak for the majority of the roles. As Mike Barrier noted in *Funnyworld*, all the Disney cartoon features that followed *The Sword in the Stone* "have been dominated by star voices." [73] * And as early as 1970 and *The Aristocats* the casting of these big names was aimed directly at the audience who had been the first television-reared generation. The "Celebrity" voices already began to include as many sitcom stars as motion picture notables.

* It could be argued that *Gay Purr-ee*, a 1962 one-off UPA cartoon feature released through Warner Bros., was technically the first to use "Celebrity Voices" (including talents the calibre of Judy Garland and Robert Goulet) for the leads. Readers are referred to the chapter on UPA cartoon voices.

There were five major names in the *Jungle Book* voice cast. They were musical entertainers Phil Harris and Louis Prima, along with screen actors George Sanders, Sterling Holloway and Sebastian Cabot. The big difference was that beyond their voices they were already famous names, instantly known to the general public from years of radio, records, Las Vegas, TV and movies. Importantly, those names were now being seen as valuable aids to promoting the film. Weren't voice artists once deemed anonymous?

Even more importantly, the characters were seemingly animated to match and catch the personality of each celebrity, rather than the other way around. Only once before, in *Alice in Wonderland* and its famous comedy stars Ed Wynn and Jerry Colonna, whose voices were so well known as to be unmistakeably unique, did cartoon character voices remind theatregoers of their actual behind-the-mike actors. In *Jungle Book* it now seemed a deliberate ploy.

Phil Harris and Disney knew each other socially. Harris was a perfect fit for cartoons. He had been a veteran bandleader and jazz singer since the twenties, but his greatest gift was as a natural comedian. Harris spent ten years in the role of the hilariously brash and egocentric orchestra leader on *The Jack Benny Program* from 1936 before inheriting his own radio series for Fitch Shampoo. *The Phil Harris-Alice Faye Show* ran for eight solid years. By the time the Rexall company assumed sponsorship in 1948 the Harris-Faye program was arguably the all-time funniest show from that great medium, and Harris worked each week with radio's top comics, many of whom were cartoon voices (Blanc, Walter Tetley, Alan Reed, Hans Conried). *The Jungle Book* role of Baloo the Bear was pure Harris personified, taking advantage of his musical talents as well via the catchy Terry Gilkyson song "The Bare Necessities." It was delivered in the relaxed Harris manner of almost gliding his whiskey baritone across the lyrics, the way he had in so many New Orleans-inspired Dixieland numbers like "Basin Street Blues."

Harris was certainly well received in this part and he was inevitably cast in subsequent Disney features like *The Aristo Cats* where he landed the lead role. He would have dominated *The Jungle Book* had it not been for the inclusion of long-time movie cad, sneering cynic and all around hissable George Sanders. Sanders was so good as Shere Khan, the menacing and imperious tiger, that to some viewers he virtually stole the show. His world weary, subtly clipped voice and his patented supercilious acting persona proved one of animation's great casting choices, as perfect in its way as Alan Reed was in the role of Hanna-Barbera's Fred Flintstone: neither character can now be imagined with any other voice. It had been Disney's idea to audition Sanders. In 1962 the urbane character star had appeared in the studio's live action Jules Verne adventure *In Search of the Castaways.*

Sanders aside, the voice of long-time Disney regular Sterling Holloway was a fine choice for the snake named Kaa, whose hissing reptilian sibilance was married to Holloway's fey, trembly tenor. Kaa's battle of wills dialogue sequence with Shere Khan was a fine demonstration of the effectiveness of totally contrasting voices enhancing superb animation. It's easy to see why Disney's master animators always spoke of how great voice acting inspired them in every area of their skills, from facial expression to character attitude and poses, caricature and uniquely distinct body movement.

Louis Prima was another famous musical name who was well used in the show as the orangutan King Louie. Prima's energetic, high and husky Italian-tinged vocals, honed in Las Vegas lounge shows since the mid-fifties, was an inspired choice for the monkey song "I Wanna Be Like You." (This was Prima's second cartoon role, because one year earlier he had gently warbled the romantic song "Pensate Amoré" in the 1966 Hanna-Barbera spin-off theatrical feature *The Man Called Flintstone.*)

Even the supporting voices were a sign of the new style of voice casting to come in the post-Golden Age. With the Beatles and British Invasion groups all the rage at the time of production it was decided to have the vultures sing as a rock group. While that idea was finally nixed by Disney in favor of a tried-and-true barbershop quartet approach, the vultures' speaking voices remained topically English. In fact one was positively Liverpudlian. Expat disc jockey "Lord" Tim Hudson supplied a most Ringo Starr-esque vulture voice, while Chad Stuart, of Chad & Jeremy fame, voiced another as a light British pop-star type. Balancing these two was the older vulture, played by veteran Disney character voice, and fellow Briton, J. Pat O'Malley.

The Jungle Book, one of the studio's notable successes and always a happy picture to revisit, ends this part of the Disney feature voices chapter. Future Disney animated features now had a brand new template for the voice casting process, and a highly successful one it has proved ever since.

Feature Voices, post-Walt Disney & post-Golden Age

As noted, the trend of using big-name voices really kicked in with *The Jungle Book*. Over half a century has passed, a longer period of time than the thirty-seven-year Golden Age of animation itself. Today cartoon geeks, industry players and movie fans alike are still arguing the merits or deficiencies of hiring "Celebrity Voices" for animation. Walt Disney had seemed happy to approve the *Jungle Book* vocal cast, and director Woolie Reitherman appeared to be all for the continuation of strong, recognizable star voices on his soundtracks: the four follow-up features he directed were the ones that determinedly continued the trend. The Disney company soon mastered the art of publicizing so-called celebrity names by making voices far more of a selling point than they had ever been. This set the future pattern of cartoon voice casting, seemingly for all time.

Indeed the first of the "post-Walt" features, *The Aristo Cats* (1970) showcased even more big names, twelve starring voices in fact. Many of the talents were familiar from current hit television shows like *Green Acres* (Eva Gabor and Pat Buttram), *The Andy Griffith Show* (George "Goober" Lindsey), *The Beverly Hillbillies* (Nancy

Kulp) and *Rowan and Martin's Laugh-In* (Roddy Maude-Roxby). Personality musicians Phil Harris, fresh from his triumph as Baloo, and Scatman Crothers added jazzy charm to the soundtrack, while from the hit movie *The Odd Couple* the studio hired Monica Evans and Carole Shelley, the two English girls who portrayed the comically scatterbrained room-mates Cecily and Gwendolyn, the Pigeon sisters. Other movie names included familiar character players like crotchety Charles Lane, Disney mainstay Sterling Holloway and the veteran British comedienne Hermione Baddeley who had already appeared in three Disney live action features of the sixties: *Mary Poppins*, *The Adventures of Bullwhip Griffin* and *The Happiest Millionaire*.

The mostly live-action musical-fantasy *Bedknobs and Broomsticks* (1972) featured a short animated sequence set on the Isle of Naboombu which was supervised by Ward Kimball. For the animated characters here it was briefly back to the old method of hiring anonymous cartoon voice specialists. Excellent voice talents Lennie Weinrib and Bob Holt, both of whom had begun amassing TV cartoons, DePatie-Freleng theatricals and commercial credits galore, were used alongside reliable voice veteran Dal McKennon. Weinrib was cast as the voice of the lion king Leonidas, while Holt played the Codfish from the island's lagoon. Dal McKennon voiced the Fisherman Bear.

The next fully animated Disney feature was 1973's *Robin Hood*, and it was top heavy with British "name" voices. They included contemporary movie star Brian Bedford who spoke the heroic title role, the distinguished and plummy-voiced character star and raconteur Peter Ustinov as villainous Prince John, and the uniquely original comedy actor Terry-Thomas as Sir Hiss. Returning to the Disney soundstage was the ditzy Broadway team of Monica Evans and Carole Shelley, although this time in separate roles. The remaining voices were a total contrast and couldn't have been more American if they tried.

The Disney staff had been surprised when southern-fried Phil Harris auditioned as Baloo for the Indian subcontinent setting of *Jungle Book*, but here he was in his third Disney feature playing the role of Sherwood Forest's largest denizen, Little John. To top that, his old *Jack Benny Program* co-star Andy Devine provided his famous strangulated vocal chords for a truly distinctive Friar Tuck. TV comedy names, and Alabama natives, Pat Buttram and George Lindsey were back to cavort in Merrie Old England while Colorado's Ken Curtis, then appearing as the unkempt and cantankerous Festus on *Gunsmoke* (a role that often sounded like a human cartoon character), played Nutsy the Vulture. Country music star Roger Miller, a Texas-born chart-topper and songwriter with a most creative comedy mind, was a fine choice for the musical member of Robin's merry men, Alan-a-Dale. Somehow the ensemble worked, but that blend of Brits and Americans was mighty eccentric casting.

The trend of big name voices begun by the Disney studio was suddenly an emerging industry. 1973 saw TV giant Hanna-Barbera release their animated feature *Charlotte's Web*, and it too boasted various "names" as the voices, with Arizona cowboy singer Rex Allen narrating, *Laugh-In*'s Henry Gibson as Wilbur, Debbie Reynolds as Charlotte and the brilliant stage and radio actress Agnes Moorehead as the Goose. The standout voice was snarky Paul Lynde as Templeton the scavenger Rat, who got to sing the amusing "A Fair is a Veritable Smorgasbord" in the sardonically campy Lynde manner. Even independent producer Fred Wolf of Murakami-Wolf made a feature in 1976, *The Mouse and His Child*. Big acting names ruled again: Peter Ustinov and Andy Devine, fresh from Disney's *Robin Hood*, were back to the cartoon field once more, and they voiced this film along with Oscar-winning Cloris Leachman and Oscar nominee Sally Kellerman. Celebrity voices had quickly become the norm beyond just the Disney organization.

"Star" casting became entrenched at Disney by 1977, more than ten years since Walt's death, as the studio released *The Rescuers*.

Again a raft of major names from TV series were prominent as voices, like Eva Gabor in her second Disney cartoon, the ever-popular stand-up comedian Bob Newhart, and sitcom standouts Pat Buttram (*Green Acres*), Joe Flynn (*McHale's Navy*) and Bernard Fox (Dr. Bombay the warlock in *Bewitched*). Accomplished Broadway and motion picture actress Geraldine Page appeared as Madame Medusa, and the aging star of old-time radio's long-running comedy vehicle *Fibber Mcgee and Molly* - Jim "Fibber" Jordan himself - was as perky and sharply comic as he had been forty years earlier. Husband & wife acting veterans John McIntire and Jeanette Nolan finally did a cartoon for the Disney company; over forty years earlier McIntire had been the junior announcer bringing on a young Disney in 1934's Christmas *Hall of Fame* radio program for Hinds Honey & Almond skin balm, "starring Walt Disney, with Mickey and the Gang."

With voice acting now considered a respectable credit for so-called "celebrity" actors, the die had been well and truly cast. The decades of Disney features to come starting in the early eighties, to say nothing of those from up and comers Pixar and DreamWorks and the rest, would all adopt the megastar voice approach and it is now, as they say, de rigueur. (So, undoubtedly, were the vastly higher fees and deals the big name stars' mangers negotiated, when compared to the one-time-only "scale" payments which the Golden Age voice experts were paid!)

Just a small sample from the Disney features of the eighties demonstrates the rapid growth of the celebrity cartoon trend, with top names from every field of entertainment, encompassing Broadway to the music industry. The choices ranged from evergreen favorites to relative showbiz newbies. They included Mickey Rooney, Pearl Bailey and Jack Albertson in *The Fox and the Hound* (1981), followed by accomplished Shakespearean thespians John Hurt and Freddie Jones emoting alongside the clever nightclub comic John Byner in *The Black Cauldron* (1985). Vincent Price, owner of one of film's most hammily recognizable voices was in characteristically fine form, obviously enjoying himself hugely as Ratigan - even singing - in *The Great Mouse Detective* (1986), while Bette Midler, Dom DeLuise and Billy Joel starred in *Oliver & Company* (1988). Even blue-tinged Vegas comedy legend Buddy Hackett worked alongside character actor Kenneth Mars in *The Little Mermaid* (1989).

The trend of casting such well-known voices continued bigger than ever through the nineties as the Disney Company, experiencing a resurgence of popularity, unfurled a record nine features over the next decade, including enormous box-office successes like *Aladdin* (1992). For that mega-hit the most memorable voices by far were supplied by two brilliant, departed comedy talents: Robin Williams played the exuberant and energetic Genie and the truly one-off Gilbert Gottfried voiced Iago the parrot. With Williams and Gottfried it was obvious that their unique comedy minds were allowed to drift from the approved script, and the film incorporated moments using riffs and improv bits created during their recording sessions. And as good as those two were, it is impossible to forget the work of actor Jonathan Freeman, with his fruitily booming theatrical voice, who was particularly good as the villainous Jafar.

In the nineties the movie and television industries were on the verge of major change as the internet began its mighty and all-pervasive climb, and CGI digital effects were in the beginning stages of development. The stakes were becoming higher than ever as cable TV companies expanded, and the stirrings of the gaming industry were already underway. Above all else the breathtakingly swift adoption of the worldwide web meant many new entertainment options, and the term "fragmented audience" had once complacent executives on edge. Movies now faced fierce competition to attract ever bigger market share. By now animated features had become a form of blockbuster with Pixar's 1995 *Toy Story* property outdoing even Disney in the popularity stakes.

Names like Robin Williams, Tom Hanks, even Don Rickles could indeed attract a huge audience to a cartoon feature just on reputation alone.

Aladdin's casting of Williams and Gottfried proved persuasively that the closest the cartoon medium of today has come to matching the old style comic voice specialty artists like Mel Blanc, are when the chosen "celebrity" voices are past masters at the art of stand-up comedy. Eddie Murphy is another example of a top tier comic talent who is not only innately funny but also endlessly creative, prone to bouts of improv at the recording dates. He spoke the role of Mushu, with almost a demented revivalist preacher delivery, in 1999's *Mulan* then topped even that over-the-top cartoony performance with his stellar job as the motormouth hanger-on Donkey in the huge *Shrek* franchise for competitor Dreamworks.

When comparing Murphy and Williams to some celebrities who came across as a little "ordinary" to cartoon connoisseurs it's obviously going to be an ever-debatable issue. Both Val Kilmer in *The Prince of Egypt* (1998) and Mel Gibson in *Pocahontas* (1995) were panned and admired equally. Indeed the topic of star voices is now so subjective and contentious that virtually every viewer will appreciate a "celebrity" voice differently, and a good or bad casting choice is ultimately decided via the ear of the beholder.

In 1995, the decade's monster-mega success *The Lion King* featured two magnificent theatrical voices emoting for a pair of the leading lions: James Earl Jones as the imposing yet tender father figure King Mufasa, and Jeremy Irons as the unctuously villainous Scar. Both artists were in top form, but an interesting point arose about a possible hazard to the casting of certain star names. It was pointed out that some viewers found the casting of Jones had unintentionally impaired their enjoyment of the story because his boomingly wonderful vocal instrument was simply too familiar and distinctive, and all they could think about was Darth Vader presiding over the African Pride Lands.

By now even TV animation had adopted the use of celebrity voices, with *The Simpsons* attracting legendary Hollywood names like Liz Taylor. Disney's *Hercules* series was a spinoff of their 1997 *Hercules* feature cartoon which had used the voices of Danny DeVito, Charlton Heston and Rip Torn. The television version featured a veritable roll call of famous and infamous cameos. It became increasingly common for name voices to appear in "guest" roles with often topical gags as part of the cartoon show experience, and anyone well-known like William Shatner, David Hyde Pierce, Eric Idle, Wayne Newton or Regis Philbin was likely to appear.

It was in one sense like revisiting those Golden Age cartoon shorts which highlighted celebrity caricatures from thirties movies and radio programs. Of course in those halcyon days the voices were almost always imitated. But in the here and now, our hyper-cool age of seen-it-all irony means that certain stars, reading self-reflexive comedy dialogue, are in a sense doing impressions of themselves. In fact "celebrity" itself would inevitably be mocked in television cartoons like *Family Guy* with famous names sending up their own images.

And so what of today's richly talented crop of the "old style" specialty cartoon actors, those anonymous multi-voice artists who had been the backbone of the animation industry for virtually their whole careers? Would they even still get a look-in? Would they be forevermore relegated to bit parts like "Henchman #3," "School Principal's Secretary" or "Telephone Receptionists A & B," with maybe just one line of dialogue apiece? Would all those funny, well-written crazy master villains and zany sidekicks - parts that voice specialists had thrived on creating, developing and honing - now automatically go to still more on-camera superstars?

When the trend began taking off there was understandable panic and occasional resentment…questions were bandied about, mostly along the lines of "did Celebrity X *really* need this gig?" or "These rich and famous people are taking our livelihoods away!" or

"Will this famous pair of actors *truly* improve the quality of a movie's voice track?" The late June Foray never got past her indignant stance that cartoon voice work should have remained the domain of the specialty artist, but many others came to accept the status quo, whether grudgingly or with graceful equanimity.

In one area certain unsung voice actors were able to fill a particular niche that the celebrity names could never do. As time inexorably marched on and the first great wave of voice experts like Mel Blanc, Daws Butler, Paul Frees and Don Messick began passing simply from old age and natural causes, the need for what was called "voice matching" arose in the late eighties. By now the classic theatre cartoons, sold to television in 1955-56, had been in constant rotation entertaining two generations who came of age watching them over and over in a manner that their original theatrical creator-directors had never envisioned. And since 1958, led by the mighty Hanna-Barbera studio, literally hundreds of newer cartoons had been made for television, creating a second wave of now-revered animation stars.

This phenomenon meant a number of vintage theatrical characters, like Popeye, Bugs Bunny and Donald Duck, had gained immortality simply due to those decades of daily television reruns. Even the earliest made-for-TV series like Hanna-Barbera favorites *The Flintstones* and *Yogi Bear* were now senior citizen cartoon stars and had joined this distinguished pantheon of animation greats. The ongoing popularity of this large menagerie meant they were also being regarded as serious nostalgic cash cows (or bunnies, ducks and pigs) by their now-salivating rights holders.

And so new opportunities arose to revive these much-loved characters from the so-called classic era, for anything: feature compilation films, animated commercials, talking toys, theme park soundtracks. There was now a retro market, and matching those famous voices became a new and highly specialized talent requiring ongoing practice and endless dedication.

The successful character matching specialists include a raft of actor-artists who had aspired their whole lives to be as versatile as their childhood voice idols. They included Jim Cummings (who took over Winnie the Pooh), Bill Farmer (Goofy), Corey Burton (Ludwig Von Drake and other Disney voices originated by Paul Frees, Bill Scott and Bill Thompson), Jeff Bergman (Bugs, Daffy, Elmer, Fred & Barney, George Jetson, Yogi Bear), Frank Welker (Scooby Doo), Bob Bergen (Porky Pig), Tony Anselmo (Donald Duck), Billy West (Elmer Fudd), Eric Bauza (various Looney Tunes voices) and the sadly departed Joe Alaskey and Greg Burson. At the risk of appearing somewhat immodest your normally humble author owns up to Bullwinkle, Dudley Do-Right, Boris Badenov, Popeye and, for the Australasian market, various Hanna-Barbera and Looney Tunes voices over the last forty years.

But beyond the matching of immortal classic-era characters, the multi-skilled vocal artists were still understandably concerned about the endless adoption of "superstar" voices in features and TV series. Many of those veterans felt they were indeed being unfairly relegated to smaller roles and a much reduced slice of the pie than what was once their daily norm. For some, like the uber-versatile Frank Welker, the new and massively popular areas of cable TV and video games opened new opportunities for reviving long-time cult adventure cartoon series like the giant Hasbro entity that is *The Transformers.*

And yet once the dust finally settled, the voice experts found they were in fact still working. It seems it wasn't all done and dusted for these versatile specialists. Old style jobs now co-existed with brand new areas for voice artists. Commercials, promos, even dubbing and looping still offered the same bread and butter work opportunities alongside new cable and syndicated tv programming. And there were two new fields, those of gaming and audiobooks, both of which became huge employers of voice people. The patterns of work may have changed but jobs were still there to be had! With luck on their side and good agents, plus the willingness to keep honing their vocal skills; with constant observation of fast changing trends in dialects, comedy and even the English language itself, they would still be able to work at their craft.

But it must be said, those dear, dead days when the truly skilled artists of the human voice got to play virtually every role, delighting and surprising their directors, colleagues and even themselves - even if they ended up with zero screen credit - were already becoming just a bittersweet and fading memory. Oh well....sic transit gloria boomers.

Chapter 7:

East Coast (Fleischer & Famous) Cartoon Voices, 1929-59

At the end of May 1941, veteran cartoon maker Max Fleischer, based in Miami since 1938, was utterly shocked when he was handed a contract by his long-time distributor, Paramount Pictures. The document stated that Fleischer's thirteen-year relationship with Paramount was now terminated, thus instantly ending the Fleischer cartoon studio. That same legal document also threatened to freeze payroll unless all assets - patents, copyrights - were turned over to Paramount. It seemed the Fleischer family name would effectively be expunged from memory, with the cartoon outfit having just been officially renamed Famous Studios. Max was suddenly living through a waking nightmare, especially when he suspected his estranged brother Dave already knew of this seemingly random decision.

Six months later in November 1941 Dave Fleischer resigned and moved to Hollywood. At the end of this annus horribilis (just following Pearl Harbor and the disappointing box office showing for his second cartoon feature Mr. Bug Goes to Town) Max was summoned to New York and told that he too would be resigning. It was the worst type of corporate bastardry: the eerie silent treatment. Literally no explanations and no answers to any of Max's queries were forthcoming. And the unspoken threat of destroying him financially was now palpable. Paramount was a Goliath with deep pockets, and Max held off any legal redress in order to see how things developed and to protect his son in law, long-time animator

Seymour Kneitel, who, having only just recovered from a heart attack, had been appointed to run Paramount's newly named cartoon facility.

Next the dirtiest part of the whole deed occurred during the Christmas shutdown of the Miami plant: twelve years of Fleischer Studios paper records and files were burned in an open fire overseen by Dick Murray, the same Paramount "suit" who had hand-delivered the fatal contract to Max seven months earlier. Studio tax records, bank statements, lab invoices, employee records for over seven hundred staff, film delivery reports and all the Fleischer cartoon production records were incinerated over a mammoth two-day operation designed to destroy any remaining chance of Max being able to prove anything in a courtroom scenario. [1]

And that, dear reader, is why this book is so maddeningly light on verified information regarding many of the voices for Fleischer and Famous Studios. To add to an author's woes, it is also light on voice talent information for other Golden Age New York cartoon shops like Van Beuren and Terrytoons. Twenty-five years of diligent research, and neither myself nor anyone else has turned up key production papers like music department payroll, outside talent requisitions, sound recording logs, indeed nothing remotely helpful to this book's topic. Surviving paper trail records for West Coast cartoons have been frustratingly incomplete, but at least there were some official documents! The great East Coast animation industry's collective sound department records appear to have totally vanished.

What we do know has been gleaned by me and several dedicated Fleischer historians from various pioneer interviews and random newspaper pieces on cartoon sound topics, in fits and starts over many years. I was determined to include one chapter on the history of New York cartoon voices and it simply had to be about those from the illustrious Fleischer studio!

At the start of this book we saw how the trailblazing cartoonist Max Fleischer (along with his brothers Dave and Lou) pioneered the first literal sound cartoons via the De Forest Phonofilm process back in the days of silent film in 1924. His *Song Car-Tunes* were singalongs featuring an ornate use of animated lettering and characters to accompany and enhance the theatre audience participation. Voices hired included vocalists like tenor Allan McDonald and The Metropolitan Quartet. ² But while these films were relatively popular, it wasn't until Walt Disney's revolutionary *Steamboat Willie* in late 1928 that cartoons with sound would finally be regarded as essential novelties for a full movie program. The Fleischers, contracted to Paramount Pictures in 1929, began to tackle the new disciplines of making "all-talking all-singing" cartoons with films emphasizing jazzy music in concert with singing cartoon characters and early attempts at humorous dialogue.

Animator Dave Tendlar pointed out that when the Fleischers moved to their expanded quarters at Broadway and Forty-ninth at Times Square, they were essentially located in show biz central. The studio workspace was above the Silver Slipper nightclub and next to a burlesque theatre. All the big-time Broadway houses, along with jazz clubs and cabaret boites were nearby. It was perfect for the new sound cartoons because the brothers had access to endless Broadway and vaudeville talent, from Ethel Merman to the Mills Quartet to Louis Armstrong. Besides Lou Fleischer's contacts they were able to book any talent already contracted to Paramount.

Certainly once the "talkies" took off in 1929 Max Fleischer was ready to solve any problems and absorb the new technical disciplines of synchronized animation. His first voice artist of note, Billy Murray, the famous entertainer nicknamed "The Denver Nightingale," had been making recordings since the shellac and wax days for Thomas Edison's phonograph records, starting in the pre-electrical recording era of 1897. A long-time member of the American Quartet, Murray was in the twilight of his recording career by 1928, as the advent of pop crooners began to make his full-bodied singing style seem outmoded. [3]

But Billy Murray's strong tenor voice and sly comic sense made him perfect for this brand new medium of sound cartoons. He and his long-time vocal colleagues Walter Van Brunt (aka Walter Scanlon), baritone James Stanley and others ended up in the new medium of radio. They then started providing voices for Fleischer, at first in the quartet which accompanied the bouncing ball singalongs which were the main part of Fleischer's new Screen Song series.* Max's brother Lou, who was musically gifted since childhood, was in charge of the studio's sound and music department. He and his bandleader associate Manny Baer hired Murray and Scanlon to do the character voices along with singing the songs in the cartoons of 1929 and 1930. [4] Murray's voice is heard in such cartoons as the 1931 commercial reel *In My Merry Oldsmobile* and in Screen Songs like *I'm Afraid to Come Home in the Dark* (1930), for which he narrates a spooky opening as well as providing a drunken voice solo, and *A Hot Time in the Old Town Tonight* (1930). Many of the titles were songs Murray himself had recorded on Edison cylinder records years before, in the period between 1902-1909.

*The late Vitaphone researcher-historian Ron Hutchinson uncovered an early typed sound report for a live action short film which used uncredited voice dubbing by Billy Murray and his vocal colleagues as well as radio animal imitators like Bradley Barker. Intriguingly, even back in the late twenties they were collectively listed on the report as "Voice Artists."

The voices of Billy Murray and Walter Scanlon were also heard in a 1929 Fleischer industrial film for Western Electric, *Finding His Voice*, which explained various facets of this new-fangled sound-on-film recording. Carlyle Ellis spoke for the "film surgeon" named

Doctor Western who coaches the two filmstrips "Talkie" (Murray) and "Mutie" (Scanlon) in the new technology.

The Fleischer studio soon moved beyond just musical content and tackled animated speech. For its new series called "Talkartoons," beginning with *Noah's Lark* (1929), Billy Murray's voice was heard doing actual cartoon dialogue, as primitive as those early efforts may have been. For *Radio Riot* (1930) he provides an Italian accent and plays a radio exercise host. Another of Murray's recording colleagues, James Stanley, sings and does a frog announcer voice. In the Talkartoon *Wise Flies* (1930) Murray does a male spider's dialogue as well as singing the opening title. Their thirty long years of experience as novelty singers meant this was relatively easy work for these seasoned vocal pros, and Murray is heard often over the next two years. [5]

When compared with the same period's cartoons produced in Los Angeles, the first thing that's noticeably unique about the early thirties Fleischer films is a prominent lack of lip-synch. Along with their trademark overlapping, rubbery action and the innumerable randomly nonsensical gags being mandated daily by supervising director Dave Fleischer, it was obvious the animators didn't work with the aid of any pre-recording. The track, including the musicians, sound effects and dialogue, was post-recorded after the picture's animation was completed.

This was markedly different to the West Coast technique in which dialogue was pre-recorded on blank film before the animation was handed out. This approach was well established in the Los Angeles studios by mid-1930, and it meant that every syllable of a speaking character's mouth movement could be broken down for the animators on exposure sheets and result in a cartoon-like approximation of realistic speech. (The animators in Hollywood were given a wax record dubbed from the master dialogue recording so they could constantly refer to the sound for timing purposes.)

At Fleischer's when an animator had a scene with a talking character, the procedure was different. They would go to the music room where Lou Fleischer, the head of sound, would set up his metronome. Lou would speak each line of the dialogue to the beat of the mechanical device, experimenting with slower and faster deliveries of the words. With his extensive musical knowledge, Lou would determine exactly how fast to adjust and set the "beat" on the device, and by using a stop watch he worked out how long each piece of dialogue would be for the accompanying animation footage. Any last minute ideas, added in the "post" recording session as the actors watched the finished animation on a large screen, would be coming from a mouth that wasn't moving. [6]

Eventually, certain musical numbers requiring accurate lip-synch were pre-recorded as animation techniques improved, but virtually all the little nonsense bits of dialogue - those bizarre Dave Fleischer touches that still charm today - were recorded at the very end of the production process. Listed as overall Director on the screen credits, Dave's major role was actually supervising the many recording sessions.

Recording the Fleischer cartoons

In the thirties the Fleischer's recording facility was in a building owned by Paramount at 9th Avenue & Broadway. It was primarily used by clients as a newsreel recording studio.

Maurice Manne was a veteran New York sound engineer. A creative self-starter with a natural flair for audio, Manne did all of the sound effects for Fleischer Studios and continued this work for Famous Studios through the forties. In the early years, when they post-recorded the dialogue and music, they also post-recorded all the sound and vocal effects.

Animator Dave Tendlar remembered Maurice Manne as "a very nice guy," and recalled, "They would run the film in a rehearsal session, so that the sound men would determine what was needed for the particular picture. Manne had a long table, about ten feet long, and he would lay out all these different gadgets - tin cans, whistles, cowbells, a rubber tire, whatever. Once they commenced recording, he would toot, whistle and plink along with the picture, as he was watching it. It was all done in one take as the picture rolled: sound, actors and musicians." [7]

It was ingenious if primitive compared to the technology which came later in the magnetic tape era, but the cornball approach worked perfectly for the thirties Fleischer cartoons. The Paramount sound studio's tracks were recorded by skilled audio engineers, still sounding vibrant and crystal-clear almost a century later, with excellent balance achieved between sound effects, the zany cartoon voices and Sammy Timberg's always bouncy orchestra and those unforgettable scores, arranged by Timberg's associates Victor Erwin and Win Sharples.

Indeed there was still much dialogue post-recording as late as 1938 when the Popeye color special *Aladdin and his Wonderful Lamp* was underway in Miami, although animator-director Dave Tendlar recalled the Genie with the zany Lew Lehr-German accent was pre-recorded in New York. He said that it was "around 1940" when the changeover to full-time pre-synched dialogue finally took place. Dave Fleischer noted that an occasional score was pre-recorded for special cartoons like *The Spinach Overture* (1935) where the plot revolved around Popeye playing piano, with each finger movement animated with extreme precision. [8]

Fleischer's first talkie star, BETTY BOOP and her Voices

When it came to prominent animated stars in the thirties it was the two immortal characters, Betty Boop and Popeye, who dominated Fleischer's sound cartoons. In the early years from 1930-33 the New York studio cartoons leapt far ahead of their West Coast rivals in terms of musical sophistication and an adult gag sensibility.

When the situation reversed and the Fleischer cartoons began lagging behind Disney's artistically superior Hollywood shorts from mid-decade, it was still their unique feel - streetwise, urban, often dark in tone and imbued with an overall grungy aura - that resonated with Depression-era audiences. The best of them had an intangibly surrealistic and sometimes even disturbing quality that elevated them to a high level of creativity, even with all their deliberately rough and ethnically cliched edges.

Starting with Betty Boop, and then three years later with Popeye, the Fleischers possessed arguably the two most unforgettably distinct voices in sound animation's first decade. These standout characters were the main reason that West Coast cartoon directors began looking for more inventive voices from 1934, in order to replace the endlessly overused male falsettos. Animator Myron Waldman noted that the idea of a female starring character initially came from Max Fleischer's wife Essie who had suggested a girlfriend for the Fleischers' first talkie star character Bimbo. [9] At first no one suspected that a nasally squeaky diva, eventually named Betty, would rapidly overtake the relatively bland Bimbo in popularity.

Betty Boop, despite the studio's denials in a 1934 lawsuit trial, was quite blatantly an animated approximation of the then-famous entertainer Helen Kane, nationally known as the "Boop-Oop-a-Doop Girl." Her uniquely babyish voice and "boop-a-doop" style of vocalizing had been imitated on stage by at least seven women, some of whom would alternate as the cartoon Betty's voice.

Sidebar, HELEN KANE

The inspiration for Betty Boop was unquestionably Bronx-born singer-actress Helen Kane who became the symbol of the Roaring twenties "flapper era." She began as a teenage performer touring with the young Marx Brothers in a revue. In the twenties she broke through to stardom in the hit Broadway show *A Night in Spain* where she introduced her scat singing boop-oop-a-doop style via the song "That's My Weakness Now." She was an instant hit and was quickly booked as a solo artist at New York's famous Paramount Theatre. In 1928 she was back on Broadway in the revue *Good Boy* where she introduced her signature number "I Wanna Be Loved By You," written by the Marx Brothers' composing team of Bert Kalmar and Harry Ruby. Her follow-up stint at the Palace Theatre made her name as a leading exponent of jazz age show business in Manhattan's chic nightclub culture, and this huge fame led to records and feature film roles for Ms Kane in a series of early sound musicals for Paramount. That studio's PR department devised the famous "Sing like Helen Kane" novelty contests which indirectly led to the creation of the animated supper club singer who soon became Betty Boop.

Helen Kane's place in the show biz firmament was meteoric but brief, and by 1931 her novelty appeal was fading just as her cartoon take-off was becoming popular. After years away from the spotlight Ms Kane had a comeback of sorts in 1950 when MGM hired her to dub the singing voice of Debbie Reynolds in *Three Little Words*, the musical biopic of her old songwriters Kalmar & Ruby.

∗∗∗

Cartoon aficionados are well aware that Betty Boop's character began her screen life as a nameless canine entertainer in the 1930 Talkartoon *Dizzy Dishes*, starring Bimbo. Animator Grim Natwick remembered Dave Fleischer giving him the sheet music to a song. On the cover was a photo portrait of Helen Kane which Fleischer asked Natwick to study, after telling him about a voice imitator they intended to hire. That mimic was a talented young singer named Marjorie "Margie" Hines, who quickly became one of the most prominent voices in early thirties East Coast animation.

Margie Hines was one of several young girls in the Paramount sponsored "Helen Kane Boop-a-Doop contest" which toured on the large RKO theatre circuit, via the Radio-Keith-Orpheum booking agency of Greater Manhattan. The show Ms Hines entered took place in a cinema cathedral in Brooklyn in 1929. When the young office worker won ("hands down, she easily out-booped all other contestants" [10]) she was offered radio spots in Pittsburgh and a national tour with Dave White's revue for several top vaudeville bookers. *The Billboard* magazine in a 1930 issue mentioned "The familiar baby-voiced Boop-a-Doop singing is contributed by Margie Hines, who handles it nicely in [the song] "Do Something." [11]

It was during the New York run of White's tour that Ms Hines was spotted by Billy Murray, who besides voicing characters for the early Fleischer Talkartoons was also scouting talent for the studio. The new medium of sound cartoons had quickly gained in popularity during 1929, and voice talent was already a constant requirement. Murray was seeking the voice for a female - and incidentally canine - nightclub singer to be part of the next Bimbo cartoon, the previously mentioned *Dizzy Dishes*, for which the animation was underway. He heard in Miss Hines's voice exactly what he had been seeking for the cartoon chanteuse, and after Dave Fleischer heard her fine vocal impression of Helen Kane, Paramount contracted her to supply the voice that would eventually become world famous as Betty Boop. She sang an actual Helen Kane number, "I Have to Have You," in the cartoon. [12]

Margie Hines began working for the studio in May of 1930. When her singing dog character received enthusiastic audience feedback, Paramount signed her to a six month contract. She provided the proto-Betty voice and some other characters for several Talkartoons and Screen Songs released over the next year.

After two further shorts featuring this early version of Betty, the character's voice underwent a brief vocal experiment when the same girl was featured in the Talkartoon *The Bum Bandit* (1931). Here she sang in a very different sound, a rich contralto voice supplied by Harriet Lee, who was known as "the Songbird of the Air." For this Bimbo short the embryonic Betty was called Dangerous Nan McGrew. This was the same role played by the real Helen Kane in the 1930 Paramount comedy *Dangerous Nan McGrew,* but in the cartoon she has a non-Kane voice!

Harriet Lee did only two more cartoons, singing for the Screen Song entries *Any Little Girl That's a Nice Little Girl* (1931) in which she was the voice of Lulubelle, then starring as herself in *You're Driving Me Crazy* (1931). After this, Ms Lee did several years of prestigious radio work before retiring from performing in the late thirties to become an in-demand vocal coach, eventually being retained in that role by actress Dorothy Lamour. Harriet Lee was still employed in the voice culture field at MGM in the forties. [13]

Meanwhile, Paramount appears to have mandated that the new Betty-like character revert to her familiar baby-voiced characterization thereafter. This would indicate she was already becoming a popular cartoon personality due in large part to that distinct squeaky sound. In *Silly Scandals* (1931) she was given her full Betty Boop name, and after several more cartoons over the next year she morphed into human form with *Dizzy Red Riding Hood* (1931). When the Talkartoon series ended in the summer of 1932, she became a Paramount star in her own Betty Boop series with her first official entry, *Stopping the Show* (1932)

Her films were easily the most grown-up of any cartoon character in the era now known as "pre-Code." Prior to mid-1934 when the film industry formalized the Production Code, Betty appeared in many scenarios in which she played an unworldly girl, innocently flaunting her sex appeal and being taken advantage of by abusive, sexist menaces who were perfect cartoon villains. Some Betty Boop cartoons cast her in backstage show biz plots, while several others boasted a dark Depression aura. Those cartoons were imbued with a subtext which seemed to scream danger in the big city, containing, in the words of Fleischer scholar Mark Langer, "a tremendous sense of fatalism." [14]

Sometime in 1931, the Fleischer Studio temporarily toyed with pre-recording cartoon dialogue for in-demand voice talents who were not always in town for a recording session. According to documents in the 1934 Helen Kane lawsuit, to be discussed soon, Margie Hines had recorded Betty Boop dialogue throughout 1931 for several cartoons which wouldn't be released until the following year. Two 1932 cartoons she voiced, *Betty Boop's Boop-Oop-a-Doop* and *Minnie the Moocher*, needed extra singing when she was unavailable and Mae Questel did the post-recording sessions.

Margie Hines's Betty voice had got her plenty of publicity, the *Decatur Daily Review* disclosing, "You've wondered perhaps who it is that speaks for Betty Boop in Max Fleischer's inkwell cartoons on the screen. Her voice is the voice of Margie Hines." [15] It appears the final cartoon of the twenty Betty Boop titles Hines recorded before her Paramount contract expired, was *I'll Be Glad When You're Dead You Rascal You* (1932).

The new-found fame resulted in a flurry of work for Ms Hines including an on-camera role in a Warner Bros. short, *The Perfect Suitor* starring comic Benny Rubin. *Film Daily* reported in 1931, "Margie Hines's contract with Paramount for the Max Fleischer cartoons has expired. She will freelance. Miss Hines is the femme voice in the majority of the Fleischer drawings." [16] The *Fitchburg Sentinel* noted she left on a vaudeville tour "on the strength of the popularity of her ghost voice*," [17] before signing a new contract to do cartoon voices for the Van Beuren company in 1932. There she played that studio's leading female star, Countess Cat.

* "Ghosting" was thirties movie industry lingo used to describe either dubbing a voice in to a picture, often to replace another voice for either technical or aesthetic reasons, or when professional singers pre-recorded a vocal track that was lip-synched by a non-singing actor during principal photography.

Mae Questel (the family name was apparently Kwestel) was the first Betty Boop voice talent to succeed Margie Hines in 1931. Questel, like Ms Hines, had entered one of the Paramount sponsored Helen Kane look-and-sound-alike contests in late 1929, egged on by friends and workmates. As with the earlier contest won by Margie Hines, this one was again hosted by Ms Kane herself at the Fordham Theatre, a Bronx movie house.

Mae Questel had been performing since age seventeen when she enrolled in a drama class sponsored by the Theatre Guild. A natural stage artist, she demonstrated her impressionist skills imitating top stars of the day like Ms Kane, Marlene Dietrich, the French-accented Irene Bordoni and even a Maurice Chevalier take-off. After winning the Kane contest, she signed for a prestigious RKO vaudeville booking for ten weeks and quickly became a draw, appearing at the Bronx Franklin Theatre, the Palace and the 81st Street venues, as well as radio's *R-K-O Program* heard on station WEAF. Mae Questel was on her way, and became a regular radio guest star over the next year. [18]

As Betty's cartoons kept gaining in popularity, Fleischer's studio in conjunction with Paramount continued auditioning talent in an attempt to perfect her sound. Max's son, the prolific film director Richard Fleischer, wrote that his father took the Betty character very seriously and tried out several voices. Paramount had advertised for a girl "with a cute voice" but none seemed exactly right. Richard Fleischer recalled, "The voice needed to be squeaky, but it also had to be cute and sexy, to sing, to do good line readings, and be able to say 'Boop-Oop-a-Doop' in exactly the right way."

When Mae Questel was booked to perform in the famous Palace Theatre at Times Square, Max Fleischer caught her show. He was highly impressed, his son writing, "Max finally found what he was looking for in 1931 when he came across the incomparable Mae Questel. Her voice and Betty became synonymous. Oddly enough, Mae looked exactly like Betty Boop." [19]

Once Margie Hines was no longer under contract to Paramount, Fleischer hired Mae Questel for the 1931 Talkartoon *Silly Scandals*. She performed the number "You're Driving Me Crazy" and it marked the sixth appearance of the character, who was given the single name Betty in the cartoon. It was the start of a long voice-over career that would see Ms Questel become the East Coast's leading female animation voice talent. Indeed Betty's screen look changed as a direct result of Ms Questel who modelled, wiggled, pouted and booped for the cartoonists at the Fleischer studio. As an *NEA* news item put it, "Betty Boop has become a caricature of the young lady who furnishes her voice." [20]

The Fleischer sound & music department considered Mae Questel a notch better at singing and improvising in the baby-doll Betty voice than Margie Hines, although both were regarded as fine performers. But it took Ms Questel a while to become the regular Betty voice. Ms Hines had already recorded dialogue for a batch of Betty cartoons in various stages of production. Meanwhile Questel had made such a name in the industry following her top placing in the Kane competition that she played the on-camera Betty Boop in a 1931 Paramount short *Musical Justice* (replacing Marjorie Hines, according to a draft in the transcript of the film). [21] For this novelty entry Questel appeared with top crooner Rudy Vallee and sang "Don't Take My Boop-Oop-a-Doop Away."

In 1932, commencing with the immortal Betty-Cab Calloway cartoon *Minnie the Moocher*, Mae Questel became the longest-running and arguably the most popular of all Betty Boop's vocal delineators. She had her own radio program, *Mae Questel The Mimic On The Air*. Later that year she starred in the first series of NBC's *Betty Boop Frolics* radio show, broadening the character's fanbase still further. [22]

The next artist in the continuing parade of Betty Boop voices was Ann Belle Little, the squeakiest high soprano Betty yet. Ann Little had been in show business since 1925 as the baby character in the *Greenwich Village Follies* revue, and for a time she and her sister Jane had a comedy act in vaudeville.

By this stage Margie Hines was under contract to rival cartoon maker Van Beuren and Mae Questel was pregnant with her first child. Paramount, aware of Betty Boop's enormous popularity and marketability, was seeking backup Betty voices. Ann Little recalled that one day in late 1932 she was "in a [music] publishing house recording [in a make-a-record booth]...when a theatrical agent [for] Paramount Studios wandered in and stopped to listen." He urged her to attend the Betty Boop voice auditions at Paramount's recording stage the following week, insisting she had exactly the type of voice for which the studio was looking.

Ann Little continued, "I went to the auditions and [Dave Fleischer] chose me. There were hundreds of girls there and most of them could sing better than I could. I suppose I had what he wanted. I was very tiny [4'10"] and very pretty [then] and I had this high pitched voice." [23] She began working as a Betty voice in March 1933, recording three cartoons in the series (*Betty Boop's Birthday Party*, *Betty Boop's May Party* and *Betty Boop's Big Boss*). She was then booked by Paramount for a variety stage show that would travel across the country starting in the summer of 1933.

For this tour, Ann Little was effectively given official Paramount approval to be billed in advertising matter as "Little Ann Little, the Original [sic] Voice of Betty Boop." [24] In typical show business fashion this questionable billing was okayed in spite of the various accurate newspaper items between 1931 and 1933 confirming that Marjorie Hines was the "original" Betty voice.

The stage appearances showcased Ms Little singing Betty Boop-style songs in full Betty makeup while a lightning-sketch cartoonist, Pauline Comanor, would draw her likeness on a large easel. [25] The in person engagements, including all the musicians, were arranged and contracted by Paramount in conjunction with Fleischer Studios.

Initially Ann Little was part of a Paramount star package headlined by veteran entertainer Manny King, billed as *The Vanity Fair Revue*. In her portion of the festivities, she sang and danced, while part of her act was a demonstration of how cartoons were made. A silent Betty Boop scene was projected as Ann, live on stage, sang the words. *The Daily Journal* reported, "This screen picture was especially made for [Little Ann Little] by Fleischer [Studios], and is done with their permission and cooperation." [26] At the conclusion of her act, a complete sound Betty Boop cartoon was screened. The performances were seen as an effective promotion for both the Betty Boop cartoons and Paramount.

The act made Ann Little something of an authority on cartoon recording, telling one interviewer the studio "makes several at once now," indicating the Fleischers did pre-record at least some dialogue when voice artists' schedules meant they would be on the road. As she explained, "Most of the time the drawings are made first. I see the film, rehearse it, and then the sound is synchronized with the picture. Once in a while, though, they record my voice first" [27] (*Sandusky Register*, 1934). However, the quotes become inaccurate from this point, with one report stating, "She does four or five [cartoons] at one time in the Fleischer studios in New York [wrong: Ann Little recorded a total of just three in 1933], and then dashes out to towns hither and yon…." [28]

Regrettably, Ann Little was one of those driven personalities who claim many more credits than was actually the case. She became somewhat delusional about her exact role as Betty, eventually repeating blatant falsehoods over several decades. These included: being "the original Betty Boop" voice, when Margie Hines was known and well publicized for the role three years before; doing the cartoon voice for twelve years when in fact there were only nine years in the entire Betty Boop ouevre; and stating that she was the original "Boop-Boop-a-Doop girl" and that "Miss Helen Kane was a later version" (!)

Ann Little continued her stage act for almost nine years, long after the Betty Boop cartoons had ended in 1939. It is plausible that Paramount's head of shorts and talent contractor Lou Diamond kept Ms Little in this handy promotional role because her ultra-squeaky voice wasn't as flexible as the other actresses, and she wouldn't be pestering him for recording dates. It would appear that her later aggrieved stance regarding her role in the Betty saga came from feelings of entitlement. Was it possible her ambitious off-mike personality was a little pushy, to the point of desperate. Was she annoying during recording sessions? Certainly in the Helen Kane trial to come a year later she embarrassed herself and the defence team, as we will see.

In the mid-forties Ann Little married a business man and retired to Florida where she taught dance for five years. Following his death she remarried and by 1954 was ordained a minister in the Unity School of Christianity. In her senior years she was still entertaining at retirement homes but had become personally embittered about her Betty Boop experience. In 1975 she even committed the cardinal show biz no-no of bad mouthing a colleague. It ended up in print in 1975: "A friend heard this Mae Questel on television. She's a little fat woman I met in Mr. Fleischer's office a few times, saying she was the original Betty Boop on the *Tom Snyder Show*." [29]

Although Mae Questel remained the particular favorite of the Fleischer brothers, she was unavailable to record while in the later stage of pregnancy. The fourth Betty voice, chronologically, was young vocalist Bonnie Poe, a third Helen Kane mimic who possessed a more flexible range than Ann Little. Poe and Questel had known each other from the Kane competitions. A precocious vocal and comedy talent, by age fourteen Poe was a singer with Borrah Minnevitch's well-known Harmonica Rascals group and sang on radio shows.

Bonnie Poe was hired as a straight-woman for comic headliner Eddie Stanley. In early 1932 they worked in a Broadway stage show starring Helen Kane herself. Ms Poe mimicked Ms Kane within the show, before entering still another lookalike contest. She recalled, "Miss Kane told me about the Helen Kane contest that was going to be held at the Riverside…and told me that she thought it would be a very good idea if I joined the contest." [30] Bonnie Poe and Mae Questel tied in first place. Ms Poe's imitation led to a Paramount Pictures contract and her turn at the Betty voice in cartoons.

Before she became a regular Fleischer voice Bonnie Poe travelled to Hollywood for a brief stint as a nightclub hostess where she dated actor George Raft. While there she did a few short films including her shot at a Betty Boop on-camera appearance: for the 1933 short subject *Hollywood on Parade No. A-8* she appeared made up as the cartoon Betty. It was for a skit with famous *Dracula* star Bela Lugosi, in which the horror icon in full vampire costume menacingly admonished her, "You have just booped your last boop," as he went to bite her neck. Soon after this film, Ms Poe returned to New York.

Soon after the Riverside Theatre Helen Kane contest, the real Ms Kane began changing her tune about all the look-and-soundalikes. During 1931 the Betty Boop cartoons were a big success, coinciding with a concomitant decline in Helen Kane's showbiz fortunes. In May 1932 she instigated a $250,000 infringement lawsuit, claiming "deliberate caricature" resulting in "unfair competition." [31] Essentially her beef was that the cartoon films had exploited her personality and image via the character of Betty leading to loss of reputation and earnings. Named were Max Fleischer, Fleischer Studios and Paramount-Publix Corp. The case came to trial two years later, and is covered in a sidebar which ends this chapter's Betty Boop section.

One 1933 news item stated that Bonnie Poe "took over the full-time role of Betty Boop in the cartoons and on [the second Betty radio series] for a short time, while Mae Questel was preparing to have a baby." [32] In fact Ms Poe's first voice job for Fleischer was the Screen Song *Boilesk* in which she played a flapper speaking in a Betty-ish voice. Her first actual Betty cartoon came immediately after that cartoon. It was *Mother Goose Land* (1933) in which she did her slightly more nasal sounding Betty and doubled as other characters. Her versatility was also on display in *Popeye the Sailor* (1933) for which she not only performed the Betty cameo singing "Yaaka Hula Hickey Dula" (in re-used animation from the 1932 *Betty Boop's Bamboo Isle*) but also provided the first voice of Popeye's "goil" Olive Oyl. It is Bonnie Poe's voice we hear singing the title song "Strike Up the Band for Popeye the Sailor."

Poe's real name was Clara Rothbart. She was heard in a number of cartoons in the 1933-34 theatrical season, including eight early Popeyes. Her Olive voice is recognizable for its cartoonishly broad New York accent which causes her to call the sailor "Pawp-eye." When Questel returned to the Fleischer microphone in 1934, she played the title role a 'la Betty for the first Color Classic entry *Poor Cinderella*. Bonnie Poe was one of several more in that cartoon, playing the Fairy Godmother. [33]

From 1935 Ms Poe's cartoon appearances decreased as she got busy with her singing career. She did nightclub work where, similar to Ann Little, she was predictably billed "The Original Betty Boop" reflecting again the all-too common industry practice whereby performers' agents are happy to use confected PR billing. Bonnie Poe returned as Betty for a few cartoons in early 1938 when Mae Questel was again on maternity leave, while her steady radio work as one of Gertrude Berg's actors in *The Rise of the Goldbergs* serial continued into the forties. (Mae Questel, too, worked with Ms Berg in that long-running radio series.)

As the Helen Kane trial loomed a 1933 news item stated, "Marjorie Hines, the first Betty Boop, was succeeded later by Mae Questel. There is now still a third Betty. All three have sung on the radio

under the cartoon name, and no one seems to have noticed the difference." [34] The "third Betty" referred to was Ms Poe, and it was this
lack of recognition for her role as an interim Betty voice that seems
to have triggered Ann Little's years of disgruntled feelings.

SIDEBAR: THE HELEN KANE TRIAL

In late April 1934, the Helen Kane case came to trial in Manhattan. While her claims of being caricatured both vocally
and visually seemed to have some validity, it was proven that
her actual appearance was not truly unique. Defence lawyers
noted that Ms Kane's hairstyle was feathered, rather than
the spit curl style Betty Boop sports on screen. Later it was
even suggested that Paramount actress Clara Bow, in films
preceding Helen Kane, resembled the plaintiff visually. Max
Fleischer only acknowledged he recalled Helen Kane from a
show he had attended in 1928.

The main claim, though, was not the visual copy, rather it
was her famous "boop-oop-a-doop" singing style and voice
quality that had been appropriated for the cartoon films.
During the trial, the various Betty Boop voice talents were
called to testify. First came Bonnie Poe, followed by Margie
Hines. They were asked to demonstrate their talents in the
boop-oop-a-doop style, with Ms Hines describing the vocal
affectation as "licks." In musical terminology "licks" refers to
a short series of half improvised notes, either instrumentally
or vocally.

Little Ann Little, who had the most babyish Kane voice of
them all, was asked by the prosecutor, "Anybody tell you to
talk in a high pitch baby voice here?"; later he inquired, "You
talk that way at home too?" According to a court reporter she
replied, "Yes indeedy, always" in her squeaky little voice. The
courtroom erupted in laughter, and she ended up annoying

the court stenographers who "glowered at her." Her naïve claim of being the first Boop-a-Doop voice was shot down when it was pointed out that "The Betty Boop cartoons were first put out in 1930." Ms Little's response was a gauche "Oh, I am not sure just when."

When Mae Questel took the stand she related the story of how she was "discovered" in a Helen Kane competition, and that she was declared the winner by Ms Kane herself. It was when Questel produced a signed photo of Helen Kane which read "To Mae Questel, the only other Helen Kane," that Ms Kane's case was weakened.

But the most telling evidence against Kane's claim to originating the scat singing style was when the names of several booping-style vocalists were proved to have preceded her. Paramount and Fleischer obtained MGM film footage of a child singer from Chicago, known as both Baby Esther Lee Jones or Little Esther. Testimony was heard that Kane and her manager attended performances by Esther at the intimate Everglades Nite Club in New York. Lou Fleischer was able to repair the out-of-synch film print in time for the next day of the trial. It showed Esther Jones performing a "Boop-oop-a-doop" style of singing chronologically earlier than Ms Kane. That footage seemed to be the clincher. Kane couldn't prove her claims beyond doubt and the case was thrown out by the judge.

Ms Kane was disappointed and appealed, unsuccessfully, in 1935. Paramount released a short called *Fleischer Victory Newsreel* in May 1934. Max Fleischer appeared on-screen along with five women who had done Betty Boop's voice: Margie Hines, Mae Questel, Ann Little, Bonnie Poe and Kate Wright. Catherine "Kate" Wright, present at the trial as another of many Boop-a-doop song stylists, was finally determined by recent discographers to be a popular Colum-

bia and Victor record artist and radio singer, who had possibly the most accurate Helen Kane voice of them all. After
years of speculation among Fleischer cartoon fans as to
which Betty Boop films she voiced, the trial documents
became available revealing that Fleischer claimed Ms Wright
"did not voice Betty Boop in any film from 1930-34." [35]

Betty's Support: "Extra" Fleischer Cartoon Voices

Without studio documents like recording logs this author admits
defeat when it comes to identifying the countless "bit part" character voices in Fleischer Studio cartoons of the thirties. We can never
know who precisely did the scores of odd little one liners which
gave those first five years of Fleischer talkies their truly identifiable
stamp. But we can at least name a few obscure, barely known contributors.

After Billy Murray and his vocal colleagues faded from the cartoon scene in 1931 to concentrate on their new radio show *Scanlon, Shields and Murray*, a singer named Claude Rees from The
Elm City Four male quartet was at first used for the voices of Koko
and Bimbo. Many of the "extra" voices in Fleischer cartoons were
uniquely suited to "sound effects" specialists like Bradley Barker,
the most famous of the New York based animal imitators. A former silent film actor-director, Barker turned to his lifelong hobby
of imitating sounds when the "talkies" arrived. In the late twenties
he vocally recorded such iconic early cinema sound effects as the
MGM lion, the Pathe crow and animal sounds for jungle films.

On radio Brad Barker could mimic the sound of virtually any
animal, and for *The March of Time* series he was called on to do hundreds, from a gorilla, a wolf call, an elephant trumpeting, a camel's
wail and tigers. [36] His 1938 publicity blurb stated he "had yapped,
meowed and quacked on fifty cartoon shorts," and an entry in the
Variety Radio Annual noted he did "Voices of the characters in the

Betty Boop cartoons." [37] Barker is heard to good advantage in classics like *Wild Elephinks* (1933) and it is likely him as the screeching Roc in the 1936 *Popeye the Sailor Meets Sindbad the Sailor* Technicolor two-reel classic. Barker prided himself on his accuracy and took his art rather seriously. So too did his competitor, a diminutive older man named Donald Bain, who had amassed years of small-town stage gigs under his belt, and who claimed "Betty Boop and Popeye cartoons" in his résumé. He was heard in some of the later shorts like *Hunky and Spunky* (1938) and *The Playful Polar Bears.* (1938). [38]

Bradley Barker (such a perfect surname for an accomplished animal mimic!) and Donald Bain became legendary along Manhattan's radio row, and each man spent several productive years rushing from a radio show to a cartoon dubbing to another radio show, doing first maybe a chicken, followed an hour later by a screeching cat, or a whinnying horse, and in Barker's case, a growling husky dog in the opening of the long-running juvenile radio serial *Renfrew of the Mounted*. A famous joke circulated among the radio acting fraternity: "I just saw Brad Barker rushing into the CBS lobby on all fours....and he was carrying Donald Bain in his mouth." [39]

Another important contributor from 1931 was Bruce "Cookie" Bowers, a novelty performer whom Max Fleischer had known since childhood. Bowers's stage act consisted of a raft of impersonated noises, ranging from a buzz saw, a mosquito, a sewing machine* and a political orator. When radio took off in the late twenties, his unique talents ("claiming 1,000 noises, with others ready on three hours' notice") were being called on. [40]

* Mark Kausler suggests it could well be Bowers doing the sewing machine noises in *Betty Boop's Crazy Inventions* (1933).

While booked on the West Coast, Cookie Bowers, along with Hollywood voices Billy Bletcher and Pete Smith, spoke as various dogs for the actual canine stars of the 1930 *Dogville* "Bar-kies" novelty shorts for MGM (*Dogway Melody, So Quiet on the Canine Front* et al). When that series ended Bowers returned to New York. A 1932 syndicated feature story via the *National Enterprise Association* noted that Bowers was working as "all of the animal sounds and incidental voices in the Betty Boop ani-mated cartoons." It quoted Max and Dave Fleischer who believed that in [recording] a cartoon, certain sound effects were "picked up and timed better" by a human voice rather than by mechanical imitations. It was noted that Bowers practiced "as rigorously as a Metropolitan diva. Just when he [has mastered] the Four Original Hawaiians, along comes a new musical instrument he is asked to imitate." [41]

Bowers was heard in cartoons starting in the 1931-32 season. He also helped "arrange" the *Betty Boop Frolics* radio show in 1932. Noticing the slow decline of vaudeville, his main arena of work, Bowers took himself to Europe where he trod the boards touring English music halls with his specialty. He was back in New York sometime in the mid-thirties and appeared on radio's big variety show, *The Royal Gelatin Program* on September 2nd 1937. Host Rudy Vallee's introduction described him, "Man of a million voices, Cookie Bowers. Cow, rooster, hen, and cat & dog fight…a great many of the animal sounds you hear in the animated cartoons are done by Cookie Bowers."* [42]

*Although the majority of Vallee's hundreds of radio pro-grams survived, it is our bad luck that this particular episode with Cookie Bowers is, to date, a missing show. The quote above was taken from the script in the Rudy Vallee collection, part of Thousand Oaks Library's American Radio Archive. If the acetate recording is ever found, Bowers's performance might just pinpoint certain Fleischer character voices with certainty.

Bowers made an interesting observation about the recording of early cartoon voices: "I learned two things essential to screen acting by being the voice of cartoons. Timing and pantomimic technique. Rhythm in speaking lines is a definite need in talkie production. In cartoon work that is drilled into us. Sometimes a [metronome] is used when synchronizing the sound in a cartoon, the better to get the timing in speaking the words assigned to the person or animal character depicted." [43]

Even more specialized talents in the Fleischer shorts were the dedicated bird imitators. Henry Boyd, mainly a serious lecturer on bird life, was also a specialty whistling performer. He contributed various chirps for cartoons of the thirties, a possible example being the Betty Boop cartoon *Baby Be Good* (1935). A straight-faced Boyd insisted, "I do forty songbirds and the cricket. I do *not* do mother hens or roosters. In the barnyard line, I will go only so far as the baby chick." [44]

Meanwhile a young actress named Frances Reynolds was on the lower-rung of Fleischer cartoon voices. Aside from ducks and roosters, she did crying baby sounds and little girls aged "about five." But Fleischer buffs know her for one part: "I have been playing the role of Pudgy, Betty Boop's dog, for Paramount now for several months" she admitted in a *New Yorker* article in the fall of 1937. [45]

There were other specialists too, like various professional singers. Wallace Clark had been a "voice on the old Bouncing Ball" Screen Songs for Max Fleischer, and a member of the Debonairs vocal quartet. He claimed he did "most of the Popeye and Betty Boop soundtracks." That sweeping statement aside, Clark next hinted that he had been "the original cartoon voice of Popeye the Sailor and Betty Boop [!!], calling on other members of the quartet when additional voices were needed." [46] He added the information that he retired from show business in 1935 to go into real estate, so make of that what you will. (A possibility: The Debonairs may indeed be the group which sings the opening theme, "Made of pen and ink, she can win you with a wink, ain't she cute?...sweet Betty.")

When it came to celebrity impressions, a stocky and energetic stage mimic named Arthur Boran could do excellent voices like President Roosevelt, Ed Wynn, Eddie Cantor and Jack Benny among his wide repertoire. In 1934 Boran was awarded the Blue Ribbon of Merit for radio work by bandleader Ben Bernie, and his brag sheet noted, "The voice in many of the Max Fleischer animated comedy picture cartoons."[47] If only these people had appended the shorts' actual titles to these calling cards. It is highly likely Boran is doing the Herbert Hoover and Governor Al Smith political impressions in the 1932 *Betty Boop for President.*

As late as 1940 the use of expedient in-house talent was still in place, with animator Myron Waldman's wife Rosalie owning up to doing voices.[48] Lou Fleischer's son Bernie recorded the voice of Andy in the 1941 *Raggedy Ann and Raggedy Andy* two-reeler (although his songs were sung by 12-year old Johnny Rogers, a soloist with the Miami Boys' Choir).[49]

There were likely several more anonymous people who performed extra voices for many of the studio's signature throwaway gags mandated by Dave Fleischer (the endless worms, moths and others who simply squeak something innocuous like, "Hi, Betty!!"). And there were broad dialect experts too, like the Yiddish-inflected Saturn in *Betty Boop's Ups and Downs* (1932) who wants to own the planet Earth. Without studio records, these countless one-off bit players are today impossible to determine. Many of the throwaway voices sound amusing but are probably not voice professionals. In fact they sound suspiciously like staff members or musicians. Historian Mark Langer noted that "Often, provision of voices was informally arranged by seconding studio staff or members of the orchestra."[50]

However, we might get an inkling of certain contributors. Fortuitously the scripts - if not the recordings - survive for both of the two Betty Boop radio series and, happily, the all-important cast pages are included. The first series, *Betty Boop Fables*, aired from November 1932 through January 1933 and starred Mae Questel as Betty. In weekly support were bass singer Gus Wicke as Gus Gorilla and a woman named Lee Brody as Gus's simian spouse. The prolific radio animal mimic Bradley Barker, whom we just met, did Koko the Clown's voice as well as a menagerie of odd critters from the Betty cartoons (a frog, a kangaroo, a lion), while veteran Fleischer sound department engineer Max Manne played Bimbo. [If Manne followed the departed singers Billy Murray and Claude Rees into the Bimbo role in the actual cartoons we might have another regular voice and not even know it.] [51]

And here's a surprise: in the radio show, Max Fleischer himself played "Uncle Max" and he helped out by supplying noises for - of all things - a baby Bear and a baby Gorilla. [52] But then again, why not? Fleischer was as much of a genial on-camera ham during the silent era as Walter Lantz had been. When "talkies" arrived Fleischer was still happy to do a cameo, appearing on-screen in a memorably avuncular turn in *Betty Boop's Rise to Fame* (1934).

Paramount, aware of Betty's popularity, was eager to continue the momentum for another "star" character. Max Fleischer envisioned great animation possibilities in the *Thimble Theatre* newspaper comic strip's character Popeye, a grizzled, tough and squint-eyed sailor created by leading cartoonist Elzie Segar. Popeye was first seen in early 1929. He was immensely popular in the *Thimble* strip by 1932. That year a deal was struck with the King Features News Syndicate, and the hard-as-nails swab was slated to be "introduced" as a special guest star in the 1933 Betty Boop entry *Popeye the Sailor*.

Meantime Betty's second radio series, renamed *The Betty Boop Frolics*, ran in the summer and fall of 1933. For this follow-up series, Mae Questel, who had just become a mother, was unavailable. The role of Betty was shared between her original voice Margie Hines and actress-singer Bonnie Poe, depending on each other's weekly availability. There were fewer supporting characters this time around and more of an emphasis on Betty's songs in this run of fifteen-minute shows. The only other regulars were NBC staff announcer Alois Havrilla, bandleader Victor Irwin, a musical associate of Sammy Timberg, and a weekly appearance by one Billy Costello as Ferdie Frog, another incidental character from the cartoons. [53] Whether coincidental or planned, this second radio series premiered July 14, 1933, the same day the new Betty cartoon *Popeye the Sailor* was released, introducing the famous seafaring tough guy, also voiced by Billy Costello.

The Popeye Voices

William A. Costello was a prominent vaudeville novelty performer. An actor and a multi-instrumental musician with big-band experience, Costello also possessed a uniquely flexible trick voice which he developed as an entertainer while serving in the Navy. He claimed he was taught various vocal tricks by his father, also a stage performer. Costello would sing pop songs in a pleasant low tenor and do alternating verses using his trick froggy voice. He also had the ability to break into comic whistling effects and the same type of zany scat-singing which made Cliff Edwards famous as "Ukulele Ike."

Costello was already well known to the Fleischers. He was a vaudeville name throughout the Roaring twenties, known variously as Billy "Uke" Carpenter or sometimes Sam Carpenter. The *New York Sun* reported "his hot brand of singing [later] brought him the [stage] name of Red Pepper Sam," and he recorded with big names like top crooner Gene Austin.

The *New York Sun* noted, "Two of his recordings were purchased for synchronized cartoons [including a scene in *Betty Boop M. D.* (1932) featuring Bimbo singing Costello's hit "I'm Nobody's Sweetheart Now"], which led to his association with Max Fleischer in the [second] Betty Boop NBC radio series" in which he played the weekly role of Ferdy Frog. [54] In early 1933 he appeared in a couple of cartoons, including the Screen Song *Boilesk*. As Lou Fleischer reflected about casting the Popeye role, "Dave and I chose the peculiar voice of Sam Carpenter [i.e., Bill Costello]."

Costello's freak vocal effects proved perfect for cartoons. There was just one problem: the Popeye series proved instantly popular, soon outstripping Betty Boop and even rival Mickey Mouse in screen fame, and success changed Costello's personality bigtime. Mae Questel noted that his behaviour became egocentric. She told one interviewer that Costello had "an inability to recognize that success had gone to his head." [55] According to Lou Fleischer, "[Costello] became entirely incorrigible after recording a couple of pictures, and I was asked to find a voice to replace him." [56] That took a while to do, yet Costello's manner remained "obstreperous."

Dave Fleischer recalled, "he wouldn't come in on time and he dressed up like a dude. He got too 'big' for us." [57] When Costello insisted on a vacation during a busy period of production, his days were well and truly numbered. Indeed he proved so troublesome that one Popeye entry, *Be Kind to Aminals* (1935), featured a poor replacement voice that must have dismayed the many fans of the cartoons, to say nothing of the King Features and Paramount executives. According to historian Ray Pointer, Dave Fleischer fired Costello for turning up drunk to the *Aminals* session. A panicked hunt was on for a new Popeye voice. [58]

Dave Fleischer, interviewed by Joe Adamson in 1968, recalled that when Costello became difficult he knew of "several" people who could do a Popeye imitation. * He cryptically added, "We had several men able to do Popeye's voice. I had about five standbys." [59] This is a pretty vague statement, but it is known that Harry Foster Welch, a New York stage entertainer and sound mimic, had among his "thousand voices" a Popeye imitation. According to veteran print cartoonist Bob Dunn, Welch was "the [approved] vaudeville

and banquet circuit King Features version of Popeye [but] not the
Fleischer animated voice." [60]

* Dave Fleischer's so-called "standby" Popeyes may have
included Frank Matalone, a young actor who did a Popeye
voice in a 1936 appearance on comedian Fred Allen's radio
show.

Dunn saw Harry F. Welch performing in person at the Hippo-
drome Theatre for a benefit function. Welch had been booked by
Dick Hyman, "the King Features publicity man." The show included
star names like Jimmy Durante and Vincent Lopez's Orchestra.
Dunn described Welch as one of those entertainers who was likable
enough but, essentially, a terrible ham. "He was great...for about
twelve minutes. But then you could feel him losing them. He didn't
know when to get off." [61]

For live appearances, Welch was approved by King Features
to dress as Popeye with "flesh colored canvas arms, a rubber nose
and a moulded rubber jaw." He would do a skit where he jumped
back and forth from Popeye's to Olive Oyl's voices. In early 1936
The Billboard reviewed him, noting he "fared very well" with
his musical sound effects and mimicry. The unsigned author
appended his review, stating, "He's the new Popeye, succeeding
Billy Costello." [62]

This is where it becomes plausible that Welch, a driven show-
off type desperate for a prestigious job, could very likely have auditioned for Paramount to replace Costello. In a 1941 *Popular Science*
article Welch claimed to have taken over the voice "in 1934, and last
year [1940] handled the part in ten of fourteen Popeye shorts." [63]
Blatantly false information except for noting the year 1934, indicating he very likely tried to get in with Fleischer. 1934 is the year Jack
Mercer, in a 1977 TV interview, recalled taking over the voice, even
though his recordings weren't heard in finished cartoons until the

following year. Could it be that Welch is one of the "several" men Dave Fleischer spoke of as Popeye backups?

But it sure isn't Welch doing the awful Popeye in *Be Kind to Aminals*. It has also been suggested that this notorious performance was by Floyd Buckley, an actor who played the sailor man in two radio series sponsored by Wheatena cereal from 1936-38. [64] But Buckley, an older man with a deeper gruff voice, was a veteran Broadway actor. He might have been a disappointing Popeye on air, but he could definitely act. He was in demand for character work on dramatic radio shows. The *Aminals* Popeye, although pitched similarly to Buckley, sounds distinctly amateurish. His speech is so poor he sounds indistinct at times, drowned out by the music, lacking the ability to project vocally like a trained professional. Unlike Buckley, who recorded novelty song records in the Popeye voice, this "actor" couldn't sing: the cartoon's ending - normally sung by Popeye - features the expected "I'm strong to the finich, 'cause I eats me spinach" closing music, but on-screen Popeye just sits there, mute. It seems plausible to suggest that, schedule wise, Dave Fleischer was so anxious after firing Costello that he settled for this abysmal performance as the Popeye short approached its delivery date.

Might this have been the unidentified person whom Lou Fleischer described when he recalled that brother Dave, when the hunt was on to replace Costello, overheard a gruff voiced man at a newsstand? As Dave Fleischer recalled, "I happened to hear a fellow buying a newspaper. When I heard his voice, I asked him what he did. He said he wasn't working, so I asked him to come to my office. I tried him on the sound recording, and he sounded pretty good. So I used his voice." [65]

As for Harry Welch he was at least a working pro, if not the world's most accurate mimic. He is heard on a Peter Pan / Rocking Horse label record from the early sixties, where he is credited on the album cover for Popeye's voice. The LP's tracks are an exact match to the voice actor who replaced Jack Mercer in a few Famous

Studios cartoons like *Island Fling* and *Rocket to Mars* in the 1944-45 period when Mercer was in the service and stationed overseas in Germany, as will be discussed. But Welch is not on any of the classic Fleischer Studios tracks despite the bunk he propagated in the *Popular Science* article.

POPEYE'S Classic Voice

Whatever the case, after various outsiders were auditioned for Popeye, the Fleischers discovered that the sailor man's perfect voice had been in the studio all along. Winfield "Jack" Mercer (1909-84) was a young man from a show business family. A seasoned stage performer since childhood he possessed a lifelong gagman's mind and comedic skills; he also had innate drawing ability. When a vaudeville opportunity fell through in the depths of the Depression, Mercer decided to use his second talent and seek an artistic job. His mother's theatrical agent knew a Paramount contact, who in turn recommended the young man apply at the Fleischer studio. He was employed in early 1932 in the cel painting ["opaquing"] department. At some point the following year Mercer was promoted to the ink-tracing division and from there to an in-between animator position. [66]

Top Fleischer animator Dave Tendlar recalled Mercer doing the sailor's voice very early, sometime in 1933 while it was still the domain of Bill Costello, "the older fellow doing the Popeye voice in the beginning. [Jack] was around [twenty two] years old, he was a slim kid, but looked only about fourteen. He was an opaquer [painting cels] at first." [67]

Mercer remembered that when he moved into the tracing department at Fleischer he "started to [mimic] voices for any character I was inking at the time ... whatever they were working on, like [for instance] a chicken squawk. Everybody [in the room with me] would laugh." [68] Tendlar said that when Mercer was promoted

to the inbetween department, he began fooling around with the studio's new star voice of Popeye "and doing his little laugh." Mercer
told historian Michael Barrier, "I started to imitate the Popeye voice
and somebody heard me." [69]

That somebody was Lou Fleischer. One day when Lou was in
the animation area he overheard a staff member singing, "'Oh, I'm
Popeye the Sailor Man' in a real good voice." [70] When he asked who
the singer was, various staffers answered him stating it was Jack
Mercer. In a letter to *Funnyworld* Lou Fleischer recalled asking the
young man to identify himself. "Knowing that we were seeking a
voice to replace [Costello], Mercer answered timidly, 'Oh I can't
do it. Just kiddin' around.'" [71] But it was a more authentic imitation than the insecure Mercer thought it was, and Fleischer was
delighted.

Lou quickly informed his brother Dave that he had found a suit-
able Popeye voice. Dave Fleischer replied that the schedule couldn't
spare any animators and to please find someone else, quickly. Under
pressure, Lou attended a Fred Waring Orchestra theatre show and
during the intermission he asked resident drummer-comedian
Poley McClintock - who had been doing a virtual clone of Costello's
froggy Popeye voice on records since the mid-twenties - if he would
consider doing some recording for the studio "in his off time, and
he agreed." [72] McClintock, possibly smelling screen fame, apparently
held his bandleader boss up for a raise that same day. Fred Waring, a big theatrical star, complained loudly to Paramount's Louis
Diamond ("Paramount's liaison with the Fleischers" [73]). Diamond
berated Lou Fleischer, assuming he had talked money, even though
he said he was simply doing his usual talent scouting.

Soon thereafter Dave Fleischer had a change of heart. He asked
Mercer to come and rehearse a picture for a while then go back to
his animation desk. Lou added, "This procedure continued until
Jack went with us to the recording room. At the first recording, after
several takes his voice gave out, but Dave was well enough satis-

fied with one of the takes and we accepted that one. In subsequent recordings Jack had no trouble at all." [74]

As Mercer recalled, "At the time I didn't think I could really do it well enough. So I went home and practiced after work. About a week later my voice cracked and I got this peculiar sound...it was the actual [Popeye] tone and quality I wanted to get so I went back the next day and told [Dave] 'I think now I can really do the voice.' Dave and Lou had me audition over the phone to someone at Paramount [shorts executive Lou Diamond]. A short time later, I started to do some incidental voices on some of the cartoons as a breaking-in period. Then, one day [in 1934] I was informed I was going to do a Popeye cartoon." * [75]

* Fleischer fans are generally agreed that Jack Mercer's first time at the Popeye voice was for *King of the Mardi Gras* released in 1935. But this author and the late Hames Ware, my original research associate and other "pair of ears," became convinced years ago that Mercer can be heard on the track of a few 1934 and 1935 Popeyes preceding that cartoon. This might possibly clarify Mercer's comment that the Fleischers had him doing incidental voices in 1934 before his first official Popeye booking. A few examples: I believe that in the Costello Popeye cartoon *The Two-Alarm Fire* we hear Mercer's familiar laugh, likely cut in from one of his auditions. In *We Aim to Please*: "One half dozen sandwiches!" and "Peek-a-boo! (laugh)" and the end sung phrase "We aim to please" are very Mercer-like. In *The Hyp-Nut-Ist* Mercer's mumbled, "No, you lose" and the Popeye laugh are apparent, and it's his jackass noise re-used from *The Dance Contest* session. *Pleased to Meet Cha!* features various mumbles that sound like Mercer. The final cartoon attributed to Bill Costello, *You Gotta Be a Football Hero*, definitely has Mercer's mumbling, laughs and scatting during Popeye's big

run to the touchdown. *Choose Your "Weppins"* has Mercer doing some mumbles and Napoleon's line, "He got me!," while he plays a matrimonial clerk in *For Better or Worser*. Some of *The Dance Contest* and *We Aim to Please* seem to be someone else, and it may well be that they did get drummer Poley McClintock in for *Beware of Barnacle Bill*. Whoever it is wasn't a true actor, and Popeye's dialogue is minimal in several. I should stress this paragraph is simply my and Hames Ware's own theory; I am happy to be dissuaded if we can ever locate sound reports, session sheets or other documentary proof.

Mercer said, "I changed the character [of Popeye] quite a bit. I didn't make it quite as gruff. [Costello's Popeye] was very militant at times." [76] Mercer plussed the voice by technically keeping the unique froggy sound but softening the delivery, thereby making Popeye less surly, far warmer and generally more happy-go-lucky. Essentially he improved upon the original, in the same way Mel Blanc "humanised" and improved on the original voice of Porky Pig in 1937.

Indeed Mercer managed to make the character likeable despite the rough, often cynical flophouse milieu in which the stories took place. Fleischer scholar Mark Langer described a typical Popeye cartoon of the mid-thirties, *For Better or Worser* (1935), as a combination of "grotesquerie and pessimism." [77] Animation historian Harvey Deneroff observed that the Popeye formula, where the menacing Bluto is always bested in the end, begat the model for all the adversarial animated series to come, including "the Bugs Bunny, Tom & Jerry and Roadrunner cartoons." [78]

In April 1935 Paramount and Fleischer offered Mercer a new contract which allowed for voice recording work along with his animator position. It was clear to the Fleischer brothers that Mercer possessed more native intelligence and a far more subtle comic mind than Costello's. He began creating a raft of amusing muttered ad libs that long-time Popeye fans now cherish. Mercer acknowledged that Costello had employed ad lib muttering, but those were more functional than comedic.

As Mercer saw it, "...I used [the muttering] as a means of putting in a funny line. In those days we used to record everything at once...[there was] no pre-recording of these things. They ran the [finished] picture and we had to do the lines as the picture ran. They used this system of a [flashing] bouncing ball as our cues. In between where the actual [scripted] lines were written we would ad lib lines to fill it up." [79] Animator Gordon Sheehan added, "Jack wrote most of that stuff himself. He'd see spots where he could put in a little comment, or gag." [80]

It was the mumbled asides that gave Popeye an extra dimension and he became more humorous and memorable. As Mercer noted, "A funny line might occur to [me] after a take and I'd make a note of it for the next take." He thought the ad libs were "Popeye thinking out loud," [81] although delivered *sotto voce* in volume. Sheehan noted, "Jack had a special little voice for that, as if [Popeye] was talking to himself." [82] There were many of these under the breath gags, as for instance when Popeye, in the middle of a fight, painted a circle around one of Bluto's eyes and mumbled, "Hm, the mark of Zero!"

Dave Tendlar said, "[Jack] had a trick voice that he could control. [After he became an established voice] he was worked to death by the staff. [When] there was an ad lib by Jack, and the director thought it was funny, he just left it in the track. At Fleischer they let the actors fool around, and Jack would constantly gag it up. He was a joker, and a funny guy, quite a comic. And very clever, a very creative guy. We very naturally took advantage of his talents." [83]

Beyond Popeye, Mercer became a studio utility voice: "Right away, I worked on the Betty Boops and any of the other cartoons they had...I would pick up any odd voices, incidental voices throughout the picture. I'd go to a recording [session], and they'd hand you a script, and say, 'You do this, you do that and whatnot.'" [84] Mercer's voice is certainly recognizable in the 1936 Color Classic *The Cobweb Hotel*.

Once Mercer was established as the invincible sailor, his ad libbing ability provided him with additional job security: in 1936 he was transferred to the Fleischer story department where he remained into the Famous Studios era for over two decades, and for which function he eventually received many screen credits, often collaborating with Carl Meyer.

By the late thirties, Mercer had gained much experience in two areas. He was both a story man and a supervisor of voice recordings. Of this role he explained, "For a time they gave me the title of Director of Dialogue." [85] Mercer was tasked with directing actors at recordings, assuming some of Dave Fleischer's earlier responsibilities. Essentially Mercer became what Hollywood's Bill Scott described as a "floor director," a role Scott had for the entire run of the Jay Ward TV cartoon sessions. The full extent of Mercer's talents was at last acknowledged by the Fleischers.

Mercer continued this function at Famous Studios throughout the forties, recalling, "Many times Izzy [Sparber] or Seymour [Kneitel] would become very confused as to how to get a certain actor to read a line, and I would butt in and say, 'Would you mind if I try to get them to say this line the way I think you would like it read?' I did an awful lot of that." [86]

As Mercer settled into the Popeye role he slowly added a few other semi-regular voices including Popeye's four nephews. They were simply Popeye's voice mechanically sped to a childlike pitch, and overdubbed in unison to sound like quadruplets. Mercer also spoke for Popeye's cantankerous old man, Poopdeck Pappy, at first in the excellent 1938 cartoon *Goonland*. That short also showcases Mercer's fine singing voice, as Popeye warbles the catchy opening, "I found out where to find my Pappy ... My Pappy who got lost when I was born!!" Mercer also claimed he took over the Wimpy role from whoever did it first; one source notes Lou Fleischer pitched in for some early Wimpy lines. [87]

As already noted, the first Olive Oyl dialogue was recorded by Bonnie Poe who had just taken over Betty Boop's voice. Her characterization was aptly described by Ray Pointer as an "oafish" sounding Olive. She remained the voice of Popeye's "goil" for several cartoons until Mae Questel did *Shoein' Hosses* (1934). Questel's unique take on Olive's voice was based on screen actress ZaSu Pitts's fluttery comic whine, which suited the pretzel shaped leading lady perfectly. Questel became Olive's full-time voice in *A Dream Walking* (1935) and she recorded Popeye cartoons for the next four years.

By late 1937, however, Questel was less available for recordings during her second pregnancy, so some proven Betty Boop voices were re-called for temporary duty in films released the following year. These included Bonnie Poe (*Out of the Inkwell*) and Little Ann Little (*Buzzy Boop*). [88] Margie Hines was also invited to sub as Olive's voice for some Popeye cartoons like *The Jeep* (1938). It appears that Mae Questel was able to return for two more 1938 Popeyes, *Mutiny Ain't Nice* and *A Date to Skate*. But with her expanded family and regular radio work in New York, she declined to move to Miami when the Fleischer studio migrated there in the summer of 1938, as will soon be discussed. For the next five years the roles of both Olive and Betty Boop were in the capable pipes of Betty's original voice artist Margie Hines, who made the move south to Florida.

As will be seen Mae Questel would return as Olive's voice in late 1943 after the cartoon facility was renamed Famous Studios and resumed operations in Manhattan, a period of major change covered later in this chapter.

Finally we get to the marvellous hulking bully Bluto and his early voice, a topic which remains a thorny issue with your author. For decades, the commonly accepted wisdom has been that William Pennell was the voice for the first Bluto. The lumbering bad guy with the unforgettably hulking presence appeared in the debut

Popeye cartoon, remaining the sailor's eternal nemesis over the quarter century of theatrical shorts, from 1933-57.

My problem is this: I have seen zero credible documentation which confirms that Bill Pennell is indeed our man as the earlier Bluto. Pennell's name first appeared in the early seventies, unsourced, in a library reference book, *Who Was Who on Screen* by Evelyn Mack Truitt. His entry stated, "the voice of Bluto." Pennell was known at first to be a radio announcer, until one source described him as a bass singer from a quartet employed by Paramount. More recently it emerged that there were indeed two men named William Pennell working in the same thirties timeframe, the older one a New York based singer, the other a radio commentator in markets as far flung as Miami and Los Angeles.

Whichever Pennell supposedly did the deep, growly voice of early Bluto had also been doing voices for Fleischer for at least two years previously. The same voice person is heard in several Betty Boop cartoons like *Bimbo's Express, Jack and the Beanstalk* and *Dizzy Red Riding Hood.* He is most prominent as a villain, a lecherous boss or a surly customer; he is for instance the belligerent hippo patron in *Betty Boop's Bizzy Bee* who constantly yells for more "Wheatcakes!!!," and it should be added he is a fine cartoon voice actor. In the earliest Popeyes it is also he who warbles the title ditty "Strike Up the Band for Popeye the Sailor."

To confuse Popeye geeks even more, another possible name appeared in the mid-nineties. In the *AFI Catalog: Feature Films, 1931-1940* there is an entry for the 1932 Paramount movie *The Big Broadcast.* This was a musical feature based on popular radio stars of that period, affording audiences the chance to see many of their home entertainment favorites like Bing Crosby, Cab Calloway and George Burns up on the big screen. The movie was unusual in that Paramount filmed parts of it in Hollywood and parts in New York, to accommodate certain radio stars who originated their weekly shows from either one Coast or the other. Duplicate interior sets were constructed for both cities to match up exactly. A note appended to the film's entry in the *AFI* volume reveals, "According to copyright records, Charles Carver, who was a character voice for Fleischer screen cartoons, made a cameo appearance in this film as the bass voice in Kate Smith's theme song, 'And You Were Mine.'" [89] (Ms Smith and her radio show were based in New York.)

So, could the early Bluto actually be bass vocalist Charles Carver, and not William Pennell? The *AFI* note seems compelling. It is credible enough for this book to nominate Carver as one probable early Bluto, but your cautious author is ever willing to be swayed if more documentation is unearthed. One Fleischer historian, Ray Pointer, is convinced that the bass voice in *The Big Broadcast* sequence is not a Bluto actor [90]. The research continues.

The next Bluto, however, is undoubtedly the most revered to any died-in-the-spinach Popeye nerd. The subterranean-toned Gus Wicke (not spelled "Wickie" as was previously assumed) was a fixture around Broadway for some three decades as a popular bass singer for various trios, quartets and quintets. These groups performed old time songs, comedy ditties, and skits in nightclubs and other stage shows. For years Wicke was a member of combos like The Westerners and The Mauve Decade Quartet, enjoying runs in legitimate Broadway musical comedies like *Ballyhoo*.

By the time Wicke began doing Bluto's voice he was a member of the full-time house quartet at Bill's Gay Nineties nightspot in the heart of Manhattan, where he was resident for over a decade. Like the earlier Bluto actor, he had already done voices for Fleischer Screen Songs like *I'd Climb the Highest Mountain* (1931) and in 1931 Talkartoons like *The Male Man* and *Silly Scandals*. In 1932 Wicke's name was listed on NBC cast sheets for the first Betty Boop radio series playing Gus Gorilla, a role he also played in a 1935 Color Classic *An Elephant Never Forgets*. Similar vocally to the earlier Bluto, Wicke's basso voice is technically superior in depth, resonance and a sonorous delivery with a marvellous mocking laugh. [91] His earliest appearance in the role is for the 1935 Popeye entry *The Hyp-Nut-Ist* and that role was followed by a non-Bluto villain in *Choose Your "Weppins."*

Once Gus Wicke and Jack Mercer were teamed in the cartoons they became the most memorable hero versus bully-boy voices of the thirties. They gave great performances in the 1936 Popeye classics *A Clean Shaven Man* and *Brotherly Love* where they sang harmony, out-machoed each other and competed in an endless series of chortles, mumbles and mutterings to hilarious effect. It took until the online era before Wicke's biography was researched in detail by cartoon scholars David Gerstein and E. O. Costello; Gerstein unearthed the ultimate Wicke description in a 1939 issue of *Charleston Daily Mail*: in the paper's "This New York" column the author praised, "Gus Wicke, whose foghorn voice makes bullfrogs green with envy." [92] Sadly Wicke couldn't continue with cartoons, admittedly an adjunct to his extensive stage work, once the Fleischer Studios operation moved to Miami in mid-1938. His final Bluto role was for *Big Chief Ugh-Amugh-Ugh.*

Fleischer Studios Moves to Miami

By the spring of 1937, the Fleischer cartoon studio was the busiest animation plant in New York with its own particular workplace bureaucracy. The lower scale employees, like inbetweeners and inkers, had routinely been expected to work long hours. Some of these people, resentful of the much larger fees paid to top echelon animators, eventually felt like Dickensian sweatshop hires under an uncaring management, and those feelings festered. When some activist union members were fired by the Fleischers over salary issues, the workplace grievances escalated rapidly into what became a particularly nasty strike (there was violence) that lasted five months. The Commercial Artists & Designers union was victorious.

Max Fleischer was a self-made, successful businessman who had no time for unions. Just like Walt Disney four years later, the paternalistic Fleischer perceived the strike action as a personal affront. The divisive event concentrated his mind, and he decided to move the entire operation to Miami, Florida, an avowedly non-union state, where for several years the Fleischer brothers had maintained holiday homes.

In February of 1938 just such a move was formally announced. Paramount Pictures financed the relocation, starting in May, and it took just six months until the brand new facility was ready for cartoon production. It was a top drawer, modern, fully equipped studio, air-conditioned (a must for Miami) and with its own cafeteria. It boasted a large sound stage.

Not only had labor unrest been a prime reason for this huge upheaval, but there had also been a concomitant game change within the cartoon industry following the release of Disney's enormously successful animated feature *Snow White and the Seven Dwarfs* (1938). Max Fleischer himself had a natural desire to compete with Disney, his chief thirties "rival," on both an artistic and a business level. Paramount sensed a huge opportunity after seeing Disney's feature cartoon triumph, and they regarded their investment in Fleischer's studio in sunny Miami as the *raison d'etre* for the making of their own cartoon feature. Following the 1936 Popeye color two reeler, and months before the move south, the Fleischers and Paramount had decided on a feature animated version of Jonathan Swift's famous story *Gulliver's Travels*.

For a studio used to a decade of producing short cartoons, the vastly different undertaking of the *Gulliver* feature would require a much larger staff. The Fleischers began seeking and hiring top West Coast artists and story talents, offering the biggest salaries in the cartoon business.

Among those making the move from California were story men Cal Howard and Ted Pierce from the Schlesinger studio, screenwriter Edmond Seward and character designer Charles Thorson, both from MGM, and freelancer Pinto Colvig. Colvig was famous as a leading Disney character voice in roles like Goofy and Grumpy from *Snow White*, as well as being a talented gag-man and musician. Soon over a hundred more came from Hollywood along with some two hundred New Yorkers who moved South to the new studio.

Eventually Fleischer Studios' staff swelled from 175 in New York to over 650 during production of the cartoon feature in Florida. In what seemed like no time the new studio was so filled to capacity that the overflow of writers had to be housed in surrounding bungalows. [93]

As early work on the *Gulliver* story proceeded, the new facility added finishing touches to ten cartoons for which production had begun in New York. These included the Betty Boop cartoon *Sally Swing* (1938), which was in effect a pilot film for a new spinoff series. It featured the voice of young radio star "Baby" Rose Marie in the title role, but in the end it remained a one-off short. The Popeye cartoon *A Date to Skate* featured the final thirties voice track recorded by Mae Questel in New York just before the move. The last of the New York cartoons requiring post production in Miami was the Popeye *Customers Wanted* (1939) before the studio completed its first full Florida production, the Betty Boop *So Does an Automobile* (1939).

The top talents from California began arriving in early 1939 and soon marked their creative territory. Inevitably, with the somewhat different approaches to story and production methods with which each group was familiar, a rift soon developed between personnel from the two Coasts. The California story men insisted on re-doing much of *Gulliver*, already storyboarded over several months by the Fleischer team. The West Coasters felt strongly that the early board was overloaded with slapstick. They also sensed the story area required a continuity overhaul. Finally a romantic musical approach was suggested which changed the direction of the film.

Much of the New York v. Hollywood territorialism subsided over time, but some resentments lingered. Dave Tendlar observed the East versus West cliques up close and he added that a third group was "a union clique." [94]

GULLIVER'S TRAVELS, Fleischer's first feature

The chief problem with the Fleischer Studio undertaking a cartoon feature was the speed with which Paramount wanted it pushed through, aiming for a Christmas 1939 release date. Characteristically, Disney had taken over five intensive years to produce *Snow White and the Seven Dwarfs*, during which time his animators attended endless art classes with an aim to honing their drawing abilities to levels they hadn't imagined themselves capable of reaching earlier. The Disney film's story and cast of characters had been constantly refined with pinpoint attention to character motivation.

Simply put, in 1938 the Disney team was far advanced artistically. Although various Fleischer artists were undeniably talented the sophistication wasn't there when it came to the kind of character analysis demanded of a feature-length cartoon, and the old habits of the New York years were overly ingrained. Thus any discussion of trying a fresh approach to animation or story problems was met at first with an attitude of disdain for anything deemed artsy-fartsy. But despite the lack of Disney's finer techniques and overall expertise, Paramount was able to release *Gulliver's Travels* in the week before Christmas 1939, just as they had wanted.

Overall, the rushed production meant the film lacked anything even approaching *Snow White*'s depth. Several characters look too much alike, many of the Lilliput citizens are shallow and ill defined, and leading figures like Gabby are simply not as likable as Disney's Seven Dwarfs. The songs composed by Paramount's contract tunesmiths Leo Robin and Ralph Rainger were tuneful and pleasant but nowhere as memorable as the songs from Disney's film. The biggest hit was "It's a Hap-Hap-Happy Day" composed by Fleischer's own musician Sammy Timberg with his long-time arranger Winston Sharples. The singing voices for the romantic leads were done by two famous radio and concert hall vocalists, Jessica Dragonette as Princess Glory and Lanny Ross as Prince David. Unfortunately these two characters have virtually no dialogue and seem chronically underdeveloped. The same problem affects King Bombo's palace spies Sneak, Snoop and Snitch. Allegedly comedy characters, there are no discernibly different personality traits between the trio, who should have been richly amusing comic relief bunglers in the Three Stooges vein.

Gabby, the Lilliputian watch-man and town crier, is the film's major supporting character. His dialogue is spoken by Pinto Colvig in a voice that is mechanically sped. But his incessant chatter is lacking in clever comedy, so that Gabby often comes across as a strident little motor mouth.

Jack Mercer's voice for King Little is a tad too timid and mild to the point of sounding flat, as if Mercer was constantly trying to home in on a more distinctive voice that he finally couldn't find. His rival, King Bombo, is played by Schlesinger story man and voice artist Ted Pierce. It's a solid characterization but again the dialogue is mainly unremarkable. The two kings seemed badly in need of a Palace joke writer. Visually, the elderly Royals were caricatured in a way that made them seem oddly unrelated to their very human-looking offspring. In *Snow White* the superior writing eased any similar perception between a realistic heroine and the cartoonish dwarfs.

As Dave Tendlar recalled of the title character's voice, "Gulliver himself was played by a local newspaper [and radio] reporter for the *Miami News* [his name was Sam Parker, and he modelled some of the live action for the animators]. The figure in Gulliver looks exactly like him. I spoke with him many times at the studio; he was an awfully nice fellow." [95]

Although flawed the film still has its attractions. Visually *Gulliver's Travels* is often attentive to finery in its detailed settings, approaching though not matching Disney's lavish second feature, *Pinocchio* (1940). Some of the animation is accomplished and worthy of kudos considering the hurried production timeframe. But the story has areas of concern that appear slapdash with some sequences seeming confused and not fully thought through. The rush to finish is often all too apparent, as animator Mark Kausler notes: "Crowd scenes of the Lilliputians tying Gulliver to the giant wooden platform were marred by drawing featureless bubble heads on them, no doubt to save time in clean-up." [96]

Certainly, the film was an undeniable achievement for the relatively small window of time it took to make and its success cannot be denied. According to historian Harvey Deneroff it was highly popular, beating *Pinocchio's* early domestic box office figures. He added that *Gulliver* "broke some box office records in Latin America" where it outdid *Snow White's* success. [97] But with war raging in Europe in late 1939, its earnings in that important market were severely restricted, a problem shared by Disney when *Pinocchio* was released soon afterwards. *Gulliver* managed to make a modest profit, but the budget overruns - it finally cost a cool $1.5 million - were seriously concerning to Paramount.

Just as concerning was a fractious and dysfunctional relationship that had developed between Max Fleischer and his younger brother Dave. Since the move to Miami they had begun clashing, and Max's old school values of propriety had hardened as he aged. To him, Dave appeared to be exhibiting a lax attitude, flaunting both his racetrack gambling habit and his patently obvious office love affair during business hours. In 1940 the brothers continued to grow further apart to the point where they finally avoided even eye contact. What was worse, they were fifty-fifty stockholders in Fleischer Studios.

Aside from the *Gulliver* feature, work continued apace on the regular Popeye, Betty Boop and Color Classic shorts. Betty's career was waning, the star a victim of the now entrenched Production Code which in the past four years had blue-nosed her unique early coquettish and sexy qualities totally off the screen. Betty, the once beloved cutie of the early Depression era, had morphed over time to the point where she was an unremarkable domestic woman who needed her dog Pudgy and Grampy, as well as younger relatives like Buzzy Boop, to bolster her now pedestrian stories.

One problem with being in Florida was that it might have boasted a town called Hollywood, but it sure wasn't Hollywood, California. The cartoons began calling out for some distinct new voices but there was no outside acting pool. The studio had to continue relying on its in-house talents for most of the dialogue. Those studio voices were top notch of course, and Jack Mercer and Margie Hines were past masters from their years voicing New York cartoons. Writer Carl Meyer, like Mercer a story man with a natural ability at character acting, contributed several voices. But as versatile as these in-house talents were, there was inevitably a monotonous sameness to the many cartoon tracks recorded in the Florida era. It was only occasionally that an outside talent, such as a nightclub impersonator doing a stint in Miami, was engaged.

Some regular characters like Bluto simply weren't the same. As we have seen, both Mae Questel and the great Bluto voice Gus Wicke were unwilling to pull up stumps and lose the plentiful work around Broadway and on radio. The first "new" Bluto, heard in *Customers Wanted* (1939), was inadequate, sounding more like a dumb gangster. The cartoon was a cheater using earlier footage: the older clips were re-scored and re-voiced with this weaker Bluto. Wicke's booming villainy was sorely missed.

When Pinto Colvig relocated to Miami from Hollywood he had specifically answered a call for a voice artist position, mainly to do Bluto, and he arrived in early May, 1939. His first Fleischer role was in the Betty Boop cartoon *Musical Mountaineers* released on May 12th which indicated that Fleischer was still post-recording much of the dialogue. Colvig ended up voicing some forty cartoons, including the Fleischer features, during his two years in Miami.

Colvig contributed some fine performances using variations of his many Disney voices, like Goofy. But it was immediately apparent in the dreamlike Popeye entry *Wotta Nitemare* (1939) that his Bluto voice just didn't work, sounding strained and artificial, lacking the hulking quality needed. He tried again in *It's the Natural Thing to Do* (1939). After that cartoon some other staffers had a go: Jack Mercer owned up to trying the Bluto role, and it occasionally sounds like Ted Pierce in a 1940 Popeye *Stealin' Ain't Honest*. Pierce is certainly recognizable doing the Walter Winchell radio imitation in *Fightin Pals* (1940).

Without the Manhattan or Hollywood talent pools, Colvig attempted a few more Blutos and he improved, but it was never his best voice. Colvig's comic ability was always strong though, and he and Mercer were funny in *Shakesperean Spinach* (1940) with Popeye and Bluto as amateur actors singing in a joyously hammy fashion. In the spring of 1939 Popeye and Olive tied the knot off-screen when Jack Mercer and Margie Hines were wed. They honeymooned briefly but evidently some urgent recording was needed while they were away. Colvig was quoted in the *Miami News* of June 11, 1939 describing how Fleischer P. R. man Hamp Howard did a fill-in voice: "They got him to talk for Popeye in the [most recent] release, as a sub for Jack Mercer. Did a good job too." [98] If only Colvig had mentioned that cartoon's title!

For these staff voices, it didn't help that the three new series which replaced Betty Boop, after she breathed her last in 1939's *Rhythm on the Reservation*, were some of the weakest cartoons in both story and character design in the entire history of Fleischer Studios. Those series comprised the Stone Age, Animated Antics and Gabby cartoons, most of which were afflicted with uninspired writing, unfunny gags and truly ugly draftsmanship. This situation arose because the top animators and layout talents were so busy on the intricate *Gulliver* feature that the shorts inevitably suffered under the studio's secondary tier of talent. Again, Colvig, Jack Mercer and Carl Meyer handled many of the voices in these B-grade cartoons, assisted in a handful by one or two unidentified nightclub comics who perform a few impressions like a Bert Lahr. But the dialogue for the shorts is totally unmemorable.

Some cartoon people were never enamored with the move to Florida. Animator Shamus Culhane told Harvey Deneroff that the decision to move was "an absolutely irrational act. There was no business advantage to moving there. They didn't have a lab; they didn't have actors - all they had down there were old vaude-villians and they were lousy actors. If a camera broke down, there was no camera place. He might as well have moved to Peacock, Kentucky." [99]

Superman and *MR. BUG GOES TO TOWN*

In the spring of 1939 during production on *Gulliver* the studio began discussing material for a second feature. After some false starts, including an unsuccessful attempt to buy the rights to Maurice Maeterlinck's book *The Life of the Bee*, the Fleischer writers developed and worked on an original treatment to feature an all-insect cast. Paramount signed off on the story *Mr. Bug Goes to Town* in December 1940. This would be another complex assignment, although the lessons that were learned in the two years since *Gulliver* commenced production showed that the animators' range and drawing abilities had improved noticeably. The new feature was scheduled to open in November 1941.

Meanwhile the long-time business relationship with Paramount was about to change markedly. The budget overruns on *Gulliver's Travels* meant that the Fleischers were in deeper debt than ever. Paramount, concerned as well about the deteriorating personal relationship between siblings Max and Dave, decided to foreclose on its Miami studio loan in May, ordering them to halt production. It then bought all Fleischer Studios' assets while a new agreement allowed the Fleischers one final year on production, with Paramount advancing the money for completion of the *Mr. Bug* feature and two dozen short cartoons. These would consist of twelve new Popeyes and twelve cartoons based on the enormously successful *Superman* comic books.

Superman had been created by two Ohio teenagers who loved science-fiction. One was writer Jerry Siegel who envisioned just such an all-powerful hero character in mid-1934. The other was Joe Shuster who was the artistic half of the creative partnership. By the summer of 1938 with the young men employed in the comics industry, their first *Superman* story appeared in Action Comics for DC Inc. Reader response was swift and overwhelmingly enthusiastic and the young team had a gigantic hit, or rather DC, as rights-holders, did. Within a year "Superman" had his own magazine, followed by a daily newspaper strip. Ancillary rights and merchandise deals were quickly underway via a subsidiary company, Superman, Inc.

Radio was the next natural showcase for the "Man of Steel" and in late 1939 audition recordings were cut by producer Bob Maxwell who joined the publishing company and paired it with a public relations firm. It took a few weeks but by February 1940 *The Adventures of Superman* bowed as a syndicated 15-minute juvenile oriented radio show, airing three times a week. With its action packed serialized stories, urgent pace and ingenious use of sound patterns, the punchy audio dramas were soon rating incredibly well for such a relatively new show.

Superman, Inc. had meantime been seeking a movie opportunity for months. In the late summer of 1940 they were approached by Paramount, keen to propose a two year series of expensively mounted short cartoons to be produced by their animation contractor Fleischer Studios. According to *Superman* historian Michael Hayde, "Paramount literally handed *Superman* over to Fleischer Studios" as an assignment. [100] The Fleischers were allocated $50,000 to produce the first episode in the series. The animation directors now faced an even bigger challenge than the *Gulliver* feature. These would be dramatic cartoons, completely different to the comedic style with which the cartoonists were long familiar. The realistically rendered human characters, the decision to use cinematic flourishes in the layouts and camera angles, and a radio technique of carefully chosen sound effects meant that an enormous investment in time and skill would be put to the test. Could the Fleischer team, after years of zany cartoon characters, lay out and animate a credible cast of realistic human figures that would generate the desired suspension of disbelief?

Work began in the fall of 1940. The original idea of a black and white series was nixed a few months into the project in favour of full Technicolor treatment. The extra work that entailed - realistic color, shading and lighting effects - meant that the initial cartoon, *Superman*, wasn't released until a year later in September 1941. But the wait was worth it, and the Fleischer *Superman* cartoon series was a triumph. The animation was excellent, the action moved at a brisk clip, and the futuristic special effects and sci-fi elements were addressed with intelligence and imagination. The cartoon was undeniably exciting. It was visually fascinating. The first entry resulted in an Oscar nomination. The second of the contracted twelve, *The Mechanical Monsters* (1941), appeared two months later and was even more impressive.

The voices were provided by the New York radio talents: Clayton Collyer had already notched up eighteen months on air in the title role of *The Adventures of Superman*. For the Paramount cartoons he performs his dual voices of Clark Kent, a light tenor delivery that vocally morphs into the booming tones of the Man of Steel, whenever he announces, "This looks like a job (change to baritone) for Superman!!" Joan Alexander, by that time the third Lois Lane voice on radio, also did the cartoons. In the first episode, character actor Jackson Beck voiced the Perry White role. [101]

The highly dramatic background narration which sets up that first entry has been credited to the radio show's director and announcer George Lowther. But some movie buffs insist the voice belongs to Broadway and New York radio drama veteran Grant Richards. Until it can be confirmed, suffice to say the opening commentary, describing the end of the planet Krypton and the origins of the title character, is a wonderfully delivered dramatic reading.

With this series and the upcoming *Mr. Bug* feature, it was obvious that the large Fleischer staff had come a long way in developing and honing their artistic abilities. It's hard to believe that the *Superman* series was made by the same studio artists who, a year earlier, had exhibitors begging on their knees for no more Stone Age or Gabby cartoons.

The second feature, *Mr. Bug Goes to Town*, was finished by late 1941. It showcased a large cast of anthropomorphized insects in a story about their struggles dealing with the big city human world. The characters were cartoon takes on familiar Hollywood movie types. The lead roles were spoken by local Miami actor Stan Freed as Hoppity the grasshopper, and studio ink & paint artist Pauline Loth as Honey Bee. The humans were played by professional voice talents, with Kenny Gardner, a crooner featured with Guy Lombardo's Orchestra, as songwriter Dick Dickens. Theatre actress Gwen Williams read the part of Mary.

Dave Tendlar commented on the excellent insect character voices, noting, "Actors never did relish the idea of coming down to Miami. They always had difficulty getting people to come down there, so [for *Mr. Bug*] Dave [Fleischer] decided to audition some people from around the studio: Jack Mercer who [as you know] had a vast repertoire of other voices, and several others. They auditioned and they had great voices. They were story men, and they knew animation, they knew character. They turned out to be very good actors. Carl Meyer was [Smack] the mosquito and Jack Mercer was [Swat] the fly. Mr. C. Bagley Beetle was done by Ted Pierce. The story men seemed to be the guys who could really act." [102]

Tendlar was spot on. These characters' voices were improvements on the ones heard in *Gulliver*. Story man Ted Pierce, who had provided many one-off voices at Schlesinger's studio in the mid to late thirties, enjoyed the largest role in his long career. He made the most of the villainous Mr. Beetle, whose design appeared to closely channel movie character star Edward Arnold. Jack Mercer doubled as the falsetto Fly and kindly old Mr. Bumble. Carl Meyer's mosquito vocally resembled a Dead End Kid, and even the straight lead of Hoppity evinced a likably youthful energy, different to many other blandly straight heroic types in other animated features. Even Mae Questel agreed to record a "Bee Scout" character and travelled down to Miami.

Importantly, *Mr. Bug* has the unique distinction of being the earliest cartoon in animation history to afford screen credit to supporting character voices: aside from the lead actors, the on-screen cast reads: "Mr Bumble - Jack Mercer, C. Bagley Beetle - Ted Pierce, Swat - Jack Mercer, Smack - Carl Meyer." No doubt Mercer and Pierce were delighted with this long-overdue voice recognition.

The on-screen credit was, however, a one-time rarity. One year later in 1942 Disney, for the first time, credited a single name, Fred Shields as "Narrator," in the opening titles of *Saludos Amigos*. After Mel Blanc began receiving Warner Bros. screen credit from early 1944, it wasn't until 1946's *The Three Caballeros* that an opening Disney cast list named prominent voice artists like Sterling Holloway, Clarence Nash and Frank Graham for the first time. It wasn't until 1949 that the Disney features began regularly listing voices in that studio's fashion ("With the Talents of..."). It's possible that, had Fleischer Studios continued, they might even have credited voices on the shorts. But such was not to be.

Sadly, *Mr. Bug* proved a major box office flop, with some staff blaming Paramount for delaying the film's release due to a large backlog of movies. The holdup meant that the unlucky feature was released to theatres just following the December 7, 1941 attack on Pearl Harbor. Overnight, the national mood became downbeat and morose, definitely not the ideal time for a whimsically optimistic Frank Capra-esque happy ending cartoon.

When the Fleischers' contract ended it was not renewed by Paramount Pictures. Max and Dave, now totally estranged as family members, were obviously unable to function as they once had, and Paramount was already aware that Dave Fleischer was heading to Hollywood to run a rival cartoon studio, Screen Gems. The brothers cut their long ties to Paramount at the end of 1941 and left the studio. It was an inglorious end to one of the greatest chapters of animation history.

Paramount, as we saw at the beginning of this chapter, was now fully rid of the Fleischer brothers. The cartoon outfit was officially renamed Famous Studios. At its helm for many years were three Fleischer studio veterans: animation director Seymour Kneitel who was also Max's son-in-law, story artist and Dave Fleischer's longtime assistant Izzy Sparber, and the long-serving business manager Sam Buchwald. While the studio's name might have changed, the staff simply continued making the contracted Popeye and Superman shorts. The final Fleischer-produced Popeye was *Baby Wants a Bottleship* (1942) and the first of the dozen remaining Popeyes made under the Famous banner was *You're a Sap, Mr. Jap* (1942). When those twelve were completed it marked the end of the black and white era for Paramount cartoons.

The West Coast staff had already started peeling away, returning home to California. Pinto Colvig's last voices for Fleischer were heard in the final entries of the Gabby and Animated Antics shorts. Earlier Colvig recorded a supporting voice for the *Mr. Bug* feature but by the time that film was released he had been back in Hollywood for months (he and Cal Howard returned by the late summer of 1941). Colvig was already busy voicing cartoons for

Lantz, Schlesinger and Screen Gems. Ted Pierce followed soon after, returning to the Schlesinger plant where his writing talents blossomed into his most productive Warner Bros. years. The final Miami tracks featuring Pierce's voice were in two of the Superman series, *Showdown* and *Destruction, Inc.* They were among the first cartoons released under the Famous Studios banner in late 1942-early 1943.

In the final Miami-produced Popeyes, Bluto's voice was still changing.* The excellent impressionist Dave Barry, then known as David Siegel, was appearing in nightspots around the country. When Barry was booked in a Miami club, Lou and Dave Fleischer caught his show and he was employed to do a Bluto; he had a skit in his stage act where he did a Popeye, Bluto and Olive routine [103]. Barry had a natural baritone voice range and was a fine comic talent. His deep-voiced Bluto was one of the better replacements, being heard in *Olive Oyl and Water Don't Mix* (1942) and *Seein' Red White 'n' Blue* (1943).

* An unsigned 1942 Miami newspaper item sourced by Popeye expert Fred Grandinetti disclosed one of the obscure Florida-based voice talents: "Lee Royce, the handsome baritone at Jimmie's on the Trail [nightclub] is the voice of Bruto [sic] the heavy jawed enemy of Popeye, in Fleischer's movie cartoons made here. He also is both voice and model for Fleischer's Superman cartoons." [104]

In January 1943 the Miami studio officially closed and the staff members started returning to New York.

Back to Broadway: Famous Studios cartoon voices

The first cartoons to emerge from Famous Studios in Manhattan commenced production while the staff was still based in Miami, reflected in those cartoons featuring Margie Hines as the voice of Olive Oyl. The move back to New York took a few months of read-justment before the studio was operational sometime in March of 1943. Later that year some dialogue was recorded in Manhattan, using talents like character voice specialist Gilbert Mack, who was both Shorty the sailor and Billy in *The Hungry Goat* (1943), one of the last Fleischer cartoons post-produced in New York. A most flexible actress named Cecil Roy was also auditioned, then hired, for a newly licensed series, Little Lulu. New York's large radio talent pool was now available to the cartoon makers, and they were both situated in the heart of the theatre district.

Dave Tendlar, recalling the Famous recording dates, said, "We'd call for a [session] at nine o'clock in the morning, and everybody would show up, and they'd record from 9:30 to 11 o'clock. Sometimes they'd record two pictures. An hour and a half, two hours tops, was the most they could rent the sound stage for. They always rented this stage on Fifth Avenue, owned by RCA. It had great sound equipment and a tremendous sound stage, and a projection room with a big screen. They used the larger room for recording the musical score, with room for maybe eight, ten, twelve musicians. We alternated back and forth. The smaller room was for dialogue sessions. It was just perfect for recording, and within walking distance from the Famous animation studio.

"We used that studio from 1943 until about 1960. All the music recording sessions were done there, too. Every theatrical had its own score. Weeks later they would rent that studio again for the mixing session. The regular musicians became very seasoned with cartoon work. They invariably had the same musicians come in, ninety per cent of the time. They knew immediately, through past experience, what the director and the conductor wanted." [105]

Once Famous was fully under way the Popeye cartoons remained the studio's top priority, and there were several fine entries in the series. From the 1943-44 season all Famous cartoons were produced in full Technicolor, starting with Popeye in *Her Honor the Mare* (1943). Bluto had one final mystery voice artist to go, a wonderful classically trained baritone vocalist in the fully musical entry *We're on Our Way to Rio* (1944), with Olive's role sung by a fine Carmen Miranda mimic.

After that cartoon Mae Questel was back on board for various female voices. Margie Hines's final appearance as Olive Oyl was in *The Marry-Go-Round* released late in 1943. Questel reclaimed the part in *The Anvil Chorus Girl* (1944) and remained the definitive Olive from 1944 all the way through the completion of 220 cheap Popeye television cartoons by 1963. She also did the voice on children's records and commercials. In fact Questel dominated much of the Famous Studios cartoon output for twenty years becoming Little Audrey and enacting several other parts. For many cartoon connoisseurs Mae Questel will always be the ultimate interpreter of both Betty Boop and Olive.

Completing Popeye's regulars, the final Bluto voice was provided by Jackson Beck, one of New York's busiest radio talents. He was also one of its finest actors. Once the Famous staff were resettled in Manhattan, Seymour Kneitel and Izzy Sparber began auditioning actors. Beck was tipped off by an agent pal. "I just answered an audition, as simple as that. I ended up doing years and years of animated voices for Seymour and the other [producers]." [106] Beck had a natural baritone which he could make gruff or smooth, perfect for his many gangster and hard bitten cop roles. Besides his radio character work he was an in-demand stentorian narrator who since early 1943 had been the long-time announcer of the thrice weekly serial *The Adventures of Superman*. Beck always recalled Bluto being his first cartoon role, but he had completely forgotten that among his endless credits he had already worked for Fleischer. He can certainly be heard in the first animated Superman episode from 1940, and in fact he was hired at least once as a Bluto voice for a pre-Miami Fleischer cartoon: back in 1937 Beck played the teenage Bluto for a flashback scene in the Popeye cartoon *The Football Toucher Downer*.

As already noted, the first Famous Popeye cartoon to feature the vocal triumvirate of Jackson Beck, Jack Mercer and Mae Questel was *The Anvil Chorus Girl* (1944). Beck's Bluto was a terrific gruff bully voice, and he was instantly a perfect fit as the dialogue became wittier in some of the mid-forties cartoons. The team of Mercer-Questel-Beck was the most prolific trio of East Coast voice artists in the forties and early fifties. But for the first two years, with Mercer in the armed forces, Questel and Beck mostly recorded either alone or as a duo.

America had entered World War II a year before Mercer was drafted in January 1943. He enlisted in mid-July, was inducted and left for training camp on August 3rd. Mercer's draft notice meant he was essentially in the Army by the time other staff members were still moving back to New York from Florida. With pre-recording of voices now an East Coast cartoon norm ("from sometime in 1940" [107] according to Dave Tendlar), Mercer had already recorded dialogue in Miami for cartoons which the staff completed once the studio was up and running in Manhattan.

While Mercer underwent basic training at Camp Edwards in Massachusetts, he recorded new material for Famous Studios whenever he could obtain a leave pass. A December 23rd Christmas letter from Sam Buchwald asks Mercer when he "will next be in town," adding, "Let me know and I will try to arrange a recording date, if you are in the mood. We have two Popeyes that could be recorded at the one session." [108] Mercer continued recording dialogue into early 1944 until his troop shipped overseas.

By the forties, animation dialogue was routinely recorded at least a year before a cartoon was finished and ready for theatrical release. This meant that, during his time away, Jack Mercer's pre-recorded Popeye voice was heard in a dozen shorts, from *Cartoons Ain't Human* released in September 1943 until *Tops in the Big Top* released in March 1945.

While Mercer was in Germany, stationed on the Elbe River in a gun division, [109] Popeye production continued apace at Famous. It was at this point that Mercer's eighteen-month absence became audibly apparent. The next twelve Popeyes, from *Shape Ahoy* released in April 1945 to *Abusement Park* released in April 1947, required another two years of Popeye recording sessions. Because dialogue tracks for these twelve cartoons were recorded with Mercer half a world away, the sailor's voice consisted of a hodgepodge of different fill-ins.

Popeye's lines were apparently voiced by at least three male replacements. It is currently impossible to determine who was who and what dialogue was recorded exactly when, because crucial Paramount studio recording logs containing dates and personnel, production numbers and talent payment slips haven't surfaced.

Mae Questel claimed she spoke for Popeye because the sound cutter managed to pitch her high voice to a "sped down" setting to pass for a male tonality. In 1989 she told the *New York Times*, "In World War II when Jack Mercer was in the service, someone dressed as Popeye was hired to fill in for [Popeye's voice] and was brought into the RCA studio, but he got mic fright so I stepped in and did the voice for Popeye." [110] She also mentioned this anecdote on a couple of TV shows, demonstrating her gruff attempt at the Popeye voice on *The Mike Douglas Show* and to Leonard Maltin on *Entertainment Tonight*. [111] It was an impressive trick, especially for a woman of her advancing age, but it still didn't sound too much like Popeye. If indeed they used her stuff, it is most likely her re-equalized voice in the first of the problem-Popeyes, *Shape Ahoy* (1945), and a slight chance she is reading Popeye lines in *Peep in the Deep* (1946).

Jack Mercer told historian Michael Barrier, "They said that [Floyd] Buckley, some guy who did it on radio years and years ago, might have done one or two. I did a lot of [dialogue lines] while I was still in Camp Edwards, on leave." [112] Adding to the confusion: some of these 1946 Popeyes contain lines that are recognizably Mercer's voice. This is obvious in parts of *Rocket to Mars* and *Rodeo Romeo*. In *The Fistic Mystic* Harry Foster Welch is doing his okay-but-not-great Popeye, then we hear some lines by Mercer. Similarly *The Island Fling* has a poor replacement, most likely Welch again, and one line by Mercer. No doubt this was because extra pickup lines added in post-production on almost finished Popeye shorts were scheduled once Mercer was back in town. He was officially discharged from the Army on October 21, 1945 so there was plenty of time for him to do post-recording for a few cartoons which weren't scheduled for release until 1946.

Whatever the case, Mercer simply couldn't and wouldn't hazard a guess as to just who did the various fill-ins, and all he could say thirty years later was, "I don't know who the heck did any of them, or whether they used repeat dialogue from old pictures, or what." [113]

A final poor Popeye voice is used in *Abusement Park* (1947) and then Mercer was back in town as a full-time civilian voice man. His first all new Popeye was *I'll Be Skiing Ya* (1947). Once Mercer returned he re-joined the Famous story department, along with recording new voice tracks, finally standing alongside his Popeye co-stars in the sound studio.

Jackson Beck hit it off immediately with Mercer and spoke glowingly of him for years afterward, considering him "a genius at the craft of voices." [114] The always confident Beck occasionally chided his co-star for being too naturally reticent to ever ask for any raises or seek more recognition for being *the* great Popeye voice. But Mercer, who always had a mild and moderate disposition, was happy to remain relatively anonymous as the one and only screen Popeye from his 1945 return to civilian life and all the way to Hanna-Barbera's 1978 TV version, as well as for record albums and licensed commercials.

Unlike the situation in Miami a few years earlier, the Famous directors could now have the pick of Broadway and radio talent.

Kneitel and Sparber sometimes hired dramatic actors for straight narration of the fairy tale-style single entries. Examples included resonant voices like Ed Begley reading the story of *Leprechaun's Gold* (1949); other top radio actors and announcers narrated some of the new travelogue spoofs. Charles Irving described *The Funshine State* (1949) while the mellifluous tones of Ken Roberts supplied commentary for *Madhattan Island* (1947). The Popeyes to one side, throughout the forties Famous Studio's new Noveltoons introduced several fresh characters, each one of which relied on a unique and memorable voice.

The first new series, replacing the Superman theatricals, was Little Lulu. It was based on Marge Buell's panel character, a stoic yet slyly mischievous young girl. Cecil Roy, the New York radio actress known as "the Girl of a Thousand Voices: from Newborn to Ninety,"[115] was cast as the childlike voice of Lulu. Born Cecile Hildegarde Roy, this talented woman, an ex-schoolteacher, had an uncanny ability to totally disguise her own vocal timbre. She could do small boy voices and she also played the roles of Lulu's mother and Mandy the house-maid, who closely resembled the regular domestic character from MGM's Tom & Jerry cartoons.

The Lulu series kicked off in Christmas 1943 with an excellent short, *Eggs Don't Bounce*, featuring a nightmare sequence aided by a catchy original spook-song, "Now You Done It, You Done, Done, Done It." Such musical numbers appeared in innumerable Famous cartoons. Often intricate and covering a wide variety of styles, they were a collaboration of master musician Winston Sharples, a longtime cartoon music expert, and a leading New York radio vocal quartet, Helen Carroll and The Satisfiers, consisting of lead singer and contractor Helen Carroll (formerly a member of The Merry Macs), backed by Bob Lange, Ted Hansen and Art "Scrappy" Lambert. [116]

In 1945 the one-shot Noveltoon *The Friendly Ghost* was released. The little boy spirit named Casper reappeared twice, in 1948's *There's Good Boos Tonight* and a year later in *A-Haunting We Will*

Go. By the time the junior ghost headlined his own series in 1950 with *Casper's Spree Under the Sea* his high, sweet voice was being provided by twelve year old professional child actor Alan Schreiber, whose stage name was Alan Shay.

Acting since the age of six, young Mr. Shay had already notched up several years of theatrical experience, including lead child roles in four Broadway plays. Interviewed years later for the Fort Lauderdale *Sun-Sentinel* Shay recalled doing about a dozen cartoons where he "uttered such memorable lines as, 'Hi, Mr. Frog, how are you?' or, 'I don't want to hurt you, I want to be your friend.'" In radio, "I was always cast as a crying orphan." [117]

Shay answered an audition to play Casper. His voice, pleasant and emotional, landed him the gig. "All you had to do was be able to read. You'd walk into the studio, they'd hand you the script and you'd go to work." He always recorded alone while the other actors, like classic radio announcer Frank Gallop, who narrated the Casper shorts, were scheduled at different sessions. "I never really knew what the thing was about until I [saw it] at the movies. I got a whopping $30 per cartoon." [118] His final Casper role was in the 1954 *Boo Ribbon Winner.* Shay enjoyed the recognition, and did other jobs like singing commercials, until his voice changed, then at seventeen he quit acting to go to college. And "that's show biz," as it was for many a child performer. Casper's later dialogue was provided by several female artists adept at realistic child voices, including Norma McMillan and Gwen Davies.

From early in the Noveltoon series the Famous team produced several shorts that were aimed more at the children's fairy tale market. *Suddenly It's Spring!* from 1944 featured youthful actress Joy Terry who eventually moved to Los Angeles (and later married Paul Frees) as the singing and dramatic voice of Raggedy Ann. Cecil Roy and Jack Mercer appeared in support roles, while the mother's dialogue was spoken by Joan Alexander, who had enacted Lois Lane in both the radio and cartoon Superman series.

As we have seen, Jack Mercer was mostly out of action for Famous Studios' first two years while serving his country overseas, which meant the cartoons weren't top heavy with his various bit voices, as was the case in the late Fleischer Miami period. Many fill-in parts were spoken at first by Mercer's story department collaborator Carl Meyer. Meyer's vocal range was similar to Mercer's for whiny and eccentric Brooklynese characters.

After making the role of Bluto his own, Jackson Beck became a virtual animation regular for the next twenty years. Beck was a standout voice actor like Hollywood's Mel Blanc. Both gave that "something extra" in their performances. Beck was a brilliant interpretive actor who gave a hundred and ten per cent to each part, no matter how tiny the role. He went far beyond his main Bluto assignment, essaying the gravel-voiced Buzzy the Crow starting with *The Stupidstitious Cat* (1947). Buzzy was based on Rochester, the sassy valet on *The Jack Benny Program*. Beck was also Little Lulu's father, a role he shared with another fine radio actor, Wendell Holmes. Essentially Beck handled any assignment he was handed, from straight narration to a range of dialect stereotypes. These ranged from French to Spanish to Irish cops, along with impressions of movie stars like Humphrey Bogart, Edward G. Robinson and Charles Boyer, and scores of other parts from one liners to leads. He even sang on occasion in Popeyes like *Vacation with Play* (1951), and for one 1949 cartoon, *The Ski's the Limit*, he was given rare on-screen credit. One character Beck voiced in 1945 was Joe the Cannibal in *Pop-Pie a La Mode*; that role would now be considered a casting no-no, but it suited Beck's rich baritone range perfectly.

Meanwhile, Famous hired expert comedy talents like the in-demand radio stooge Arnold Stang and Sid Raymond, a zany impressionist. They gave the wilder Noveltoon entries a fresh and quirky sound that was the essence of New York attitude. Stang was a favorite foil of comedy stars like Milton Berle and Henry Morgan. He voiced Shorty the sailor in a couple of Popeyes like *Moving Aweigh* (1944), and he was also cast as Blackie the sheep. Stang's longest-running Famous role, the wise-guy mouse named Herman, sounded like a scratchy, whiny combination of all the Dead End Kids rolled into one. Cartoon fans remember him for starring years later in the title role of TV's *Top Cat* for Hanna-Barbera.

Sid Raymond was a veteran comedy mimic who did stage, night-clubs and early TV sketch shows. Jackson Beck, who worked with him on many cartoons, described Raymond as "pure vaudeville." [119] Unlike some impressionists who are technically good at the voice imitations, Raymond was genuinely funny and his loud, silly voices and trademark Bert Lahr "nyong nyong!!!" sound became a familiar feature on many of the cartoons. His first Famous cartoon was *Lulu's Indoor Outing* (1944).

Raymond retained pleasant memories of the recording sessions from half a century earlier: "They were wonderful. The directors [Sparber, Kneitel, Tendlar, Waldman] were in the control room, and they could see me and I could see them. I did one line at a time, and I'd look at the director and he'd put his finger up meaning 'do one more,' and then he'd say over the loudspeaker, 'Sid, give it with more emphasis.' Then he put his hand up in a circle [meaning] 'okay.' Then I'd do the next line. If we had dialogue, the other guy, like Jackson Beck would be at the other microphone, and he would pick it up." Recalling his freedom to ad lib lines which were often used in the finished cartoon, he added, "They always liked my timing." Raymond could never understand the policy of voice actors not being given screen credit.

Starting with *Naughty But Mice* (1947) Raymond played Katnip to Stang's Herman the Mouse, and his dense feline logic produced the braindead catchphrase, "Duuuuuhhhh, that's logical." The Herman and Katnip cartoons resembled an evil cousin to Tom & Jerry, with ultra-violent gags and smartass attitude. In the fifties Raymond's most prominent character for Famous was the huge and clumsy duckling Baby Huey who debuted in *Quack A Doodle Do*

(1950). It was another in his long line of chronically dopey voices. Raymond even voiced an occasional bit part in a close imitation of cartoon veteran Pinto Colvig's Goofy voice.

These were the vocal talents comprising the basic Famous Studios stock company in its first decade. Occasionally another voice was used like the unique veteran Phil Kramer in *Robin Hood-winked* (1948), or mimics like Ward Wilson who was the likely voice of an occasional celebrity like Fred Allen in *Land of the Lost Jewels* (1950) or the Jack Benny imitation in *Our Funny Finny Friends* (1949). But mostly it was the versatile group covered to this point. As late as 1959 many of the cartoons still boasted long serving Famous voices like Jackson Beck, Sid Raymond, Jack Mercer, Cecil Roy and Gwen Davies. That year a few newer voice specialists began sharing the Noveltoon microphone into the new decade.

The newbies included accomplished nightclub voice impressionists like Bob McFadden and Will Jordan. Notably actor Allen Swift, who was the East Coast's undisputed voice-over king of commercials in this period, voiced one late fifties entry, the clever *La Petite Parade* (1959), which has become an accepted classic and a favorite of vintage cartoon lovers. Other talents began speaking for the Famous cartoons including Herb Duncan, Corinne Orr, and comedy LP star Eddie "The Old Philosopher" Lawrence. Lawrence, like Sid Raymond, had also begun his career as a movie star impressionist on radio's *Original Amateur Hour* circa 1935 under his real name of Lawrence Eisler. Various cartoon animal sounds came from the talented larynx of specialty sound imitator Frank Milano.

While Famous Studios was never in MGM's league, their character based Noveltoons - especially in the first few years - were often fast, furious and funny. The films were unpretentious entertainment that did their job, until, like all the Famous series, they began to resemble earlier cartoons and they quickly became unimaginative and repetitive. Plots, formulas and gags were recycled. Certainly the Casper entries were from the start virtual clones of each other with mechanically formulaic gags, like the endlessly identical reactions of everyone with whom the ghost came in contact, invariably shrieking "A g-g-g-g-ghost!!!" Similarly, many of the Little Audrey cartoons ended with the young girl simply collapsing into a laughing jag in lieu of a clever comic punchline.

The problem with later period Famous was that the studio's animators, a skilled and talented group of animation artists including Marty Taras and Johnny Gentilella, were themselves vastly better than what they had to churn out year after year.

Before his low budgeted TV cartoons kicked off in 1960, Popeye's mid-fifties Famous theatricals had also lost much of the "vim, vigor and vitality" they exhibited in the forties. The once mighty sailor man's final cinema entry was the pedestrian *Spooky Swabs* released in 1957. To be fair some late fifties Famous entries still showed sparks of energy and originality. Occasional entries benefitted from offbeat and inventive story material written by newer talents like animator-gag specialist Irv Spector, who came up with amusing one shot cartoon ideas like *Chew Chew Baby* (1958).

The Famous Studios theatrical schedule settled into a pattern for their final decade, with the long-running Noveltoons eventually joined by a sister series called Modern Madcaps. Cost-cutting techniques meant that the full animation of the mid-forties inexorably gave way to a New York version of UPA's representational style and these late era Paramount releases soon resembled the various made-for-TV cartoons which began taking off from 1958. While the releases of 1959 still benefitted from voice artists who had begun with Famous sixteen years earlier, it was a time of imminent change: 1959 was the final year to feature long-established star characters like Baby Huey, Casper the Friendly Ghost and the team of Herman and Katnip.

We now reach the end of the East Coast classic period covered by this book. The original aim was to cover just the Fleischer studio's voices, but the early Famous period was an inevitable part of the continuum. It is a source of considerable frustration that Hames Ware and I were not able to learn more about the uncredited Famous Studios voices. Hopefully I can eventually source key Paramount production and sound department documents for the Famous years. If so, a fuller chapter on the excellent voice roster covering the complete studio run spanning 1943-67, with extra identifications for various frustrating "unknowns," will be the first item for a revised edition of this book. And of course if anyone knows of a Terrytoons paper collection archive with sound department data, please reach out.

To conclude this still-inconclusive survey of Golden Age New York cartoon voices I append the following checklists of people who we either know for certain, or suspect, did voice work for East Coast animation houses.

FLEISCHER STUDIOS Cartoon Voices, 1929-42

Joan Alexander, Donald Bain, Bradley Barker, Dave Barry Siegel (a Bluto voice, Stone Age series), Arthur Boran, Bruce "Cookie" Bowers, Henry Boyd, Floyd Buckley?, Charles Carver (bass singer, circa 1932), Everett Clark (singer - voice of Grampy), Wallace Clark & the Debonairs (vocal quartet), Clayton "Bud" Collyer, Pinto Colvig (from 5-12-39 to 8-15-41, as Bluto, etc.), Billy Costello, Gwen Davies, Jimmy Donnelly, Leo Donnelly, Jessica Dragonette, Carlyle Ellis, Bernie Fleischer (child voice), Lou Fleischer, The Four Marshals (quartet), Stan Freed, Kenny Gardner, Dolores Gillen, Margie Hines (Betty Boop, 1930-32 & Betty and Olive Oyl, 1938-43), Cal Howard (1939-41), Hamp Howard (studio publicity director), Arthur Kay, Harriet Lee (Betty Boop once, in 1931), Ann Belle Little (Betty Boop, in 1933 & 1938), Pauline Loth, George Lowther, Rose Marie (voice of Sally Swing), Frank Matalone, Poley McClintock, Jack Mercer, Carl "Mike" Meyer, Billy Murray, Joe Oriolo, Sam Parker, William Pennell, Madeline Pierce, Ted Pierce (1939-41),

Bonnie Poe (Betty Boop, 1933 & 1938), Purves Pullen, Mae Questel (Betty Boop and Olive Oyl, 1931-38, 1943-61), Claude Rees & The Elm City Four (Quartet), Alice Remsen, Frances Reynolds (voice of Pudgy), Grant Richards (*Superman* opening narrator?), Johnny Rogers (boy singer), David Ross (radio announcer, in some Color Classics), Lanny Ross, The Royal Guards (quartet), Lee Royce (a Superman and Bluto voice), Walter Scanlon, Monroe Silver?, Rosalie Waldman, Gus Wicke & his quartet (Fred Bishop, Jerry White, Frank Bessinger), Gwen Williams, Kate Wright (a post-1934 Betty Boop?), The Three X Sisters (Pearl & Vi Hamilton, Jess Fordyce: sang for Color Classics including *The Little Stranger*, Betty Boop cartoons [close harmony, character singing], 1933 Screen Song *Sing, Sisters, Sing*), Lou Zukor

FAMOUS STUDIOS Cartoon Voices, 1943-60

Joan Alexander, Dayton Allen, Dave Barry, Jackson Beck, Ed Begley, Larry Best, Helen Carroll & the Satisfiers: Helen Carroll [leader], Bob Lange, Ted Hansen & Art Lambert (the vocal group in Little Lulu & Screen Songs), Clayton "Bud" Collyer, Bill Dana, Gwen Davies, Herb Duncan, Michael Fitzmaurice, Frank Gallop, Hermione Gingold, Valerie Harper, Margie Hines, Wendell Holmes, Charles Irving, Will Jordan, Phil Kramer, Eddie Lawrence, Shari Lewis, Gilbert Mack, George Mathews, Bob McFadden, Norma McMillan, Jack Mercer, Carl Meyer, Frank Milano, Mae Questel, Sid Raymond, Ken Roberts, Cecil Roy, Lee Royce, Alan Shay (Casper), Arnold Stang, Joy Terry, Cal Tinney, Harry Foster Welch, Ward Wilson

TERRYTOONS: Known Cartoon Voices, 1930-60s

Dayton Allen (comedian and impressionist: Heckle and Jeckle, Deputy Dawg Voices, various impressions), Bern Bennett, John Gurney (basso vocalist), Roy Halee (lead tenor) & his Quartet, Roy Halee (Mighty Mouse's operatic singing voice), Margie Hines, Boris Karloff (once), Arthur Kay (prolific impressionist in late thirties-early forties Terrytoons, notably voice of Gandy Goose), Bob McFadden, Norma McMillan, Jo Miller (Terrytoons cartoon *The Wolf's Side of the Story*, 1938 or *A Wolf's Tale*, 1944 / *The Wolf's Pardon*, 1947), Tom Morrison (long-time studio employee, who did Mighty Mouse speaking, Little Roquefort, Sourpuss, Percy the cat, Dimwit the dog, one of the Terry Bears), Douglas Moye (studio camera operator who played the Terry Bears' father and other roles), John Myhers (Hector Heathcoat), Philip Scheib (Terrytoons musical director; played the other Terry Bear, various voices in the thirties), Judy Stahr (voice of Nancy), Allen Swift, Patricia Terry (Paul Terry's daughter: she was ten in September 1939, when her mother Irma confirmed she did child voices for her father's cartoons), Lionel Wilson (Tom Terrific) **Unconfirmed:** Bill Beach, Arthur Elmer (voice impersonator), Trudy Gale, Dolores Gillen, Owen Jordan, Athena Lorde, Danny Merrill, Bryna Raeburn. Each of these radio artists claimed "Cartoons" in mid-forties New York radio casting books, and are thus contenders for both Paramount and Terrytoons. The research continues....

CODA: Cartoon Voice Actors migrate to Television

As animation's great theatrical era inexorably wound down in the early sixties, the new television cartoons reigned supreme. They were a different type of cartoon, highly cost conscious and done to the new "planned animation" formula: endless close ups of two heads conversing back and forth, eye blinks, single body parts moving, overused walk and run cycles, endlessly repeated backgrounds, canned music. It was recognized from the outset that dialogue, and lots of it, would be what kept the audience interested. Ideally, the dialogue would be clever, and the voices had to be unique and funny. And so cartoons became far more voice driven than they ever were in the theatricals. And for the first few years the dialogue was indeed good.

For several voice actors covered in this book, TV cartoons were the greatest gig of them all. It was virtually like returning to their dear, dead medium of radio. Talk, talk and more talk. Unlimited opportunities to create funny voices. This was what these actors trained themselves for, and it was what they thrived on. If the dialogue was witty and attracted an adult following along with the targeted kiddie audience, all the better. Early writers like Charles Shows, Michael Maltese and Warren Foster were soon providing funny and subtle scripts.

For the first couple of years Daws Butler, Don Messick and a few others like Julie Bennett had it almost to themselves as Hanna-Barbera established the basic made-for-TV form. With the debut of *Huckleberry Hound* in 1958, Butler became the undisputed king of TV cartoon voices, in the same way Mel Blanc had so dominated the theatricals. His lead characters (like Huck, Yogi, Mr. Jinks, Quick

Draw and Snagglepuss) were as vocally memorable as any of the older cartoon stars. Most importantly, from *Huckleberry* onwards the television voice artists were given on-screen credit! Youngsters from the first TV generation grew up actually knowing the voice actors' names, after daily exposure to each series' end titles. With seasonal continuity of work, plus big companies like Kellogg's paying the bills and a guarantee of twenty six episodes per series, this certainly seemed like paradise for freelance specialty voices. And as the cherry on top, residual fees were paid for the first few reruns. That never happened with the theatricals.

Butler and Messick were soon joined by Jay Ward's excellent stock company: June Foray, Paul Frees, Walter Tetley, Hans Conried and Bill Scott. Then the floodgates opened: UPA, Hal Seeger, Total Television, Pantomime Pictures, Format, Filmation and other studios joined the Hanna-Barbera bandwagon. In 1960 when cartoons went primetime with *The Flintstones* not only radio big-timers like Alan Reed but the great Mel Blanc himself joined television's vocal ranks.

From that point animation acting was a wide open field, and the list of voice specialists swelled from a handful of reliable old pros to a very long list indeed. TV cartoons mushroomed in the late sixties and as the sheer quantity of writing increased the quality inevitably dropped. After a few years, the TV cartoon treadmill was being perceived even by its practitioners as an industry akin to a Detroit auto assembly line.

Several actors who dominated early theatricals didn't make it to the in-crowd of TV cartoon voices. Perhaps it was their age, but Martha Wentworth, Billy Bletcher, Pinto Colvig, Pat McGeehan and others were conspicuously missing from tele-animation casting. Bill Thompson did a handful (remember *Touche Turtle?*) but he was easing away from performing and entering the business world. A now older Stan Freberg was far too busy with his successful ad agency Freberg Limited, although he hired various talents for his radio and TV spots.

Vocal groups like the Sportsmen Quartet and the Mello Men now relied on endless commercial jingles for a living; TV cartoon shows used vocal ensembles only once for their opening-closing theme songs (The Rhythmaires and the Randy Van Horn singers handled many of these). Meanwhile the vibrant full orchestras from the theatrical days were now a distant memory; their TV offspring either used Capitol's licensed cues for background music, or commissioned tracking libraries composed by talented musicians like Hoyt Curtin.

A few actors who had done theatricals didn't last long in TV cartoons. Jerry Mann only did some season One *Flintstones* while Jerry Hausner worked in UPA's decidedly inferior 130 *Magoo* and 130 *Dick Tracy* TV episodes. Jack Mercer was super busy on the East Coast as every voice in 260 threadbare new Trans-Lux *Felix the Cat* cartoons. He, along with Mae Questel and Jackson Beck, toiled on an additional 220 el-cheapo *Popeye* cartoons for King Features TV. A fresh group of actors began auditioning for Hanna-Barbera, and newly appointed voice directors began expanding the available talent pool. Many sixties cartoons were being voiced by actors who had never done a theatrical, like Doug Young, John Stephenson, Allan Melvin, Jean Vanderpyl and Harvey Korman.

It is beyond this book's Golden Age brief to do a historical study of voices from the TV cartoon dynasty. Suffice to say the vocal torch had been well and truly passed, and the theatrical shorts came to their sad but expected end in the seventies. A new age had dawned, and with it a new animation epoch.

NOTES / BIBLIOGRAPHY

This book's topic is one of the least documented in film studies. The author's initial research was sparked by recognizing many animation voice artists from their work in old-time radio, starting in 1972. It became a serious study in 1990. After I teamed with the late Hames Ware in 1994, we pooled our research and decided to write a book on the topic. Assisted by Hames's long-time research associate Graham Webb in England, our earliest sources were our collections of audio tapes containing 30,000 Golden Age radio broadcasts, along with personal correspondence with top Golden Age voice artists including Daws Butler, June Foray, Paul Frees, Billy Bletcher and Bill Scott.

Over a three-year period, I was able to create reference audio of virtually all theatrical cartoons from 1930-60, by extracting just their spoken word portions and matching many voices to radio shows and movie soundtracks (remember, we're talking the analog era!).

Animation historians generously loaned transcripts of over one hundred key interviews with veteran cartoon studio personnel (directors, story artists and voice actors, all now deceased). My principal debt regarding interview transcripts is to historian and animation scholar Michael Barrier, whose generosity was truly boundless.

Once these methods were exhausted, I undertook primary research at various repositories: USC's Cinema-TV Library, UCLA's Arts-Special Collections Library, the clubroom of Pacific Pioneer Broadcasters, the Margaret Herrick Library at the Center for Motion Picture Studies, Walt Disney Archives (just in time, before it was ordered off-limits to freelance researchers), and the Billy Rose Theatre Collection's clipping files, New York Public Library at Lincoln Centre. Each of these institutions yielded obscure but helpful documents including sound department reports, casting file cards, music department payroll records, vintage articles from clipping files, and inter-studio correspondence.

Key industry casting publications were *The Academy Players Directory* and *National Radio Artists Directory*. Since the advent of online search engines, historians have access to Newspapers.com, and computer literate cartoon buffs (in particular the indefatigable Don M. Yowp) have unearthed even more long-buried confirmation of certain voices.

Chapter 1: WARNER BROS. Cartoon Voices

Jack L. Warner paper collection, Warner Bros. Archive, USC Special Collections: Actor File Card Index, 1940 to 1960s in Doheny Library; Music Department payroll files housed in Annex building (Music cue sheets; cartoon notes, 1942-49: dialogue session dates & fees; extra talent requisitions), Leon Schlesinger material [courtesy Ned Comstock, Stuart Ng, Leith Adams, Noelle Carter]). Author on-site research: USC, School of Cinema-Television library (March 1997, January 1999), Warner Annex (June 2002, May 2004).

Interview transcripts: Rudolph Ising and Bob Clampett, Carman G. Maxwell, Fred MacAlpin, Hugh Harman and Bob Clampett, Hugh Harman & Rudolf Ising with Bob Clampett, Friz Freleng, Bob McKimson, Chuck Jones, Virgil Ross, Tex Avery, Bernard Brown and Bob Clampett, Treg Brown and Bob Clampett, Michael Sasanoff, Frank Tashlin, Carl Stalling, Lloyd Turner, Michael Maltese, Bill Scott, Arthur Davis, Bill Melendez, Norman McCabe, Don Christensen, Nelson Demorest, Mel Blanc, Billy Bletcher, Daws Butler, Robert Bruce.

In-house journals: *The Inbetweener* (1938-40, courtesy Martha Sigall, copies via Mark Kausler); *Warner Club News* (copies courtesy Ned Comstock, USC).

1. Ray Pointer, *The Art and Inventions of Max Fleischer, American Animation Pioneer* (North Carolina: McFarland, 2017), p. 59. David Gerstein, email to author, 29 January 2022. Gerstein undertook further research on this remake that Ray Pointer was the first to mention. Gerstein notes there is more to discover, but concluded, "A large number of [so-called] Song Car-Tunes are actually 'Popular Song Parodies,' a rival bouncing ball series Alfred Weiss produced before his team up with Fleischer."

2. Rudolf Ising interview with Michael Barrier, Milton Gray & Mark Kausler (Bob Clampett sat in), 2 June 1971. Hugh Harman interview with Michael Barrier & Mark Kausler (Bob Clampett sat in), 3 December 1973.

3. Ising 1971 interview. Harman 1973 interview. In the Harman interview Bob Clampett recalled that in the first year of Looney Tunes, when Harman and Ising were pre-recording dialogue, Disney still recorded dialogue, effects and music, everything "all at once." Harman responded, "When we were working on our first experimental reel, *Bosko the Talkink Kid*, the head of Disney's inking department - she was his sister-in-law, Hazel Sewell - came over to our studio, and she said, 'It's the oddest thing in the world, Walt is disparaging your pushing this talking thing. He doesn't think talking will be worth a thing in cartoons, ever. He's ridiculing it.'" Disney's cartoons were notably lighter on dialogue than the Warner cartoons, for at least two years.

4. Leith Adams to author, Warner Bros. Studio, Burbank (Martha Sigall also present), 29 June 2001.

5. Ibid. In June 2002 Leith Adams was primarily responsible for my locating and researching the cartoon dialogue and music recording reports (covering the years 1942-49) included in the Warner Bros. collection housed at USC.

6. Steve Schneider, *That's All Folks! The Art of Warner Bros. Animation* (New York: Henry Holt, 1988), p. 35.

7. Pinto Colvig Paramount Pictures studio biography, 10 October 1939. Tom Klein, "Bolivar the Ostrich Outspoken," online at Cartoonresearch.com, 21 January 2017. "Cartoon Film Demands Increased Productions," *The Billboard*, 12 July 1930.
8. Ibid. Hugh Harman interview, 1973.
9. Ising interview with Barrier & Milton Gray (Bob Clampett sat in), 30 November 1973. Harman and Ising joint interview with Barrier & Gray (Bob Clampett sat in), 29 October 1976.
10. James R. Silke, *You Must Remember This: Fifty Years of Fighting, Working and Dreaming at Warner Bros.* (Boston: Little, Brown, 1976). The Harms-Remick-Witmark purchase was also noted in Clive Hirschorn, *The Warner Bros. Story* (London: Octopus Books, 1979), mentioning that the acquisition gave them $100 million worth of music for use in films.
11. C. G. Maxwell interview with Milton Gray, 6 April 1977.
12. John Scott, "Depression Weathered Nicely," *Los Angeles Times*, 7 December 1930. An earlier article, "How Funny Loony [sic] Tunes are Made," 25 June 1930, appeared in a special *Variety* issue celebrating the Warner brothers' 25th anniversary in the entertainment business.
13. Harman & Ising joint interview, 1976.
14. Maxwell interview.
15. Ising interview 1973. Harman interview 1973.
16. Ising interview, 1973.
17. Maxwell interview.
18. Fred MacAlpin interview with Michael Barrier, 15 January 1979.
19. Ising interviews, 1971 and 1973.
20. Marguerite Tazelaar, "Animated Cartoons in Person," *New York Herald Tribune*, 1 March 1931.
21. Ising 1971 & 1973 interviews. Harman & Ising joint interview 31 October 1976.
22. Ising interview 1971.

23. Bob Clampett 1969 interview with Michael Barrier and Milton Gray.

24. *Herald-Tribune*, Frank Marsales article.

25. Jonathan T. Caldwell, "And Now Bosko is Dancing," *The American Dancer*, March 1932. Ising interview, 1973. Harman interview, 1973.

26. Will Friedwald, "Hugh Harman at Cinecon" 30 August 1980, published in *Animania* No. 22, 1981.

27. Harman interview, 1973.

28. Maxwell interview.

29. Scott Bradley interview, 11 March 1977.

30. Ising interviews, 1971 & 1973.

31. MacAlpin interview.

32. Ibid.

33. Ibid

34. Maxwell interview.

35. *Herald-Tribune*, Drummer's sound kit report.

36. Leon Schlesinger quoted in *Hollywood* magazine, December 1936.

37. Friz Freleng telephone interview with author, Hollywood-Sydney, March 1994.

38. MacAlpin interview.

39. Ising on Marsales, 1973.

40. Ising interview, 1971.

41. Page Cook, "Ken Darby career article," *Films in Review*, Vol. XX, No. 6, June-July 1969, pp. 335-356. "Biography of Ken Darby" (autobiographical career profile), 10 June 1974. This document notes the radio show from which Rudolf Ising and Frank Marsales hired the early Merrie Melodies voices: "Franco Hi-Jinks & Staff Artists, KFWB Hollywood, 1931-32-33-34."

42. Ising interview, 1971.

43. Harman and Ising joint interview, 1976.

44. Ibid.

45. Ising interview 1971.

46. Leon Schlesinger quote, *Hollywood* magazine, December 1936.

47. Ising 1971.

48. Ibid. Introduction to Art Scott interview, *Walt's People*, Volume 9 (Xlibris Publishing)

49. MacAlpin interview.

50. Harman, 1973 interview.

51. Bob Clampett, 1 June 1979 interview.

52. Harman, in 1976 interview.

53. Harman, 1973 interview.

54. Harman & Ising interviews, 1973, 1971.

55. MacAlpin interview.

56. Bob Clampett. Clampett's files included detailed drawings he made of the Warner Bros. Sunset Boulevard lot and the Schlesinger cartoon studio's buildings at various times between 1933-41.

57. Bernard B. Brown interview with Michael Barrier (Bob Clampett sat in), 28 November 1973. Brown unsigned newspaper feature, *Toronto Globe and Mail*, 24 May 1980.

58. Friz Freleng, Joe Adamson interview, 1969.

59. Bob Clampett interview, 30 April 1972.

60. Friz Freleng, interview with Jerry Beck, 2 August 1988. Published in *Animato!* No. 18, Spring 1989.

61. Michael Mallory, "Arthur Davis," *Comics Scene*, No. 13 (undated, circa 1985).

62. Bernard Brown, 1973 interview.

63. Bob Clampett, in Brown interview.

64. Brown interview.

65. Norman McCabe, interview with Milton Gray, 8 December 1976.

66. Philip K. Scheuer, "Nasty Little Jane Withers Has to Be Nice," *Los Angeles Times*, 7 July 1935.

67. Bob Clampett, Bernard Brown interview, 1973. Schlesinger on Jane Withers, *Hollywood Magazine*, December 1936.

(On a 1978 TV coast-to-coast appearance themed around commercial actors, Jane Withers, in Burbank, spoke to Mae Questel in New York, and noted that when she did voices in Looney Tunes, she sought out Betty Boop cartoons for tips on vocal delivery.)

68. Clampett, Bernard Brown interview.

69. In a letter to Hames Ware, Clampett clarified that Jack Carr "joined us at Schlesinger's in late 1933 and used to leave his animation desk to go over and do some voices. He did do the voice of Buddy after he arrived." 8 August 1972. In an earlier letter to Hames Ware dated 16 March 1972 he wrote: "I'm going to call Jack Carr for you, since he did some voices for us at Leon's in the 1933, 34 era and I will double check which ones." Carr was ill and died in early 1974 so the contact with Clampett didn't happen (unreliable online sources note Carr's death in 1967, but they appear to be conflating the animator with an actor of the same name). Bob Clampett, letter to Graham Webb, 19 August 1972. Jack Kinney recalled King "had a very high, funny voice...kind of nasal." Kinney interview with Michael Barrier, 28 November 1973.

70. Bob Clampett TV interview (mid-1950s), included on DVD "Bob Clampett's Beany and Cecil, The Special Edition," 1999.

71. Martha Sigall to author, 29 June 2001.

72. Donald Hayworth, "A One-Man Menagerie [Purv Pullen]," Screen & Radio Weekly (undated, circa 1935), p. 14. The article notes recent feature films with Pullen's "sound effects and animal calls [include] Sequoia, Jalna, The Crusades, Tarzan and His Mate, and he has worked with Walt Disney, Aesop's Fables [Van Beuren], Leon Schlesinger and Betty Boop [Fleischer]." Because Pullen was contracted to Ben Bernie's touring show he was one of the rare cartoon voice talents who worked animation jobs on both Coasts.

73. Film Daily, March 1935.

74. Friz Freleng telephone interview with author, March 1994.

75. Friz Freleng interview with Reg Hartt, Toronto, 1980.

76. Tex Avery, interview with Milton Gray, 18 February 1977.

77. Philip K. Scheuer, "Business of Ghosting Now Hollywood's Oddest," *Los Angeles Times*, 21 April 1935. "Ghosting" was a sound department expression which referred to dubbing voices onto film, such as off-screen narration or cartoon characters; replacing an actor's voice with another voice by matching lip-synch while watching playback; or a pre-recorded singing voice which was mimed by a non-singing actor to an audio playback, during live action photography.

78. Treg Brown, interview with Michael Barrier (Bob Clampett sits in), 20 January 1979.

79. Avery, interview with Gray. Tom Klein, "Apprenticing the Master: Tex Avery at Universal, 1929-1935," *Animation Journal*, Fall 1997, p.14-15. Cal Howard, interview with Michael Barrier, 1 November 1976.

80. Tex Avery interview with Joe Adamson, *Tex Avery, King of Cartoons* (New York: Popular Library, 1975). The run-down building Avery first occupied was the one famously nicknamed "Termite Terrace," but he and his crew were only there for about a year. In 1936 Avery's unit moved to the main building on the Sunset Boulevard studio lot. Virtually every reference to Warner Bros. cartoons mistakenly names the entire cartoon studio Termite Terrace, even referring to it by that name in the fifties after the studio relocated to Burbank.

81. Ibid.

82. Chuck Jones to author in Sydney, March 1990.

83. Billy Bletcher, interview with Michael Barrier & Milton Gray, 7 June 1969. Audiotape.

84. Bob Clampett letter to Hames Ware, 1972.

85. Tralfaz blogspot, 3 April 2012, "The Bernice Hansen [sic] Mystery Solved" (cited are *Associated Press*, April 1936; Alice

L. Tidesley, Ledger Syndicate - *Baltimore Sun*, 20 June 1937; "Mickey Mouse's 'Voice' in Court," United Press, unsigned, December 1934 (this article named her Berneice Hansell).

86. Hames Ware letter to author, 1996.

87. Friz Freleng, interview with Joe Adamson, UCLA Oral History Project, 28 July 1968-26 June 1969. Freleng, interview with Reg Hartt, Toronto, 1980.

88. Bob Clampett interview, 30 April 1972.

89. Friz Freleng to Adamson. Clampett interview, 1972.

90. *N. Y. Herald Tribune*, "Count Cutelli, Sound Effects Expert Is Dead," 17 July 1944 (unsigned). *Variety* obituary, 19 July 1944: "Cutelli was probably best known for his Porky sound effects in Leon Schlesinger's Looney Tunes."

91. Schlesinger's autographed photo (flanked by two superimposed images of Porky Pig) is dated 2 November 1937. The photo was part of a printed program which Cutelli gave out at a live performance entitled "The Sound Effects Department." Cutelli was also responsible for inventing mechanical devices to be used for reproducing sound effects of all kinds, from explosions and battles to an avalanche and a quiet river. Vocally he demonstrated "various imitations of fowl and animals." The autographed photo is intriguing because its date is several months after Mel Blanc had taken over Porky's voice, indicating Cutelli was still doing vocal noises for some cartoon tracks.

92. "Cartoons Kidding Stars Hit by Crosby Action," *Hollywood Reporter*, 5 August 1936.

93. Paul Harrison, syndicated entertainment column, *National Enterprise Assoc. Service Inc.*, 3 July 1937.

94. Frank Tashlin interview with Michael Barrier, 29 May 1971. In 1969 at a Hollywood tribute screening of his cartoons Tashlin told Hames Ware that he truly wished he could recall some of the voices he had hired thirty years earlier, noting, "I can see

them all in my mind's eye, I just can't remember their names."
Hames Ware phone call to author, 1995.
95. Bob Clampett telephone interview with Hames Ware, 6 February 1972.
96. Schneider, *That's All Folks!*, p. 56-57.
97. Michael Barrier, "The Moving Drawing Speaks," *Funnyworld* No. 18, 1978, p. 18.
98. Ronald L. Smith, *Who's Who in Comedy* (New York: Facts on File, 1992), p. 54 ("On the Warner Bros. lot, [Mel Blanc] first turned up in the 1930s as a violinist in their music department.") Blanc had been musically trained as a child, his instruments being violin, tuba and sousaphone.
99. Friz Freleng, interview with Joe Adamson, 1968-69.
100. Treg Brown interview, 1979.
101. Tex Avery, interview with Gray, 18 February 1977.
102. Bob Clampett telephone interview with Barrier, 8 June 1979.
103. Bob Clampett, Animafeastival Toronto, Summer 1979.
104. Treg Brown interview.
105. Ibid.
106. Ibid.
107. Tex Avery at Chapman College, 17 August 1974.
108. Friz Freleng, interview with Reg Hartt, Toronto 1980.
109. Bob Clampett, interview with Walter C. Brasch, 18 June 1975.
110. Bob Clampett interview, Animafeastival, Toronto, Summer 1979.
111. Mel Blanc, interview with Michael Barrier, Milton Gray 4 June 1969.
112. Dave Barry to author, Pacific Pioneer Broadcasters, Hollywood 5 January 1995. Barry, guest speaker, SPERDVAC Presents, Encino 28 July 1995.
113. Bob Clampett interview, 6 June 1969.
114. Bob Clampett's son Rob located a dialogue script for *Porky in Egypt* indicating "Camel Mad Scene." On the back of the page

was a list in Clampett's hand of various movie and radio names who Dave Weber imitated in a voice audition for this cartoon. In an email to the author he quoted from the page: "[Edward G.] Robinson, [Fred] Allen, [Joe] Penner, Lionel Barrymore, [Eddie] Cantor, The Mad Russian, Parkyakarkus, Boake Carter [radio newscaster], Ed Wynn, [Jimmy] Durante, and then at the bottom the name Weber was circled." This indicates Bob Clampett's final decision to use Weber's straight voice, which he deemed more effective for the camel's crazed hallucination scene rather than the potential distraction of a well-known celebrity imitation. Rob Clampett, email to author, 31 July 2002.

115. Bob Clampett, telephone interview with Hames Ware, 6 February 1972.

116. Carl Stalling, interview with Michael Barrier and Bill Spicer, June 1969. Published in *Funnyworld* No. 13.

117. Leroy Hurte, letter to author, 25 July 1999.

118. Tashlin, interview with Barrier.

119. Thurl Ravenscroft, November 1995 telephone interview with author and follow-up letter to author, December 24, 1995.

120. Ibid.

121. Carl Stalling, interview with Barrier, 1969.

122. Treg Brown interview.

123. Friz Freleng with David Weber, *Animation: The Art of Friz Freleng* (Newport Beach: Donovan Publishing, 1994), p. 100.

124. Ibid. p. 97: "That was Tex Avery's voice. He sang this, but he had no sense of rhythm. I'd beat out the rhythm for him, and he'd get way off, and I shook the dressing room and said now you've got the rhythm, so sing to that rhythm. He never got it. So we used it just as it was. I guess it was funny, after all it wasn't *supposed* to be good singing."

125. Tim Onosko, "Bob Clampett: Cartoonist," *The Velvet Light Trap* No. 15, 1975.

126. Chuck Jones to author, Sydney May 1990.

127. Robert Bruce, interview with Michael Barrier, 25 June 1990. Bruce, telephone interview with author December 1994 and follow-up letter, 3 January 1995. In Bruce, Audio-cassette biography: *Life as a Third Banana*, he discusses being a member of the KFWB stock company (including Arthur Q. Bryan and Jack Lescoulie), which led directly to his doing cartoons.

128. Bob Clampett letter to Hames Ware, 15 March 1974.

129. Chuck Jones, *Chuck Amuck: The* (New York: Farrar-Straus-Giroux, 1989).

130. Avery

131. Avery interview with Gray, 27 April 1977.

132. Chuck Jones, telephone interview with author, March 1995. Letter to author, 28 February 1996.

133. Robert McKimson, interview with Michael Barrier, 28 May 1971.

134. Bob Clampett, 31 October 1976 interview.

135. Carl Stalling document courtesy Daniel Goldmark, 1997.

136. Pinto Colvig paper collection (25 June 1938 letter to Fred Strang), Southern Oregon Historical Society.

137. Cal Howard, interview with Barrier, 1 November 1976.

138. Avery interview with Gray, April 1977.

139. Rhys Talbot, interview with author, Burbank, 26 April 2007. Talbot noted that his mother kept payment stubs from Lantz and Schlesinger engagements as a reminder of her days as a performer. Chuck Jones couldn't recall the name of the woman who spoke for Sniffles, but said "she had a voice like a charming six year old" (Letter to Graham Webb, 7 February 1972).

140. Mel Blanc, *The Mike Walsh Show* TV interview, Sydney Australia, May 1985. On this show Blanc, unusually, demonstrated the "interim" voice of Bugs he used in *Elmer's Candid Camera* and *Elmer's Pet Rabbit*, demonstrating the differences between his Bugs Bunny voices. Tape from TV audio.

141. Avery, Chapman College appearance / Q&A session, 17 August 1974.

142. Avery interview with Gray, April 1977.

143. Ibid.

144. Ibid. Also notes from Bob Clampett telephone interview with Michael Barrier, 25 May 1971.

145. Don Christensen, interview with Milton Gray, 12 August 1978.

146. Bob Clampett interview with Walter Brasch, 18 June 1975.

147. Chuck Jones, interview with Michael Barrier (date unknown).

148. *Daily Variety*, 25 April 1941. USC Jack Warner Collection, Mel Blanc contract agreement file. See author's article, "Mel Blanc: From Anonymity to Offscreen Superstar (The Advent of On-screen Voice Credits)," Cartoonresearch.com, Keith Scott tab, 12 September 2016.

149. Treg Brown interview.

150. Robert Givens interview, 16 August 1990, published in Jim Korkis & John Cawley, *How to Create Animation: Lessons from the Masters* (Las Vegas: Pioneer Books, 1990), p. 78. "[The finished storyboards] were pretty close to the finished product, at least in the expressions. Mel Blanc recorded from those damned things!"

151. Don Christensen, interview with Gray.

152. Norman McCabe, interview with Milton Gray, 8 December 1976

153. Norman McCabe, interview with Michael Barrier & Milton Gray, 10 February 1990. McCabe telephone interview with author, Van Nuys September 1996.

154. Ibid.

155. Clampett, *Velvet Light Trap* interview, 1975.

156. June Foray, telephone interview with author, Hollywood September 1996.

157. Stan Freberg, telephone interview with author, Hollywood July 2001.

158. Leonard Maltin to author, Toluca Lake 2010.

159. "Atomic Comic" quote by Jack Bundy, *Jack Bundy's Album* radio show (guest, Danny Webb), 7 May 1945 (audiotape in author's collection). Hames Ware *Animato!*, No. 40, Winter 1999. Bob Clampett letter to Graham Webb, 1977.

160. Bob Clampett interviews, 31 October 1976, 8 June 1979. Sody Clampett to author, Hollywood September 1995.

161. Ibid. Regarding the "problematic" nature of *Coal Black*, it is instructive and revealing to note that actress Vivian Dandridge wrote an affectionate letter to Bob Clampett dated 9 June 1952. This was a simple note wanting to catch up and chat after nine years. (Vivian Dandridge letter, Bob Clampett Archive, copy courtesy Michael Barrier); Lillian Randolph and other black artists retained happy memories of this cartoon. Sody Clampett said that Eddie Beal, the music adviser-talent contractor for *Coal Black* and *Tin Pan Alley Cats*, became a close friend of Bob Clampett and they and Beal's brother Charlie socialized for several decades until Eddie Beal's passing. (Sody Clampett to author, Hollywood, September 1995.) Clampett's son Rob noted that, "maybe 1962, Eddie Beal invited Dad to an NAACP meeting. I think Dad went to that meeting. Eddie was certainly part of the fabric of the Central Avenue [black music] scene." (Email to author 21 November 2008.) In February 2003 Rob Clampett and Milt Gray intended to make a digital mini-documentary on *Coal Black*. The star of the original musical "Jump for Joy," which inspired Clampett's cartoon, was Herb Jeffries, who was among several actors who auditioned for the cartoon in 1941 (Clampett interview, 1979). In 2003 Jeffries was 91 years young and attended a screening of *Coal Black* with Rob Clampett and Gray at which he expressed his admiration for the film and wanted to be a part of the documentary. The cartoons were, and remain, controversial, but certain individuals were evidently more equanimous about them than

some latter day critics on race and representation might care to admit.

162. Ibid.

163. Michael Barrier, *Hollywood Cartoons: American Animation in its Golden Age* (New York, 1999), p. 437.

164. Clampett, interviews, 6 June 1969, 8 June 1979. USC Warner Collection: Music payroll records for *Tin Pan Alley Cats* recording sessions, 1 & 8 August 1942.

165. Billy Bletcher interview, June 1969 (the full audiotape via Hames Ware). Bob Clampett letter to Mike Barrier, 15 May 1970.

166. Bob Clampett, Toronto appearance, summer 1979.

167. Ibid.

168. Ibid.

169. *Warner Club News*, "What's Cookin'" column by Michael Maltese, December 1944.

170. Bob Clampett, interview, 31 October 1976.

171. Bob Clampett, *Velvet Light Trap* interview, 1975. Clampett Toronto interview, summer 1979.

172. Dave Barry, letter to Bob Clampett, 14 May 1945.

173. Chuck Jones, letter to author, 28 February 1996.

174. Robert Bruce, telephone interview with author, December 1994.

175. Bob Clampett, 6 June 1969 interview.

176. Michael Maltese, interview with Michael Barrier, 31 May 1971.

177. USC Jack L. Warner Collection. Murray Kinnell SAG document, 1945.

178. Lloyd Turner, interview with Michael Barrier, 13 May 1989. Turner, tape letter to author, October 1991.

179. Ibid.

180. Freleng interview with Beck, 1988.

181. Freleng telephone interview with author, March 1994. Jones to author, Sydney September 1990.

182. Barrier, *Hollywood Cartoons*, p. 477.

183. *Warner Club News*, Michael Maltese quotation, December 1944, p. 4.

184. Freleng & Weber, *The Art of Friz Freleng*, pp. 100-101.

185. Maltese, interview with Barrier, 1971.

186. McKimson, interview with Barrier.

187. Ibid.

188. Robert McKimson, letter to Graham Webb, 1 June 1970.

189. Stan Freberg, telephone interview with author, July 2001.

190. Treg Brown interview.

191. Lloyd Turner, tape letter to author, October 1991.

192. Bill Scott, interview with Paul Etcheverry, November 1981. Published in *Animania* No. 20, 1983.

193. McKimson, letter to Webb.

194. Ibid. June Foray telephone interview with author, August 1996. Daws Butler to author, June 1979.

195. Chuck Jones, letter to Graham Webb, 7 February 1972.

196. Chuck Jones, interview with Greg Ford & Richard Thompson, published in *Film Comment*, Jan-Feb. 1975 special issue on cartoons.

197. Chuck Jones, interview with Michael Barrier, date unknown. Audio excerpt played during Barrier's commentary track for *One Froggy Evening*, Looney Tunes Platinum Collection Vol. 1, Disc 2 Blu-ray.

198. Chuck Jones, telephone interview with author, March 1995.

199. Chuck Jones, interview with Ford & Thompson, 1972. Jones, letter to Graham Webb.

200. Treg Brown interview.

201. Paul Julian, interview with Michael Barrier, 18 December 1976.

202. Treg Brown, interview. Maltese to Daws Butler, *The Carole Hemingway Show* (radio), July 1975.

203. McKimson, quoted by Joe Adamson, *Bugs Bunny: Fifty Years and Only One Grey Hare* (New York: Henry Holt, 1991), possibly from McKimson interview with David Butler.

204. Mark Evanier to author, Hollywood, October 12 1998.

205. Chuck Jones, letter to Linda Jones, March 1955.

206. Daws Butler, interview with Milton Gray, 20 March 1976.

207. Bob Clampett, letter to Hames Ware, 1974.

208. Chuck Jones, telephone interview with author, March 1995.

209. Daws Butler, tape letters to author, April 1974, October 1974.

210. Barrier, "The Moving Drawing Speaks," *Funnyworld*, 1978, p.18.

Chapter 2: MGM Cartoon Voices

Metro-Goldwyn-Mayer Music Department records (Arthur Freed paper collection): card file index [courtesy Ned Comstock], cartoon notes (dubbing vocalists, vocal groups, dates and fees; production numbers, inter-office correspondence), author research on-site, USC Cinema-TV Department, Edward L. Doheny Library, USC Cinematic Arts Library (February 1999, June 2002, May 2004).

Interview transcripts: Robert Allen (with Allen's annotations), Tex Avery, Michael Lah & George Gordon, Hugh Harman & Rudolph Ising (Bob Clampett sits in on four interviews), Bill Hanna, Friz Freleng, C. G. Maxwell, Fred MacAlpin, Scott Bradley, Dick Bickenbach. Correspondence and audio interviews: Daws Butler, Paul Frees, June Foray, Don Messick, Leroy Hurte, Lillian Randolph, Jameson "Jerry" Brewer, Billy Bletcher.

Articles: Will Friedwald, "Hugh Harman (1903-1982)," *Graffiti*, Spring 1984; Mike Barrier, "Silly Stuff: An interview with Hugh Harman," *Graffiti*, Spring 1984; Mike Barrier: "The Careers of Hugh Harman & Rudolf Ising," *Millimeter*, February 1976; Mark Mayerson, "The Lion Began with a Frog," *The Velvet Light Trap* 1977; Will Friedwald, "Hugh Harman at Cinecon 16," August 1980, *Animania*

#22, 1981; Jim Korkis, David Mruz, Nancy Beiman, various articles in *Mindrot* #19 (the Tex Avery Memorial issue, 1980); Greg Ford: *Tex Avery: Arch-Radicalizer of the Hollywood Cartoon*, 1978.

Trade papers: Anne M. McIlhenney, "Filmland Rambles," *Buffalo Courier-Express* November 19, 1939; Hubbard Keavy, "New Cartoon Enters Movies," *Associated Press* May 5, 1940; cartoon reviews in trade publications: *Motion Picture Reviews, Motion Picture Herald, The Billboard, Box Office*. Tex Avery: *The Exhibitor*, 9-17-41; *Box Office*, 10-23-43

1. Hugh Harman interview (moderator Will Friedwald), "Hugh Harman at Cinecon 16," 30 August 1980. Published in *Animania*, issue 22, 1981.
2. Fred MacAlpin interview with Michael Barrier, 15 January 1979.
3. Rudolph Ising interview with Michael Barrier, Milton Gray & Mark Kausler (Bob Clampett sat in), 2 June 1971.
4. USC Cinema-Television Library: MGM Music Department files, Arthur Freed collection. Bill Hanna interview with Paul Maher, 1978 (Children's Television Archive). Bill Hanna to author, Sydney September 1991.
5. Ising, 1971 interview.
6. Graham Webb letter to author, August 1994.
7. Scott Bradley interview, 11 March 1977.
8. MacAlpin interview.
9. Philip K. Scheuer column, "Business of 'Ghosting' Hollywood's Oddest," *Los Angeles Times*, 4-21-35.
10. Rudolf Ising interview with Michael Barrier & Milton Gray (Bob Clampett sat in), 30 November 1973
11. Bob Clampett telephone interview with Hames Ware, 6 February 1972. Letters between Hames Ware and Graham Webb in the seventies refer regularly to Harman and Ising's absent minded description of "the girls" when asked about cute little voices.

12. Ising, 1973 interview.
13. Ising, 1971 interview.
14. MacAlpin interview.
15. Jack Zander, interview with Michael Barrier, 24 March 1982.
16. MacAlpin interview.
17. Friz Freleng, telephone interview with author, March 1994.
18. MacAlpin interview.
19. MGM in house journal: "Whimsy by the Mile (MGM Establishes Cartoon Factory to Animate Famous Comic Strip The Captain and the Kids)," 1937, unsigned.
20. Robbin Coons, "Billy Bletcher Sells One Voice - That Leaves Him Just 999," *Associated Press*, 27 November 1937.
21. C. G. Maxwell, interview with Milton Gray, 6 April 1977.
22. Ibid.
23. Ibid.
24. Hugh Harman and Rudolph Ising, interview with Michael Barrier & Milton Gray (Bob Clampett sat in), 29 & 31 October 1976.
25. Friz Freleng, telephone interview with author, Hollywood-Sydney, March 1994.
26. Michael Barrier, *Hollywood Cartoons* (New York: Oxford University Press, 1999), p. 614 n.2
27. MGM Cartoons, various trade articles: Frederick C. Othman, "They Make Faces at Themselves, Then Draw Movies," *United Press*, 1938; Marney McCaskill, "Harman-Ising," *Film Daily*, 1939; "Cartoon Staff," *Motion Picture Herald* ("The Hollywood Scene"); Fred Quimby Studio biography; "Animating Mother Nature," MGM Shorts in-house journal
28. Ising, 1973 interview
29. *National Radio Artists Directory*, 1945. *AFRA Guide*, October 1950.
30. USC Cinema-TV Library: MGM Music Department Records, cartoon entries, Arthur Freed Collection.

31. Ibid.
32. Joe Barbera, *My Life in Toons: From Flatbush to Bedrock in Under a Century* (Atlanta: Turner Publishing, 1994), p. 76.
33. Thurl Ravenscroft, letter to author, 24 December 1995.
34. Jameson "Jerry" Brewer, letter to author, 21 February 2000: "It was indeed Pedro de Cordoba who narrated and was the Padre's voice in *The First Swallow*."
35. Mike Maltese column in *The Exposure Sheet*, Vol. 2, No. 3, 12 February 1940.
36. Elmore Vincent entry in *AFTRA Guide* 1956. Bob Clampett letter to Hames Ware, 16 March 1972 (Clampett wrote: "Did I mention Elmore Vincent to you? He played old men characters in radio and in some of the cartoons such as the Harman-Ising MGM's. Until quite recently he has been in the vending business and I let him instal one of his candy and cigarette machines in my Studio. I'd chat with him when he came in to fill the machines.").
37. Jerry Mann clipping file, Billy Rose Theatre Collection, NY Public Library at Lincoln Center. Whitney Bolton, "Broadway Gets Its Mann" (*New York Literary Digest*, undated, early 1950s): "[Mann] finally got a six-months jolt at M-G-M [circa 1942], but they never put him in front of a camera... he [found a job] in the Cartoon Building, writing cartoon comedy gags and doing the noises for Tom and Jerry cartoons." The article indicates he did that for several years in MGM cartoons.
38. USC Cinema-TV Library, MGM Music Department files, Cartoons. Courtesy Ned Comstock.
39. Bill Hanna (with Tom Ito), *A Cast of Friends* (Dallas: Taylor Publishing, 1996), pp. 47-48.
40. MacAlpin interview.
41. Tex Avery, interview with Joe Adamson, 19 June 1969, 13 November 1969, 25 March 1971, in *Tex Avery: King of Cartoons* (New York: Popular Library, 1975).

42. Heck Allen, interview with Adamson, 1 April 1971 in *Tex Avery: King of Cartoons* (1975).

43. Tex Avery interview with Gray, 2-18-77.

44. Ibid.

45. Audiotapes of radio shows featuring Wally Maher as the character Wilbur (Avery's template for the Screwy Squirrel voice): *The Tommy Riggs and Betty Lou Show, Request Performance, The Jack Benny Program*. Avery had completely forgotten Maher's name and never did recollect it (Maher died relatively young years before on 27 December 1951). When June Foray, on behalf of Graham Webb, asked Avery about the Screwy voice, he told her, "Oh we just got some nut off the street." For a time, according to Hames Ware, the young researchers took him literally. In 1991 George Balzer, the writer of the *Tommy Riggs and Betty Lou Show*, was the first to confirm it was Maher doing Screwy's voice to the late comedian-radio historian Ken Greenwald, who had sensed it was Maher's voice.

46. Avery, interview with Gray, 4-27-77.

47. Heck Allen interview.

48. Allen, *Tex Avery, the King of Cartoons* TV documentary, 1988.

49. Avery, interview with Gray, 4-27-77.

50. Adamson, *Tex Avery: The King of Cartoons*, note p. 142.

51. Avery, interview with Gray, 4-27-77.

52. John Brown's casting for *Symphony in Slang* was confirmed in *Variety*, 5 August 1949.

53. Daws Butler, interviews with Milton Gray, 20 March and 5 April 1976.

54. Avery, interview with Gray, 27 April 1977. Avery interviews with Joe Adamson, published in *Tex Avery: King of Cartoons*.

55. Butler interview with Gray, 20 March 1976.

56. Tex Avery at Chapman College, 17 August 1974.

57. Michael Lah, 1988 documentary, *Tex Avery (The King of Cartoons)* (Moondance Productions).

58. Avery interview, 17 April 1977.

59. The casting of Shug Fisher and his Hillbillies in *Pecos Pest* was noted in *Variety*, 30 October and 14 December, 1953.

60. USC Music Department files, Cartoons; entry for *Magical Maestro*.

61. Ibid.

62. Fred Karbo, "professional laugher," noted in *Variety*, 24 December 1952,

63. Wes Harrison, undated publicity biography (circa 1960s). Patrick Kampert, *Tribune*, "The Man with the Golden Throat," 27 November 2005: "His versatile vocal chords graced Tom and Jerry shorts (the sound of a mighty tree falling)." www.mrsoundeffects.com/about.

64. Paul Frees, tape letter to author, 10 August 1972. Frees, letter to Graham Webb, 1974.

65. Colleen Collins entry in *The AFRA Guide*; the 1952 and 1954 volumes mention her work in MGM cartoons. Trade paper items later confirmed her casting.

66. Francoise Brun-Cottan, online Cartoon forum, 2005. As a child actress voicing the tiny French mouse in several Tom & Jerry cartoons, her professional name was noted as Marie Francoise.

67. Michael Lah, 1988 TV interview.

Chapter 3: COLUMBIA-SCREEN GEMS Cartoon Voices

Interview transcripts: Sid Marcus, Cal Howard, Harry Love, Art Davis, Dick Huemer, Howard Swift, Paul Sommer, Paul Fennell, John Hubley, Frank Tashlin, Bob Clampett. Articles and interviews by Paul Etcheverry and Will Friedwald in *Mindrot* and *Animania*, *The Velvet Light Trap #15*, 1975, *Animatrix*. Columbia Pictures corporate records archive at Sony Pictures Archives, Culver City [courtesy Nick Szech], author's research on-site, January & February 1999, August 2012. Scrappy website Scrappyland.com maintained by Harry McCracken.

1. Richard Huemer interview with Joe Adamson (1968-69), Oral History Collection, UCLA.
2. Sid Marcus, interview with Milton Gray (Harry Love sat in), 24 February 1977. Marcus, letter to Graham Webb, 14 February 1977: "When sound was added [to cartoons], if voices were needed we all pitched in, usually [all] in falsetto."
3. Ibid.
4. Bob Clampett, letters to Hames Ware, 16 March 1972 and 8 August 1972. Clampett wrote: "Jack Carr, who was an animator dating back to 1923 in N. Y., was a voice of Krazy Kat for Mintz in around 1930."
5. Marcus interview.
6. Harry Love, interview with Milton Gray, 16 January, 1977.
7. *Los Angeles Times*, 21 April 1935, Philip Scheuer's column: "Business of Ghosting Hollywood's Oddest."
8. Ibid.
9. Sid Marcus, letter to Graham Webb, 14 February 1977: "Later [from the mid-thirties] when more dialogue was needed, professionals were used, including Mel Blanc, Smiley Burnette and many others."
10. Harry Love, interview with Paul Etcheverry, 23 January 1981. Published in *Animania*, issue 23, 5 March 1982.
11. Ibid.
12. Ted Okuda, *The Columbia Comedy Shorts: Two-Reel Hollywood Film Comedies, 1933-1958* (North Carolina, 1986).
13. Dave Weber PR items were plentiful in the 1937-39 period, including *Academy Players Directory* entries for 1937 and 1938, listing his cartoon credits. *Variety*, "Weber's Voice Disguises in Mintz short," 2 July 1937. *Variety*, "Weber Dialogs

cartoons," 2 December 1937. *Los Angeles Times*, "A Town Called Hollywood," 16 January 1938. *Variety*, "Weber Ends Krazy Tales," 9 July 1938.

14. Robert Winkler, guest speaker at *SPERDVAC Presents*, 10 January 1987 (Audiotape). SPERDVAC (Society for the Preservation and Encouragement of Radio Drama, Variety and Comedy) is a Southern California based old-time radio organization.

15. Ibid.

16. Sid Marcus, interview with Gray.

17. Harry Love interview with Etcheverry.

18. Hugh Harman & Rudolf Ising, interview with Michael Barrier & Milton Gray (Bob Clampett sat in), 29 October 1976.

19. Harry Love letter to *Funnyworld*, No. 21

20. Harry Love interview with Etcheverry.

21. Hugh Harman & Rudolf Ising interview.

22. Frank Tashlin, interview with Michael Barrier, 29 May 1971. *Frank Tashlin* (British Film Institute publication, 1994) has Michael Barrier's annotations to the cartoon section of Tashlin's filmography, and publishes his interview with Tashlin.

23. Arthur Davis, interview with Michael Barrier, 24 November 1986.

24. *Daily Variety*, April 25, 1941. *The Hollywood Reporter*, April 25, 1941. Creation of cartoon series "The Fox and Crow," 1958 legal document in Columbia Corporate Archive, Sony Pictures Television, Culver City. Author research 29 January 1999.

25. Dave Fleischer, interview with Joe Adamson (1968), Oral History Collection, UCLA.

26. Ibid.

27. *National Radio Artists Directory*, October 1943 issue. Paul Sommer, interview with Milt Gray, 30 March 1977 (Sommer identified voice artists hired for Screen Gems cartoons).

28. *Hollywood Digest*, 1 December 1943 ("Dave Barry, voice impressionist, to Columbia cartoon studio").